Saints and Postmodernism

Religion and Postmodernism
a series edited by Mark C. Taylor

Edith Wyschogrod

Saints and Postmodernism

Revisioning Moral Philosophy

 The University of Chicago Press
Chicago and London

The University of Chicago Press, Chicago 60637
The University of Chicago Press, Ltd., London
© 1990 by The University of Chicago
All rights reserved. Published 1990
Printed in the United States of America

07 06 05 04 03 02 01 00 99 98   3 4 5 6 7 8

Library of Congress Cataloging-in-Publication Data

Wyschogrod, Edith.
  Saints and postmodernism : revisioning moral philosophy / Edith
Wyschogrod.
      p.   cm.—(Religion and postmodernism)
  Includes bibliographical references and index.
  ISBN 0-226-92043-7 (paperback)
  1. Ethics.   2. Postmodernism.   3. Altruism.   4. Analysis
(Philosophy)   I. Title.   II. Series
BJ1012.W97   1990
170—dc20   90-36721
                                                      CIP

For Daniel, Abigail, Tamar, and Margaret Hannah

Contents

Acknowledgments

I should like to express my indebtedness to all those who so generously contributed to the shaping of this work. I am especially grateful to Thomas J. J. Altizer for his fiery criticisms of postmodernism, to Ray L. Hart for his illuminating reflections on the problem of nonbeing, to Rodolphe Gasché for his helpful remarks on the problem of unity and difference in postmodernism, to Lucia Lermond for her remarkable insights into Deleuze's thought and the spirit of postmodernism generally. Ralph Sleeper's observations on antifoundationalism and the structure of theory, Thelma Z. Lavine's discussions of Enlightenment rationality, Jeffrey Reiman's accounts of recent debates in moral philosophy, and Naomi Miller's counsel on art historical matters were especially useful. My debt to Mark C. Taylor for having contributed so much to "shaping" the idiom of postmodernism and for his encouragement of the present project is immense. Luncheon conversations at the Wilson Center with Robert L. Belknap, Renee Fox, and Jeffrey and Barbara Diefendorf were fruitful in ways that are hard to pinpoint. I should also like to thank James Waller for his assistance with the index. Thanks are owed those others—family, friends, and colleagues—who have unstintingly fostered this project. The shortcomings of this work should, of course, be attributed to me alone.

I wish to thank the Wilson Center for the opportunity to conduct my research under its auspices from September 1988 to January 1989 and to convey my appreciation to Ann Sheffield, head of the History, Culture and Society Program, to Patricia B. Wood of the Center's staff, and to my research assistant, Adrienne Safran, for their help in matters large and small.

This book was prepared (in part) under a grant from the Woodrow Wilson International Center for Scholars, Washington, D.C. The statements and views expressed herein are those of the author and are not necessarily those of the Wilson Center.

Instead of . . . its "roads, its seas, its clouds, as if they were those of freedom and justice," read " . . . its roads, its seas, its clouds, as if those of repression and absence." Because the reality of the text and the text of the real are a long way from forming a single world.

Letter of Marcel Broodthaers, 31 October 1969

Moissac, Saint Pierre, exterior narthex portal, figure of Jeremiah.
Giraudon/Art Resource, New York.

Prelude

A POSTMODERN ethics? Is this not a contradiction in terms? If post-modernism is a critical expression describing the subversion of philosophical language, a "mutant of Western humanism,"[1] then how can one hope for an ethics when the conditions for meaning are themselves under attack? But is not this paradox—the paradox of a postmodern ethic—just what is required if an ethic is to be postmodern? Does not the term *postmodern* so qualify the term *ethics* that the idea of ethics, the stipulation of what is to count as lawful conduct, is subverted? And is a postmodern ethics then not an ethics of the subversion of ethics so that ethics turns into its opposite, a nihilism that is unconstrained by rules? Yet, if postmodernism succeeds modernism as the term implies, nihilism is not *post*modern in any straightforward chronological sense because it flourished in the nineteenth century and, as a species of antinomianism, has ancient roots in Greek Sophism and Roman Cynicism.

The matter is therefore not simple. The word *postmodern* prefixed to ethics as its qualifier becomes neither the mere negation of what has, at various times, been interpreted as lawful conduct nor the sign of a dialectical reverberation between normative ethics and its opposite, the negation or defiance of norms. This is because the term *postmodern* is not an innocuous modifier, a word that is subordinated to the word it modifies. The relation between "ethics" and "postmodern" is complex and requires a radical rethinking of the syntactic and semiotic possibilities of each. A postmodern ethic must look not to some opposite of ethics but elsewhere, to life narratives, specifically those of saints, defined in terms that both overlap and overturn traditional normative stipulations and that defy the normative structure of moral theory.

Why a postmodern ethic now? The twentieth century is witness to the deaths of millions within ever more compressed time frames:

death through nuclear, chemical, and biological warfare, through death camps, through concentration and slave labor camps, and by means of conventional weapons. Newly emerging biological and chemical instruments for mass destruction are in the process of development. Conflicts that have thus far remained local offer no guarantee of containment but, instead, may constitute potential flash points for global war. Elsewhere I have called this new historical horizon the *death event*.[2] Because these happenings constitute the often unconscious apperceptive background of daily existence, life is held cheap. When natural calamity occurs, the affective responses to it are blunted even when efforts to mitigate suffering are mobilized. Thus earthquake, the AIDS epidemic, famine, and other disasters strike without the resonance of awe that accompanied previous disasters. This normalization of death is abetted by the fact that it is nightly fare on television, as a remark overheard in a Washington D.C. supermarket attests: "Blood and mayhem, mayhem and blood, the same tonight as every night. Only the names are different."

Effective debate in political and academic forums seems futile when the world's ills are such that they require extreme measures: urban MASH units to treat gunshot wounds on city streets, AIDS clinics, international investigations of and protests against human rights violations, to name only a few. The list is long and its contents enervatingly familiar. The crises constituted by the death event, by disease and natural disaster, require total and radical responses. The world's religious traditions have in the past addressed the problems of the wretched of the earth in the persons of saints, those who put themselves totally at the disposal of the Other. I shall argue not for the retention of the historical contexts in which saintliness has arisen with their often deeply rooted prejudices against other claimants to transcendent truth, but for the saint's recognition of the primacy of the other person and the dissolution of self-interest.

I shall argue too that the antiseptic atmosphere of modernism does not allow saints to breathe, for despite modernism's extraordinary aesthetic and technological achievements, it disdains the artifacts and conditions of the New Age: supermarkets and television, poverty and glitz, Concorde jets and the homeless asleep in airport lounges. This is the ambiance that postmodern thinkers and artists recognize as the backdrop of contemporary existence and are willing to encounter.

The question, "What is postmodernism?" has generally been taken up in the context of art and architecture, of literary theory, of political critique, and of philosophical—specifically metaphysical or epistemological—inquiry, but rarely in its relation to ethics as such. The present effort would seem to fall naturally within the sphere of philosophical inquiry because, according to the traditional scheme, ethics as the investigation of the nomos of conduct is a branch of philosophy. But if, as I mean to argue, ethics is the sphere of transactions between "self" and "Other" and is to be construed non-nomologically, it cannot look to traditional philosophical discourse for a perspective on human conduct.[3] Instead it must turn to what postmodernism means in some of its other manifestations, especially the visual arts and literary narrative, because in these concrete expressions postmodernism exposes the presuppositions of the conventions of modernism as modernism runs up against the actuality of our "mascara and soap-opera age."[4]

How then will postmodernism be viewed in the present inquiry? Although philosophical, psychological, political, aesthetic, and culture-critical postmodernisms have been distinguished from one another, postmodernism's breaking of boundaries does not encourage easy classification. Instead, postmodernist thinking invites the engagement of strategies drawn from various quarters and whose deployment issues in new ways of thinking and acting. The old does not simply disappear. It is displaced within specifiable discursive contexts—art, literature, philosophy—through critique. In the epigraph of this section, Marcel Broodthaers, a Belgian postmodern artist, affirms this slippage when he suggests that the real is unattainable, that the nineteenth-century organization of the real as freedom and justice has been displaced in our own age by a repression and absence that, paradoxically, expresses this inexpressibility.[5]

Because postmodernism is contrasted with modernism, it may be useful to pinpoint the differences between them. According to Jean-François Lyotard, the modern aesthetic is one of form in which what cannot be presented is put forward as a missing part of a pattern that provides the source of aesthetic delight. He identifies this patterning with the Kantian sublime. "The real sublime sentiment is a combination of pleasure and pain: the pleasure that reason should exceed all presentation, the pain that imagination or sensibility should not be equal to the concept."[6] The postmodern, by contrast, becomes reflexive about the presentational process itself:

The postmodern . . . puts forward the unpresentable in presentation itself: that which denies itself the solace of good forms, the consensus of a taste which would make it possible to share collectively the nostalgia for the unattainable; that which searches for new presentations, not in order to enjoy them but in order to impart a stronger sense of the unpresentable. . . . [The] rules and categories are what the work of art itself is looking for. The artist and the writer then are working without rules in order to formulate the rules of *what will have been done*. Hence the fact that work and text have the character of an *event*. Hence also they have always come too late for the author, or, what amounts to the same thing, their realization (*mise en oeuvre*) always begins too soon. *Postmodern* would have to be understood according to the paradox of the future (*post*) anterior (*modo*).[7]

Lyotard's account highlights the conflation of art and philosophy, for now art in its concern with meta-aesthetic statement becomes a kind of categorial inquiry. Built into this mode of artistic shaping is a chronological skewing: the rules for creating the artwork are not fore-disclosed but come to light only after they have already been put to use. I hope to show in the body of this study that the life habits of saints are temporally orchestrated in the same way: saintly work is defined "(post) anterior (modo)" in the sense Lyotard attributes to these words.

Six impulses or tendencies drawn from the differing manifestations of postmodernism appear repeatedly in the present study because of their bearing upon the sphere of moral action: differentiality, double coding, eclecticism, alterity, empowerment (and its opposite), and materialism.

The first, differentiality, consists of a group of tactics that call into question the standard canons of reason, the possibility of a totalizing discourse capable of presenting an account of the real. Also called into question is the primacy of the present, the privileging of present time by understanding past and future as modalities of the present. The result of these analyses is the emergence of a differential infrastructure that underlies the unity of theoretical reason and of a language whose oddities reflect the break with closed thought structures.

Postmodernism brings to light a certain circularity of standard modes of rationality, a problem that can be stated in the terms of standard rationality itself. If reason—construed as logic in the broad sense—is the complex of rules that classify and relate the elements of language so that it issues in understandable patterns, these patterns are legitimated by appeal to the very rules that constitute them. Reason, unable to go outside itself, can only spin its wheels. Yet argument as a thought form has become the dominant mode of philosophical speech through which both truth and meaning are said to be established.

This has crucial consequences for the sphere of moral philosophy. Questions of compelling life urgency, it is held, can be settled by debate, yet the result is often a quagmire of conflicting views. Narrative conceptions of ethics have been brought forward in part as a response to the impasses created by the confrontation of various moral theories.

Although the move to the use of life story is an important step, the idea of narrative as the encompassing framework for moral philosophy is captive of the same naïveté as moral theory, if it is conceived, as Lyotard points out, as master narrative.[8] Like the metaphysical presuppositions of theoretical thought, the philosophical biases in which narrative has heretofore been grounded must be brought into critical perspective. Postmodern literary theory highlights the traits of narrative such as the multiplicity of its voices and its openendedness by exposing narrative's grammatical, semiotic, and lexical tactics.

Here the second tendency of postmodernism, the strategy of double coding, takes on considerable importance. Postmodern criticism shows the ambiguity, the encrypting of meaning in art, architecture, and literary narrative. In the context of postmodern architecture, Charles Jencks defines double coding as "the combination of Modern techniques with something else," whatever can communicate with a wide public,[9] a move undertaken because modern art and architecture failed to make contact with a broad audience or to create continuity with the past. Yet postmodernism, having passed through modernism, retains something of modernism's critical sensibility so that postmodern works are distinguishable from the kitsch of sheer revivalism. Thus popular elements are used selectively and with pointed intent.

Two examples should help bring this reflexiveness to light. Consider first a postmodern work that appears to take the perspective of modernism as its point of departure. A 1989 dance performance by the Basel Ballet entitled "La belle vie," a work set in the period just before the Revolution of 1848, seems to be the very embodiment of modernist ballet. Yet, in a bordello scene that opens on a note of balletic formalism, an Apache-like duet indebted to acrobatics, musical comedy, and other popular art forms, as well as to the modernist idiom of George Balanchine, interrupts the action and is punctuated by a dancer shrieking in Korean. This introduction of popular and disruptive fragments, sometimes quasi-political, creates new theatrical and choreographic effects. Dennis Potter, in the TV series "The Singing Detective," begins at the opposite end, not with high modernism but with an already popular art form, the TV detective story. He places a modernist frame around a murder mystery through the artful use of flashback, spatial dislocation, and the display, not of the blood and gore that has become a convention of the genre, but of deforming disease in undisguised clinical detail. The combination of modernism and popular entertainment yields a new postmodern television idiom.

I cite these examples not only because they highlight the eclectic character of aesthetic postmodernism but also because they help clear up a possible objection to a postmodern ethics based on narratives of saints' lives. It is not possible, it could be argued, to renew interest in hagiography because as a literary form such narratives have become kitsch. This criticism is not without merit. Only if hagiography is read as doubly coded, that is, only if it has passed through the lens of modern and postmodern criticism so that it is no longer offered in its first naïveté, can it surmount this charge. High modernism *and* the popular must reciprocally penetrate, fissure, and retract one another so that hagiography becomes a living art form.

Double coding is linked to postmodernism's tolerance, its democratic eclecticism, the third tendency of postmodernism referred to earlier. In the present study the deconstructive tactics of Jacques Derrida, the social and historical epistemology of Michel Foucault, the "kynical" or disruptive criticisms of culture of Peter Sloterdijk, the dismantling of psychological structure by Jacques Lacan, Gilles Deleuze, and Felix Guattari—all will be deployed side by side as needed for the interpretation of saintly existence. I shall not try for iron-clad arguments since that is just what postmodern critique hopes to expose as fruitless. Instead I shall be guided by context, by the problems as they outline themselves in actual lives. Nor will I remain equally well-disposed toward all postmodern trends and tendencies, especially those that propose not the disclosure of a cataclysm that has begun in the hope of a new dawn but the revelation of an apocalypse that is taken for the new dawn itself.

If eclecticism is to be far-reaching, it must include and engage the philosophical voices of its time. Such engagement should not be confused with treating the various modes of philosophical discourse as strands in an ongoing philosophical conversation. In the context of ethics, conceptual positions do not float in a vacuum but bear upon the sphere of life and action. I am therefore compelled to engage a dominant strand of recent philosophical discourse, analytic philosophy of language and ethics, in order to bring the protocols and policies of this philosophy into polemical contact with postmodern criticism. This project requires the redescription of arguments for altruism developed in the context of analytic ethics in a way that will elicit the differences between analytic and postmodern narratological—sequential event oriented—approaches to altruism. Because almost no work at all has been done along these lines, this project demands the invention of new strategies of language for thinking through the problems raised by such contextual transposition.

The comparative work that exists has generally been undertaken, in the spirit of Richard Rorty, as an analytic recasting of recent continental thinkers to fit the prior notion of philosophy as conversation. The result is often a straitjacketing of Heidegger, Derrida, and Foucault, the only continental thinkers of whom any extended notice has been taken, by passing over their more subtle strategies and restructuring what remains as a series of arguments. It is as if, to notice their work at all (to borrow an analogy from the computer world), it must be rewritten to accommodate the software of philosophical analysis.[10]

Yet, if postmodernism is to be genuinely eclectic, it cannot remain isolated from a dominant strain of thought in the English-speaking world. It must expand its terrain and recognize that modern philosophy has not stood still since its framing in the work of Descartes, the British Empiricists, and Kant and Hegel, the philosophers dealt with by Heidegger and his successors. Postmodernism is challenged to show and not merely assert both the constancies and the alterations in the history of Western thought. This I shall try to do not only because the task is itself engrossing but because it has the most crucial bearing upon the problem of the relation of saintly life to moral theory.

Eclecticism will thus express itself at several levels, first as the juxtaposition of widely differing genres, second intraphilosophically by considering different philosophical idioms: phenomenological and post-phenomenological philosophy, analytic philosophy and the work of such traditional thinkers as Plato, Aristotle, and Descartes. Attention to a wide range of philosophical voices will help to uncover both the failures of moral theory and what remains to be thought through afresh. Once the microstructures of theory have been exposed, and philosophical argument shown to be unavailing in the context of moral life, an appeal to the first type of eclecticism, the use of a broad spectrum of textual forms, is virtually mandated. Jean-François Lyotard, who not only brings the term postmodernism into prominence but remains one of its most provocative voices, makes the necessity for multiple texts and styles a moral issue. He considers the effort to render the multiplicity of language games commensurable, to suppress their differences, an act of terror.

Yet texts and genres are not randomly selected either by Lyotard or in the present work, where they help to express and interpret saintly altruism. Thus, for example, if the question of saintly compassion is to be addressed in a postmodern fashion, the fictions of Jean Genet provide a useful focus for inquiry in that they show a relationship between altruism and deviance. But the theme of compassion is also the subject of theoretical investigation by the analytic philosophers whose theories are subjected to postmodern critical scrutiny. Thus Genet's convict-saints must be considered along with the arguments of Nicholas Rescher or Thomas Nagel if the role of altruism in saintly life as well as the limitations of theoretical approaches to the problem are to be exhibited. The textual oddities such juxtaposition creates are intended not as jolts for their own sake but to help the reader see what is at stake when altruism is endorsed in a contemporary context. The reader will be forced to reflect that the altruism that is the result of postmodern analysis is a far cry from the salvaging of the altruism either of an older hagiography often marked by sentimentality and parochialism or of the liberal altruism endorsed by John Stuart Mill or some recent analytic ethicists. Instead, saintliness will be seen to bear within itself the traces of the distortions brought out by postmodern analysis. Thus, in the case of Genet's "saints," I discuss them not only because of Genet's contribution to the stylistics of hagiography but in order to show that transgressive saintliness now marks or is inscribed within traditional acts of altruism: altruism has become reflexive and saintliness marked by negation and ambiguity.

The fourth strand of postmodernism is that of alterity, an old word used for otherness, that is generally used to refer to the otherness of persons. I distinguish an ethic that appeals to alterity from one that leans on some conception of the good. It has often been argued that actions are seen to be right or wrong in terms of a prior stipulation about what is to count as good. In the language of recent ethical debate, de-ontologists "eat lotus" with the Platonists by assuming some things to be good in their own right whereas consequentialists assume that some things are good because of what happens later because of them. Even many narrative ethicists think some stories are more worth heeding than others and offer criteria for distinguishing good from bad stories. An ethics that offers no anchorage can be interpreted as useless, yet conceptual moorings seem to be what postmodernism attacks. Must not a postmodern ethics offer some *point d'appui*, some anchorage that could guide moral deliberation and choice?

This question cannot be answered without first considering what it means to say that the languages of narrative and of the visual arts are discourses of power. Empowerment, it may be recalled, is the fifth tendency in my earlier enumeration of the impulses of postmodernism. In an age grown cynical and tired of official versions of events, the question of what individual or group authorizes a discourse, of whose power supports what discourse, is of considerable importance. It is just here, I shall argue, that there are deep disagreements among postmodernists. Because metaphysical language and moral norms can be described as discourses about the distribution of power, postmodernism may be thought to endorse a ruthless battle of power in which might determines right, an interpretation generally attributed to Nietzsche, who is often seen as a pathbreaker of philosophical postmodernism. If there is no stopping the dynamics of power, must a world subject to postmodern critique not go under in an orgy of conflicting and self-destructive struggles for power?

This is indeed one possibility of postmodernism. Ihab Hassan shows that, on the one hand, postmodernism "veers towards open, playful, optative, disjunctive, displaced or indeterminate forms."[11] Yet, on the other hand, built into postmodernism is an opposing tendency: "Postmodernism depends on the violent transhumanization of the Earth, wherein terror and totalitarianism, fractions and wholes, poverty and power summon each other. The end may be cataclysm and/or the beginning of genuine planetization."[12] This characterization seems to mandate as the sensible alternative to apocalypse a return to moral theory.

There is no denying that postmodernism is fine-tuned to the apocalyptic dimension of twentieth-century history. Postmodern artists and writers have peered into the abyss-like character of this century and have seen, heard, and tried to communicate, in fragmented critical writings and artworks, what lies beyond language. I shall consider in detail the resulting fissure within postmodernism itself, the difference in the way in which the abyss-like is appropriated by postmodern thinkers, who often differ radically from one another. At present I want only to suggest that heedfulness to what is abyss-like in history need not produce an eros for it but can elicit a postmodern ethic that is sensitive to the postmodern cry for difference.

Earlier I spoke about ethics as the sphere of relations between self and Other. The other person opens the venue of ethics, the place where ethical existence occurs. To answer the question about whether postmodernism requires some *point d'appui*, this Other, the touchstone of moral existence, is not a conceptual anchorage but a living force. The Other is different from oneself; her/his existence will be shown to carry compelling moral weight. In the context of a postmodern ethics, the Other functions as a critical solvent in much the same way as the notion of difference functions in postmodern metaphysics. I have capitalized the term Other when it refers to the other person not because this use of the Other is to be thought of as a master concept but to distinguish it from the many possible significations of the term.

Materialism, the sixth and last tendency of postmodernism, is often linked to an ethics of power. In the present context materialism will be associated with the sphere of the Other as bound up with the other's need, and thus with her/his material body. The term Other can be given a collective sense as referring to the wretched of the earth. The Other, both individually and collectively as the precondition for moral existence, is the Other in her or his corporeal being. The saintly response to the Other entails putting her/his own body and material goods at the disposal of the Other.

There is another less obvious role that materialism plays. Whatever else it may be, language, because it is made up of sounds or written marks, is something material. Even the language of *agape* is, as it were, shot through with the materiality of its medium. The sounds and marks of hagiographic narrative constitute a linguistic artifact that saints or those who are deputized by them offer as a tangible gift to the Other in the Other's interest. Having considered the characteristics of postmodernism, I believe it may be useful to state some of the main claims of the present work. A study that purports to be postmodern is not, I have insisted, a straightforward chain of arguments. It may therefore help to consider these claims as a paratactic arrangement of some of the work's main contentions:

1. Moral theory is an unsatisfactory way of addressing matters that require action in contemporary life. As Heidegger argues, the notion of theory in modern philosophy is derived from the ontology of modern science and, as such, assumes that truth is to be exhibited in propositions that assert causal relations, that these linguistic chains of argument directly or indirectly mirror the world, and that they explain phenomena. Narratives of saintly life steer clear of this difficulty. Yet, if the nomological character of moral theory is to be avoided, the presuppositions of narrative cannot be taken for granted but must be exposed through literary analysis of narrative structure. This alteration of perspective from theory to narrative and its implications for actual existence is one meaning I attribute to revisioning ethics. I shall return to the move away from theory in due course in order to bring out some specific aspects of revisioning so that the interdependence of various phases of the process described in the body of this study will come to the fore.

2. Saints' lives should not be imagined as emanating from some

specific religious community but as found across a broad spectrum of belief systems and institutional practices. A saintly life is defined as one in which compassion for the Other, irrespective of cost to the saint, is the primary trait. Such lives unfold in tension with institutional frameworks that may nevertheless later absorb them. Not only do saints contest the practices and beliefs of institutions, but in a more subtle way they contest the order of narrativity itself. Their lives exhibit two types of negation: the negation of self and the lack of what is needful but absent in the life of the Other. These expressions of negation are not just the subject matter of hagiography; they also enter its formal structure because negative content requires new modes of narrative expression.

3. The saint's addressees are acutely sensitive to the problem of interpreting hagiography. They believe that understanding hagiography consists not in recounting its meaning but in being swept up by its imperative force. The comprehension of a saint's life understood from within the sphere of hagiography is a *practice* through which the addressee is gathered into the narrative so as to extend and elaborate it with her/his own life. In this context I consider the risks and gains when the life of a political figure is interpreted hagiographically.

4. The body of the saint is accorded special meaning. The practice of asceticism should not be interpreted psychoanalytically as the reflection of repressed sexual desire even if such repression is a factor in saintly practice. Instead, the saint's body is to be taken as the unit of significance in saintly life. Not proclamation or argument, but the flesh acquires general meaning. I show that the peculiar mode of generality exhibited by the body, carnal generality, is to be distinguished from exemplarity, a concept that stems from theoretical understanding.

5. The saint's life is doubly coded with respect to her/his existence in time. On the one hand saints' lives express the time that belongs to work and achievement but on the other saints also live time as pure flux or passage. The latter mode of temporalization is not at all easy to see. It is discernible in certain primordial sensory experiences that have been generally ignored because of philosophy's stress on the relation of sensing to knowledge. Yet, not only is sensing a mode of cognition that brings to light some present content but also it is the body's sensitivity to pain and wounding. This passive and receptive structure has its own mode of temporalization, that of irrecoverable or lapsed time, of a flux that passes away and that constitutes the temporal framework of the saint's relation with the Other.

6. Double coding is also exhibited by the gender of saints. Although

the saint is a being who has a specific sexual identity, because saintly generosity consists in the abnegation of her/his own being, the saint speaks, as it were, with the voice of the Other. The body from which this thinking and speaking issues, neither that of self nor Other, becomes a nongendered body. This complex relationship to gender is explored in the context of specific saintly lives.

7. A startling claim is made by the postmodern philosopher Gilles Deleuze and his psychoanalyst collaborator Felix Guattari that desire is a mode of production and, as such, constitutes the underpinning of culture and history. Desire is hypostatized and treated not as lack but as pure positivity. Because Deleuze and Guattari also recognize the dynamic character of desire—desire is not only being but also motion—this positivity is conceived of as pure void. Like some Neoplatonists whom they resemble, they deploy this metaphysical pattern in the service of their quest for ecstasy. Postmodernism will be split along a fault line with the ecstatics, Deleuze and Guattari, Kristeva, and other postmoderns, on the one side and the philosophers of difference, Derrida, Levinas, and Blanchot, on the other. I shall argue that only the latter postmodernism can provide a language and interpretive context for saintly existence.

8. The reservations expressed regarding moral theory do not preclude insightful observation into the character of other-directed existence by analytic ethicists. In mining their arguments for such insights, I show that they run into difficulty because the Other is treated as another self. The accounts that derive from this perspective develop an altruism qualified by self-interest. Recent historical events will inevitably impact differently on altruism that begins with the self as the unit of significance and altruism that takes the Other as its starting point. A postmodern altruism must appeal to radical saintly generosity, to a benevolence that will not be brought to a close. Such saintliness is not a nostalgic return to premodern hagiography but a postmodern expression of excessive desire, a desire on behalf of the Other that seeks the cessation of another's suffering and the birth of another's joy.

There is a further problem still to be considered, that of revisioning as it is bound up with the relation of theory to philosophical method. Earlier I indicated that revisioning ethics entails a move away from moral theory. It is important to examine the character of the *specific pathways* along which philosophical meanings are created and deployed, the tracks along which the language of theory runs, in order to see how moral reason functions. The metaphor of the pathway is not accidental. It is by now a truism that philosophy from Descartes to the present is preoccupied with questions of method, a term made up of the prefix *meta*, "within," and *hodos*, "way" or "journey." To remain or abide within philosophy's way is to be constrained by conditions of philosophical method, by the turn to theory understood as systematically organized knowledge. The inextricability of moral theory from the conditions governing the organization of philosophical thinking generally, from the laws of spin so to speak of this thinking, is a central contention of the present work.

Although it is hoped that the work itself will make clear the relationships of moral theory to moral lives, it may be useful to sketch in advance the ways in which the critique of theory as part of revisioning ethics will be focused. My investigation will work itself free of theory by undertaking a three-pronged critique of theory: a pragmatic criticism of moral theory; an ontological criticism of its infrastructure; and a criticism of normative reason as belonging to the philosophy of reflection.

Consider first the pragmatic criticism, the easiest to see. As Alasdair MacIntyre and others have pointed out, moral theories do not result in moral actions. What is more, the increasing complexity of contemporary life generates new moral problems so that the arguments about moral issues increase in intricacy without resulting in solutions. Even the terms in which these arguments are couched cannot be decided upon because the background claims, claims belonging to the context in which they arise, cannot be agreed upon. If there is no common frame of reference, no cultural consensus in terms of which these disputes can be settled, the disputants can only go on arguing without altering moral dispositions or generating moral actions.

The pragmatic critique I have described reflects a well-worn philosophical distinction, that of means and ends. Based on the concept of utility, the pragmatic argument suggests that moral theory is an instrument that fails to achieve an already predetermined goal: the transformation of moral conduct. It describes the failure of theory as a means, an important first step, but it cannot account for the deficiencies of theory. Thus philosophers like MacIntyre or Bernard Williams, despite a richness of argumentation, remain phenomenologists of the failure of moral theory rather than thinkers who forge a new ethic in response to the radical transformation of historical circumstance.

Paradoxically it is Heidegger, the phenomenological thinker in the technical sense, who is the diagnostician of the failure of theory because he brings to the fore its infrastructures, its metaphysical protocols, or, in his terms, the way in which being is interpreted by theory. Thus the pragmatic critique is not independent of the uncovering of theory's ontological presuppositions, its underpinnings that preordain the character of specifically moral theories. For Heidegger, being in modern thought is viewed in terms of the being of nature as conceptualized by modern technology, a nature that is thought of in terms of calculable homogeneous units. The aim of theory is the manipulation and control of nature by means of an all-comprehensive account of being that includes human being. Once the meaning of being is determined by modern technology, the access routes to being will be construed along lines compatible with this ontology. A relation to being other than that established by the ontology of technique is precluded. Within such a world, the ligatures that connect one being to another are bonds of calculation and control.

Although it would seem that when philosophy is dominated by technology's mode of knowing it would turn its attention to the object of knowledge, contemporary philosophy in actuality exhibits a peculiar type of reflexivity: the subject of knowledge or consciousness is seen as apprehending the world and in the act of world-apprehension, as orienting itself toward self-apprehension, a recursiveness of consciousness especially evident in the philosophies of Kant and Husserl. This turn in the history of philosophy—the transcendental turn—is already criticized by Hegel and designated by him as the philosophy of reflection. The damaging result of reflection is its suppression of the time-tied encounter with the Other in that its standpoint is that of an omniscient and timeless observer. Such an observer is a disinterested spectator oblivious, among other things, to the pain and suffering of the Other.

The triple critique of moral theory I have sketched, the pragmatic critique of its utility, the ontological criticism of its infrastructure, and the attack upon knowledge as reflection, taken together constitutes the "argument" or "justification" for the break with theoretical discourse as the "ground" for generating moral lives and is a crucial component of the revisioning process.

Although the critique itself still falls within the recognizable boundaries of philosophical discourse, the fact is that I have undertaken a *postmodern* revisioning. Thus there is another face of revisioning, the one that treats moral life from the standpoint of hagiographic narrative. As I suggested earlier, this aspect of my text will often differ from standard philosophical writing, even from the work of the philosophers to whom I am deeply indebted, Heidegger, Merleau-Ponty, and especially Emmanuel Levinas. Life histories are recast in hagiographic form in the interest of exploring hagiography's narrative structure, its exhortative force, its network of practices. The conventions of postmodernism are put into the service of explicating moral dilemmas, and saintly responses are themselves part of the revisioning process. Such conventions include quotation marks used not only in the standard manner but to enclose doubly coded words, generally metaphysical posits expressing unity, totality, or closure, to indicate the displacement of the word's conventional use. The crossing out of a word indicates that it is written under erasure (*sous rature*) so that its historical meaning, although crossed out, is allowed a partial appearance. This brings to light not only the time-bound character of language but also its alienation, for a term under erasure is an alienated linguistic fragment.

In conformity with postmodern practice, the remarks here, although prefatory, do not constitute a preface. This calls attention to the fact that, even if they precede the "main body" of the work, they in fact reflect an act of stepping back from the work and, as in a musical prelude, striking its themes. All these moves taken together are nondifferent from the revisioning itself but constitute what I hope is its novelty.

In roaming freely through the world's religious traditions, I have discovered saintly lives among the canonized and among those who neither sought nor found institutional sanction. At the same time, I turn to a number of thinkers in the history of Western philosophy who, on the face of it, are unlikely candidates for providing insights into postmodern saintly existence: Aristotle, Plotinus, Damascius, Descartes, to name a few. Following Heidegger, I try to think through what has remained unthought in their philosophies, especially their treatments of time, of possibility and necessity, and of self, in order to wrest insights from their work that bear on saintly lives. This too is part of the revisioning process. In confronting present-day formulations of the problem of altruism, I have tried to show why a theoretical ethic must be supplanted by a narratological and a specifically hagiographic one. The recent phenomenological and postmodern thinkers to whom I appeal, Heidegger, Merleau-Ponty, Levinas, Derrida, Bataille, Blanchot, and others, have been my teachers in this task. It could be argued that in trying to think through a postmodern ethic the departures and hesitations, the errancies of my efforts, are the measure of what has been gleaned from their work. I am already in their debt because it is through their voices and silences, their marks and re-marks, that a postmodern ethic speaks.

1

There is a thought that has haunted me for a long time. . . . It is to portray a wholly good man. Nothing is more difficult . . . especially in our time.

Feodor Dostoevsky in a letter to Maikov,
31 December 1867

Giovanni di Paolo, Saint Catherine of Siena Giving Her Cloak to a Beggar. Cleveland Museum of Art, gift of the John Huntington Art and Polytechnic Trust, 66.3.

Why Saints?

THE REFLECTIONS in this epigraph are noteworthy not only because of their content but also because of the probable circumstances under which Dostoevsky thought of portraying a figure of ethical perfection. It is likely that he first heard of Saint Tikhon, the subject of these comments, in Siberia.[1] This would give special significance to the phrase "especially in our time," for the turmoil of the time—political and social—is reflected in Siberia's penal institutions. Then, as now, Siberia is both site and symbol of punitive exile. It is not unreasonable to speculate that Dostoevsky's desire to depict "a wholly good man" is bound up with the moral decay he sees around him. This moral decay may also account for his pessimism about the difficulties of the task in that one is likely to be moved by the life of a saint in an age of depravity but still unlikely to know how to give an account of it. These very difficulties suggest that depicting "a positive holy figure" is not only an aesthetic challenge but a matter of moral urgency. This suspicion is encouraged by the further fact that Dostoevsky in a letter to Maikov on 25 March 1870 announces "I am not going to create, I am only going to portray a real Tikhon whom long ago, with deep delight, I received into my heart."[2] Not a character out of whole cloth but "a real Tikhon"! Is it possible that Dostoevsky, like Kierkegaard in his account of Abraham, thought that *describing* the saint's life meant "making the movements after him?" To lead a moral life one does not need a theory about how one should live, but a flesh and blood existent.

To see better how Dostoevsky's approach may be helpful in thinking about the moral life, it may be useful to consider in a preliminary way some criticisms, not of any specific moral theory, but of moral theory generally as an instrument for gaining insight into what moral lives are or how they might be pursued. One difficulty connected with moral theory is the gap between the theory (even when it is a theory about practice) and life. The aporia between theory and practice is particularly apparent in modern theories from Hume to the present. This problem can be attributed to an underlying assumption about the relationship between scientific and ethical theories. Ethical theories are thought to be something like theories in science. The answer to a scientific inquiry can be agreed upon because it is interpreted as somehow representing the way things are. But as Bernard Williams argues, "in the area of the ethical, at least at a high level of generality, there is no such coherent hope."[3] There is a deeper layer of philosophical difficulty at which the confusion of the structure of moral theory with that of scientific theory occurs that is bound up with the way in which scientific understanding becomes the dominant model for thinking. I shall return to this question in detail later. At present I cite their conflation because it suggests a reason for the gap between moral theory and life.

A second problem is the failure of recent moral theories not only to settle moral questions but, more significantly, even to agree upon the terms of moral disputes. This is not a lexical failure but the result of the heterogeneous philosophical background claims that govern attempts to resolve disputed questions. Alasdair MacIntyre has called attention to this problem and correctly notices that such heterogeneity is still another reason why theories "fail to produce dispositions not only to act but to feel in particular ways. . . . Moral education is an *education sentimentale*."[4] Unlike legal disputes, incommensurable claims cannot be settled by adjudication if they are genuinely incommensurable. What is more, the attempted resolution may only proliferate the number of claims by adding on conditions thought to be required by the compromise.

Can recourse to the lives of saints offer insight into what moral lives are and how one might go about living a moral life while still avoiding the two difficulties associated with moral theory, the gap between theory and practice resulting from the confusion of moral and scientific discourse and the incommensurate presuppositions of theories from which follows the failure to produce moral dispositions? Each of these problems demands a different mode of attack. The first dilemma requires a genealogical analysis of theory. By tracking the turning points in the history of philosophy that permit the world picture from which modern science emerges, one can bring out the way moral theory comes to be dominated by the properties of scientific inquiry. The analyses of Heidegger and Derrida are especially pertinent to an understanding of the process and the result of this conflation. The aim of my investigation is not to liberate moral theory from an embedding matrix with the hope of producing a better theory. Such a project would permit a general theory of morality to emerge unscathed and would point to a possibly deeper concealment of the root problem. Instead, a genealogical analysis should facilitate proceeding by a different route, that of attentiveness to concrete social experience, to encounters with other persons. The results of considering the concrete social plane are general results, but this generality is to be interpreted differently from the kind of generality striven for by moral theories, a matter I shall take up in later chapters.

The second difficulty cited, that heterogeneous background claims make it impossible to attain accord about moral practice, is parasitic on the first (that moral theory and scientific discourse are intertwined) in that such background claims are themselves covert moral theories or are bound up with moral theories. But by appealing directly to concrete moral lives, a different nontheoretical discursive framework can be brought to bear on questions of moral practice. To be sure, pending the promised account of theory, the question of why moral lives cannot be accounted for by a theory about moral life remains open. But it is both possible and important for what is to follow, to describe in a preliminary way and in postmodern terms what one is appealing to when invoking the lives of saints: *narrativity, corporeality, textuality, historicality.*

In considering the structural features of saintly lives, I shall not only discuss a variety of religious traditions but also transgress historical boundaries. That hagiographic texts are specific to their context I do not contest here. Instead, I hope to bring out the manner in which some features of saintly lives impinge on what is integral to time-bound social and political praxes and, in fact, may serve to undermine them. It should also be apparent that I do not endorse many culturally related expressions of saintly lives but turn to these features of experience in order to illuminate the structural conditions of those lives.

Narrativity

The term narrative comes from the Latin *narrare,* "to relate or recount." Through its probable earlier form, *gnarare,* it may be linked to *gnarus,* "knowing," "skilled," and thus conceptually to knowledge. In English one of the earliest uses of the word occurs in the context of Scottish law and refers to "that part of a deed or document which contains the relevant or essential facts."[5] Although he does not allude to the etymological link, Jacques Derrida notices that narrative is in part a juridical discourse. "[Someone] demand[s] the narrative of the other, seek[s] to extort from him . . . something that they call the truth of what has taken place: 'Tell us exactly what happened.'"[6]

Because hagiographic texts are narratives, they are also in the sense described by Derrida juridical discourses purporting to relate events. I define hagiography as a narrative linguistic practice that recounts the lives of saints so that the reader or hearer can experience their imperative power. According to this definition, some factual biographies of saints may not be hagiographic whereas some works of fiction may be at least partially so, especially if the narrative is recast to exhibit the compelling force of a life. Hagiography is limited neither to a historical period such as the Western European Middle Ages nor to a specific genre, the tale of a holy life. Instead, hagiography is a widely disseminated discursive form found not only in religious literature but in biography, autobiography, and the novel. For the purpose of the present study, the value and utility of saints' lives in building moral lives, I shall restrict my account of narrativity to three features of the hagiographic story: its temporal character or event structure, the grammatical mood that governs the story, and the social formations it exhibits.

Because narrative is that discourse whose main purpose is to relate events—unlike both eulogy, in which facts are subordinated to arousing memory, and argument, in which facts are in the service of inference—narrative has a sequential structure. Hagiographic narrative exhibits a tripartite chronological ordering: the time of the matter narrated, the life of the saint from birth to death with both its quotidian and exceptional episodes; "authorial" time, or the time of recounting; and the order of time into which the story falls, that of the listener or reader. Even when these strands overlap temporally, they may still be differentiated. Thus in oral cultures the time of narrator and the time of hearer may coincide but they are distinguishable through the heterogeneity of the tale's voices, that of teller and addressee. On the other hand a single life may display multiple temporal scissions. In autobiographical narrative, protagonist and narrator are the same but the time of narration and that of the matters related will differ. These chronological layers are generally distinguishable intratextually to the narrative's protagonists as well as to the tale's extratextual addressees.

This account would, on the face of it, seem to support a straightforwardly representational theory of narrative. According to the received view, the events of the saint's life constitute the tale's referents and are mirrored or reflected in the narrative as events antedating their representation in language. But if these events are imagined as lacking discursive embodiment, how are they to be construed? Before the tale comes into being, "events" are nothing more than a shapeless flux, an an-archic and inchoate nonground. It is only through narrative articulation that events are disclosed as such and take on the character of an ontological matrix. Maurice Blanchot's view of narrative generally applies *pari passu* to stories of saints' lives:

[I]f we regard the tale [*le récit*] as the true telling of an exceptional event which has taken place and which someone is trying to report, then we have not come close to sensing the true nature of the tale. The tale is not the narration of an event, but the event itself, the approach to that event, the place where that event is made to happen—an event which is yet to come and through whose power of attraction the tale can hope to come into being too.

. . . The tale is a movement towards a point . . . unknown, obscure, foreign [and] such that apart from this movement it does not seem to have any real prior existence, and yet it is so imperious that the tale derives its power of attraction only from this point and cannot even "begin" before reaching it.[7]

In the tale (*le récit*), an event is a nodal point or "lure" that brings into being both itself and the narrative of which it is the focus.

It is important to stress that in the case of saintly lives the claim that events are textually constituted does not imply that saints have not lived, suffered, and worked in actuality. However, *recounted* saintly lives depend on the general conditions of textuality and the context-laden conventions of hagiographic discourse. I shall consider the ontological and discursive conditions of hagiographic textuality in detail later. At present it suffices to notice that although "facts" constituting saintly lives may be independent of textual reference, these "facts" cannot in any straightforward way cash out recounted events.

In hagiography this situation is complicated by the deliberate reworking of the facts of saintly life and by hagiographic invention *tout court*. In historical investigations of saintly lives, it has been noted that religious communities often fabricate hagiographies for saints who never existed. Speaking of Roman Catholic tradition, Pierre Delooz writes:

Most saints were once real people, about whom objective facts may be established: their sex, their place of birth, and particularly of death. . . . But beside the real saints are what we may call the *constructed* saints. All saints are more or less *constructed* in that, being necessarily saints *for other people*, they are remodelled in the collective representation which is made of them.[8]

What is more, if the narrative continues to remain vital to the life of a community, this shaping and reshaping continues. Thus Saint Anthony of Padua, who was, in the common sense meaning of the term, a "real"

saint, is depicted in the Later Middle Ages long after his death as carrying the child Jesus in his arms, perhaps, Delooz speculates, because
family feeling was becoming important in the Europe of that period.[9]
At least for Christian Europe of the Later Middle Ages where interest
in hagiography is intense, the life that is recounted is shaped in conformity with social expectations connected with saintly acts.

Like many other narrative forms, the hagiographic tale is organized
around some matter or upshot, the story's point, even when a story
seems to do no more than replicate the events of a life. The narrative
that is intentionally utterly pointless is rare. Narrated events are generally believed to have significance not only to protagonists and recoun-
ters but to addressees and are shaped with these multiple constituencies
in mind. The upshot of a hagiographic narrative may be (and often is)
bound up with a moral point.

Could it then be argued that saints' lives are didactic stories, fables
without genuine chronological articulation? If so, is hagiography linked
more closely to moral theory than to narrative in that purely didactic
tales may be vehicles for the expression of moral maxims that are themselves theories or embedded in theories? In that case a fable's sequential
structure would subserve its moral claims. Aesop's story about the crow
who succumbs to the fox's flattery so that, as she tries to sing, she drops
the cheese from her beak is not a genuine narrative but an illustration
of a prudential maxim about flattery deduced from a theory about egoism and self-interest.[10] The fable or purely didactic story is actually
an argument and the moral, a conclusion arrived at deductively.[11] But
the essential structure of *narrative* is to bring something to fruition
through its temporal development. The moral lesson of the didactic tale
is alien to narrative as such, interrupts its flow, and remains a dead
element within the story.

Because saints' lives have a temporal structure, becoming and change
are intrinsic to them. Something happens, then something else: the
structure of the "then" is the order of narration and is plotted in terms
of that toward which the sequence tends. (Some narratives are more
purposive than others. Open narratives do not coerce the reader or
hearer through prefabricated leads or inferences toward already determined conclusions but permit the *reader* to resolve the narrative's ambiguities.) In true narrative discourse the chronological character of
events is integral to the story's point, whereas in the relation of theory
to example the independence of the example—its own coming to temporal fruition—is suppressed in the interest of theory, an abstract formulation having general import. Even the most static narrative cannot

lose its temporal movement, whereas an example is designed to arrest time in the service of the theory it instantiates. Even when they are models of time-tied processes, examples are not meant to draw the hearer into their sequential structure, to "make the movements" of a series of thens. Instead, they are intended to be "seen through," as transparent toward theory. A moral dictum embedded in a narrative becomes, as Bakhtin remarks, "an object, a relic, a thing."[12]

In sum, the sequential structure of hagiography is such that the story's denouement is not a theory built up from events that serve as the theory's supports but a coming to fruition of a life by way of the story's time-tied events. A grasp of this structure is significant not only for understanding particular narratives but also for envisioning the relation of narrative to moral practice.

To see how the intratextual orchestration of time is intended to grip its addressees, consider the life of Mary the Egyptian as derived from a twelfth-century French source.

Listen to the true story of Mary the Egyptian. . . . [She] was born in Egypt and was shameful even in her youth. She was enamored of pleasure and gave herself to all men. . . . It's a wonder that her parents did not die of grief. . . . At the age of 12 she left her family. . . . [and] came to Alexandria. . . . One day. . . . she went to the port where a ship of pilgrims was arriving [and] asks to go with them to Jerusalem. . . . offering to pay her passage with her body. . . . Shortly after [she came to Jerusalem] it was the Feast of the Ascension. . . . [When] she was barred entry into the Temple . . . she comes to a realization of her sins. . . . cries for mercy . . . [and is able to enter]. There a statue speaks to her: ". . . Spend the rest of your life in the desert."

. . . For more than forty years she lived nude . . . like an animal. . . . Zozima, a saintly monk, [sees Mary]. The wind rose and revealed her flesh burned by sun and frost. Mary took to flight, with Zozima . . . close behind. . . . He calls out to God . . . and give[s] her a cloth to wrap herself in. . . . [Mary prays and rises] a full two and one half feet. [The next year Mary returns and prays for death. She dies but her body does not decompose. After another year Zozima looks for her. Led on by a bright light, he finds the body and a letter instructing him to bury her but the earth is too hard.] A lion came up to him. . . . The lion dug out the grave. . . . [and] disappeared into the great desert. Zozima returns [and] recounts the life of Mary. We pray that Mary will intercede for us and ask God to forgive our sins. Amen.[13]

The story of Mary comprises three strands of narration, each exhibiting its own mode of temporality. First, there is the strand of Mary's life ("she was born in Egypt," and so on) that recounts a transformation from sin to redemption. As Bakhtin argues in connection with tales of metamorphosis, individual fate is portrayed in chronological sequence and explicated as a "life-long destiny . . . at all its critical turning points."[14] Life is transformed not because of chance events but because the individual assumes responsibility for her/his actions.[15] By contrast with literary forms in which character remains static (such as the epic), action inscribes its *traces* in the lives of saints and affects the world the saints inhabit.[16] Second, the authorial strand, "Listen to the true story," points to a narrator-witness who is outside the story and different from the tale's characters.[17] The text is complicated by an "earlier" telling by Zozima, who is both protagonist and the first narrator. The final narrator appeals to a "we," a community embracing himself and his addressees, who are to pray for Mary's intercession. From Mary's perspective, her life is lived in a forward progression—early promiscuity, the ship of pilgrims, the voyage to Jerusalem, the encounter with the statue, the Feast of the Ascension, wandering in the desert—and only with the passage of time does she come to see her old life as sinful. The narrator and his eleventh-century addressees are likely to constitute a community that is familiar with the tale's hagiographic conventions and is never in the dark about the saint's spiritual condition. For them Mary is retrospectively interpreted as always already sinful and always already redeemed, a life making and unmaking itself.

The tale's chronological strands and textual voices may appear to the reader to convey information and, as such, to reflect an attitude of factuality toward what is recounted even when the events reported are out of the ordinary. But even if what occurs is brought to light in the indicative mood, the hagiographic material is united and framed by the imperative mood. Thus in the command "Listen" and in the demand that all pray for Mary's intercession, the imperative mood of the tale solicits others to transform their lives. The narrative voices together with the temporal scissions they reflect are organized to display Mary's remarkable spiritual rebirth and transformation. The story's success is not measured in aesthetic or cognitive terms but rather in regard to whether the addressees experience the saint's spiritual rebirth as an existential demand. The tale is not intended to elicit replication but to inspire a new catena of moral events appropriate to the addressee's life.

Not only does hagiography exhibit an event structure plotted along a chronological axis, but through its narrative voices it expresses diverse social functions. Lyotard suggests that the social agenda of narrative is the transmission of customary knowledge without having to formulate this knowledge theoretically. This is the single point, Lyotard claims, about which widely divergent accounts of narrative agree:

Some study the form for its own sake [Propp]; others see it as the diachronic costume of the structural operators that . . . properly constitute the knowledge in question [Lévi-Strauss]; still others bring to it an "economic" interpretation in the Freudian sense of the term. . . . Narration is the quintessential form of customary knowledge, in more ways than one.[18]

This hypothesis is applicable to the myths of nonliterate societies as well as to tales and legends of heroic apprenticeship (*Bildungen*). It is also relevant to understanding the function of custom or socially sanctioned moral practices encompassed in saints' lives. But it is crucial to notice that institutional norms often thwart saintly intentions and, conversely, that saintly acts frequently impinge on entrenched custom and explicitly articulated practice. To see the way in which narrative discourse forwards the purposes of moral insurgency, it is useful to consider hagiography not as folktale or legend of apprenticeship (despite some superficial resemblances) but as a proto-novelistic discourse. Because the novel articulates the various strands of social existence, it incorporates a multiplicity of social utterances, each occupying its own social space and each contesting the multiple voices of others. Mikhail Bakhtin's account of the heterogeneity of fictional prose shows that, far from being devoted exclusively to customary knowledge as Lyotard thinks, novelistic discourse contains voices that sabotage received knowledge. Bakhtin writes:

The novel can be defined as a diversity of social speech types . . . and a diversity of individual voices, artistically organized. The internal stratification of . . . characteristic group behavior, professional jargons, generic languages, languages of generations and age groups, languages of the authorities, languages that serve the socio-political purposes of the day. . . . is the indispensable prerequisite for the novel as a genre. The novel orchestrates all its themes, the totality of all its objects depicted and expressed in it, by means of the social diversity of speech types and by the differing individual voices that flourish under such conditions. [These voices are] those fundamental compositional unities with whose help heteroglossia can enter the novel. . . . [The] dispersion into the rivulets and droplets of social heteroglossia, its dialogization—this is the basic distinguishing feature of the stylistics of the novel.[19]

Heteroglossia, the interplay of a novel's multiple voices, is often expressed as a conflict between confessors and others representing institutional claims who speak out against saintly practice whereas the saint insists on going her/his own way. Consider Saint Margaret of Cortona's rebellious response to her confessor's suggestion that she cease starving herself: "I have no intention of making peace between my body and my soul. . . . [A]llow me to tame my body by not altering my diet. I will not stop for the rest of my life until there is no life left."[20] In a letter from the thirteenth century, Saint Clare of Assisi, to whom ascetic practice was not foreign, writes to the more extreme Blessed Agnes of Prague: "Since we do not have *a body of bronze* nor is ours the strength of granite . . . I pray you and beseech you in the name of the Lord, oh dearest one, to moderate . . . the impossible austerity . . . you have embarked upon so that . . . your sacrifice will be *seasoned with the salt of prudence*."[21] The ecclesiastical wariness with which ascetic extremes are regarded cannot be attributed exclusively to concerns of prudence about health or even to the background theological consideration that the body, insofar as it is part of divine creation, cannot be totally corrupt. Instead, ecclesiastical worry about self-mortification can be attributed largely to the conflict it poses with another institutional norm, that of recognizing and obeying the Church's authority to determine appropriateness in matters connected with ascetic practice. Thus self-mortification is by no means univocally understood in this period because, as Bakhtin argues, "no living word relates to its object in a *singular* way; between the word and its object, between the word and the speaking subject, there exists an elastic environment of the other, alien words about the same object, the same theme, and that is an environment that it is often difficult to penetrate."[22]

Not only is ecclesiastical reproach ignored but the pieties of everyday life, especially submission to parental authority, are similarly flouted. Consider the account of the life of Saint Theodosius, the first monastic saint canonized by the Russian church and recounted by Nestor, a monk of the same Kievan cloister to which his subject belonged. Theodosius was born to "Christians of exemplary piety" but decided to join a group of pilgrims against his mother's wishes. The point about his parent's piety is important because it tells against the argument that Theodosius is merely following the Gospel precept to leave even one's parents if they lack faith in Christ. The struggle is intense: "Carried away by fury, [Theodosius's mother] seized him by the hair, flung him to the ground . . . trampled on him, [and led him home] bound like a criminal. . . . [She] flung him into a room, shackled him and locked the door."[23] Hagiographic narrative is replete with such instances of rebellious conduct. The legitimation of customary morality cannot have been the sole intent of the story, and, conversely, if such narratives highlight deviation from custom, morality grounded in custom cannot be said to support them. Bound up with the issue of the legitimation of custom is a further question: Can a cultic community that has preserved the narrative of a saint's life intend it to become a scenario for straight-forward reenactment?

If narrations of saints' lives constitute, at least in part, exceptions to what is generally believed about narrative discourse and are legitimated by neither the theological nor the prudential structures of their epoch, what does legitimate saintly practices? The validating rules for the so-cially disruptive and institutionally destabilizing features of saintly life are not to be looked for *outside* that life but are *immanent* to it. In fact, such rules are rules of thumb that are established *intradiscursively* in the context-specific local determinations of the life itself.

To see this in the Christian context, consider the underlying theo-logical motif common to Christian saintly lives of widely differing re-gional and historical provenance. A background belief of virtually all Christian hagiography is that saints live their lives in the light of Christ's life. *Imitatio Christi* is the apothegm that illuminates saintly contempla-tion and the command that guides saintly conduct. But if this is the imperative under which Christian saints labor, there is an insuperable obstacle to the success of their efforts. The infinite wisdom, power, and goodness of Christ are not re-presentable even by a spiritual elite. To the extent that the earthly ministry and passion of Jesus are paradig-matic, they are so in and through their transcendent ground. Human nature, however, cannot conform itself to divine perfection. Thus *Imi-tatio Christi* is an unrealizable imperative because the life of Christ can-not be replicated.

The saint's task is to undertake two intersecting lines of endeavor. The first strategy is to *construct* a content, necessarily extreme—self-mortification, voluntary poverty, and the like—to reach for what is in-herently refractory to representation, a life like that of Jesus. The second strategy, parasitic on the first, is, paradoxically, to "*show*" unrepresent-ability itself, in this case to display how impossible it is to bring the divine life into plenary presence.[24] A similar case can be made out for Buddhist sanctity. The Buddhist saint or Enlightenment Being devel-ops "skill in means," the ability to design measures for enlightening sentient beings in the manner of the historical Buddha, but is unable to depict the Buddha nature that is itself beyond description or enactment. In the nonincarnational theology of Judaism, saintly presence expresses itself in the intersubjective realm as a response to the *imago dei* that marks each person. Even when saintly life is an expression of obedience to institutional norms or revealed laws, there can be no rules to guide that aspect of saintly work which admits of no conceivable realization, to *fully* re-present the divine life or to *fully* realize the divine will. The life itself *is* the quest for rules. Like the postmodern writer, the saint "is working without rules in order to formulate the rules of what *will have been.*"[25]

Saintly Bodies

Saintly life, like any other existent, requires material conditions for its emergence. For any entity to exist as a discrete individual, Aristotle argued, there must be matter. But in the case of saintly life, corporeality plays a complex role. This is as true for Buddhist devotional traditions in which the life of a saint may stretch across innumerable bodily transformations as it is for both Eastern and Western Christianity. Most hagiographic accounts think of the body as a hindrance to the development of a sought-for spiritual inwardness. In fact, the suspicion with which traditional conceptions of sainthood are regarded is, in part, the result of the naturalistic attitude most modern thinkers hold toward the body. Self-mortification is viewed as an obstruction to natural and spontaneous human development, a tendency reflected, for example, in Rousseau's pedagogical recommendation to allow for the expression of natural freedom in childhood:

Since civil servitude begins with the age of reason, why precede it with a servitude of privation? Let us endure a moment of life exempt from this yoke that nature has not imposed on us and allow childhood the exercise of natural freedom that distances it, for a while at least, from the vices one contracts in slavery [translation mine].[26]

Nietzsche and Freud fit ascetic practice into a pattern of psychological pathology continuing and deepening the Enlightenment account. It is easy enough to understand the repugnance inspired by such practices as self-starvation, wearing painful garments for years at a time, nudity under harsh environmental conditions, self-flagellation and burning. The hagiographic accounts themselves supply as reasons for ascetic practice, expiation of sin, avoidance of further temptation, and, in a general way, the testing of faith. Speaking of the Christian communities of the fifth and sixth centuries, Peter Brown writes:

We should not forget the speed with which in all areas of the Mediterranean world, the ascetic movement had articulated and, in so doing, amplified, Christian anxieties about sin and the last judgment. . . . not because more sin was happening or because the last judgment was thought to have drawn appreciably nearer. . . . [but because] Christian leaders presented the world and the play of human action within it in terms of a single all-embracing principle of explanation, as so many consequences of sin and its admission.[27]

Torture inflicted by others often serves the same ends as asceticism. Consider the practices inflicted on Saint George to make him renounce his faith in the Trinity: "George is placed on a bench. Weights of iron and lead are attached to his feet, a fire is lighted beneath him, he is pierced with lances, and poison is poured into his wounds. . . . He is whipped and salt is put on his open wounds."[28] The role that both torture and ascetic practice fill for a spiritual elite is, as Weinstein and Bell comment, "the mastery over bodily demands [as] the avenue of communion with the godhead; for the humble believer it was the outer sign of spiritual election."[29]

Recent interpretations treating ascetic practice as reinforcing institutional norms do not, as I argued earlier, account for asceticism's frequently antinomian role. Psychological interpretations single out the repression or sublimation of sexual impulses but fail to include socio-historical factors. Can asceticism be explained in still another way, one that links its practices to a view of corporeality that can accommodate features integral to these practices as described in the hagiographic materials themselves? If such a conception of corporeality can be provided, is it possible to show how asceticism is a possible outcome of saintly life but not integral to it? In order to take up these questions, it is important to consider how the body is ordinarily experienced without losing sight of the fact that the saint does not experience body-as-such but a time-bound, socially and historically conditioned saintly body. This is not a further fact added on to saintly life but inextricably bound up with who and how saints are. Before turning to saintly corporeality, it is useful for the conceptual analysis of the body in asceticism to examine bodily existence *tout court*.

It is by now a commonplace that the way in which the human body is conceived in modern philosophy can be traced to a sharp distinction drawn by Descartes between the subject that thinks and the object of knowledge. While Greek philosophy takes account of this distinction, it comes to play a pivotal role in philosophical thought when Descartes makes the thinking subject the Archimedean point for the foundation of knowledge. In so doing, the thinking subject, the guarantor of truth and certainty, is interpreted as an internal world of consciousness and the physical world, a world present to it. Objects are thought of as spread out side by side before consciousness. Because the subject of experience, the true subject, is identified with consciousness, the body is interpreted on analogy with physical objects as another object, a fragment of the not-self inserted into mechanistic space. This view of the body as object loses sight of the body's character as the subject of experience.

In his analysis of the genesis of the object in visual perception, Merleau-Ponty offers a description of visual experience that helps to account for the Cartesian interpretation.[30] The way objects have been thought of is, at least in part, the result of the built-in double character of the visual process itself. Merleau-Ponty shows that there is a discrepancy between the way in which objects actually originate in visual perception, reach the observer, and the way in which objects are finally seen. It is the first question, how objects originate for us, that constitutes the novel feature of Merleau-Ponty's analysis. He claims that two primary factors govern perceiving, first, the horizon factor, the idea that objects are not seen by themselves but are picked out against a background, and, second, the wholeness factor, the idea that each object is perceptually discriminated as a totality.

Consider first the horizon factor: "I see the next door house from a certain angle, but it would be seen differently from the right bank of the Seine, or from the inside or from an airplane," Merleau-Ponty writes.[31] The house is given against a backdrop which both stations and limits it, a visual horizon against which it comes forward or recedes and can be distinguished from other objects. Consider next the second characteristic of perception, the feature of wholeness. It is bound up with the first, but instead of focusing on the figure-and-ground character of the visual field, the object itself is of primary concern. In the often cited example of a six-sided cube, the cube is not given all at once, in *ein Augenblick*. Instead, individual faces of the cube present themselves successively in conformity with the observer's position. Yet the observer claims to see a whole cube. The absent sides that would be seen if the object were circumnavigated and that are attributed to it are the product of a visual inference, an inference that is not something consciously performed but is simply a property of the way visual perception works.[32]

Of course the genealogical analysis of the percept just undertaken does not figure consciously in actual perceptual acts. But vision in its ordinary functioning opens the way for conceiving objects as wholes and is capable of complex acts of unconscious abstraction. In the case of the multiple views of the house, "the house *itself* is none of [its] appearances; it is as Leibniz said, the flat projection of these perspectives, that is the perspectiveless position from which all can be derived, the house seen from nowhere."[33] The phenomenon of the horizon as well as the multifaceted character of entities is integral to perception because human beings *are* their bodies. The view from nowhere and the inference to wholeness reflect perception's attempt to transcend the limitations of embodiment.

Because the body, integral to the manner in which perception occurs, can itself be seen, it is in that respect no different from the house or the cube or any other visible object that can be inserted into a world of objects. But as Merleau-Ponty argues, the body is not an object like others because one cannot distance oneself from one's own body so that it can give itself as a totality. I myself am that body. I do not see my body in the way I see the bodies of others nor do I move it as I would push a cart. "Movement is not thought about movement and bodily space is not space thought of or represented. . . . A movement has been learned when the body has understood it. . . . We must avoid saying that our body is in space or in time. It inhabits space and time." [34] Similarly William James writes: "The body is the storm center, the origin of coordinates, the constant place of stress. . . . Everything circles round it and is felt from its point of view." [35]

It is possible to interpret Merleau-Ponty's analysis as itself vulnerable to a Cartesian-like interpretation: instead of making the rational subject, the ego cogito, the foundation of knowledge, now this role is attributed to the perceptual subject. But a closer look shows that if the untotalizability of the perceptual field, the way in which objects come to be seen, is attended to, perception is always undoing itself. As Descombes writes, "[T]he perceiving subject sees its empire disintegrate around it. Cubes shed their sides, things dwindle away into the distance, becoming miniscule, faces have an 'ambiguous' air, others only exist in the infinite. The world frays at the edges." [36]

With this account of the perceptual field and embodiment as a conceptual backdrop, the question of saintly corporeality can be considered afresh. I argued earlier that the saint did not experience first a body and then something saintly added on to it but instead was his or her body, lived it so to speak, in a unique way. Thrown into saintly experience are not only the ensemble of perceptual, tactile, and kinesthetic structures that constitute everyday bodily experience but the viscera and bones, in short the saint's entire body. In Christian tradition, the concern of fourteenth-century piety with Christ's passion provides numerous examples of such total involvement. Most striking is Saint Catherine of Sienna's description of entering directly into Christ's wounds "and [finding] such sweetness and knowledge of the divinity there that if you could ever appreciate it you would marvel that my heart did not break." [37] When the entire body is implicated in saintly experience, the *body as a whole* functions as a sensorium. It does not help to say Saint Catherine *saw* the passion, although visions of the passion are common. Instead, truer to her own account, she entered into the passion, felt it with her whole being. Nothing intervened between herself and it. The lack of distance that informs her encounter is experienced as pain. If sense is to be made of Saint Catherine's perceptual acts, her brand of seeing must be redescribed as the body's seeing.

I argued earlier that seeing has two aspects, an abstract or cognitive side that suspends the actual spatial and temporal conditions of perception, and a genealogical side that reflects the spatio-temporal character of the perceiving acts. Saintly asceticism reflects these two dimensions of the structure of perceiving in the manner through which pain is experienced. Consider again Saint Catherine's description of pain as sweet. Standard psychoanalytic explanation, by relying solely on the transformation of sexual feeling to explain the sweetness she describes, does not go far enough in its account of body. To be sure, the body is a field for the expression of desire, but its cognitive and perceptual dimensions cannot be ignored. Just as the diachronic or moment-to-moment character of perceiving is suspended when objects are perceived as wholes, so too pulsations of pain can be put out of play. But at the same time, this infrastructure of pain is invasive even when set aside and does not simply disappear. The pain pulses are, so to speak, the price paid for sanctity and may in some contexts become intrinsic to it. This question will recur in connection with saintly compassion in chapter 2. At present it is enough to notice that pain and its suspension are the mode of realization of the saintly body's perceptual structure.

These two aspects of saintly corporeality are illustrated in Saint Teresa's description of her bodily states. "I can testify that after rapture my body often seemed as light as if all weight had left it; sometimes this was so noticeable that I could hardly tell when my feet were touching the ground. For while the rapture lasts, the body often remains as if dead and unable of itself to do anything."[38] The entire body as a pain sensorium is suspended and becomes self-transcending just as vision transcends temporal and perspectival specificity by suspending them. Saint Teresa has been lifted to the view from nowhere to which her body as a whole aspires. But when her soul is still yearning for God she recounts untold distress. "The pain is so excessive one can hardly bear it. . . . [M]y pulses almost cease to beat, my bones are all disjointed and my hands are so stiff that sometimes I cannot clasp them together. Until the next day I have pains in my wrists and in my entire body as though my bones had been wrenched asunder," she cries.[39] As Michel de Certeau argues, the semantic order is linked to torture and pain: "The defoliation of meaning and torture are not just what is said in the discourse. They define its mode of production."[40] Extremes of ecstasy and distress express the organic range of saintly corporeality, quite literally the systole and diastole of saintly consciousness in which the body as a whole expresses itself.

Textuality

From the standpoint of understanding saints' lives as hagiographic texts, it is worth pondering the use of text as metaphor in the fiction of Henry James. Consider the tropes in the following passages from James's *Wings of the Dove*:

The sense was constant for her that their relation was as if afloat, like some island of the south, in a great warm sea that made for every conceivable chance, a margin, an outer sphere of general emotion, and the effect of the occurrence of anything in particular was to make the sea submerge the island, the margin flood the text. (Text A)

She had long been conscious with shame for her thin blood, . . . of her unused margin as an American girl closely indeed as, in English air, the text might appear to cover the page. She still had reserves of spontaneity, if not of comicality; so that now all this cash in hand could find employment. (Text B)

There was always doubtless a moment . . . at which it was beyond disproof that one was back. His full parenthesis was closed, and he was once more but a sentence, of a sort, in the general text, the text that from his momentary street corner, showed as a great grey page of print that somehow managed to be crowded without being "fine." The grey however was more or less the blur of a point of view not yet quite seized again. (Text C)
Henry James, *The Wings of the Dove*

Long before postmodern critics fastened theoretical attention on texts, Henry James noticed three properties of texts, as these citations show: first that a text is a piece of discourse fixed in writing (Text B), second that texts comprise marks and spaces whose boundaries are frangible (Text A), and finally that it is useful to apply the concept of texts to persons and their relations (Texts A, B, and C). The last property shows that lives treated as texts double up recursively, bend back upon themselves, in that the life in the text is itself a text (Text C). To show the pertinence of the question of textuality in saintly life, I shall consider each of these properties of texts: their written character, the role of presence and absence in texts as signified by their marks and spacing, and the relation of textuality to persons. James's astonishing references to the concept of the text in the passages cited open the question of the time and space of writing as they bear on the hermeneutics of "character." In chapter 2, I shall treat the life of Millie, the poor little rich girl in James's *Wings of the Dove*, as hagiographic and shall recur to these citations as bearing on the semantics of moral practice.

James's remarks presuppose the commonsense notion that texts are linguistic objects fixed in writing. Philosophers from Plato to the recent past have paid scant attention to writing, preferring instead to consider speech the primary manifestation of language. The function of writing has generally been interpreted by philosophers as the imitation of living speech. The locus classicus for this view is *Phaedrus*, the dialogue in which Plato treats the question in some detail. There Socrates criticizes writing, an invention of the Egyptian god Thoth, as eroding the power of living speech. In bringing writing to the fore as a problem for thinking, Derrida demonstrates the paradoxical character of Plato's interpretation: Socratic truth is established not in speech but in Platonic writing. The description of living speech falls back on a scriptic metaphor in that the truth of vocal utterance depends on its being *inscribed* in the soul.[41] Writing is a *pharmakon*, the Greek word for both remedy and poison, because it is the proposed cure for lapses of memory, but injurious in that it deepens the disease it is intended to heal. On Plato's account its status is determined by its relationship to full speech, which alone can bring truth into plenary presence. Writing is the other of the living logos. But the mutual relations of the two are such that speech can no longer claim primacy. If writing merely imitates speech it is secondary, but if speech is already inscription—written in the soul—then speech is ancillary to writing.

Derrida claims that the history of philosophy contains many opposing paired motifs in addition to speech and writing such as inside/outside, present/absent, universal/particular. The first member of the pair is both conceptually and practically privileged, a status acquired as a result of its distance from the spatio-temporal specificity of concrete facts and one that cannot simply be reversed:

It is not a question of returning to writing its rights, its superiority or its dignity. Plato said of writing that it was an orphan or a bastard, as opposed to speech, the legitimate and high born son. . . . At the moment when one attempts to interrogate this family scene, and to investigate all the investments, ethical and otherwise, of this entire history, nothing would be more ridiculously mystifying than such an ethical or axiological reversal.[42]

Not only can writing never be a re-presentation of phonic speech but there is a second, more radical meaning ascribed to the term. Writing is a kind of common root of both speech and actual writing. Does such writing, "arche-writing," provide a linkage between language and truth? Is there a prelapsarian writing that avoids the pitfalls of paradox and ambiguity attached to the concepts of speech and writing in the ordinary sense? Derrida thinks not, because we are already bound by a philosophical history which generated them and which cannot be abandoned at will. Any straightforward attempt to transgress these limits is bound to fail. But we can bring to light the dissimulations of a philosophical language that pretends a fullness without breach in its expression of concepts such as logos and speech. Derrida's claim is that not only are these notions to be found in the more or less unitary tradition from Plato to Hegel but that they are maintained in altered configurations in contemporary philosophy as well. Thus, bringing to light the presuppositions of speech and writing is pertinent to any contemporary reading of their significance.

Bound up with the problem of writing is the notion of the text. The term may simply refer to the material text, marks inscribed on a sensible medium. But if texts are to be thought of as material, the term *material* itself must be reworked so that it does not connote that which things ultimately are, the objective stuff that is the foundation of language. Otherwise a metaphysical materialism would guarantee the truth of the text in the sense that matter, something existing outside the text itself, would become the ultimate referent through which the text would be understood. It is still possible, however, to give an account of materialism that avoids the pitfalls of the straightforward view of matter as grounding linguistic reference. Matter can be thought of as the expression of a radical alterity, other than spirit but also other than itself in any straightforward sense.[43]

What account can be given of matter that would bring this alterity to light, and how would such an interpretation affect the concept of text? Such an analysis must so configure the idea of text that negation or nonpresence as it bears on textuality is brought to light. The material text is to be seen not only as a system of marks but also as the blank spaces that surround them.

The fact that marks and spaces are juxtaposed and that both go to make up the physical text is obvious, but its significance requires considerable explication. From a commonsense standpoint the blank spaces are devoid of meaning. Derrida comments: "In the constellation of blanks, the place of the semic content remains practically empty: it is that of the 'blank' meaning insofar as it refers to the non-sense of spacing, the place where nothing takes place but the place."[44] If the disposition of the blanks becomes a focus, it can be seen that they recur throughout the material text as a pattern of spacing. This pattern does not show itself as "whiteness" first and then examples of it, but rather as disseminated "whites." Where do the "whites" stop? Do they overrun the page, the print, the "material" text now that it is seen to be riddled by blanks? The effect of spacing is to decenter the text so that there is no total or proper text.

But if the white spaces are not copies of an original whiteness, still they appear to be unmarked, impossible to differentiate from one another. If so, it could be argued that there is an undifferentiated white Oneness, a privileging of blank space, something like a "center" of textual absence. This would be the case if the blanks, the textual spacings, did not have a singular capacity for themselves becoming marked not by the black marks of script but in a manner intrinsic to their character as disseminated whites. The blank spaces can be folded over.[45]

The fold is not an accident that happens to the blank. From the moment the blank (is) white or bleaches (itself) out, as soon as there is something (there) to see (or not to see) having to do with a *mark* . . . whether the white is marked . . . or unmarked, merely demarcated (the *entre*, the void, the blank, the space, etc.) it remarks itself twice.[46]

The fold is not exterior to the blank; it is its outside as well as its inside, the text's reinscription of itself as it were. Derrida thinks of this as the feminine folding back upon the masculine, black-marked text. This white space, without which there would be no text, is a kind of originary white, an "origin" required by the black marks. Without it there would be a purely black text as materially empty as a white text. The white spaces are not beyond or exterior to the text but always reappropriated by it. They are a reserve that stands ready to overwhelm the text but, so long as there is text, are ever and again refolded into it.

Consider again the citations on textuality from *The Wings of the Dove*. Lives are described as the black and white spaces of texts, as the relations of marks to margins. Human relations are encountered phenomenologically as the boundaries of texts permeable in their intertextual openness. In James's novel, Susan Shepherd, Millie's friend and chaperone, is overcome by Millie's vulnerability and offers a surfeit of "general emotion" (perhaps compassion) to protect Millie against the vicissitudes of fortune, "the effect of the occurrence of anything in particular" or "any conceivable chance" (Text A). This is the margin, the reserve, that she hopes will save Millie from fate on the one hand and human evil on the other. The margin is a powerful force, a flooding of the shore by the sea. Compare Derrida's comment that "the question of the text . . . has not merely 'touched' 'shore' [*le bord*] [but] what has happened . . . is a sort of overrun [*débordement*] that spoiled these boundaries and divisions."[47] Susan's protective love is the overrun, that which "makes the sea submerge the island, the margin flood the text."

James also describes the life of Densher (the Englishman who is loved by Millie) in textual terms (Text C). Densher has been living for a time in America and has thus briefly entered another text, that of American life. Although Millie is now living in England as an American, America is still intrinsic to her text (Text B). This places Densher briefly inside another text, Millie's, one that he will ultimately betray. Densher's text is without reserve, one from which the white spaces are largely absent, a "great grey page of print," "a blur" (Text B). He cannot fully conceal the white spaces, but the effort results in a dissimulated masculine (nearly black) text, "grey without being fine." In returning to the "general text," "the grey blur," Densher shows that he has not yet discovered how to read another's life (Millie's). He will learn this much later when he sees that repatriation to his own text, his own language, is impossible because the language of the Other (Millie's) riddles his own through and through. When he speaks, he will utter words so novel that they no longer belong to the "general text" (Densher/England) but are transformed by the strangeness of the Other.

The pattern of paradox and discursive complexity revealed when the material character of texts is considered can also be found when texts are interpreted as differential systems of signs. Borrowing from the linguistic theories of Saussure and Jakobsen, Derrida interprets signs as the "simples" of linguistic structure.[48] According to the classical theory, signs represent the present in its absence. "When we cannot take hold of the thing, we go through the detour of signs."[49] This suggests that signs, by substituting presence for what cannot become present, dissimulate in the same fashion as the material text. Every sign comprises two elements, a signifier, an acoustical linguistic bit, and a signified, the concept to which it refers. The advantage of Saussure's interpretation is its departure from the classical view that signs refer to extratextual objects in that Saussure sees signs as arbitrary. Meaning is not grounded in an object that is signified, an ontic referent, but derives instead from the differences among signs, which themselves circulate in an open-ended system of signs. For Derrida, "signs function not by virtue of the compact force of their cores but by the network of oppositions that distinguish them and relate them to one another."[50] Concepts lack independent signification; they have meaning only as signs that relate to one another rather than by virtue of their transparency toward an ontological ground. Instead of signs and ontological referents "there is nothing but a field of indefinite substitutions in the closure of a finite ensemble."[51]

While Saussure's analysis is helpful, it does not go far enough. For Derrida the indicative power of signs is unstable from the start. Meaning depends upon differences within signs and among them. *Différance* (with an "a") is the term used to point to these differences. It is an undecidable term which does not designate anything but describes an absence. Neither a concept which can be cashed out by some anterior meaning, nor a negative particle (because there is no original to negate), "*différance* is the nonfull, nonsimple 'origin'; it is the structured and differing origin of differences."[52] *Différance* includes the sense of postponing until later as well as dissimilarity or alterity as determined by spatial criteria. Both meanings are important since *différance* embraces economic calculation (with its connotations of delay and deferring), detour, respite, reserve, and re-presentation. While *différance* produces differences such as those in and among signs, it is prior to phenomenologically accessible differences. It is the "movement by which language or any code, any system of references in general, becomes historically constituted as a fabric of differences."[53]

Différance has no ontic status nor is it the transcendental ground of a system. In fact, Derrida turns to specific texts to discover the tracks or traces of *différance*. Yet what can they be tracks or traces of? The structure of time, concealed though not obliterated by the time-scheme of the present or by the structure of the subject as source point from which the nows of the present appear to spring. What is the concealing structure, and what does it conceal? Each new now seems to be something that is, a being or a produced object. Time appears as a hypostatized series of instants produced by an autonomous subject. But for Derrida the present carries the trace of a more primordial structure reflecting the dependence of time on space, the periodicity of time, which can only be thought of in terms of intervals or spacing. This opens time out, as it were, from its purely subjectively generated now-points to an outside:

Since the trace is the intimate relation of the living present with its outside, the openness upon exteriority in general, upon the sphere of what is not one's own, etc. *the temporalization of sense is, from the outset, a 'spacing.'* As soon as we admit spacing both as interval and difference, and as openness upon the outside, there can no longer be an absolute inside, for the 'outside' has insinuated itself into the movement by which the inside of the nonspatial, which is called 'time,' appears.[54]

This analysis of temporality assumes that time is parasitic on space and therefore that space is more primordial than time. But if so, then *textual* space—both the space that figures in textual content as well as the material space of the text—rather than the space of the *world* is the field of reference. Paul Ricoeur points to the difficulty of suspending the referential function of language so that literature (the text) signifies only itself. Citing Genette, who writes that "language *spatializes itself* in order that space, having become language, may speak and inscribe itself in it," Ricoeur argues that the question of the ontological character of intratextual figural language has been begged on behalf of the primacy of the text.[55] The same criticism applies to Derrida's often cited remark that there is no *hors texte*, nothing outside the text. But Derrida considers himself exempt from this criticism in that his comment refers only to a philosophical presupposition of textuality, the view that texts cannot be cashed out by extratextual ontic reference. But this, he insists, does not entail the more radical claim that everything that can be referred to is text. "It was never our intention to extend the reassuring notion of the text to a whole extra-textual realm and to transform the world into a library."[56]

If, however, signification arises only within a textual field, Ricoeur's critique of Genette applies mutatis mutandis to Derrida and cannot be dismissed without further consideration. If there is an *hors texte* after all but it cannot be brought into community with the text, it becomes something like a Kantian thing-in-itself. If on the other hand an extratextual ontic referent enters the text, it acquires signification only intratextually and there is no *hors texte*. In short, what is the ontic status of extratextual objects and events? This question is particularly vexing in the case of texts about saintly lives. Is the question about the veracity, the historical accuracy of a hagiographic text, an empty question? To consider this issue, we must examine the sense in which saintly life is historical in the context of moral practice.

Historical Truth

Earlier it was argued that hagiographic textuality both situates saintly lives within theological discourse and gives them reserves or margins which not only test the limits of theological concepts but contest the very possibility of theological discourse itself. But how is independence from theological embedding possible unless saints' lives are detached from context, from the narratives that communicate them, and are subjected to extratextual verification?

For many historians, saints' lives are historical texts to be deciphered and evaluated from the standpoint of their factuality. This is because a presupposition thought to be required by historical discourse is the belief that ontic referents cash out what is recounted in historical texts even when the narratological structuring of these events is acknowledged. Such a position can be congenial to an analytical philosophy of history in that historical narratives can be interpreted as orchestrating extratextual events in much the same way that scientific theories may be seen to assemble and organize extradiscursive facts.[57] Does an account of textual historicality then depend on the belief that historical texts represent extratextual matters? Such an account is, of necessity, parasitic on a general theory of truth that claims propositions mirror an antecedent ontic ground. I shall consider this representational theory of truth in detail in chapter 6. At present it is enough to grant that, if one subscribes to this view, narrative sentences can be interpreted in the same way as any other sentences that purport to describe the world. Once the temporal layering and multiplicity of voices found in hagiography are disentangled from narrative sequences, tense-free narrative sentences expressing "the view from nowhere" could be discriminated and these would constitute the narrative's historical core.

Consider the proposition "Thomas More was imprisoned in the Tower of London in 1534." On the representational view of truth an event external to the belief occurred and the ascription of truth or falsity to the sentence depends on matching extratextual facts with linguistic items. Thus as a minimum it could be established that a certain x existed and that, at time t, x was incarcerated. But such interpretive neutralization only embeds the sentence in another, far thinner narrative so that the thicker description required for understanding the sentence about Thomas More is lost. Judging the sentence's truth or falsity is not independent of its narrative embedding. "Thomas More" in the sentence cited is more than a linguistic bit that can be cashed out by a material body that existed some time in the past. Instead, "Thomas More" designates an open-ended social artifact whose meaning cannot be brought to closure and is articulated through multiple frameworks: theologically in terms of Henry VIII's quarrels with the papacy, economically and politically in terms of England's relations with Spain, and theo-politically in the context of the Act of Supremacy and Cromwell's view of it, to name only a few possibilities. Were the hagiographic account of Thomas More not nested in other historical narratives, the significance of the proposition affirming his incarceration would remain largely incomprehensible.

The hagiographic text's veracity (understood, of course, as a function of its *narratological* factuality) is also integral to its *moral* authority. How does this show itself inter- and intratextually? A moral hermeneutic of a moral text must factor in the question of veridical reportage so that the text's addressees may feel impelled to "make the saint's movements" after her. Contemporary hagiographic reading is especially sensitive to the issue of plausibility so that even when extraordinary moral or ontic claims are propagated, they are rendered credible through the believability of context.

To see this it may be useful to compare the life of Saint Giles with that of Maksymilian Kolbe, referred to by some sources as the Saint of Auschwitz. Saint Giles is a Greek nobleman who gives up a luxurious life to perform meritorious acts of healing and charity. He is nourished by a supernatural doe, becomes confessor to the emperor Charlemagne, founds an abbey, and dies after having lived a sanctified life. According to the best historical evidence, the major eleventh-century source for his life, the *Vita Sancti Egedii*, is "a legendary fabrication," based on an earlier Latin version written to confer prestige on a monastery in the Flavian valley.[58] Consider now the life of Maksymilian Kolbe as hagiographically recounted:

Maksymilyan is born into a devout family in a town near Lodz. As a student he shows great aptitude in mathematics and science but elects to become a Fransiscan. He enters the novitiate in 1910, is sent to study in Rome in 1912 and completes his doctorate in philosophy in 1915. In 1917 he organizes a group, the Militia Immaculate, for spreading the faith and in 1919 returns to Poland to become Professor of Church History in Cracow. He contracts tuberculosis but is cured. He makes visits to the sick, founds a journal, and later a village for printing religious materials. In 1930 he embarks on a mission to Japan where he publishes a journal and organizes a small friary. There he has a vision of the virgin, one of several in his lifetime. Recalled to Poland in 1936, he heads the community he founded there earlier. With the Nazi invasion in 1939, he is arrested, released, and ultimately rearrested and sent to Auschwitz. There Kolbe persuades a camp official to permit him to substitute for a fellow prisoner sentenced to death. He is killed on August 14, 1941.[59]

There is general agreement about the "facts of the case" and about the way in which they have been established: appealing to official documents, examining contemporary accounts of events alluded to, and the like. These criteria of factuality organize the narrative but are cashed out, as it were, by other narratives. This is not to say there is no *hors texte* but rather to stress that, apart from *some* narrative chain in which it is articulated, the event, fact, or person referred to is an empty *Ding an sich*. The story of Kolbe gains plausibility because the narrative text leans on the strategies of historical writing. What is more, because of this historicality, the hagiographic reading of his life is open to serious criticism because of the character Kolbe attributes to Judaism in certain of his published writings and to further inquiry about whether his missionizing activities reflected an insensitivity to Japanese religious traditions.

There is no question of such issues arising in connection with the life of Saint Giles, since the very same historical strategies that provide the warranty for the account of Kolbe's life reveal that the sources for the life of Saint Giles are specious and that its hagiographic symbols and stock accounts of supernatural interventions command belief only among the most credulous.

Earlier I stressed that it is misguided to look to hagiography as straightforwardly historical, as if its overriding purpose were the assembling, reporting, and interpretation of a narratively regulated past. At the same time, saints' lives, even when punctuated by miraculous interventions and rhetorical strategies reflecting specific literary contexts, appear to be informed by a will to historicity. That is to say, whether unconsciously or artfully inserted into the text, the political, economic, and social conditions of the time of writing are exhibited in hagiography. This rich detail, hagiographically orchestrated, occurs even when it is inert so far as the narrative's denouement is concerned. Such concrete contexts announcing the story's provenance are not mere embellishment but are bound up with the fact that hagiographic discourse purports to disclose a life. Contemporary social existence therefore serves both as a system of placeholders and reference points against which changes in saintly consciousness and behavior are marked off, and as a catalyst of these transformations. "In-text-ured," as it were, in social catenae, the saint's life becomes transparent as a *life* when memory and expectation, desire and hope interact in wider contexts.

Hagiography requires historicality for still another reason. The beliefs and actions of saints constitute an unmediated appeal to the lives of their addressees without recourse to laws, moral rules, or maxims even when intratextual reference to such juridical structures occurs. It is the life as narrated that exhorts the text's addressees to "make the movements" of the saint's existence after her/him. The success of the life's appeal is in part the result of sheer perlocutionary force: the indicative mood of the narrative's sentences carries imperative weight. Hagiography is historical to the extent necessary for saintly praxes to be experienced as imposing realizable demands on the lives of its addressees.

Consider, by contrast, the function of mythological texts. Without entering into detail, it suffices to notice that many myths are etiological, explaining the origin of groups, natural phenomena, or cultic practices and, as such, propagate ontic claims. On this account, as Lévi-Strauss argues, myths have an explanatory function similar to that of scientific hypotheses.[60] Mircea Eliade insists that myths depict the time and space of cultic origins by re-creating in present time and space an originary spatio-temporal configuration.[61] Hagiography, to the contrary, is "lived forward." Even Buddhist accounts of saints with their background assumption of many lives presuppose that saints' moral and meditational practices are forward-directed, with liberation from rebirth and suffering as their goal. The imperative claims of hagiographic texts depend on a certain factuality, not because they are inherently logocentric (privileging truth dependent on speech and presence) but because historical plausibility is a first step in securing attention to moral practice. For this reason the fact of factuality is an intratextual condition of hagiography.

FOUR CRITERIA determine the infrastructure or conditions of saintly lives: narrativity, corporeality, textuality, and historicality. Narrativity refers to a quasi-juridical discursive form in which the "facts" (or "truth") about a life are brought to light. Its complex temporal structure includes the time of the life narrated and the time of the recounting, as well as that of the addressee. Narrative does not issue in a didactic conclusion in the form of either moral laws or prudential maxims. One difficulty with the "moral lesson" view is that it results in an arresting of the chronological sequentiality of the story. Law-like properties are attributed to didactic conclusions, and moral dilemmas are treated as if they were instances to which such laws could be applied. This tactic contravenes the structure of narrative itself through which something temporal comes to fruition and in which time does not stop.

Saints' lives do not transmit customary knowledge even if hagiographic texts include such material. Instead, they often come into conflict with standard theological discourse. What legitimates antinomian saintly practices is not theological or social concepts but rules of thumb immanent to the lived life itself. To be sure, saints in many of the world's religions try to re-present the transcendent—for example, the life of Christ or the Buddha nature—but these are inherently unrepresentable. Because there can be no such concretization of transcendence, the saint's life also folds back upon itself and becomes to a significant degree a quest for moral praxes.

Saintly corporeality can be understood by appealing to Merleau-

Ponty's account of the body and of perception. He depicts perception as having a double character, diachronic or sequential on the one hand and synchronic or essentialist on the other. These are replicated in the saint's experience of the body, especially in traditional contexts, as ascetic practice. For the saint the whole body is a sensorium in which pain and its suspension alternate. Just as ordinary perceptual processes can be interpreted either from the standpoint of how they arise or from that of the percept *tout court*, so too the corporeal structure of asceticism can be seen to reflect this double perspective.

Saints' lives are not only communicated *in* texts but *as* texts so that the character of textuality is pertinent to grasping saintly life and practice. Because these texts are written, a fact that, until recently, has gone unnoticed, the character of writing itself must be displayed. Derrida shows how writing, seen as an imitation of speech, has been systematically debased in Western philosophy. He does not endorse reversing the relations of writing and speech but argues instead for a more primordial writing which unmasks the claim that speech founds truth. Texts, like writing, are material, but such materiality must be grasped as incorporating absence or negation, in this case the blank spaces and margins with which texts are riddled. As some suggestive comments in Henry James's fiction show, human lives can be thought of as the markings and blank spaces of texts.

Not only do texts have a material structure, but they have a semiotic structure as well. Texts as a system of signs do not point to extratextual ontic referents. Instead, they acquire meaning only intrasignificatively by way of the difference between one sign and another. Derrida uses the term *différance* to signal a cluster of differences—spatial and temporal—that destabilize the field of signs. But if texts are unstable and saints' lives are texts, then the question of the factuality of saints' lives—whether and how they lived—is begged. This issue raises the further question of historicality.

Like the Kantian *Ding an sich*, historical facts are seen to be inaccessible unless narratologically orchestrated. Factuality, textually derived, is important in hagiographic discourse, in part on its own account but more significantly because a sense of historical veracity is necessary to generate moral practices in the text's addressees. The *fact* of factuality, so to speak, is indirectly inscribed in the text as part of the intratextual fabric authorizing saintly practice in the community to which the text appeals.

2

This very thing the heavenly voice of thunder repeats, "*Da da, da,*" that is, control yourselves, give, be compassionate.

Bṛhadaranyika Upaniṣad

These fragments I have shored against my ruin. . . .
Datta, Dyadhvam, Damyatta.

T. S. Eliot, *The Wasteland*

Après ma mort, je ferai tomber une pluie de roses.

Motto on a statue of Saint Teresa of Jesus, Paris

Bodhisattva. Metropolitan Museum of Art, New York, Rogers Rund, 1922.

Saintly Influence

IT IS easy to forget that the primary purpose of hagiographic discourse is not a re-presentation of the events of saintly existence. Stories about saintly life are descriptive of event sequences that, taken together, constitute a double discourse, that of narrative factuality, a story *tout court*, and of hagiographic imperative authorized by the events and acts of the story that show the saint as being at the disposal of the Other. "Here I am," is the hagiographic indicative—the saint's avowal of her/his availability—that empowers and sanctions the hagiographic imperative, "Come, follow me." The saint forgoes self-interest claims, or, in Christian hagiographic language, the soul empties itself of self. For theistic hagiography, the "interior space" that is thus hollowed is filled by a transcendent Other. But human others, the recipients of saintly benevolence, may also come to occupy this void.

In the present chapter, I consider the *mechanism* by which saints affect others rather than the way in which saintly life comes into being. This procedure is justified in that it begins with what is easiest to see, the effects of saintly action as socially manifested. These matters are not unrelated, but they are functionally, if not ontologically, distinct. I shall focus, first, on how saints as discrete individuals come to embody "universal" significations and, second, on how these significations are communicated. Saintly acts are interpreted as practices that provide a point of contact between saints and other persons. Henry James's novel *The Wings of the Dove* is treated as hagiographic fiction that illustrates the influence of altruistic action on moral self-interpretation and practice.

The saint's relation to the Other generates a paradox bound up with saintly self-emptying. If the transcendent or human Other fills the place of the self, substituting for the self as a content, then the Other's claim to alterity is undermined. The Other is swallowed up by the self as an object of utility, desire, or representation and becomes part of the self's conative, affective, or cognitive structure. If, on the other hand, saintliness is a total emptying without replenishment, there is no subject to engage the Other. In either case the alterity of the Other disappears, is reduced to the homogeneity of the Same. This paradox opened up by saintly selflessness will be seen to dissolve once the relationship between power and powerlessness in saintly existence is clarified. Powerlessness will be viewed as renunciation and suffering, the expressions of self-negation in saintly life, whereas, by contrast, the field of moral action will be interpreted as requiring empowerment.

Connected with the problem of the suppression of otherness is the association of saintly practice with mystical tenets. The background convictions that guide the lives of many Christian saints as well as some individuals in other traditions include the belief in the possibility of mystical union with the godhead. Far from supporting an absolute distance from transcendence, some saints seek to diminish the space between the self and a divine source of goodness and knowledge. It is therefore useful to consider the relation of saintly life to mysticism before turning to the main theme of the present chapter, the way in which the saint's life impacts on the lives of others.

Mysticism, Theism, and Saintly Life

The English word *saint* as well as Romance language equivalents derive from the Latin *sanctum*, dedicated or set apart for the worship of deity. Thus, in Western Christian tradition, a linguistic link connects the saints with theistic belief. I shall, however, define the saint—the subject of hagiographic narrative—as *one whose adult life in its entirety is devoted to the alleviation of sorrow (the psychological suffering) and pain (the physical suffering) that afflicts other persons without distinction of rank or group or, alternatively, that afflicts sentient beings, whatever the cost to the saint in pain or sorrow.* On this view theistic belief may but need not be a component of the saint's belief system.

Mysticism, like theism, has in its multiple expressions been of the greatest historical importance in providing the conceptual language for the moral vision I have described. Despite the assertions by many saints that they have had unmediated experiences of some divine power or source, not all saints are mystics nor are all mystics saints. To be sure, many who led selfless lives were both mystics and theists and some who lived selflessly and have been thought of as saints, like Dorothy Day and Mother Teresa, were or are at least theists. Nevertheless, contemporary believers who performed selfless acts in slave labor and concentration camps, and nonbelievers or Buddhists who alleviated suffering in epidemics and wars meet the criteria I propose for sainthood. In short, my account of who saints are does not mandate any given religious or cultural context, even if saints have traditionally emerged within specifiable theological and institutional frameworks.

Because historically the texts of Christian hagiographic tradition are often bound up with mystical doctrines, it is worth noting some interpretive strictures proposed by recent scholarship in connection with the comparative study of mystical texts in order to determine whether these constraints affect the consideration of saints' lives. Arguing against an older generation of theorists such as W. T. Stace, R. C. Zaehner, and William James who endorse a common core of mystical experience that cross-cuts cultural and theological lines, recent investigations support a difference of experience as well as of doctrinal claims.[1] Thus Carl A. Keller suggests an analysis of literary genres to pinpoint thematic and stylistic differences in accounts of mystical experience[2] while Steven Katz argues that specific religious traditions not only influence postexperiential reports of the mystic but also define in advance what the mystic will hear, see, or feel.[3] Thus Katz contrasts the Christian mystic's unitive experience with the retaining of discrete individuality on the part of Jewish mystics.[4]

A seeming uniformity of expression may conceal differences of experience and underlying doctrine so that such terms as God, being, union, or nothingness become vacuous in the absence of supporting context. These caveats provide an important corrective to earlier studies which presuppose a common core of experiences such as merging with an absolute center of power and goodness, a claim not always present in reports of experiences which match in other respects. Still, if mystical encounters are defined only intrareligiously, any effort at comparison is precluded. In an effort to overcome this difficulty, Wayne Proudfoot claims that, even if the distinction between unmediated core experiences and interpretation is artificial, the language used to describe mystical experience is meaningful. Far from being vague, the terms *ineffable* and *paradoxical*, common to numerous reports of mystical experiences in different religious traditions, are the products of complex grammatical rules. These terms are not interpretations of mystical experience but constitutive of it.[5]

Although the warnings I have cited remain pertinent to the analysis of mystical texts, they are less crucial to the interpretation of saints' lives and utterances. Once the distinction between mystic and saint is drawn, the saint's experience can be considered in terms of her/his actual or envisioned acts. To be sure, these are incorporated into a conceptual framework but, more important, they are articulated within a context anchored in human *need* and, therefore, one which remains relatively constant. The description of saintly life suggested earlier—self-sacrifice in the interest of alleviating the suffering of persons and/or sentient beings in disregard of the cost to the saint's own life—is also distinct from both historical and present-day criteria for canonization within the Roman Catholic church even if some whose cults are institutionally sanctioned may meet the stipulated condition of radical altruism.[6]

Because the contemplative and often mystical strain in saints' lives on the one hand and active tendencies on the other are often found intertwined in many Christian sources, they must be distinguished if we are to see what is distinctive to saintliness. One strand is concerned with truth or knowledge of the divine, knowledge generally arrived at through interior contemplation, the other with moral matters in which love, charity, and compassion figure. In the case of the former, a language of considerable semantic density together with attestations of the experience's ineffability must be penetrated. Saint Teresa of Avila focuses largely on the truth aspect of her experience and says little about morality. But a close reading shows that, in describing the third stage of prayer, Saint Teresa differentiates the soul's union with God from the soul's other faculties, which remain intact:

It happens that when the will is in union, the soul realizes that the will is captive and rejoicing, and that it alone is experiencing great quiet, while on the other hand understanding and memory are so free that they can attend to business and do works of charity. . . . The soul is both Mary and Martha. Thus the soul is, as it were, occupied in the active and the contemplative life. It is doing works of charity and business pertaining to its life.[7]

The unitive aspect of Saint Teresa's experience, although distinct from its cognitive dimension, plays a role in her saintliness in that selflessness is required if the divine Other is to be received. In his account of sixteenth-century mystic speech, Michel de Certeau writes: "The *I* of autobiographical discourse is 'an organizing factor.' Its role is to mark *in* the text the *empty* place (empty of world) where the *other* speaks."[8] The space from which the language of alterity issues is hollowed out in the recesses of Saint Teresa's inner life, an "interior castle" made of a single diamond or of clear crystal. As de Certeau suggests, "it is a place where one dwells without dwelling there—and whose center is also exteriority (God)."[9] The other now speaks not from outside but from the heart of the self, from an outside that is inside. This double placement is made possible by the divine Other's incorporeality.

Saint Teresa's journey is also undertaken as a breaking away from ecclesiastical authority. She can enter her castle and roam about it without permission. De Certeau argues that "her itinerary combines the normality of an *order* imposed from without (. . . a series of institutional and rational dependencies) and the *gaps* created in it by irruptions of 'folly' (coming from within, from the other . . .)."[10] In this context, recall the point made earlier: although hagiographic texts endorsed by religious traditions are often idealized biography or autobiography, saints' antinomian acts provide an intratextual counterdiscourse to the constructed artifacts of already well-developed theological and institutional frameworks. The conflict between saintly desire and institutional norms that manifests itself in hagiographic plot constitutes a nodal point for the emergence of saintly achievement. Institutional structure and saintly will are rival sources of power. The obligating, the nonindividual, social, or juridical narrative strand, requires the full counterweight of divine endorsement for the optative, the strand of saintly desire, to be realized.[11] In the life of Saint Teresa, her desire can speak through two "islands of utterance," the convent that she founds and the optative strand of her autobiography, both of which open avenues to the world.[12]

On the face of it, the fourth stage of prayer described as an elevation of the soul, rapture, is distinguishable from union and entirely free of moral concerns. It is irresistible: "I felt as if I were being ground to powder," Saint Teresa writes.[13] But careful reading of her report shows that, even in rapture, the moral can be distinguished from the contemplative and remain distinct from it while, at the same time, remaining bound up with it. In describing the fourth stage she insists that "the soul rejoices in some good thing, in which are comprised all good things at once, but it cannot comprehend this good thing."[14] What can the fruits of this incomprehensible good thing be? Not the bliss of divine proximity, which is mixed with intense bodily pain. Rather, it must be the detachment this "good thing" provides to do God's work. The soul now gives scant weight to earthly values such as honors and money, which are singled out as particularly worthless. Instead, these special favors granted by God are interpreted as proofs that God wants to use her "in order to help a great many people."[15]

In the Dominican religiosity of Saint Catherine of Siena, truth subserves the piety of the heart. Truth is required "to show her the world's need and how storm tossed and offensive this is to God"[16] so that truth is in the service of the other's suffering. In the life of Saint Catherine, the soul's transformation occurs in a three-phase process: first, immersion in the divine life; then, self-castigation, a result of the first step; and finally, an opening out of the soul into the spirit of charity. She speaks of communion with God "when the soul is in God and God is in the soul as the fish is in the sea and the sea is in the fish." [17] From her new self-knowledge "a holy justice gave birth to hatred and displeasure against herself . . . her imperfection . . . which seems to be the cause of all the evils of the world." [18] Thus her purpose may be to address the world's need, but she must undergo acute suffering before she can do so.

There is a paradox connected with the *imitatio Christi* aspect of Christian saintliness bound up with saintly suffering that is worth noting: on the one hand the saint alleviates suffering but on the other imposes it on herself/himself. Is it not the obligation of another, if not the saint's own responsibility, to alleviate this personal suffering? In chapter 1, I concluded that self-mortification, while not a necessary component of saintly corporeality, expresses the saint's use of the entire body as a sensorium. While this accounts for asceticism's psychological utility, it does not address the question of whether such suffering is desirable on its own account. The paradox of saintly suffering is not directly considered by Saint Catherine, but a suggested resolution can be found in her remark that "in this life guilt is not atoned for by suffering as suffering but rather by suffering borne with desire, love and contrition of heart. . . . The value is not in the suffering but in the soul's desire." [19] This text foreshadows a possible response to modern psychological criticisms of saintly asceticism by disclaiming any independent value for suffering. Saint Catherine's comment disposes of the argument that if saints suffer, they must attribute value to suffering, that suffering is undertaken for its own sake. But this response fails to blunt the force of Nietzsche's interpretation of asceticism as a reorientation of wills to power or of Freudian-inspired descriptions of ascetic suffering as enhancing and reinforcing desire. A response to these criticisms will be developed later in the context of modern and postmodern accounts of desire and repression. At present it suffices only to notice that, even if the relationship between pain, power, and desire remains to be explicated, no account of this relationship can alter the fact that saints interpret the suffering bound up with poverty and disease as an ill and seek to alleviate it.

The conclusion that may be drawn thus far with regard to the problem of the Other is that saintly acts *simpliciter* are concerned with the needs of others and, as such, may be separated from the mystical discourse with which they are intratextually bound up. In Buddhist spirituality these functions are separated in that they are ascribed to different beings. Thus, in the main, the task of the *arhant* and the *pratyeka* buddhas of early Buddhism is to overcome individual suffering by sublating individuality through meditative practice whereas the bodhisattva of the Mahayana tradition postpones enlightenment in order to bring an end to the suffering of others. Although Judaism rejects a unitive experience of transcendence, the Hasidic strand of the tradition that stresses joyful worship distinguishes between the *nistar*, the hidden contemplative holy man, and the *meshulam*, who reveals himself and engages in communal activity.[20] When the functions are combined in a single figure, as they often are in classical Christianity, mystical discourse describes submersion of the self in the transcendent Other or, conversely, an engulfing of transcendence by the self. But the mystical aspect of experience is functionally distinct from the radical altruism that is *constitutive* of saintly praxis and depends on the *need* of the Other. What is more, because mystical experience itself is diverse, the sublation of alterity is not invariably entailed.

Moral Discourse and Hagiographic Fiction

Once saintliness is distinguished from mysticism, a large body of literature in which mystical concerns do not figure can be treated as hagiography. Not only are historical examples of saintly lives in which unitive experience is absent but in which altruism is central—the Confucian sage or the *Zadik* of Jewish tradition—relevant to an understanding of saintly consciousness and activity; the novel and other literary genres depicting saintly existence can also illuminate the relationship between saints and the moral practices they influence. Fiction may be hagiographic and reveal the relationship between moral belief and action where discursive analysis fails.

Before turning to hagiographic fiction, let us consider first a systematic account of the frequently observed gap between belief and action. In his analysis of altruism Thomas Nagel focuses on this problem. He observes that moral beliefs do not regularly eventuate in moral actions: "Although everyone presumably recognizes the reality of other persons altruism is not remotely universal, for we continually block the effects of that recognition."[21] Why is moral argument so often ineffective in persuading people to behave morally? It is worth considering briefly Nagel's effort to repattern moral discourse so as to account for the discrepancy between belief and action.

In his discussion of altruism, Nagel distinguishes epistemological from moral skepticism.[22] The moral skeptic refuses to be persuaded by moral reasons about the objects of moral arguments, that is, *action* or *desire*, whereas the epistemological skeptic rejects particular arguments or evidence intended to induce *belief*. In the case of moral (rather than epistemological) argument, it is not enough to convince someone that a moral statement is true because she/he may still not be motivated to act differently. Ruling out intuition, taste, and sentiment as possible grounds for moral choice, Nagel rightly perceives that a defense for altruism depends on attacking volitional rather than cognitive skepticism.

The problem of overcoming volitional skepticism is bound up with Nagel's claim that altruism is based on the stipulation that our moral arguments are subject to formal conditions of objectivity. We depend, he contends, on the ability to reason both from personal and from impersonal standpoints. The same data viewed from one or the other of these perspectives may lead to different moral judgments. Altruism requires the impersonal standpoint, the ability to put oneself in the other person's place. Such an exchange of places enables one to view oneself objectively as having interests commensurate with those of the other person, to weigh these interests, and to act dispassionately.

The trouble with Nagel's position is that it ultimately conflates what it purports to distinguish: moral and cognitive concerns. By introducing the "formal condition of objectivity" as a criterion for moral judgments, Nagel makes moral discourse parasitic on epistemological discourse so that moral discourse is ultimately swallowed up. The ability to sift personal from impersonal considerations and apply the latter to a (putatively) constant core may produce *epistemological* conviction. But, it must be countered, the objective standpoint, or putting oneself in another's shoes, facilitates seeing what the other *believes*. This may produce *cognitive* conviction, but Nagel has already admitted that cognitive conviction generally fails to *motivate* altruistic action.

This response to Nagel's analysis is still determined by the epistemological patterning of the argument itself and is not yet a postmodern response. If deeper difficulties integral to the relations between belief and practice are to be brought out, the argument must be made self-reflexive and its discursive framing rendered transparent. The fissure between belief and action is embedded in taken-for-granted policies and protocols expressed in social, economic, linguistic, and metaphysical meaning patterns. Taken together, they form the concrete constellation or moral design through which moral significations that eventuate in actions emerge, a schematism, as it were, of the moral life. These patterns of meaning constitute a historical a priori that is on the one hand a time-tied epistemic grid and on the other an observable cultural product.[23] Such features make up a long-run ontic and epistemological mise-en-scène against and through which moral actions are staged.

As we saw earlier, Nagel argued that, although we recognize the reality of others, our moral performances are not generally based on that recognition. The failure to act altruistically was posited by Nagel as a kind of blockage. The reasons for the sense of obstruction Nagel describes can be brought to light by exploring the background epistemic patterning, the *doxei* or epistemic beliefs of postmodernity. In considering these beliefs, Peter Sloterdijk argues that our age is characterized by a pervasive, if diffuse, cynicism that penetrates social existence at every level.[24] Contemporary cynicism is resistant to critique, outfoxing both ideology (epistemic and moral error that clings to its own conditions of existence) and the unmasking of ideology. Although morally asocial, the cynic is integrated into society: "Today the cynic appears as a mass figure: an average social character. . . . Modern cynics are no longer outsiders."[25] They do not see themselves as evil but merely as "participat[ing] in a collective, realistically attuned way of seeing things. It is the universally widespread way in which enlightened people see to it that they are not taken for suckers."[26] The "wised-up" attitude of the cynic who supplants naïveté with cunning simulates a certain health in that it conspires with the interest of self-preservation.

The ability to work, come what may, is an expression of this cynicism. But because he is not naive, the cynic comprehends the emptiness of what he does but sees himself as forced to accede to circumstances. Thus cynical consciousness is self-reflexive at the same time that it is false: "Cynicism is an *enlightened false consciousness*. . . . a modernized, unhappy consciousness."[27] The cynic is both well-off and miserable. Such cynicism cannot be changed by critique because "its falseness is already reflexively buffered."[28]

The aporia between belief and action pinpointed in Nagel's argument cannot be dissolved by providing a mediating link between moral and epistemic argument chains. On Nagel's interpretation, action can be explained, as Aristotle had already maintained, as the conclusion of a practical syllogism. Instead, a recontextualization of the difficulty shows that Nagel's argument is lodged in a particular historical discourse, that of cynicism, that has already run ahead of the arguments, so to speak, a discourse that has situated itself in advance of moral action inhibiting its consummation. Sloterdijk shows that the cynic evinces a "radical ironic treatment (*Ironisierung*) of ethics and social conventions, as if universal laws existed only for the stupid."[29] He goes on to contrast the postmodern cynic with the *kynic*, a term invented to designate the ancient cynic (among others) who, finding moral ills repugnant, resorts to parody, ridicule, and scatological gesture as protest. I shall return to this aspect of Sloterdijk's account in another connection. At present it suffices to notice that moral judgments are rendered not false but vacuous by cynical reason.

The Wings of the Dove

To see cynicism practiced as well as to study techniques for its circumvention, it is helpful to observe successful and failed moral transformation in situ. By recasting a specific work of modern fiction as hagiographic narrative, we can illuminate the impasse of moral discourse—the gap between belief and practice—positively by shedding light on successful saintly pedagogy, and negatively by exhibiting how predicative moral knowledge fails. Intratextual relations bring to light not only the connections between rectitude and depravity, altruism and selfishness, cynical wisdom and saintly wisdom but, as an ancillary benefit, the extratextual link between narrative and reader.

Premodern hagiographic literature does not consider the inability of moral discourse to motivate moral action puzzling. The standard description of this failure in Pauline Christianity, "the spirit willeth but the flesh nilleth," a *Zweideutigkeit* or split moral disposition, is explained by positing a special ontic realm: in Western religious traditions, the demonic or satanic; in Hindu and Buddhist religions, the hypostatization of karmic action and the like. But it is just this failure that becomes problematic for modern and postmodern moral thought. In novels from the eighteenth century to the present, the struggle of exemplary individuals against the experiential configuration of moral *Zweideutigkeit* provides a picture of how moral action is blocked.

Because the arena of action in fiction is so often the sphere of life designated as private, I shall consider saintliness in an interpersonal context and reserve for separate treatment the phenomenologically unique confrontation of saintly life with social evil on a vast scale in the twentieth century. While the social and personal spheres are by no means solidly partitioned, practitioners of public evil may evince compassion in interpersonal relations and, conversely, those who inflict deadly damage in interpersonal transactions may be public benefactors. By segregating small-scale moral transactions from the moral concerns of large-scale social events, I differ from a view that has largely dominated moral discourse from Plato to Kant, that the spheres of individual and social morality are homologous. My standpoint in this regard is also different from many Marxist accounts in that, on the standard Marxist view, moral behavior affecting individuals cannot be a matter of indifference to society because such behavior either expresses or is generative of class conflict. Although the public and private spheres are bound up with each other sociologically and culturally, it is the contention that they are homologous *en principe* to which I object.

Earlier I suggested that *The Wings of the Dove* lends itself to hagiographic recasting and that this hagiographic core brings out interactions of saint and cynic as well as relationships of the text to its addressees. James's work has the additional advantage of depicting the efficacy of exemplary action even after the death of its altruistic protagonist. In Roman Catholic and Eastern Orthodox traditions, the cultic veneration of saints through prayer and offerings attests the ongoing character of their moral influence. It is just this postmortem effectiveness that enables them to become historical figures. Similarly relics and holy sites play a role in Hindu and Buddhist commemorative worship. This observation is by no means intended as an endorsement of such practices but is meant to highlight the often ongoing effects of saintly lives. James's novel depicts the spillover of saintly generosity that carries beyond an individual lifetime. The point is expressed in an epigraph of the present chapter: after her death Saint Teresa will cause rose petals to rain down, a metaphor suggesting a postmortem moral effluvium, as it were, extending into the future.

The account of James's novel that follows is a hagiographic skeletalization intended to organize its events so as to highlight the struggle between treachery and beneficence, betrayal and fidelity, cynical cunning and saintly subtlety:

Kate is a young Englishwoman without fortune. Lest she be compelled to live in the style of her semidestitute father and sister, she prefers to accept the charity of an overbearing aunt. She has fallen in love with Densher, an English journalist who, like herself, also lacks means. The two are secretly engaged but choose not to marry against the wishes of Kate's wealthy aunt, who prefers a more advantageous marriage. By secrecy and delay, Kate plans to bring the aunt round so that if Kate and Densher are careful they may "do all": both marry and acquire wealth. Millie is a young American woman in possession of a vast fortune who has met Densher in New York, comes to London, and falls in love with him. In love also with life, Millie learns she will die of an unspecified malady. Outwardly calm and accepting, inwardly "she is like a creature dragged shrieking to the guillotine."[30] Kate, who guesses her despair, prevents Densher from letting Millie know she and Densher are engaged. Instead, Kate urges Densher to toy with Millie's affections in order later to inherit her fortune. Densher pities Millie, but "makes up" to her. Lord Mark, a penniless peer and Kate's former suitor, opens Millie's eyes to this situation, but Millie stubbornly clings to her passion.[31] The girl dies leaving Densher her fortune. Now Densher is able to measure the depth of Millie's devotion. He agrees to marry Kate on condition that they renounce the money or, if Kate should reject these terms, that he himself renounce Millie's wealth and make over the money to Kate. Kate refuses to marry on Densher's condition. What is more, her ties to her old suitor, Lord Mark, have not been cleanly severed, suggesting possible further treachery, perhaps marriage to Lord Mark, thereby breaking faith with both Millie and Densher. Kate sees that Millie's memory is now Densher's love. The dove "stretched out her wings" to cover them so that they shall never be as they were.

Saintly life was earlier defined as the determination to alleviate the suffering of humankind or, alternatively, of all sentient beings whereas Millie's generosity fixes on the few individuals of her immediate acquaintance to whom she is passionately attached. The narrative's hagiographic import lies not in bringing to light the character of a more fully realized saintliness, but in the way in which a figure of flesh and blood, acquires generality and moral significance against the cynical wisdom (in Sloterdijk's terms) of others.

The effort to relieve suffering that is *constitutive* of saintly existence may fulfill or fall short of its aim. But even when this effort does not entirely succeed, saintly power can still be *effective* and its results may go deeper: saintly effort, even when it misfires, can morally transfigure other lives. Transformation is achieved by an appeal neither to rational norms nor to a taken-for-granted moral ethos which, in this case, is that of European cynicism, often a source of moral depravity in James's work. For Kate (and at first for Densher) the law of self-preservation overrides other concerns. The allure of Kate's position is that self-preservation demands strength, whereas altruism is bound up with disease and weakness. Kate's sexual and physical vitality, her seemingly boundless health, is not, however, what opposes Millie's "nobility of soul," thus pitting moral against physical force. Instead, the narrative concurs in the Nietzschean point that only homogeneous quanta of forces, wills to power, can oppose one another. Although Millie's disposition is selfless, it is not impotent selflessness but wealth that gives impetus to her actions and is the counterforce to Kate's vitality. Millie's vast fortune empowers her moral actions so that Densher's transfiguration can be consummated.

To see how hagiographic discourse communicates *general* meaning, consider first the intratextual signs that segregate Millie from others. The saint is marked off through the use of hyperbole and by metaphoric or metonymic substitution. The dove metaphor expresses Millie's sense of chosenness. Thus, when Kate calls Millie a dove, she feels herself "embraced . . . almost ceremonially and in the manner of an *accolade*."[32] Millie finds herself "accepting as the right one . . . the name so given her. She met it . . . as she would have met the revealed truth. . . . She was a dove."[33]

So well-worn is the dove metaphor that it would seem to resist continued use. The Fifty-fourth Psalm refers to the wings of the dove who would fly away, and the Sixty-eighth Psalm describes the silver and gold of the dove's wings.[34] A familiar symbol of the Holy Spirit, the dove is interpreted in Christian iconography as entering into and redeeming human existence. Yet, when these accretions of historical meaning are retained, they are "made new" with Millie's altruism and saintly calling.

A quite different range of symbols orchestrates saintly empowerment. On the one hand Millie is a dove emptied of force, but on the other she is in charge of a great fortune which she can call upon when the time is ripe. In Jewish and Christian saintly narratives, power ultimately derives from transcendence and is channeled through saintly practice. By contrast, in a novel reflecting its nineteenth-century capitalist provenance, power is derived from wealth. At the very moment her saintly calling is revealed, Millie fingers her priceless chain of pearls, symbol of her fortune:

Millie was indeed a dove; this was the figure though it most applied to her spirit. But . . . Kate was just now . . . exceptionally under the impression of wealth . . . which was dove-like only so far as one remembered that doves have wings and wondrous flights. . . . that such wings could . . . *had*, in fact, in the case in which [Densher] was concerned—spread themselves for protection.[35]

Through synecdoche, Millie's pearls are seen to represent the whole of her wealth, the enabling medium of moral transfiguration. This widening sphere of reference is also characteristic of theistic hagiography in which some ritual object, through a nexus of broadening significations, comes to stand for transcendent power. What gives wealth as a hagiographic trope its specifically moral force is negation. Millie's fortune is, on James's account, spiritually transformed once it is handed over to others or renounced.

These relationships can be usefully stated in still another way. It may be recalled that the grammar of narrative as discussed by Tzvetan Todorov focuses on a property of sentences, mood, which expresses the relation a character sustains with some proposition in the narrative. The indicative mood, for instance, signals that what is said is alleged really to have taken place. What is of special interest in the context of hagiographic fiction are two contrasting moods bound up with human will. The obligative is "the mood of a proposition which must occur . . . a coded, nonindividual will which constitutes the law of a society"[36] but is never explicitly stated. Such tacit laws comprise what can be called a historical a priori. By contrast, "the optative [mood] corresponds to the actions desired by the character."[37] Kate's actions—her choice to live with her wealthy aunt, to maintain the secrecy of her engagement to Densher come what may, her plan to involve Densher with Millie, and her continuing relation with Lord Mark—all express the conformation of her will with the law of society. For Kate, the optative mood of her desires and intentions coincides with the obligative mood, society's iron rule that wealth guarantees self-preservation. All tension vanishes between the private maxim according to which Kate acts, and what she perceives as the universal law of society. Desire—her love for Densher—is, in the end, subordinated to calculation. For Millie, by contrast, desire is expressed through generosity and renunciation.

Cynical reason finds Millie's acts hard to grasp. Shrewd enough to distinguish saintly magnanimity from naïveté, the cynic is depraved enough to turn it to advantage. Densher's transfiguration occurs when the interplay of cynical reason and saintly generosity becomes transparent. Self-sacrifice (and, in many traditional hagiographies, self-mortification) is a mode in which the hagiographic optative regularly expresses itself. Millie bequeaths not only her fortune but, on Kate's interpretation, her life as well: "She gave up her life that you might understand her,"[38] Kate tells Densher.

In James's fiction, death as renunciation takes on multiple layers of meaning that help to clarify the role of negation in hagiography. Jamesian narrative, Todorov argues "is always based on the *quest for an absolute and absent cause*."[39] Such a cause may be a character, event, or object. The narrative is the *effect* of this cause, itself absent or unknown, and consists in the search for it. When the cause is found, the narrative stops. The secret of Jamesian plot is the postponement of revelation, which in some cases is never fully attained. The absent cause is an intratextual presence, the force that propels the plot along.[40] Even if this hypothesis fails to do justice to the complexity of *Wings of the Dove*—to the novel's psychological, linguistic, and epistemic density—it is pertinent to the work's hagiographic character. Millie's death constitutes "an absence both absolute and natural . . . pure absence."[41] Once Millie dies, she is to be found nowhere but in the artifacts of her former presence: the letter about her bequest whose full content is never revealed, the Bronzini portrait that depicts someone long ago who resembles her, and so on. More important, the traces of Millie—her presence in absentia—are written into the lives of others. There is still another less obvious absence, the love for Densher that never announces itself. Romantic at the start, it becomes increasingly disinterested with her impending death and fully altruistic when it persists in the face of Densher's and Kate's treachery.

I have stressed that neither saintly practice nor saintly power is, for the most part, transmitted in standard normative discourse. In addition to the interpretive frameworks already proposed, saintly communication can also be understood as nonverbal pedagogy. Thus—leaning on an analogy of Wittgenstein's—seeing the meaning of saintly work is less like grasping an argument and more like understanding a musical theme. The hearer must first have some notion of music and of how people respond to it before the theme can be grasped. Similarly, before saintly practice can be understood, a prereflective comprehension of the sphere of moral action is required. This means that, for example, weeding a garden should generally be seen as a different sort of act from telling lies. Recognition of a moral dimension in human life is a necessary backdrop for discriminating acts as saintly, a criterion that is met even by the cynic.

Understanding music falls into two parts, an appreciative aspect and a performative one.[42] To gain appreciation, the listener is not to look inside herself/himself but rather at the performer to see what the artist is doing and feeling. By attending to what prompts her/his own view about the performer's experiences—their manifestations in interpretation, expression, or gesture—the hearer begins to see what the theme might mean. Now something happens to the listener. As the theme is experienced intensely, it points to something beyond itself connecting up with the total fabric of music—music's rhythmic, harmonic, and melodic capacities, its emotional power, and its previous literature.

In James's novel, Kate has achieved a certain level of appreciative understanding of what counts as a moral act in that she is regularly able to distinguish prudential from moral acts. Cynical reason (on Sloterdijk's description of it) comprehends this difference. Kate sees well enough (and long before Densher) the moral force of Millie's intentions and the transfiguring power of her presence. It is she who draws attention to the morally relevant fact that Millie died for Densher and for her. ("She died for you that you might understand her. From that hour you *did*.")[43]

At this point a breach begins to appear between musical and moral understanding. In the case of musical understanding, the comparisons that are drawn and the images used to illustrate the musical theme signal the appreciative grasp of a musical phrase and show that understanding is halfway there. Playing or singing the piece is perhaps a deeper indication that a theme has been understood. Appreciation and performance are mutually reinforcing. But in the case of moral acts, appreciation need neither prompt nor reinforce moral action. In hagiographic discourse immoral acts are all the more striking not when moral insight is absent but when it is present but fails to generate moral actions. Densher is "awed" at Kate's "high grasp," her appreciation of Millie's saintliness.[44] Still, by refusing to renounce Millie's wealth, she reveals her deficiency in moral understanding. Moral understanding misfires when appreciation, severed from performance, does not result in "making the movements" after the saintly individual. What counts as a grasp of saintliness in this context is the renunciation of power, becoming dove-like, by abjuring the source of power, wealth.

For both Kate and Densher, there has been no moral paradigm *apart* from Millie's life, just as there is no "glassy essence" apart from the musical score to be read or performed. Yet in another sense there is some pattern apart from Millie herself in that Millie's moral practice is now (somehow) repeated in Densher's life. He has learned a new moral gesture. If Millie's life is "paradigmatic," it is not replicated in any straightforward way in that simple repetition would not count as understanding moral acts but as slavish copying.

It is not argued here that the gift of great wealth to secure the private happiness of a few is equivalent to the self-sacrificial altruism stipulated earlier as a requirement of sainthood. No great suffering, the result of need, is alleviated, nor is there an intention to benefit large numbers of people. What hagiographic skeletalization highlights is the *mechanism* of saintly action and the strategies for uncovering it. These strategies, phenomenological and linguistic, include, first, bringing to light the historical a priori framing of moral beliefs, their backdrop of cynical reason; second, the analysis of the grammatical moods exhibited in hagiographic narrative, especially those expressing human will; and, finally, by considering saintliness as a kind of art, determining what is to count as having learned it.

Word as Flesh

Hagiographic discourse consists of a body of writings that have moral force for their addressees because of the larger-than-life individuals whom they describe. The lives of these individuals are read as embodying saintly qualities—as having or expressing *value*—and are interpreted by the recipients and observers of saintly action as hagiography. Although narratively articulated, the lives of actual saints nevertheless touch on real bodies, exhibit real pain, and address flesh and blood listeners. The recipient is now the destitute sufferer and the saint, one who relieves actually felt distress. The hagiographic field, the concrete arena of value transactions, is thus also, so to speak, a text of flesh in which the body takes on a signifying role: it is now a sign, a composite of signifier (a linguistic bit) and signified (what language points to) in a field of value creation. Verbal signifiers give way to the concrete graphic signifiers of the body upon which lack, pain, and desire are inscribed. But at the same time, the body is a sign that undoes itself. Michel de Certeau's comment about mystical language can be applied *pari passu* to saintly language: "[It] is the outcome of an entire set of operations on and in the shared social text. It is an *artifact* (a production) created by the labor of putting language [verbal signifiers] to death."[45]

If the saint's life "secretes" value, how is the universality of meaning attributed to saintly lives grasped without recourse to propositional truth? And if saintly language often bypasses straightforward propositional content, what do observers or sufferers see when observing saints? How is the generality of value to be accounted for when lawlike propositions are bypassed? Because the saint—in life, religious hagiography, or hagiographic fiction—is incarnate, such "generality" communicates itself in a distinctive way.

Phenomenological efforts to resolve the problem of generality in connection with moral problems have begun from two diverse starting points. The first, a tack taken by Max Scheler, Nicolai Hartmann, and others, assumes that values are instantiated in the world and have properties that are open to intuitive grasp. Values are singled out as having independent being and as accessible without having an actual locus in things. The second approach begins with the embodied existent's actual encounters with other persons and finds an empirical locus for these transactions. Martin Buber, Gabriel Marcel, and Emmanuel Levinas turn to the experience of the Other to develop an account of social existence in which concrete interactions with others disclose a sphere of responsibility prior to propositional language or moral action. The first standpoint presupposes that values are like classes or kinds and that these are real even if they are never actualized. Values may be simultaneously disclosed as universal and essential or as possibly, but not necessarily, inhering in specific phenomenologically accessible complexes. But once values are separable from concrete phenomena and can be intuited apart from context, they function as metaphysical constructs accounting for perceived identities.

By contrast, the second approach uncovers concrete social phenomena and precludes hypostatized values, a course that necessitates a language that disarticulates, "vibrates and disjoins" in conformity with what it manifests.[46] The problem of generality is not avoided. Instead, a new mode of generality that precedes the reification of universals—goodness, justice, and so on—is exhibited. I call this type of generality *carnal generality*, a conception developed *nolens volens* as it were in the work of Merleau-Ponty and Emmanuel Levinas, and the phenomena that exhibit it, *carnal generals*. Because carnal generality is rarely made thematic in post-Husserlian phenomenology, it must be tracked down in the philosophical contexts in which it occurs.

The notion of carnal generality arises in the work of both Levinas and Merleau-Ponty in connection with the search for access to meaning that cannot be manifested in concepts because, although concepts may be discursively primitive, they are not themselves ultimate. Propositional language, the language of concepts, presupposes a logos "more fundamental than the logos of objective thought endowing the latter with its relative validity."[47] To be sure, the idea of generality can be framed in discursive language. Merleau-Ponty argues, however, that generality is more primordially exhibited in the incarnate subject, an ensemble of self-transcending acts and lingual capacities. Levinas too seeks a more primitive locus for generality and finds it not in the subject but in the alterity of other persons as the Other impacts on the self. Levinas and Merleau-Ponty agree that the psycho-physiological primordium that is the incarnate subject is a primordial expression of generality. Universals and essences are abstractions derived from this more primitive experiential matrix.

This distinctive mode of generality is exhibited by context-specific complexes, carnal generals. It is important to distinguish the latter term from two others that influenced both Levinas and Merleau-Ponty and with which it might therefore be confused, Hegel's *concrete universals* and Husserl's *material essences*.[48] Carnal generality is not exhibited by concrete universals, self-particularizing or self-specifying universals, because, for Hegel, these express the self-development of the whole, the Absolute. As such, they do not require the human body as an unsurpassable condition for thought and language. Similarly the term *carnal general* is not an equivalent for *material essence*, a designation for the structural limits of an object that, when surpassed, entail the object's destruction. The term *material essence* can apply only to the body as object but not to the body as incarnate subject.

In his analyses of social existence Merleau-Ponty speaks of essences and occasionally carnal essences, intelligible structures whose meaning comes to light through successive exfoliations of the context in which they are embedded. He attributes positive significance to the term *essence*, preferring it to *universal* because for Merleau-Ponty universals derive from a spectator theory of knowledge, a gaze without a body. What universals gain in comprehensiveness they lose in complexity, the capacity to express lived experience. The term *carnal generality* occurs only once, so far as I know, in Merleau-Ponty's work, in an account of living conversation. Dialogue, he argues, introduces a new dimension into language, the encounter with other persons as the condition for communication. The Other with whom I speak becomes another myself: "Language is founded upon the phenomenon of the mirror, ego, alter ego, or of the echo, in other words of a *carnal generality* [emphasis mine]."[49] This generality is constituted by the power of the self to inhabit the body of the Other. Language is the "magic machine" which effects this mobility, makes carnal generality possible, and is its expression. Together, another and I form an ensemble of significations that is traversed by and expresses meaning.

The blurring of the distinction between self and Other is bound up with another relation, that of visible and invisible. The elements of this dyad are inseparable from the start and constitute the field—a primordium of sensibility prior to the subject-object distinction—where carnal generality arises. The difference between perceiver and perceived, subject and other, loosens and shifts so that the body sensing and the body sensed, looking and looked at, overlap. Body and world intersect in a "chiasmatic" crossing over. But there is also a difference within this unity of the visible field, one that bypasses the mind-matter and subject-object distinctions. Merleau-Ponty claims:

To designate [this unity] we should need the old term "element" in the sense it was used to speak of water, air, earth and fire, that is, in the sense of a *general thing* midway between the spatio-temporal individual and the idea, a sort of incarnate principle that brings a style of being wherever there is a fragment of being. The flesh is in this sense an "element" of being.[50]

For Levinas, although the difference between subject and object is overcome in cognition, the breach between self and Other is unsurpassable. It is this difference rather than the resemblance between self and Other that opens discourse. Even if Merleau-Ponty has grasped the significance of prediscursive corporeality for the emergence of generality, he has suppressed the condition of difference between self and Other that makes moral relations possible. Levinas, like Merleau-Ponty, uses the term *universal* to denote a derivative form of generality, the unity of classes or kinds. Still, for him authentic generality depends not on shared properties but on other persons who open up the possibility for generality. Levinas argues:

The relation with the other does not only stimulate, provoke generalization, does not only supply it with the pretext and the occasion . . . but is this generalization itself. Generalization is a universalization—but universalization is not the entry of a sensible thing into a no-man's land of the ideal.[51]

The ideality of genus is parasitic upon concrete relations with others rather than the converse. Intersubjective encounter together with the conditions of emergence constitutes the space in which carnal generals are manifested. Millie exhibits for Densher a carnal generality, a disinterested saintly love for which her entire corporeal being is the expressive vehicle. Mortal illness, compassion, renunciation, and generosity are not qualities added on to Millie or that she represents. Her corporeal existence *is* these properties.

If saintly lives are to have meaning, they must express moral value in a fashion that can be communicated to their addressees. The preceding analysis shows that it is possible to bypass propositional form and still communicate moral significations that have general meaning. What is transmitted must on the one hand be interpreted as binding upon those who are addressed and on the other be imparted in a recognizable way to a community of addressees. The saintly body acts as a signifier, as a carnal general that condenses and channels meaning, a signifier that expresses extremes of love, compassion, and generosity. In their disclosure of what is morally possible, saintly bodies "fill" the discursive plane of ethics.

Ethics, Fiction, and Possibility

It was argued earlier that moral beliefs and judgments are bound up with epistemological discourse and frequently fail to induce moral acts. By contrast, exemplary lives in which saintly power and its renunciation figure teach moral practice by way of practice. This has been exhibited intratextually but without taking account of the discursive and ontological links between ethics—a name for the field of moral action in actual human lives—and hagiographic fiction. Because action in human life is an effort to bring something about which does not yet exist and hagiographic fiction narrates the way in which such actions come into being, both are concerned with the realm of what Aristotle distinguishes as the possible. To see the connection between the two, both the field of moral action, or ethics, and of fictional saintly lives must be delineated as related spheres of possibility. No postmodern analysis can conclude with a straightforwardly Aristotelian account, but it is the essential historical starting point for an understanding of the question. By considering possibility in Aristotle's terms, a grasp of the idea of possibility marked or fissured by an anterior negation can be brought to light.

Consider as a point of departure, then, the relationship between moral practice and representation. Michel de Certeau writes: "Ethics is articulated through effective operations, and it defines a distance between what is and what ought to be. This distance designates a space where we have something to do."[52] By contrast, epistemological discourse or representation has historically been interpreted as mirroring already existing actualities so that propositions—whatever the ontic status of their objects—reflect an anterior content. But reflective or mirroring discourse cannot, even on the classical view, take account of the ethical "object," some change in the moral field, which is yet to be created. It can *image* the result of moral action as if this result were present fact, but in so doing, reflection hypostatizes a desired state of affairs still to be brought into being. The sphere between *is* and *ought* cannot (strictly speaking) be re-presented by cognitive discourse in that it is not concerned with the actual but with what may or may not come into being, what Aristotle calls possibility.

In *De Interpretatione*, Aristotle considers the meaning of possibility in the context of a discussion of the logical difficulties connected with denying certain propositions that affirm possibility, actuality, and necessity.[53] His aim is to show that the possible cannot be necessary but that there is a sense in which the necessary has to be possible. He argues that the contradictory of the proposition "It may be" ("It is possible that *x*") is *not* "It may not be" ("It is possible that *x* will not"). These two propositions are compatible because in speaking of things that are possible but not yet actual both can be true ("It may rain or it may not rain tomorrow"). Instead, the contradictory of "It is possible" is "It *cannot* be," that is, "It is impossible."[54] But impossibility ("It *cannot* rain tomorrow") is synonymous with the necessity of its not raining tomorrow. Thus Aristotle prevents the possible from being necessary.

Whereas possibility does not imply necessity, necessity may imply possibility. (If necessity did not imply possibility, it would imply either impossibility or possibility of the opposite, both incompatible with necessity.) But there is a difficulty connected with the claim that necessity may imply possibility. Possibility ("It may be") has been shown to be compatible with its opposite ("It may not be"). But the opposite of possibility ("It may not be") is clearly not compatible with necessity. Aristotle is forced to distinguish between two types of possibility, one bound up with becoming, the other bound up with actual existence.[55] When possibility is predicated of something actual, its opposite ("It may not be") cannot also be predicated of that thing. Necessity is compatible with this latter form of possibility. Aristotle writes:

> The term possible is ambiguous being used in the one case with reference to facts, to that which is actualized, as when a man is said to find walking possible because he is actually walking . . . in the other case, with reference to a state in which realization is conditionally practicable, as when a man is said to find walking possible because under certain conditions he would walk . . . [It can truly be said of both cases] that it is not impossible he should walk. . . . We cannot predicate the latter kind of [conditionally practicable] potentiality of that which is necessary in the unqualified sense of the word, [but] we can predicate it of the former.[56]

Aristotle's analysis privileges the type of possibility bound up with actuality in that it is compatible with what is for him the highest kind of existence, necessary existence. But it is a possibility that is unlike the *sheer* possibility that Aristotle describes as "conditionally practicable." What distinguishes sheer possibility, possibility *tout court*, is its openness with regard to existence and nonexistence. It is this latter sheer or fully open possibility that will be seen to unite ethics and hagiographic fiction.

Kierkegaard is struck by the lengths to which Aristotle goes to make necessity and possibility compatible.[57] Once the meaning of coming into existence, becoming, is understood, Kierkegaard asserts, Aristotle's claim, that the necessary is compatible with the possible, founders. In fact, both the actual and the possible are entirely different from the necessary so that the actual can be no more necessary than the possible. This is because Kierkegaard's analysis posits a radical discontinuity between possibility and actuality. Coming into being is interpreted by Kierkegaard as a radical transition from not existing to existing. But, it can be argued, every change presupposes something that changes. What can it mean to speak of prior nonexistence of what now exists?

The nonbeing left behind must have some kind of being. "[S]uch a being, which is nevertheless a non-being, is precisely what possibility is; and a being which is indeed actual being is indeed actual being or actuality; and the change of coming into existence is a transition from possibility to actuality," Kierkegaard writes.[58] By contrast, the necessary neither comes into being nor changes but is always related to itself in an identical way. "All coming into existence is a *suffering*, and the necessary cannot suffer; it cannot undergo the suffering of the actual, which is that the possible (not only the excluded possibility) reveals itself as nothing the moment it becomes actual, for the possible is made into nothing by the actual."[59] The actual and the necessary are distinguished in that the actual has been subjected to coming into existence, but there is no point at which the necessary has not been. Coming into being is the result of causal action whereas necessity is determined on logical grounds.

On the basis of this analysis, I take the sphere of ethics to be a holding open of a discursive and ontic space for becoming, specifically the becoming of moral change. Taking up the second type of possibility in Aristotle's account, what I called earlier *sheer* possibility, the *capacity* for action, Kierkegaard is able to maintain the conceptual independence of possibility, actuality, and necessity. This conceptual segregation of possibility provides the "ground" for ethics. It also opens the way for positing possibility as the common space for ethics and fiction.

Aristotle's depiction of the character of ethics on the one hand and imaginary discourse or *poesis* on the other is to be understood against the backdrop of the concept of possibility explicated in the *De Interpretatione*. Ethics, Aristotle argues, is concerned with things that are for the most part so. Moral ends are brought into being by choice, and the object of choice must be a *possible* object. Choosing is to be distinguished from wishing and opinion, both of which may relate to the *impossible*. "If anyone said he would choose the impossible," Aristotle argues, "he would be thought silly."[60] Opinion may relate to a variety of objects, "no less to eternal things and impossible things than to things in our own power," but choice must relate to what we ourselves can bring about.[61]

Aristotle also argues that poetry, like ethics, is concerned not with what has happened but with what might happen. Tragedy in particular describes human possibility in terms of what a person of a given character will typically—probably or necessarily—say or do.[62] In fact, Aristotle declares, the figures of tragedy are given historical names to make the incidents of the plot more plausible because something that has

happened is convincing in that it is established as being possible.⁶³
Ethics and poetry are linked for Aristotle in that both are concerned
with possible objects, ethics with the field of human choice, tragedy
with a double possibility, ontic and volitional: what could happen, and
what could be chosen. Both ethics and tragedy interpret possibility in
terms of the subject's own power to bring something that is prized or
valued into being.

Fiction and ethics are fields of multivalent possibilities. Fiction depends on the stratification of meaning in which matters are recounted
in order to gather them into some upshot or meaning. Ethics is bound
up with the unrealized imperatives or oughts intrinsic to a situation.
These diverse fields of possibility overlap intratextually in hagiographic fiction.

Consider the episode in which Densher learns that Millie knows of
his relationship with Kate. Having stayed on in a Venice turned cold
and stormy to court Millie, Densher is puzzled by Millie's withdrawal.
Appearing at last at the loggia of her palazzo, he is informed by her
Italian servant: "'The ladies [Millie and her companion] . . . were a
"leetle" fatigued' . . . and without any cause named for it. . . . It was a
Venice all of evil. . . . [I]t was to have been a moment, for Densher, that
nothing could ease off."⁶⁴ Millie's realization of her betrayal and not the
event recounted—the shutting of a door—is the meaning constellation
that is *fictionally* signified or pointed to. As *saintly pedagogy* leading to
moral choices, the shutting of the door is an opening of Densher's heart
and the beginning of his redemption. Ambiguity moves backward and
forward across a chain of events that are at once plot—shutting the
door in Densher's face—and ethical field—the disclosure of Densher's
turpitude and the beginning of his moral transformation.

Beyond Possibility

There are two ways in which the sphere of ethics as a field of sheer
possibility can be transcended. First, what is beyond possibility may be
what is *anterior* to it or before it but is not related to moral action as its
cause. Second, what is beyond it may come *after* what is brought about
through moral actions, an altered field of social relations. These further
questions, because they concern what is beyond possibility, cannot be
advanced within the discursive framework of ethics, the field of possibility itself.

Consider first the matter of what, if anything, precedes moral action,
that of both saints and those they influence. Earlier it was argued that
the saint empowers others to become different from what they now are.

Thus, for example, Millie brings about a transformation in Densher by means of the power she wields through the possession of wealth. If saintly action were explicable solely in terms of possibility, Aristotle's account of ethics would suffice to explain the exemplary individual's capacity to effect moral change. The saint whose moral excellence is actual would bring about an alteration in someone who is potentially moral so that she/he would become actually so. But saintly action is not an empowering in its basic structure. Kierkegaard grasps this point in his analysis of possibility, particularly in regard to the antecedents of change. Recall that genuine possibility for Kierkegaard is not an anterior *foundation* that undergirds subsequent ontic alteration but a non-being that is made nothing by the actual. The Aristotelian metaphysics of substance fails to explain saintly transformation because change can never, for Aristotle, be radical or catastrophic. For Kierkegaard nothing short of the nonbeing of possibility can be the "that" that has always already become.

Although saintly *action* occurs through an empowering, it is bound up with antecedent nonbeing that, as Kierkegaard shows, has a kind of being peculiar to itself. If saintly existence is a self-emptying, as argued earlier, there is a nonbeing that precedes the coming-into-being of change brought about through the saint's moral action. This nonbeing cannot be a cause in that nonbeing lacks power and cannot cause something else. What is more, the temporal structure of possibility shows that its existence as a nullity occurs in the wake of or *after* the new actuality has been brought about, and not before, as in the case of a cause. Thus saintly moral activity is not caused by a nullity, by the renunciation of power.

The upshot of this analysis is that a double "coding" of saintly moral activity can be perceived: first there is the self-emptying of the saint that is the mark of saintly life, and second the character of saintly action itself (like other actions) belongs within a causal nexus. The former (a nullity) is bound up with the latter, but it cannot be the *cause* of the latter. Instead, it marks or fissures saintly work.

Consider next how this marking or fissuring comes about. Saintly action is connected with the abnegation of power in that the authorization of saintly work derives from the *renunciation* of power. On the face of it, such renunciation appears to preclude action altogether so that saintly work has an apparently paradoxical character: it appears to be an exercise of power but depends on the abnegation of power. However, the nonpower of saintly action is not simply the negation of power but an impotence "that can never be mastered, accomplished or achieved but can only be suffered patiently."[65] *The power to bring about new moral configurations is authorized by the prior renunciation of power.* Authorization alone is incomplete without saintly action whereas saintly action without self-renunciation is allied to the spheres in which nonmoral or amoral power is expressed: polity, economy, work, and factual knowledge, the subject of chapter 3.

The discursive space both of ethics and of its authorizing structure is the life story, the narration of saintly renunciation and empowerment. The nonbeing of possibility, the field of ethics, and of the renunciation of power, the authorizing "structure" of saintly action, cannot be incorporated into standard cognitive discourse but taken together are exposed in hagiography. The life story is a kind of fiction that, as de Certeau asserts, "has no proper place of its own. It is metaphoric."[66] The discursive ambiguity attaching to ethics and the beyond, that is, the nonbeing of possibility, that precedes it disclosed in hagiography "moves elusively in the domain of the other."[67] The time and space of this alterity are considered in detail in chapter 4.

The second "beyond" of possibility is the sphere of completed moral actions. Once moral actions have been brought to their conclusion, the resulting state of affairs no longer belongs to the ontic/discursive space of ethics or possibility. Instead, completed moral action rejoins the realm of the actual, the historical sphere open to phenomenological description. To see this it is useful to consider the moral acts of saints and those influenced by them in terms of a twofold mode of temporalization. On the one hand, moral action insofar as it is bound up with the ethical as a field of possibility is ahead of itself as looking out toward the state of affairs to be created. On the other hand, once moral change is effected, the newly patterned social configuration is related *backward* toward the ethical as a field of nihilated possibilities. This newly fashioned moral reality is part of an ontic field to which saintly activity has contributed and can be described in the language of factual propositions.

SAINTLY LIFE has often been thought to be inseparable from mystical experience. In order to see how saints influence others, we must distinguish between the two and disclose the unique features of saintliness. The saint is defined as a radical altruist, one who is dedicated to the alleviation of the suffering of others irrespective of the cost to herself/himself. Whereas differences of language and experience must be accounted for in connection with mysticism, human need is universal.

Thus cross-cultural differences are less significant for a phenomenology of sainthood than for one of mysticism.

Once sainthood has been distinguished as a discrete phenomenon, its advantages for generating moral practice can be explored. Recent moral philosophy has for the most part failed to account for the breach between moral belief and practice. One proposed way to overcome this difficulty is by developing a type of objectivity appropriate to moral discourse: putting oneself in another's shoes. But this strategy is shown to reveal another's moral belief and no more motivates moral action than any other belief. Furthermore, moral problems are still discussed in unreflective cognitive language. Recontextualizing the problem of belief and practice in order to see the larger postmodern social and moral framework in and through which moral actions occur can bring to light the character of the rift. Such self-reflexiveness is useful, yet it may expose a cynicism that inhibits moral action.

Hagiographic fiction offers a means for highlighting the breach between belief and practice and the cynicism of recent moral frameworks. Henry James's *The Wings of the Dove* shows how saintly acts of generosity may restore a kind of moral equilibrium to moral interactions by generating selflessness in others who were previously motivated by self-interest. The conflict between cynical reason and altruism comes to the fore through a hagiographic recasting of the work. This conflict is reflected in the narrative, the use of grammatical mood to express personal desire on the one hand and social obligation on the other. While this analysis describes the conflicts articulated in hagiography, the way saintly action is transmitted has still to be explained. A key to grasping how saintly practice is transmitted is to see how performance functions in communicating a musical phrase. Both the appreciative and the performative aspects of musical practice are examined and appreciation alone is found to be wanting in bringing forth new practices. The inadequacy of appreciation alone and the necessity for performance in generating musical practice hold a fortiori for moral practice.

How individual saintly acts are communicated has been accounted for, but the saint's life must still acquire general meaning if others are to grasp its significance. A distinctive mode of exhibiting generality by way of context-specific complexes is developed in the philosophy of Merleau-Ponty and Emmanuel Levinas. Generality of this type, carnal generality, depends upon the human body as an unsurpassable condition of meaning. Saints are carnal generals, fleshly signifiers of compassion, generosity, and self-sacrifice.

When saints' lives are interpreted as carnal generals, ethical signification is integrated into their life stories. But the relationship between
ethics and the life story requires further clarification. The key question
of whether ethics and fiction actually belong to a common discursive
and ontic space is considered in terms of both Aristotle's and Kierkegaard's analyses of possibility. "Sheer" or "open" possibility, the capacity either to become or not to become *x*, is seen to define the sphere of
both ethics and fiction.

The saint's life is not simply one of action but one of authorized
action. The authorization of moral action in a postmodern context in
which the general presuppositions for authoritative discourse fall under
criticism requires renouncing power. Saints abjure power as the precondition of moral acts and as their warranty. Thus saintly lives display a
three-tiered structure: the renunciation of power which authorizes its
subsequent use; ethics, the sphere of pure possibility in which the
power to act awaits realization; the ontic sphere of completed acts or
nihilated possibilities. This structure is revealed in the narratological
orchestration of actual saintly lives as well as in hagiographic fiction.

3

[The children] played. They did not stop playing except to go and die. To die of destitution. Everywhere and in all times. . . . No doubt children died everywhere like that—in the Mississippi River Valley, in the Amazon, in the cadaverous villages of Manchuria, in the Sudan and on the plain of Kam. And everywhere throughout the world, as here, they died of misery. The mangoes of misery. The rice of misery. The milk of misery.

Marguerite Duras, *The Sea Wall*

Francisco de Goya, Lo Mismo. Disaster of War series. Metropolitan Museum of Art, New York, Rogers Fund, 1922.

Time without the Other

DOES ALTERITY, the "otherness" of other persons, show itself through a distinctive time scheme? If so, does the saint experience this time scheme differently from others? Does not everyone after all inhabit a common temporal framework that makes the coordination of the multiple acts and events that constitute individual lives possible? And if there is such a common framework, how can there be a difference between my time and the time of the Other? If there is an experience of time that is inaccessible to another, would that mode of temporalization not articulate the differential structure of self and Other?

In this chapter I explore the temporality of work, the temporal framework of everyday life that, to borrow a phrase of Heraclitus, is common to all. I consider too how this mode of temporalization is infiltrated by traces of alterity. Because work expresses the self's effort to make the world manageable, despite these traces of the Other, the world's otherness is necessarily lost.

I also argue that ethical theories that take for granted the time frame of work or agency do not bring to the fore the Other as an ethical datum. It is therefore crucial to distinguish the time scheme of agency from that of alterity. To be sure, moral acts are the work of agents, but I hope to show that agency as such is a property of the self in its efforts to maintain its own interests. To show this I examine two complex moral theories, each different from the other, in which altruism figures, that of Rawls and that of Gewirth. In considering these theories I focus on the question of agency in order to suggest the misdirection of their efforts: in both the Other is articulated in terms of agency and thus ultimately of the self. Rawls's and Gewirth's failure to breach the gap in moral theory between agent and Other requires a response from a postmodern perspective. The idea is not to add to the already extensive literature on their work by mounting a series of counterarguments but rather to appeal to hagiographic narrative in contrast to their views.

Death and the Time That Is Left

On the face of it, the anticipation of my death seems to qualify as a mode of temporal experience that precludes its being experienced by another. Heidegger calls this relation to my death my ownmost possibility. Similarly the Other also anticipates her/his own death, a relation from which I am excluded. I cannot die for another in the sense that my dying will take the place of the other's death because at some time the Other must die for herself/himself.

What is omitted from Heidegger's account, however, is that the force of the relation to my own death derives from an awareness of *the time that is left*, the gap between my life now and the event that is my dying and is yet to come. This is true even if the length of time I have left is indeterminable. When my death is thought of in this way as the always dwindling time that is left to me rather than as the coming to an end of my life, then the death of the Other and my death become *commensurable*. This is because all along the way, each has a certain quantum of time left. The other's death and mine are now integrated into a common framework in that each of us has a certain portion of time still outstanding.

Death is the nonbeing of a being who first must exist; and to exist is to have time left over. But, it can be argued, such time may be experienced qualitatively—for example, as hanging heavily or passing quickly. Yet that which is lends itself to quantification and calculative judgment in that the qualitative is transposable into quantity. This by no means implies that a given quality is identical with some specific quantity. Thus ten minutes may be a long time if one is waiting to hear about the outcome of a surgical procedure but ten years may not be a long time when training for a profession. If the qualitative can be expressed as quantity, qualitative temporal duration can be cashed out in terms of homogeneous units. This contention, although not identical to Quine's by now well-worn dictum that to be is to be the value of a variable, strengthens a seemingly perverse claim. Existents may be described in terms of the more and the less, which, in turn, can be given expression with the help of the quantification rules of formal logic.

In sum, death does not cordon off the time of the Other from my time but, to the contrary, opens up the possibility for commensurable although not necessarily uniform temporality. This temporality is the time that lies ahead before each life comes to an end. The preceding assertion can be put another way: each of us lays claim to a measure of time, has a stake or interest in time, a contention expressed by both

Aristotle and Spinoza as the interest of every existing thing to persevere in time. *The claim on time is the foundation of other self-interest claims.* These claims then are not grounded in an inauthentic refusal to face death, shutting out one's coming to an end, but rather in staking out a portion of time. Because death is anticipated, I see remaining time as my time, as my due. But others also anticipate death in the same way as I and, no less than I, want to persevere in existence. Because "pure" time is not inherently unshareable, there is no necessary conflict about the ownership of time. But the desire for more time generates ancillary claims of use that can be and often are opposed, thus establishing the conditions for conflicts of interest. This state of affairs is suggested in Emmanuel Levinas's comment:

Each has a right to forestall his own death. This being interested does not appear only to the mind surprised by its own negation and to the man resigned to the meaninglessness of his own death. . . . It is confirmed positively to be the *conatus* of beings. Being's interest takes the form of beings struggling with one another, each against all.[1]

A seemingly promising criterion for preserving alterity through a time scheme that reflects the differential structure of self and Other, the time scheme of one's own death, falls short of its aim. Far from preserving the difference of the Other, my death is shown to eventuate in a unitary time frame encompassing self and Other. When "time left" becomes the common measure of self and Other, it opens up the possibility for staking a self-interested claim on time founded on the desire for self-preservation. The result is a conflicting field of self-interest claims.

Moral Law and Radical Altruism: Rawls and Gewirth

Although saintly morality excludes self-interest, would it not be better to develop a moral theory that provides a means for adjudicating competing self-interest claims rather than to renounce such claims? In considering this question I shall for the moment set aside my reservations about moral theory generally. Instead, I shall briefly examine two recent theories, a social contract theory and a theory of rational agency. Each of these theories, held respectively by Rawls and Gewirth, is based to some degree on self-interest.

My aim is not to contribute new arguments to ongoing debates, thus adding to an already extensive literature, but rather to fasten on several existing objections that make the theories problematic in order to bring out the deeper difficulties these objections reveal. The criticisms upon which I shall focus render transparent the notion of the Other that undergirds Rawls's revisionist utilitarianism and Gewirth's reconceived Kantian rationalism. The views of the two are of particular interest in that altruism has occupied an important place in traditional utilitarian ethics and in Kant's practical philosophy. If reconceptualizations by Rawls and Gewirth provide satisfactory accounts of altruism, it may be unnecessary to resort to saintly lives in order to understand how moral beliefs and practices are generated. If, on the other hand, their theories should turn out to be parasitic upon interpretations of other persons that miss the singular character of the Other, then the appeal to phenomenological and postmodern conceptions of alterity may be justified.

The first, Rawls's social contract theory, assumes that an accord among self-interested parties can be reached when unlimited self-interest is abandoned in favor of self-preservation and social order. On this view self-preservation is less primordial than unlimited self-interest in that the one (unlimited self-interest) precedes the other (self-preservation) and can be abandoned in its favor. This aspect of Rawls's theory is classically represented in descriptions of the state of nature in the moral and political philosophies of Hobbes, Locke, and Rousseau, among others.[2] Rawls's view conflicts with my earlier conclusion that *self-preservation*, because it is based on the most primitive of human relations, the relation to death and time, is the precondition of other self-interest claims. More important, I shall show later that neither self-interest nor self-preservation can provide "starting points" for the moral life. Only the prior relation with the Other can cut across the claims of the self either to preserve its existence or to stake out further claims parasitic upon self-preservation.

The second theory, Gewirth's rationalist ethics, presupposes that the goodness of an individual's act is measured by whether that act is good for a community of others, a position taken historically by Kant. On the face of it, Gewirth's view of the Other seems closer to the mark in that a normative character is ascribed to the community of others. I shall argue, however, that without a prior relation to the Other, the starting point of moral action is only social secondarily and that moral action so conceived is, albeit unreflectively, entangled in self-preservation and self-interest.

Consider first Rawls's by now familiar claim that the principles of justice are those that "a rational agent situated behind a veil of ignorance" will choose. The veil conceals what social or economic position the agent will hold, what talent or dispositions the agent will have, and what type of society the agent will come to inhabit. When confronted with the problem of distributing a society's goods, no matter what social order is to prevail, a rational agent will operate on two principles: first, each person will have an equal right to the "most extensive total system of equal basic liberties compatible with a similar system of liberty for all," and second, "social and economic inequalities are to be arranged so that (a) they are both to the greatest benefit of the least advantaged"[3] consistent with providing for the interest of future generations and (b) "equal opportunity is to govern the society's distribution of positions of power."[4] Rawls concludes that "all social primary goods—liberty and opportunity, income and wealth—are to be distributed equally, unless an unequal distribution . . . is to the advantage of the least favored."[5] He grounds his view of justice on the entitlement of each member of a society to have certain basic needs met and on the right of the worst off to benefit the most from a society's resources.

A basic flaw in this position pointed to by Alasdair MacIntyre is that "individuals are . . . primary and society secondary and the identification of individual interests is prior to and independent of any moral or social bonds between them."[6] Such an asocial self, a cognitive and conative monad, would have no reason to benefit the least advantaged in the absence of an earlier social bond. What is more, without prior reasons for benevolence, benefiting the least advantaged would violate the claims of dessert, what is owed to individuals as based on effort and accomplishment.

In criticizing Rawls's view, Alasdair MacIntyre claims that the question of needs and rights is begged. Rawls's rational agent could not know the conditions of social existence—what needs and rights are or, a fortiori, exercise benevolence—prior to the act of choosing. Such concepts as needs and rights already presuppose social existence as a condition for availing oneself of the latter or satisfying the former. As Emmanuel Levinas argues in another context, "For phenomenologists . . . a meaning cannot be separated from the access leading to it. *The access is part of the meaning itself.*"[7] Social existence provides the access to the exercise of benevolence.

But there is a deeper difficulty that MacIntyre's objection helps to disinter. The self, on Rawls's interpretation, is an isolated epistemological subject upon whom the claims of the Other can only impinge *contingently*. Should there happen to be others, a rational agent might choose to take the Other into account. But the Other, on Rawls's view, is not *constitutive* of the field of moral transactions. The needs of the

Other, and a fortiori of the least advantaged, may come into view, but such a fortuitous arising of the other's needs in advance of social existence would render them inscrutable and uninterpretable.

Existential philosophies avoid this difficulty by stressing the social character of the self. There is not first an isolated subject and later a crossing-over to others. "By 'Others,'" Heidegger argues, "we do not only mean everyone else but me—those over against whom the 'I' stands out . . . but those among whom one is too. . . . The world is always one I share with Others."[8] Sartre's account departs from Heidegger's in that the Other is interpreted as "a system of meanings and experiences radically distinct from my own" and in tension with it.[9] Because Sartre holds that the Other can constitute me as an object, I am at the mercy of another's power to objectify me. What is more, I have no access to another's consciousness so that the Other is, on principle, an absence. Despite these differences, for both Heidegger and Sartre the self is transactionally constituted so that a social dimension is presupposed from the start, one to which one's social and economic "situation" are integral.

Heidegger's account by no means provides a starting point for thinking through the question of moral existence in terms of saintly altruism. But his view of the primordiality of being-with-others at least rules out one of the defining conditions of justice as laid down by Rawls, an asocial self. In fact, Heidegger has renounced the project of ethics. Standing in the way of importing Heidegger's description of social existence into an account of saintly exemplarity is not only his repudiation of ethics as an enterprise but also his delineation of the Other as another myself nondifferent from me. This similitude, established through what constitutes self and Other as a "we" (a *Mitsein*), namely our joint ventures in a shared world, undermines the alterity of the Other. Although Sartre interprets self and Other as inimical to one another, his view is an advance over Heidegger's in that the Other is different from me *en principe* and irreducible to a cognitive content.

How alterity impinges upon the self will be clarified in detail in chapter 4, where I will again take up the interest of the least advantaged from another standpoint. In the present context Rawls's view that justice benefits the least favored may nevertheless be seen as an entering wedge in grasping the relation of self and Other. But contrary to Rawls's claim that *rational deliberation* about the distribution of a society's goods under the veil of ignorance will accrue to the interest of the least advantaged, I will maintain that indigence and disadvantage are constitutive conditions of alterity and affect the way in which the Other is apprehended. For the present it is enough to notice that Rawls's insight is weakened by positing the veil of ignorance. By contrast, existential accounts of human life have shown that the Other is integral to what selves are and that, in the absence of a social existence that is existentially primordial, there may be body-objects but not a being who could make determinations about justice.

If social contract theories fail because they assume that there is a neutral ground from which ethical choices can originate, perhaps a rationalist ethic that avoids this difficulty, one that begins by presupposing a community of others, can successfully establish the claims of alterity. Alan Gewirth asserts that there is a supreme principle of morality the denial of which is self-contradictory and from which all other moral principles follow.[10] He begins by arguing that every agent has purposes which require the goods of freedom and well-being for their fulfillment. This requirement is entailed by the conditions of agency themselves because without freedom and well-being purposive action would be impossible. But others also have a right to these goods because they too are purposive agents. It follows from claiming them for oneself that it would be self-contradictory to deny them to others. In refusing others the goods of freedom and well-being, one denies what one has already affirmed, that being a prospective agent who acts in accordance with ends is a sufficient condition for having these goods.

This position is expressed in the Principle of Generic Consistency (PGC), the supreme principle of morality: "Act in accord with the generic rights of your recipients as well as of yourself."[11] Negatively the PGC entails refraining from harming or coercing others, and positively it enjoins assisting them in having freedom and well-being "whenever they cannot otherwise have these necessary goods and he can help them at no comparable cost to himself."[12]

A difficulty with Gewirth's formulation of the PGC that has received considerable attention is his assertion that agents have a *right* to freedom and well-being. In fact, it is objected, all he has shown is that agents *want* and *need* these goods. Kai Nielsen argues that the claim that it is rational to want and need freedom and well-being differs from the claim that one has a right to them.[13] If I *desire* X, there is no reason why others ought not to try and prevent my getting X; but if I have a *right* to X, others ought not to interfere with my acquiring it. The appeal to universalizability does not help because the property of necessary universalizability is precisely what does not belong to needing or desiring a good, even one which may be universally necessary. Furthermore, even if freedom and well-being are necessary to me and to another, it does not follow that it is irrational for either of us to refuse to acknowledge the other's rights to these goods. As Nielson claims, "Gewirth has not built such a logical bridge here, and he fares no better than Kant did in showing how, or even that, the immoralist or amoralist must . . . have acted contrary to reason."[14]

A further difficulty emerges from Gewirth's account of prudential judgments. Prudential "ought" judgments are "self-directed, laying a practical judgment only on the agent or the person whose well-being is directly at stake." But he believes that it is possible to move from "a self-directed 'ought' judgment to an other-directed 'ought' judgment" because "correlative requirements on others" follow from the agent's "self-directed requirement."[15] How then are prudence and morality to be distinguished? Gewirth's account fails to show how a transition is made from the level of prudence or self-interest to the level of morality, the taking account of persons other than oneself.

I cite these criticisms because they reflect *in nuce* difficulties bound up with an issue of interest to a postmodern ethic, an insufficiently reflexive grasp of alterity. The shift from prudential to moral judgments should be seen against the background of the relation of self and Other. Gewirth's view presupposes the symmetry of self and Other so that features of the self relevant to a given moral context are also features attributed to an analogous Other. The agent extends the conditions of agency to the Other as a matter of course because the Other is another myself. The freedom and well-being granted to another are ceded to a reposited self, numerically distinct from, but otherwise identical to, oneself. Unless the distinction between self and Other is radically drawn, the difference between prudential and moral judgments is blurred. Because in law multiple persons and interests must be considered, the parity of self and Other is a necessary fiction. When moral rather than juridical relations are considered, the term Other loses its force unless there is an incommensurability, an asymmetry, between self and Other.

This difficulty is itself parasitic upon the deeper question of agency. Both Gewirth and his critics take for granted that what is morally problematic is how the conditions of agency are to be distributed but not agency simpliciter. Moral value is attributed to what may be a "*natural*" but not a *moral* necessity. If the starting point of ethics is not the self but the Other, the conditions of agency, conditions stemming from one's own freedom and well-being, cannot provide the criteria for moral action. Beginning with the Other entails not only constraints on freedom and well-being, but the recognition of the *constitutive* character of alterity for the moral discourse and practice presupposed by these constraints. By contrast, saintly lives presuppose that the Other places a demand on them rather than that the Other is a second self to whom the conditions of agency are to be extended.

But, it could be argued, if altruism can be shown to be a duty deducible from the conditions of agency alone, even if there are more primordial conditions bound up with altruism, no more than the conditions of agency may be needed to establish altruism as morally required. Postmodern analyses of radical alterity would then be otiose. It is therefore worth considering in some detail Gewirth's account of an altruistic action based on an imperative frequently invoked in law, the duty to rescue.

Gewirth contends that limited altruism as expressed in the duty to rescue can be seen to follow from the PGC.[16] If one knows that unless one undertakes certain actions, others will suffer basic harms, it is one's duty to prevent these harms. Thus, for example, if X, who is an excellent swimmer, sees Y about to drown and, without endangerment, can save Y, X is obliged to do so. Under appropriately stipulated conditions, agents have a duty to rescue. But, Gewirth thinks, four variables should be taken into account: "(i) the kind or degree of harm impending to the recipient (ii) the agent's knowledge of this harm (iii) his ability to ward off the harm (iv) the cost to the agent of doing so."[17]

A difficulty attaching to Gewirth's view of the duty to rescue hangs on the question of responsibility for Y's death: whether, if X fails to rescue Y, X has *caused* Y's death. The objection to Gewirth's description is that a violation of the PGC (the refusal to accept the duty of rescuing Y), a *moral* principle, will count as ground for ascribing *causal* responsibility for the death of Y by drowning.[18] This objection astutely recognizes that the PGC is both a formal and a material principle, combining logical consistency with material rights, rights to the goods of action. Material considerations (those connected with causing Y's death) infiltrate deontological claims, claims about goodness and duty.

The problem is particularly vexing when, in a multicausal situation, X's failing to rescue Y is singled out as determining the harmful upshot, Y's drowning. Gewirth counters this objection by arguing that when the PGC assigns moral responsibility to X, it "provides the clue as to which among the multiple necessary conditions of [Y's] drowning is held to be the cause."[19] But by making the PGC do the work of deciding, it is reduced to a quasi-cognitive concept having material content and thus weakening its deontological force. In sum, objections to his account of the duty to rescue show that Gewirth fails to forge a link between a violation of the PGC, a moral consideration, and the determination of responsibility for a harmful outcome, a matter bound up with the ascription of cause. Gewirth concedes that the claim "X's inaction caused Y's death "is only *"evidenced* but not *constituted"* by the moral responsibility ascribed by the PGC to X.[20] But this concession shows that X's inaction is cut off from the constitutive principle of morality on its deontological side, just the side that is to have remained "uncontaminated" by material considerations.

Might it not be argued that saintly activity too is enmeshed in causal sequences? Even if this is so, because of the narrative character of their interconnectedness, saintly acts are not referred to a supreme moral principle. Instead, the saint's life is appealed to and, as such, saintly altruism is never cut off from material conditions. To the contrary, the saint's supreme *moral* principle is the *material* condition of the Other.

If this is acknowledged, is there not a danger of extremism in another direction, namely that saintly acts will be divested of moral worth and interpreted as merely another species of work: alleviating another's material need? Will this not reduce saintly acts and their consequences to the status of commodities? If not, how is the difference between saintly and ordinary work to be understood? Is it possible that the saint's entire life is a kind of work?

A fruitful starting point for an inquiry into these questions is an investigation of the time scheme of everyday work in order to see whether the differences between radically altruistic and everyday work are unsurpassable. Such an inquiry can uncover the temporal conditions of agency presupposed by accounts in which these conditions are never interrogated so that, if there are the differences between agency and saintly altruism, they can be brought to light.

The Time Scheme of Everyday Work

Earlier I argued that the time of the Other is not introduced through death because death allows for the commensurability of self and Other. Consider as an alternative the possibility that work in which the world is acted upon by a self opens up the temporal structure of alterity. I shall use the phrase "tasks of time" to provide a guidepost in considering this possibility and interpret the expression as containing a double genitive: the tasks belonging *to* time, time's tasks, on the one hand, and time *as* itself a series of tasks, on the other. The latter—time as a series of tasks—will demand an analysis of the differences between work and labor.

A preliminary distinction can be drawn between work and labor in terms of their range. Work refers not only to the exertions of persons but also to the activities of machines and of natural forces. Labor is generally restricted to human effort and frequently connotes pains-taking striving. It is also the term used to describe parturition with its attendant pain and eventuation in new life. The saint's project as appre-hended by the addressees of a hagiographic narrative is seen as a work, as an undertaking of tasks in time that are articulated as a unitary goal-oriented enterprise. From the perspective of the saint, "work" is toil, the arduous effort to reduce human suffering, a kind of parturition in which a rebirth for both healer and sufferer comes into being—in short, work that is labor. Time is itself the medium to be worked up, to be transformed from moment to moment. The passing of time is experienced as an extreme urgency to begin the tasks of saintly life over and over again.

The distinction between work and labor constitutes a partial parallel to the difference between the optative and the obligative narratological strands considered in chapter 1 and explored there in the context of the grammar of narratives. Recall that the obligative, according to Todorov, expresses a nonindividual will that encodes the law of a society, in con-trast to the optative, which corresponds to the actions a character de-sires or renounces. Once saintly actions are incorporated in a work, to the extent that they reflect the linguistic properties of hagiography and are subject to the conditions of institutional preservation, they take on a quasi-obligative character. A story thus *encodes* the saint's project in communicable form and provides an account of the tasks belonging to time. The optative strand of saintly singularity *encrypts* this singularity, conceals the secret of saintly labor and of the saintly transformation of time.

Before turning to the time scheme of work, we may find it useful to begin with the everyday conception of work as setting about to make something, an object. The entities that result from the shaping acts that produced them can be objects of knowledge, utility, or enjoyment. Once freed from the acts that brought it into being, an object can ac-quire new functions distinct from those inherent in the original for-mative intentions.

Is there a way of regarding work which does not conceive of it as issuing in a product? While the term *work* receives its full range of sig-nifications only in modern philosophy, Aristotle's analysis of activity lays the groundwork for a consideration of this question. For Aristotle the principal meaning of actuality is activity (*energeia*), motion or process. The difference between something actual and something merely potential is that what is actual is engaged in the exercise of its function while what is potential can come to be something else but has not attained its completed form. In his analysis of actuality, Aristotle stretches the meaning of activity to include a variety of functions in which no visible change of form, condition, or place occurs:

The actual is to the potential as a man building is to a man who can build, as waking to sleeping, as one who is seeing to one who possesses sight but has his eyes closed, as that which has been separated out of matter is to the matter, and as the accomplished to the unaccomplished. To one of the terms in each case let us assign operation or functioning (*energeia*), to the other power (*dynamis*). Not all things are said to be functioning in the same way, but only by analogy: as that is in that or to that, so this is in this or to this. For some are as motion is to power, others as *ousia* is to some matter.[21]

According to this analysis, the relation of *ousia* to matter is, on analogy with making or sensing, a process. When a thing's function is simply to exist, as in the case of a statue or a star, existence is construed as an activity. The scope of what is to count as activity now extends to the being of entities.

Modern notions of work include the Aristotelian idea of activity but also comprise two further notions. First, deriving from its interpretation in Newtonian physics, work involves an expenditure of mechanical energy. Something is used up or is depleted in order for something else, heat, to come into being. Second, originating in late medieval notions of the will and later carried over into modern philosophy, work takes on the meaning of effort as an exercise of will.[22] The modern notion derives from an older theological context in which creation is the work of a divine will whereas sin is the work of Satan in conjunction with the flesh. As such, work in modern philosophy not only brings forth existing things but also values and disvalues. It can now be asked whether the self's existing is a work and, if so, whether work carries the range of significations thus far attributed to the term: sheer subsisting interpreted as a dynamic activity; expenditure of energy; a conatus or voluntary effort bound up with the creation of objects having or lacking value.

Consider first the question of whether the self can be interpreted as a work. If it can, is it a unitary thing? How does any entity come to be a unitary thing? Against what does its singularity emerge? If out of nothing, how could it come to be at all? And if from something, as classical philosophy claimed, then from what?

For Aristotle natural and manufactured things emerge from matter when matter is informed by intelligible pattern. In the case of non-material objects, the object is identical to its function: the purpose of the activity and the activity itself are in the agent. In his analysis of the subject as a consciousness whose function is thinking, Descartes continues the Aristotelian tradition: the end of the operation, thinking, and the operation itself are contained in the agent.

The Self as a Work: Descartes

The Cartesian self exhibits a conative element absent from the Aristotelian pattern in that the thinking subject posits or wills itself over and over again. In order to establish itself as existing, the cogito must re-will itself every time it thinks: "I am, I exist, that is certain. But how often? Just when I think; for it might possibly be the case if I ceased entirely to think, that I should likewise cease altogether to exist."[23] Descartes shows the coming into being of the singular subject as a self-positing act.

But against or out of what does the singularity of the subject emerge? The Cartesian answer is God, who is "the cause of created things." Elaborating on the sense in which God's agency is to be interpreted, Descartes writes to Gassendi:

An architect is the cause of a house and a father of his son *in respect of coming into being* . . . and for this reason when it is an absolute production, an effect can remain in existence without any cause of this kind; but the sun is the cause of the light proceeding from it, and God is the cause of created things not only *in respect of their coming into existence* but also *in respect of their continuing to exist*, and must always expend his activity on the effect in the same way in order to make it stay the same thing.[24]

Descartes distinguishes between the causes of coming into being and being *tout court*. In the former case, the cause shapes an entity which can continue to exist without the activity of the shaping agency. But in the case of the sun and its light or with God and his supporting activity for man's continued existence, the cause continues to operate through the whole process. God maintains the self's existence by renewing it at every instant. What is more, self-knowledge exhibits a structure parallel to that of the self's existence. Just as God acts to ensure the self's perdurance, so too the cogito continues to posit itself each time it makes certain of its existence.

This interpretation of a self-positing cogito and a sustaining divine activity requires a new conception of time. Traditional interpretations of time like Gassendi's attribute a "necessary character . . . to . . . the connections between the parts of time," a valid view, Descartes argues, if time is considered in the abstract.[25] But "[h]ere it is not a question of abstract time, but of the time or duration of something which endures; and you will not deny the single moments of this time can be separated from their neighbors, i.e. that a thing which endures through particular moments may cease to exist."[26] The structure of the Cartesian subject calls for a mode of temporalization in which the subject's existence is continually sustained by divine action. Self-actualization consists in the moment-to-moment perdurance of a cogito that assures itself of its existence by repeating in the order of knowledge what God has guaranteed in the order of existence. Thinking and existence are determined as a taking hold of each instant, instant by instant. We will consider this aspect of Descartes' thought again after examining some crucial objections to the Cartesian position.

Contemporary philosophy—whether naturalist, positivist, phenomenological, or poststructuralist—claims that, when the self is identified with the cogito, the experienced unity of mind and body becomes inexplicable. This is because the existence attested by thought is not the body's existence but that of a consciousness, the subject of mental acts. The body is then interpreted as something outside of and apart from the subject.

The standard form of the familiar mind-body problem is stated by Gassendi:

[*Y*]*ou say* that nature teaches you by the sensation of pain, hunger, thirst, etc. that you are not lodged in the body as a sailor in a ship but that you are very closely united with it and so to speak, intermingle with it so as to compose on whole along with it. [B]ut it still remains to be explained how that union . . . can be found in you if you are incorporeal, unextended, indivisible.[27]

Another criticism of the Cartesian account of the cogito is its reification of the subject. Gilbert Ryle's by now familiar objection to Descartes' view that the cogito exists independently of the thoughts, doubts, wishes, and the like that are its content appeals to the principle of parsimony. Just as it is misleading to think of Oxford University as something distinct from its constituents, Ryle argues, positing the cogito as an entity different from mental content attributes actual existence to what is merely a useful descriptive term. The idea that the cogito is an extant entity should be dismissed as a "ghost in the machine."[28]

There is still another difficulty connected with the cogito as subject. Once the cogito is defined in terms of thought, every other kind of being becomes an object for the thinking subject. The result is a distinction between subject and object that privileges the subject. This stress on the subject determines the character of subsequent modern philosophy. Heidegger argues that the distinction itself is the result of Descartes' interpretation of the kind of being that human beings are.[29] For Heidegger the human being is not a thinking thing, the subject of cognitive acts, but a being that is already in the world, enmeshed in social and utilitarian networks as well as by a unique connection to its own death.

Bound up with this view of human being is a further question about the meaning of being. For Heidegger the Cartesian account of being reflects an unavoidable misprision that is locked into being's history, the grounding of ontology in the subject: "Man becomes that being upon which all that is, is grounded as regards the manner of its Being and its truth. Man becomes the relational center of that which is."[30] In sum, otherwise diverse philosophers agree that the reification of the cogito, the mind-body problem, and the "subjectism" of modern philosophy count against salvaging any important aspect of Cartesian thought.

At the same time what remains unthought in the work of a major thinker is worth pondering. If so, is it possible that the cogito's positing of itself as well as the ground of this epistemological self-positing in God's sustaining activity offers a new approach to the matter of work and the self's relation to it? In fact, the Cartesian cogito may be interpreted in a less damaging way than the standard objections would indicate. Consider Descartes' actual language about the self as a *thing* that thinks. If thought has a material base, it need not be seen as disembodied. To the contrary, thought has a locus; it is here, where my body is. It can be argued that the body excluded by Cartesian doubt is not the body as subject but the body as object. Far from barring experienced corporeality from the cogito, Descartes has instead cordoned off the body as thing. Emmanuel Levinas argues:

The cogito does not lead to the impersonal position, "There is thought," but to the first person in the present: "I am something that thinks." The word thing here is admirably exact. For the most profound teaching of the Cartesian cogito consists in discovering thought . . . as something that is posited. Thought has a point of departure. There is not only a consciousness of localization but a localization of consciousness.[31]

A material condition is required if thinking is to occur or, to express this in a more graphic if queer way, "a protuberance, a head," is necessary if there is to be thought. This should not be confused with the epiphenomenalist position that the brain is a prerequisite for thought but that neurophysiological processes are not identical with thinking. By contrast, my claim is that thinking is felt as coming from a place, a corporeal locus. The thinking subject *begins* from a position, a situatedness that is not a passive condition but a keeping of oneself in readiness. In Cartesian terms, each and every time there is thinking, consciousness reposits itself, takes up its place once again.

This interpretation of the cogito as a self-positing subject is bound up with Descartes' claim that remaining in existence entails assuming each instant afresh. It is also rooted in the Aristotelian idea that sheer existence is a dynamic activity. The localization of thinking starting from a specific body region makes possible the alternation of the felt fixity of a corporeal starting point of thought and the continually renewed efforts of thought to reposit itself.

If the self resumes its existence each moment, then the everyday understanding of the present as vanishing into past or future is altered. Instead of a continuum from which present time is always vanishing, each instant is experienced as stretched or extended. This is because an instant is a bit of immobilized time that interrupts the temporal flux. But the instant is also evanescent in that it falls back into the stream of time. The self's positing and repositing of itself are experienced as a succession of instants. Descartes' analysis of the cogito need not give rise to a mechanistic interpretation of time but may be viewed phenomenologically as the experienced rhythm of self-temporalization.

It can be objected that, even if the cogito is a dynamic and recurrent self-positing, it is still a consciousness rather than an agent that transforms the world through work. One distinction has merely been replaced by a comparable distinction. Instead of a distinction between mind and body, a differentiation of thought and action is presupposed. Closer analysis of the instant should, however, reveal a common infrastructure of thinking and activity.

Consider again the character of the instant as distended, as a stretch of time.[32] The cogito in positing itself takes possession of the instant, thus distancing itself—for the space of that instant—from the flux of time. But how is it possible to distance oneself from that in which one is always already immersed? To say, by taking possession of the instant, begs the question, for such taking possession is what remains to be explained. Instead, what calls for inquiry is how creating an instant distances one from the stream of time. This distancing is achieved by holding the body at bay and disincarnating the self for the interim of the instant. The subject does not lose or cease to be a body but swings free from its corporeal locus, opens out from it and returns to it. The interval released from the stream created by the act of going forth and returning exhibits a twofold structure. On the one hand the instant is itself work in that it requires an expenditure of effort as it begins to be by unbinding itself from itself as a self-identical positioned subject. On the other hand the interval that is released is free for use.[33] Rather than something spatially extended, the instant is the most primordial object of utility. When considered entitatively, the instant is a product, but when seen functionally as time stretching itself, it becomes a means through which goal-directed and world-implicating acts—work in the straightforward sense of the term—are initiated. For there to be a formative act, there must first be an enabling interval since an immediate blind collision of forces produces nothing.

It is now possible to take up in greater detail the double genitive at work in the interpretation of the task of time. The phrase can signify time's task, the task belonging to an interval of time, to its stretch or extendedness as holding the body at bay. On the other hand, an interval of time may be interpreted as itself *being* a task. On this reading, time is the task of beginning, of the cogito's first move of self-temporalization as the distended interval.

Does either account of the double genitive reflect the time of the Other? There are two grounds on which the time of work must be rejected as opening the time scheme of alterity. First, the manner in which the cogito lives time is as a succession of instants. This mode of self-temporalization is prior to any *actual* engagement with the world in that it is an infrastructure that makes world involvement possible. The instant is the defining condition of selfhood and therefore cannot be taken as a condition for alterity.

The second ground is that actual world-transforming work made possible by the self's temporal infrastructure is only an extension of the subject's aims, a fitting of the world to its projects. Still, it could be objected, work in the everyday sense involves transactions with a material world, an intersecting with conditions and objects other than the self. Furthermore, it may be objected, the view that the world's otherness becomes part of the self through work posits a counterintuitive claim about the way the world is actually experienced, one that is cognitively implausible and pragmatically useless.

To counter this objection by showing that work fails to provide access to alterity even though work entails transactions with the world, it is useful to examine the character of primordial work acts. Consider the hand that engages the world in a complex process of altering what it finds in accordance with some goal, one which need not be pre-set but may be modified as the hand feels its way about in completing its task. Just as consciousness is the exerting of an effort to assume the interval, so the hand strives to master the materials it finds. Objects can, of course, be viewed as separate from the hand, but when they are so interpreted, they are not oriented toward a task's completion. Instead, they are simply objects existing side by side with only external spatial relationships linking them to one another. But once hand and world are orchestrated teleologically, coordinated into an enterprise, the world is subjected to a system of significations imposed by the act of work.

Work subordinates the object's otherness to a plan. It is not necessary to press the radical claim that objects are engulfed by shaping intentions so as to merge with the self. Instead, it is enough to show that, in work, the world is altered in accordance with the self's designs to preclude the possibility that work provides an access route to alterity.

The question of work and its temporalization poses important difficulties for understanding saintly action. If saintly life is saintly work but work is tied to the structure of the self's world shaping, how can saintly action open out into the sphere of the Other? And, conversely, if saintly practice reflects alterity, does it cease to be effective as action? Work calls for an orienting aim. In the absence of such a purpose, action ceases to be work altogether or is abortive or incomplete work. Even when it falls short of its ends or these ends change, work remains goal-directed. These questions can be considered by explicating the second part of the distinction between work and labor.

Thinking, Animality, and the Saintly Hand

The inquiry into the character of work was sparked by the difficulties connected with Gewirth's theory: the appeal to a deontological moral principle that was found to be enmeshed in the material conditions of agency. If saints' lives are world altering, they too are involved in the sublation of the world's otherness. How does saintly action differ from ordinary work? If saintly work is to be distinguished from work in its various usual senses, that is, if work is to be construed as *labor*, it should be useful to analyze in detail the relation of hand and world sketched earlier in the example of the simple task. An account of the hand's connection to thought and action should help determine whether there are some characteristics of the manual shaping of the world that have been overlooked and that would link the hand to saintly labor.

Derrida's interpretation of Heidegger's phenomenology of the hand offers strategic clues for such a transvaluation of the function of the hand.[34] Central to Heidegger's inquiry is the distinction between the purely human use of the hand—giving, receiving, and welcoming— and the animal's use, in particular, the ape's paw that grasps or grips. Deploying the human hand in a human way is, for Heidegger, bound up with thinking, whereas the ape may display manual dexterity but, in the true sense of the term, has no hand. Derrida, playing on the double sense of monstration as "a showing" and as "grotesque," asserts that, for Heidegger, the hand is a monstrous sign, "the proper of man."[35]

The hand's performative capacity for Heidegger comes to fruition in *Handwerk*, with which thinking is compared. Thinking is a craft like that of the joiner: "Perhaps thinking, too, is something like building a cabinet (*wie das Bauen einem Schrein*)."[36] But if thinking is to be *Handwerk*, then craft must be allowed to conform with the being of what is crafted. The true joiner is attuned to "the hidden plenitude of the wood's essence and not with the tool or the use value."[37] By implication what is to be pondered is whatever is comparable in the crafting of thought to the wood's essence. This cannot be a mere means—a tool or a use value—but that with which thought must place itself in accord, the difference between Being and beings.

Derrida does not refer to a difficulty that arises in connection with Heidegger's assertion about the necessary accord between the craftsman and his material. The full conformation to the wood's essence that Heidegger proposes would leave the wood as it is in nature, untouched. Only by having some end in view—an idea of what the thing is for—and by using tools to bring about this end in conformity with some plan does craft eventuate in objects. But aesthetic and utilitarian concerns do not simply dissipate in Heidegger's analysis. Instead, Heidegger appeals to something extrinsic to craft itself but that, like craft, is linked to the essence of thinking. This is, for Heidegger, the fact that man does not simply seek shelter but stands in need of an abode. Utility must itself conform to the more primordial interest of what Heidegger sees as integral to the human essence, being at home in the world. Craft domesticates technique by subordinating the object to what is most essential to man as one who dwells. Thus the hand "that designs and signs, . . . because man is a sign (*Die Hand zeichnet, vermutlich weil der Mensch ein Zeichen ist*),"[38] unites thinking and craft in the object through the mediating influence of dwelling. I shall return shortly to this point since it is of cardinal importance for my analysis.

Consider again Derrida's discussion of the animal in Heidegger's thought, the ape that has organs for grasping (*Greiforgane)* but no hand (*Hand*)[39] and, as such, lacks the capacity for thought, language, and the bestowing of gifts. The superordinate character of the human is established by excluding animality from the essence of man.[40] Heidegger refrains from commenting on the significance of this exclusion: animal existence characterized by sentience, brute need, and repletion; feelings of hunger, thirst, and pain; and an impulse to procreate— whatever the animal's construal of these may be. Derrida observes that Heidegger does not think through the meaning of the hand in connection with need because need lies outside the hand's functions of giving and welcoming.

The striking entailment of this position is that the hand, bound up with the welcome for the Other and gift-giving, is divorced from need and destitution. Thus the gift is not, for Heidegger, grounded in lack, need, or desire but is the result of an overflow of the self's good feelings about itself. Gift-giving is bound up with the hand that works, and that, Heidegger declares, clears a path to genuine thinking. It is counterintuitive to divorce the hand from gift-giving, but Heidegger's analysis neglects what is primordial in gift-giving. The saintly gift is a response of the saint's total being to the sheer animal destitution, the vulnerability, of the Other. The hand of the saint that gives, welcomes, blesses, heals, and redeems is, by synecdoche, a condensation of the total charismatic power of the saintly body.

Not only does Heidegger exclude the animality of the ape from functions derived from the hand, Derrida claims, but Heidegger also sets men apart from another kind of animal, migratory birds: "Once we are drawn into the withdrawal (*in den Zug Enziehens*) we are—but completely otherwise than the migratory birds."[41] This exclusion returns the analysis to a point stressed earlier, Heidegger's inclusion of dwelling in the human essence. In his comments on Hölderlin's poem, "Homecoming," Heidegger interprets dwelling as a relation of physical to historical space:

"The house" is intended to mean the space which for men houses that wherein alone they can be "at home" and so fulfill their destiny. This space is given by the immaculate earth. The earth houses the people in its historical space. The earth serenifies "the house."[42]

Animals do not dwell; to the contrary, their taking shelter is a response to some need. Having no history apart from species continuity, they develop simple, unmediated relations to their environment. Without stretching the term too much, they can be said to labor rather than to work.

I stress Heidegger's account of dwelling because rootedness has generally been taken for granted as that which is distinctively human whereas nomadic existence is considered aberrant in Western philosophical and literary tradition. The Modernist voice in art and literature has tracked the upheavals in contemporary existence that have destroyed the sense of being at home in the world, but modernism interprets exilic existence as alienated, as a dislocated form of life. But the desirability of dwelling, the often unstated backdrop of a long tradition of moral and social philosophy, is foreign to both the postmodern and the saintly points if view. On the contrary, it is the absence of dwelling that becomes a central feature of many hagiographic accounts. To accept corporeal vulnerability by divesting oneself of home and history so far as possible is to transcend the essence of man through its underside, by taking on sheer animal sentience. The forest wanderers in Hindu and Buddhist traditions, the desert nomads of Christianity, and the exilic motif in the tales of Jewish sages attest the wide dispersion of the nomadic theme in accounts of saintly existence.

Work, Violence, and Saintly Labor

Is violent action a form of world shaping, of making the world anew by unmaking it? Is violence an activity to be understood along the same conceptual lines as work? In transforming something by means of work, force is applied in conformity with physical laws in order to bring something that did not exist into being.[43] Work is finding the "point of application" that will result in the creation of an entity that will conform to the worker's intentions such that a novel material or conceptual complex is brought into being, a feature of work that can be designated as its technicity. This general description of work holds not only for the craftsman's shaping of simple objects of use but also for the organization of industrial processes that may eventuate in complex entities, aircraft or industrial plants for the further production of objects or systems for generating information, for example.[44] In each case, the way in which force is applied is determined by instrumental intentions: the measurement of the resistance of what is to be altered is weighed off against the force needed to overcome it.

The same calculus of forces and counterforces found in work characterizes both individual violence and war. Work eventuates in some entity that is perceived as useful or desirable whereas war is aimed at the destruction of persons and industrial and habitable complexes. Small-scale confrontations and violence on a grand scale—genocide; nuclear, biological, and chemical warfare; and conventional war—also differ from work in that the results of violence are less manageable than those of relatively stable projects of production. Enforced instrumentalization or technicity is intrinsic to both work and violence. In the case of violence the intentions of agents are directed not against the refractoriness of a material complex but against the will of the other experienced as counterforce. The actions of another are less predictable than the conceptual or tangible entities to be transformed in work. To be sure, the material constraints that limit an adversary are open to calculation just as they are in complex acts of making, but discerning the pattern in a nexus of human actions is not a dependable guide to the prediction of future behavior. Descriptions of individual or national psychology have been notoriously untrustworthy in assessing an adversary's strength.

Violent action is the application of force not to some ontic constellation but to human beings. Nevertheless it cannot aim at the other's alterity because the Other is encountered as a quantum of power homogeneous with one's own power. While it simulates immediacy, violence fails to touch the recipient of action in her/his singularity because, when force is applied, the agent has not grasped that the recipient is not *exclusively* a counterforce.[45] The failure to grasp the character of the one at whom force is aimed constitutes a category mistake in which the singularity of the Other is understood reductively as a will to power. That the structure of work and the structure of violence are related is reflected in such colloquialisms as "She worked on him until he agreed," suggesting that work connotes the coercive use of language in order to persuade, and "Thugs worked him over," referring to work as the use of physical force against another.

Labor, as opposed to both work and violence, entails the corporeal involvement of the laborer but minimizes the input of forces extraneous to the laborer, for example, the input of machinery. This is reflected in such sentences as "Word processing is less labor intensive than writing" and "Machine labor is cheaper than handwork." When the achievement of an end in the sphere of economy or production is at stake, it is generally preferable to minimize human input. Thus *work* as I have described it obeys the law of parsimony. By contrast, maximizing the use of the agent's corporeality is integral to *labor*.[46] In the case of saintly labor, the totality of the psychological and corporeal resources of the subject are dedicated to the alleviation of suffering expressed (as suggested in the preceding section) in the hand that responds to destitution rather than the hand that is the prototype of cognitive and intellectual functions. Saintly activity reverses the principle of parsimony that governs work and remains labor intensive. Paradoxically the saint's labors may appear effortless because the saint often sees labor as rooted in a source greater than herself/himself. The deontological character of saintly action—what is good about it irrespective of its outcomes—is directly proportional to its labor intensiveness: saintly labor gives altruism its moral character.

This by no means implies that altruistic labor is doomed to inefficiency. Labor in the form of dedication to the Other is what *authorizes* the everyday work needed for altruistic accomplishment, the alleviation of pain and suffering. This dedication is not to be confused with something psychological, empathy, for example, in that empathy enters another's psyche as another myself. The effort to identify with another cannot authorize and may as psychological praxis even obstruct saintly work. Consider the comment framed in the psychological language of William Hart MacNichols, who devotes his life to working with AIDS patients: "'In the beginning I cried with them. Now I have a better sense of separation . . . I was over-identifying. . . . I can't become callous, but I can't fall apart. It's a fine line.'"[47]

In sum, saintly action is orchestrated as *labor*, the total corporeal and psychological involvement in the needs and interests of others. Saintly *work*, the achievement of ends in conformity with a plan, should be seen against this backdrop. Saintly labor is not a ghost in the machine that inhabits everyday works of generosity but *is* simply the psychological, social, and corporeal investment of the self's total resources when they are committed to altruistic existence.

SAINTLY LIFE is characterized by a distinctive mode of temporalization. To see this, various forms of temporality connected with the relation to one's own death, work, and cognition have been considered and found to suppress alterity. Existential philosophies have interpreted time as bound up with my death, but what is omitted from existential accounts is the experience of the "time left" or still outstanding between the present and the moment of death. Although this time is indeterminate, it is quantifiable and, as such, renders my death and the other's commensurable. The idea of the "time that is left" stakes a claim on time in that each person sees this time as owned by herself/himself and expresses this claim as the demand to persevere in existence. The desire under usual circumstances to continue one's life is the foundation of conflicting self-interest claims.

The question of whether morality can be founded by adjudicating such self-interest claims is examined in the context of two powerful moral theories, the revisionist utilitarianism of Rawls and Gewirth's rationalist ethics, his account of the Principle of Generic Consistency from which all other moral principles are deduced. Rawls's theory founders when it takes as its starting point a self that is an asocial monad and makes this self the founding condition for justice. Gewirth's deductive ethics based on the conditions of agency is unpersuasive because agency simpliciter is a condition of life, not a moral state. Gewirth examines how the goods of agency are to be distributed but not what provides the warranty for agency itself.

Because agency cannot be denied to a moral subject, the status of agency *tout court* comes to the fore. Are moral actions a kind of work and, if so, what kind? Work is distinguished from labor in terms of the corporeal and symbolic involvement of the agent. The pain and suffering of the latter is contrasted with the self-interested outcomes of the former. Saintly effort at alleviating suffering is described as necessarily labor intensive.

The foundations of work in modern philosophy are traced to the Cartesian conception of the subject. It is shown that for Descartes the subject interprets the constitution of the self as itself a work, first because the cogito is engaged in the act of positing itself, second because the cogito rewills or remakes itself at every instant, and finally because divine work is seen to sustain the self's existence.

Derrida shows that Heidegger too regards thinking as a work but that animality is excluded from this work. Instead, Heidegger links work to the human hand and to dwelling. The Derridean analysis highlights thought and action as the essence of the human in Heidegger and contrasts them with animality. This distinction opens the way for stressing the nonconceptual character of the animal's relation to its world and for linking animal existence to the unsheltered and destitute character of the saintly life depicted in many hagiographic accounts. I interpret animality as bound up with the alleviation of need and as related to labor whereas I see work, although distinguishable from violence, as showing structural affinities with it.

4

And I (the stutterer) travel around and collect all true deeds of
kindness and bring them to the True Man of Kindness. . . .
And from this, time becomes.

Now there is a mountain. On the mountain stands a rock.
From the rock flows a spring. And everything has a heart. The
world taken as a whole has a heart. . . .

[But] the spring has no time. It does not exist in time. . . .
The only time the spring has is the one day which the heart
grants it as a gift. The moment that day is finished, the spring
too will be without time and it will disappear. And without
the spring, the heart too will perish. . . . Thus close to the end
of the day, they start to take leave one from the other with
much love and longing. . . . As the day is about to . . . end before it finishes . . . the True Man of Kindness comes and gives
a gift of a day to the heart. And the heart gives the day to the
spring. And again the spring has time.

Nahman of Bratslav

I say to myself the earth is extinguished, though I never saw
it lit.

Samuel Beckett, *Endgame*

Giotto, Saint Francis Preaching to the Birds. Alinari/Art Resource, New York.

Diachrony and the Neuter

THE EVERYDAY lives of saints are enmeshed in the language and work of ordinary existence, sharing in what Heraclitus called the common cosmos. The time scheme of work was seen to interrupt the temporal flow in that the instant or moment breaks the ongoing rush of temporality. As a distended stretch of time, the instant becomes a means for the initiation of effort before falling back into the stream of time.

But saintly life belongs not only to the stream of everyday affective, cognitive, and active experience. Saints occupy multiple frames of temporal articulation: quotidian time; the time that is determined wholly by the Other; and the time of passage that flows between the time of the Other and everyday time. The last is especially important in that it is the mark, trace, or track of time within language that brings alterity into relation with the everyday world. Saintly corporeality and language as depicted in hagiographic narrative are a conduit between the Other and ordinary existence. This chapter will consider ways in which diachronic time, the time of becoming, reveals itself in saintly life: in physiological processes, in time's capacity for reversibility, and in the unique form of the hypostatization of time, as a gift.

With the help of the thought of Levinas and Blanchot, the notion of the neuter, a term I shall apply to passivity, to nonwork, and to an ungenderedness that dismantles egoity will be examined. Not only is the neuter to be "described" by way of the allusive strategies of Blanchot's postmodern fiction, but it can be shown as strikingly in evidence in a much older hagiographic literature. If saintly life is life lived on behalf of the destitute, then the powerlessness of destitution must be integral to the structure of saintly time and labor. The dissemination or scattering of egoity in the neuter *is* this powerlessness, one that is expressed through affective registers that tax the limits of language.

Neoplatonism and Time

Because Neoplatonic conceptions of time carry forward Plato's static view of eternity, especially as it is described in the *Timaeus*, these conceptions would seem far removed from the dynamic time design of the saintly lives depicted in hagiographic narrative. Still less does Plato's view of the unbroken fullness of eternity appear as an apt metaphor for the need and destitution of the Other. What remains unthought in Plato is brought out in the work of the Neoplatonists, a restlessness within eternity and a fissuring of its static character. In chapter 7, I shall consider in detail some postmodern articulations of the Neoplatonic scheme. In the present context I shall discuss only the relation of this tumult within eternity itself to saintly life.

Plotinus recognizes that the coming to be of time is related to the question of being, that it is an intraontological drama. "Before" there is time, being cannot be nonbeing or other than being but must be always the same or "undivided totality," being without difference.[1] But what would it mean for being *not* to be always the same, always without difference? And if (counterfactually) being were not the same, how could difference enter being? Not as something spatial because primordial being does not admit of extension: to be otherwise than being could only mean to "be" as something nonextended, to be as time. Unlike Plotinus, Plato takes as his ontological starting point not the fullness of being but the being of the multiple forms that provide the dynamic principle not only for conceptual entities but also for the bodying forth of extended things. It is only with Neoplatonism that pure difference as "pure" time is born.

But how can time infiltrate a plenum without fissure? Since there is as yet no before and after in being, how could being have fallen into time? Plotinus depicts an internal restlessness in being. But this restlessness could not have any specific point of origin in a plenum. Being must always already have been riddled by time, shot through with time's roiling motion. In a powerful allegorizing of this ontological primal scene, Plotinus writes:

Time itself can best tell us how it rose and became manifest; something thus its story would run:

Time at first—in reality before that "first" was produced by desire of succession—Time, all self-concentrated, at rest within the Authentic Existent: it was not yet Time; it was merged in the Authentic and motionless with it. But there was an active principle there, one set on governing itself and realizing itself, and it chose to aim at something more than its present: it stirred from its rest and Time stirred within it. And we, we stirring to a ceaseless succession, to a next, to the discrimination of identity and the establishment of ever new difference, traversed a portion of the outgoing path and produced an image of Eternity, produced Time. (*En* III.7.11)

This restless nature is a principle of activity, or soul, that, in its unquietness, generates time. But how is soul to be conceived, and how did it come to inhabit the plenum? Plotinus calls it "an unquiet faculty, always desirous of translating elsewhere what it saw in the authentic realm [that] could not bear to retain within itself all the dense fullness of its possession" (*En* III.7.11). How can this desire of soul be envisioned if there is as yet nothing extended within the plenum, nothing that can reveal itself as difference other than time, if there is only the plenum and difference or time? Although Plotinus does not articulate this thought, soul can only be time withholding itself, hypostatized, prior to its expenditure in the activity of self-unfolding. Using a startling postmodern metaphor, that of dissemination, to describe the process of time's unfolding, Plotinus writes: "A Seed is at rest; the nature-principle within, uncoiling outwards, makes way towards what seems to it a large life; but by that partition it loses; it was a unity self-gathered, and now, in going forth from itself it fritters its unity away; it advances into a weaker greatness" (*En* III.7.11).

In a move which will receive its full modern expression in Kant, Plotinus insists that time must not be conceived as something alongside of but extrinsic to the soul as accompanying it, but rather as something existing in it and with it, "a thing seen upon soul, inherent, coeval to it" (*En* III.7.11). Time is not a cosmological phenomenon, something that is produced by the sun's circuit (*En* III.7.12). Instead, cosmological processes are used as the measure of a time that arises as the soul's prior self-temporalization.

The intimacy of being and time is declared, but time's ramifications for the temporal character of human existence remain unthought within the framework of Plotinian philosophy. Hampered by the Greek doctrine of soul as a principle of activity or causal agent, soul is made to do double duty: as causal agency, in conformity with the Greek understanding of soul as a principle of life, it is responsible for the existence of the world of sense, but as pure self-temporalization it is the rift or fissure in the plenum of being and equiprimordial with the plenum itself. When the former interpretation is uppermost, Plotinus thinks of soul as having made time and then, having enslaved itself to its own monstrous creation, the soul "put[s] forth its energy in act after act, in a constant progress of novelty, . . . producing succession as well as act" (*En* III.7.11).

It is Plotinian time as rift or fissure that brings to light *in nuce* recent conceptions of erring and dissemination that are integral to saintly self-temporalization. A system of metonymic substitution strikingly similar to that of Plotinus begins to emerge when Heidegger's description of errancy is compared with the nomadic character of Plotinian time. Consider first Heidegger's account of errance:

> Being sets beings adrift in errance [*Irre*]. Beings come to pass in that errancy by which they circumvent Being and establish the realm of error [*Irrtum*]. . . . Error is the space in which history unfolds. In error what happens in history bypasses what is like Being. Therefore whatever unfolds historically is necessarily misinterpreted.[2]

Plotinus's restlessly active nature, always moving on to the "next" and the "after," sends time forth in errancy to escape the sameness of eternity. For Plotinus, not history but the realm of sense is the space of time's passage. It is here that error or misinterpretation in the usual sense necessarily comes to pass.

"During this misinterpretation," or history, Heidegger writes, "destiny awaits what will become of its seed." Heidegger's image of the seed's sprouting for the destining of being is identical to Plotinus's unquiet power that, in its work of diffraction and rejection of wholeness as that which is present all at once, "unfolds" as from "a quiet seed." From the metaphor of being's "mittance" (being sent forth) as a setting adrift like a vessel, Heidegger turns to the Plotinian trope of a seed and its coming to fruition, its fate determined, integral to it from the start. "Without errancy," Heidegger goes on to say, "there would be no connection from destiny to destiny; there would be no history"[3] just as for Plotinus there would be no cosmos if the seed did not "advance to largeness" through difference and diffusion. Both metaphors, setting adrift and seeding, presuppose a breaking up in order to send forth as well as the uncharted character of becoming.

In "Dissemination," an essay on Mallarmé, Derrida follows a similarly Plotinian pattern.[4] In commenting on Mallarmé's *Numbers* he claims that it is impossible to ascertain the point of origin of *Numbers* because the first and last sentences of the text as well as its epigraphs have been wrenched from other texts, thus forming relationships and continuities with prior writings. Thus Mallarmé's text is, paradoxically, older than itself. Plotinian temporality generates comparable paradoxes.

It too must preexist itself (as I suggested earlier); it too must be "straightaway plural, divided and multiplied." This is the result of its "power of germination or seminal differentiation."[5]

Equally strategic is Plotinus's transformation of time into a personage in a drama who reconstitutes events after the fact. This rhetorical strategy is only secondarily enlisted to heighten the reader's interest. It is used primarily because of a metaphysical necessity: to break with the unity of the One. As Derrida claims, "The exit out of the primitive mythical unity . . . is always reconstituted retrospectively in the aftermath of the break [*dans l'après-coupure*], the scission, the decision— which is both deciding and decided." It is this break that "parts the seed as it projects it."[6]

The idea of time that Plotinus begins to explore is not everyday temporalization in which work is attributable to a unified self homogeneous with other selves and belongs to a time frame common to others. It is only through attentiveness to traces within the everyday that another "infrastructure" is brought to the fore, one of temporal fissuring that cannot dominate work in its everyday expressions because the end or goal of work would be so broken up as to defy both actualization and comprehension. Temporal diffraction, the mode in which primordial saintly time is lived, is altogether different and must be tracked down both in its corporeal and linguistic unfolding.

To see better how to imagine the time of saintly existence, it is useful to consider the further development of Plotinian thought in later Neoplatonism. In the *Timaeus*, Plato developed the classical position that time is a moving image of eternity. Plotinus later showed that time must already (somehow) be integral to eternity and in so doing opened up the possibility for the thinking of time as a mittance or erring, although Plotinus did not see this notion through to the end. The danger inherent in the idea of a truly mobile disseminated time was held in check by later Neoplatonism in its substantializing and doubling of time. First, the eternal was cordoned off as something absolutely static, and then Iamblichus posited an additional mode of time that is intermediate between the ceaseless flow of time in the sensible world and pure, undifferentiated, motionless eternity. The latter is the time scheme perceived in the regularities of the cosmos that establish the principle of order in time. Thus there is first, eternity; second, true time, the principle of order, an earlier and later belonging to the intellectual sphere; and, finally, sensible time, the unreal time of physical becoming. Sensible time in its passage is in contact with the now of the intellectual order.

Paradoxically, the unwieldy doubling of time, the effort to hold dissemination in check, opens a space for a consideration of temporality that is de facto, if not de jure, released from the constraints of eternity. Thus Proclus can say of time that it is both at rest and in motion. The hypostatization and doubling of time raises unprecedented questions which will fall into semioblivion when Neoplatonism is (for good reason) largely abandoned by the mainstream of Western thought. But just as what seemed least promising in Descartes' view of the cogito opened a new way for understanding work (as I argued earlier), so too an interrogation of late Neoplatonism breaks a path for the understanding of saintly time.

Damascius, perhaps the most interesting of these thinkers for present purposes, interrogates the notion of primary time, the tertium quid between eternity and sensible time. On the face of it, the multiplication of levels of being would seem to vitiate the gains of Plotinus's analysis. But by questioning the nature of primary time, unsuspected aspects of temporality come to the fore. What, Damascius wonders, can primary time be, "if not time's whole presence at once." He notices that "at different moments the present is different, although time per se is one and continuous."[7] This idea is developed through an elaboration of Heraclitus's metaphor of time as a river into which one never steps twice. For Damascius, intellectual or primary time is like a river from source to mouth with its flow halted. Elaborating this analogy brings to light the real agenda for positing intellectual or primary time.

A river can be seen in two ways, Damascius argues: in the diachronicity of its flow, "its being in the process of becoming," or as a whole in a state of rest. But if an actual river, the river as it is here, is seen as motionless, he concludes "*there will be no river any more* [emphasis mine]."[8] Like the river, the past, present, and future are held together in "one form of time . . . unrolled in becoming."[9] The whole of time is continuously moving, but "taking away the present as being actually limited by the Nows from both sides" would force a halt to time, "which has its being in becoming."[10] For Damascius the great aporia of time arises as the soul tries to know time as a form in the Platonic sense rather than in accordance with the way in which it unfolds.

Time, for Damascius, can never (in contemporary language) become reflexive about its own diachronicity; it is a bleeding, as it were, that can never be stanched. Such radical diachronicity means that time as it unfolds is always new. What is retrieved in memory could, because of the lapse in time, never be a recurrence of some original. Of course Neoplatonic thought cannot dispense with memory. The strategy of positing primary or intellectual time that opened the space for thinking the dark thought of time's radical diachronicity also enables the Neoplatonists to evade the implications of diachronicity. Time's form does not exist at the level of actual becoming but as primary time. But if time is thought of both as diachronic and as reversible in a way other than through memory or recollection, new strategies must be devised. Saintly lives will be seen to experience this dark diachronicity first through the temporal structure of vulnerability to the Other that can never be synchronized with common time and second by reversing the order of time through such structures as apology and pardon.

Damascius's thinking presages postmodern thought in still another regard. Recall that the time scheme of work analyzed in chapter 3 was seen as bringing together two properties of everyday time: time's flux on the one hand and the swinging free of the individual moment from time's continuity on the other. The moment, released from the stream of time, has duration. Damascius makes notable progress in understanding this duration by analyzing one of Zeno's paradoxes. Zeno had argued that the now is indivisible and that, in order to cross it, one would have to subdivide it indefinitely. Because each new now is similarly indivisible, one could never hope to move across *any* now. Damascius contends that, since motion occurs, "the movement is not completed in indivisible units" but progresses by whole steps at once. "Movement leaps over both the whole and its part." What the followers of Zeno do not see, Damascius argues, is that the "indivisible" now "is also in time" and that time "coexists with movement, . . . and advances together with it . . . by means of whole continuous leaps."[11] Each finite indivisible unit is a quantum of time. The time of everyday work described earlier can be construed in terms of Damascius's analysis of time's movement, as cumulative progress, of the movement of time that takes place section by section.

Saints and the Renunciation of Power

How are we to think of time's dark diachronicity? In chapter 3 work was seen as lived in accordance with present time. It is now possible to pick up the thread of that analysis in order to explore the time of saintly labor as distinguished from that of work. Earlier I discussed work phenomenologically in its own right, without exploring in detail how it is bound up with saintly labor. Consider first how work is linked to the logic of presence by way of the future. In work the projected goal of some specific task is kept in view as an orienting point of present activity. Still, the completion of the task is brought about in the future:

what comes into being has future utility and an economic value that hinge on a completion that is yet to come. Work is always already ahead of itself, an investment of effort with the hope of future return, in the form either of a commodity or of money or of aesthetic value. Work swings back and forth between present effort and an envisioned future product. Present time is, in the context of work, "raw material" invested in the hope of bringing forth some value such as utility when the work is completed. In the context of many types of contemporary work— that of the consultant, for example—expertise is interpreted as the expenditure of time.

When the fruits of work are inequitably distributed, the producer can be thought of as alienated from the product. The extreme case is that of slavery in which only subsistence is offered to the one who works and sometimes, as in the case of slave labor camps, not even subsistence in that slave labor is seen as easily replaceable. Although they are differently orchestrated in the writings of classical and Marxist economists, the notional constructs of the analysis of economy such as need, utility, capital, labor, production, consumption, and exchange remain relatively constant.

Saintly activity insofar as it is an expenditure of effort may bring about alterations in the relations of these factors by eliminating the exploitative and alienating aspects of work. What is more, saints may ally themselves with a variety of social forces to bring about such changes. But the distinctive mark of saintly work as described in hagiography is its self-renouncing character. Although powerful persons of royal birth have been canonized in Western Christianity, saintly work across a broad range of religious traditions typically abandons self-empowerment and wealth. Voluntary poverty is a commonly reported feature of saintly life in widely divergent traditions of hagiographic narrative. A radical Buddhist text, the *Visuddhi Magga*, makes this point:

> Misery only doth exist, none miserable,
> No doer is there; naught save the deed is found.
> Nirvana is, but not the man who seeks it.
> The path exists, but not the traveler on it.[12]

Self-renunciation to the point of effacement is the mark or trace of saintly labor.

Is there a basis for breaking up the egoity of everyday existence that provides an enabling "infrastructure" for saintly labor and its dark diachronicity? Is this nonfoundational trait or property common to all and, if so, why are all not saints?

In uncovering the mode of temporalization of saintly existence, the time scheme of non-egoity, it is useful to consider from a fresh point of view the problem of corporeality discussed in chapters 1 and 2. It is by now a commonplace in the history of Western thought that an overturning and transvaluation of the Platonic conception of sense experience came to fruition in the philosophy of modern empiricism in the work of Locke, Berkeley, Hume, Condillac, and others. This tendency converges with a rehabilitation of the body in recent twentieth-century phenomenological thought. These recent analyses of corporeality make it possible to interpret time's dark diachronicity, the terror before time's irrecoverability, that, I argued in chapter 3, prevented Neoplatonism from developing its insights about the nature of time.

Work can be regarded as stanching the hemorrhaging of time by providing relatively permanent structures that can be called up at will. But a careful analysis of the relation between sensation and corporeality, made possible first by modernist phenomenological thinking and later by postmodern thought, may open up an indirect seeing (since direct confrontation converts the infrastructure of diachronicity into a present phenomenon) of what makes saintly labor possible and of the time scheme of the Other.

Consider first Levinas's analysis of the structure of sense impressions. Sensibility or sensation, he asserts, has a twofold aspect. First, the sense impression is connected to meaning, an aspect of sensation recoverable by phenomenological means. Second, sensation is also the capacity for being affected. This ambiguity of sensation is lodged within the sense impression itself as a difference between the feeling and the felt, between the temporal flow of sensation, on the one hand, and the stopping of the flow through the use of words, the conferring of meaning on the lived element, on the other. "The sensorial qualities are not only the sensed; as affective states they are the sensing" (*OBBE*, pp. 31–32). The sensing or being affected is an irreducible noncognitive dimension of sensation, is itself the blue of the water or the loudness of the crash; sensing and being affected are not what they are designated as being by language.

Between the lived and the meaning-laden sensation, there is an "open chasm of meaning." The pure flow of experience, of being affected, is at the level of the primordial impression subject to the bestowal of a meaning by consciousness across the split or scissiparity within the impression itself. This differing within the impression is expressed as time, the time in which the intention awaits its fulfillment or has already been fulfilled. Levinas thinks of this difference within the

identity of the sense impression as a plugging and unplugging. "Differing within identity, modifying itself without changing," the impression
always catches up with itself. There is temporal difference, but it is
"time in which nothing is lost" (*OBBE*, p. 32). Because the sense impression involves the *recovery* of time, it is still temporalized through
the time scheme of presence.

But what of the purely affective dimension of sensing? Can this aspect of sensation be considered independently of sensation's relation to
cognition? The affective side of sensation can also be experienced as
pure vulnerability: what is other than the self can affect the self through
pain or wounding. In this context, being affected means exposure to
what is other without the other's coming to fruition in a linguistic
meaning or fully realized sense content so that the other cannot be
phenomenologically recovered. Such exposure, made possible by the
body as a sensorium, is the very capacity of corporeality to become
open or vulnerable to the Other. This dimension of corporeal existence
is common to all, but saints, by posing no obstacle to experiencing this
vulnerability, permit it to acquire primacy in their lives so that it imperceptibly orchestrates saintly life and hagiographic narrative. The saint is
without defenses, unsheltered, exposed to insult and outrage.

This analysis of vulnerability as the beyond of sensation, as what is
irreducible to sensation's cognitive role, stresses passivity and receptive-
ness. The saint is the one who is totally at the disposal of the Other,
and lives this exposure as response to the Other by stripping the self of
its egoity or formal unity. Once self-interest is renounced, the one who
is thus divested of egoity becomes dis-interested (*OBBE*, p. 49). The
Buddhist expresses this denucleation of self in such phrases as, "There
is no self (*anatman*)." Nagasena, a Buddhist sage, declares, "[The
word] Nagasena is but a way of counting, term, appellation, convenient
designation, mere name for the hair of my head, hair of my body . . .
brain of the head. . . . But in the absolute sense there is no ego here to
be found." [13]

Such denuding of the self's form, such stripping it of empowerment,
would appear to leave the self open to the violence and aggression of
others. But the Other to whom the self is vulnerable is the Other of
lack and destitution. This by no means precludes that defenselessness
will not be met by aggression. To the contrary: violence is a frequent
response to vulnerability and constitutes the risk of saintly life. The
saint does not court the violence of the Other in order to be exposed
to it but responds rather to the Other's destitution. Thus saints are
not masochistic in the usual sense of the term, seeking pain in order

to derive satisfaction in suffering. The two types of vulnerability—masochistic and saintly—may resemble one another and, in historical periods when the body is denigrated, may actually come to be conflated. But it is the need and lack of the Other, not pleasure in the experience of pain, that constitutes an appeal to the saint and authorizes or provides the warranty for saintly activity in the everyday world.

The mode of temporalization integral to saintly life based on the body's vulnerability differs from that of the sense impression tied to consciousness and language. The pure experience of being affected, of vulnerability, is not subject to closure as is the sensation when taken as a sense datum in which sensing merely fills out an intention of consciousness or is incorporated into language. Vulnerability as the body's radical capacity for affect separates the self from itself. Levinas describes this condition: "This being torn up from oneself in the core of one's unity, this absolute noncoinciding, this diachrony of the instant, signifies in the form of the one-penetrated-by-the-other. . . . This existence, with sacrifice imposed on it, is without conditions" (*OBBE*, pp. 49–50).

The vulnerability of the subject opens up the contrast between the self-empowerment described earlier as characterizing work and the renunciation of power that attaches to the exposure to the Other. This renunciation of power expresses itself as patience, a condition in which time passes without recovery. The "lapse" of time, its irreversible moving on, is also inscribed in the self's corporeal existence as aging (*OBBE*, p. 55). When it is bound up with the Other, time imprints itself as the pain and suffering the enucleated self accepts in the interest of the Other. Time that impresses itself in this way does not come to fruition in pain so that pain is a culmination of the work of time, but rather time throbs without ceasing. Saintly labor is this "throbbing" passivity before the Other and is temporalized as patience. The irrecoverable time of aging and of waiting are what I call time's dark diachronicity.

Nietzsche's Objections

Perhaps the most powerful critique in Western thought that has been leveled against altruism is Nietzsche's account of it as a hypocritical masking of weakness. Nietzsche develops a trenchant analysis of time and *ressentiment* that bears directly on my interpretation of dark diachronicity. Both of Nietzsche's challenges require a response if altruism is to retain its cogency in the context of postmodern thought. It is not my purpose to examine the ultimate role of Nietzsche's arguments in their embedding contexts, however interesting these matters may be, or to decide such questions as whether Nietzsche thinks asceticism and the ethics of pity are separable, whether asceticism is in the end integral to mastery or, to the contrary, demands overcoming.[14] Instead, I shall lift the arguments from their place in Nietzsche's text because the arguments themselves have been recontextualized and constitute part of a new modern idiom in which altruism is viewed with suspicion by a broad range of thinkers.

Altruism has historically been rooted in affect, in compassion or pity for another. Pity is, according to Aristotle, "occasioned by undeserved misfortune."[15] On this view, if I pity the other I must see the other as blameless so that the other's suffering cannot be attributed to a self-generated error or moral failing. Nietzsche, however, argues that pity is a far less straightforward feeling than this description allows. In *The Genealogy of Morals* Nietzsche claims: "We need a critique of all moral values; the intrinsic worth of these values must first of all, be called in question. To this end we need to know the conditions from which these values have sprung."[16] On his view, pity is the emotion that is felt when a desire for revenge is suppressed. If someone injures me, I may strike back directly or I may delay my response. When I strike back, I spontaneously discharge my vengeful feeling so that it no longer acts upon my psychological life, but when weakness or fear prevents this direct discharge of affect, my frustrated rage turns into *ressentiment*. Pity is the fruit of this emotion (*Gen* I, 14). So long as I cannot avenge myself against the stronger, I have an interest in supporting the weaker. To maintain the object of pity and to justify this support, I turn pity into a value. "Impotence which cannot retaliate," Nietzsche declares, "is turned into kindness; pusillanimity into humility" (*Gen* I, 14).

One reason for the inability to express hostile instincts directly, Nietzsche contends, is that they are no longer healthy. This instinctual degeneration is bound up with the excessive development of consciousness and the hypertrophy of reason. This position is reinforced by a history of philosophy in which truth is identified with the beliefs of a "pure, will-less, painless, timeless knower," the view from nowhere, "an eye such as no living being can imagine, an eye required to have no direction, to abrogate its active and interpretive powers" (*Gen* III, 12). An all-embracing rationality comes to constitute a constraint that tyrannizes over instinctual life. Reinforcing these internal restrictions are the laws society imposes upon the individual that further inhibit instinctual expression. As a result of both inner and institutional repression, a new human type is created, the man of *ressentiment*.[17]

But how can a sick and reactive will triumph over the noble and self-affirming instincts? The invention of conscience by the weak drives the strong to self-doubt, so much so that the strong must be protected against the weak. The master is self-legislating whereas, by contrast, the rancorous man declares what is other or self-affirming to be evil. By making the good coincide with what is good for him, the master expresses a healthy will to power, but in the course of time the expression of *ressentiment* itself becomes an alternative will. Only after aristocratic values begin to decline does it become possible for the difference between egoism and altruism to assert itself.

Two counterarguments, one based on the balance of wills to power, the other, Max Scheler's well-known account of *ressentiment* grounded in Nietzsche's alleged misunderstanding of Christian morality, have been leveled against Nietzsche's view.[18] Both, I believe, fail in that they do not go deep enough. Because they leave unexamined some tacit presuppositions in Nietzsche's description of the body, they cannot come to grips with his understanding of sickness and health, one of the linchpins of his analysis.

Consider first the counterargument based on Nietzsche's conception of wills to power. Ultimately everything that exists, he contends, is nothing but some conformation of the will to power. As Michel Haar explains, "the locution applies to every possible kind of force," not only to psychological phenomena but to "all the phenomena of the world."[19] The term thus refers to ontological and cosmic as well as psychological forces. The internal directive of the will to power is to will its own augmentation. If it fails to increase its power, it is destined to sicken and decline. What is more, the process of willing never comes to an end. Could it not be argued against Nietzsche that, if willing is ceaseless and if rancor too is the expression of a decadent will as Nietzsche proclaims, the triumph of *ressentiment* is itself the deserved—deserved because more forceful—result of a stronger will? Is not decadent will simply another and stronger conformation of the will to power, one strong enough to triumph over instinctual forces?

In his analysis of the reactive forces, Gilles Deleuze indirectly provides a response to this criticism.[20] The argument based on the comparison of forces would be conclusive only if the reactive ones combined to become dominant and, together with strength derived from the overthrown active forces, constituted a greater active force.

But nothing like this occurs. Instead, reactive power is parasitic on active forces and this in a double sense. First, the reactive exist alongside the active forces as the principle of their negation. Second, a reactive force will "decompose [and] separate the active force from what it can do."[21] Thus reactive force is, first, subtractive and divisive and, second, by crippling the active forces, able to annex and transform them into reactive forces. The strength of Deleuze's argument lies in its interpretation of reactive forces as subtractive rather than additive and presupposes that what is subtractive can be discounted as a genuine will to power.

The second argument against Nietzsche's view is grounded in a reinterpretation of Christian pity and compassion so that these affects are exempted from Nietzsche's criticisms of them in his description of *ressentiment*. Nietzsche's view acquired considerable prestige from the early part of the twentieth century to the present—in no small measure because of its importation in altered form into psychoanalytic theory, which claimed to offer empirical support for the phenomenon of repression on which *ressentiment* is based. Against the Nietzschean and psychoanalytic interpretations, a religious and philosophical tradition remained in place which suggests that pity and compassion are valuable in themselves and that they are the source of many of our moral acts. In response to this conflict, Max Scheler and others have argued that there is a difference between the spurious emotion which actually springs from *ressentiment* and genuine pity. We tend to confuse them only because we observe no difference in the actions they motivate. The difference between them is actually in their psychological origin. Genuine pity derives from a position of strength and superior power whereas the other emotion, its nameless double, springs from repressed rage.[22]

My objection to Scheler's position is grounded in a weakness in his account of the relation between motives and behavior. Although it may be true that an identical act x, for example, helping the homeless, might spring from different motives—let us say love of one's neighbor or the desire to appear benevolent—it is unlikely that different motives would produce an identical *chain of acts*. The difference of motives could be expected to derive from a difference in disposition which would not show itself in one act but would manifest itself in numerous acts. If X strikes Y, X would not be thought of as dispositionally hostile and aggressive unless this sort of behavior was characteristic of X. It is unlikely that over the *long run* the degenerate form of pity would produce a behavioral pattern similar to the one produced by a magnanimous disposition.

In sum, the two objections against Nietzsche's attack on altruism—first, that reactive forces themselves exhibit strength; second, Scheler's argument that genuine pity is distinguishable from *ressentiment*—fail to dispose of Nietzsche's attack on altruism as a response of the weak to the strong. By looking more closely at Nietzsche's notion of life, we may elicit some presuppositions bound up with Nietzsche's vitalism that will clear the way for a fresh interpretation of saintly compassion and pity. It is particularly important to develop a postmodern response to Nietzsche's trenchant observations about altruism because Nietzsche's thought is often considered a linchpin of postmodernism,[23] so much so that even Neomarxist postmodernism has been penetrated by Nietzsche's analysis. Thus Sloterdijk, for example, alleges that although Nietzsche's critique is a reaction to the suffocating bourgeois morality of the nineteenth century and is itself an instrument of imperialism, its insights remain useful. "The psychologist in Nietzsche's sense," he writes, "sees the self-pity and resentment shine through the compassion that is shown. A form of egoism shines through every act of altruism."[24]

Because Nietzsche's thinking about wills to power has become integral to the contemporary spirit of critique itself, any counterthought rooted in that spirit is parasitic upon the conceptions he develops. Such criticism need not be viciously circular, however, in that the interrogation of a significant thinker relies on categories embedded in the presuppositions of that thought. A response to Nietzsche's *ressentiment* theory must aim at concepts integral to Nietzsche's thought, in this case his view of life as one of the manifestations of the will to power.

In Nietzsche's account of *ressentiment* the passions are interpreted as an expression of the will to life defined as "an enduring form of the processes of the establishment of forces, in which the different contenders grow unequally."[25] The will to life "rejoices in its own inexhaustibility," not to get rid of dangerous affects, as Aristotle had argued, but to "be oneself the eternal joy of becoming." On this interpretation, although individuals may die, the life process continues. Not the preservation of the species but the joy of becoming is the aim of life.

If the will to life is to express itself, it cannot be something ethereal, a consciousness without a body. The joy of becoming is a corporeal joy, the will to power nothing less than the body's self-expression as force. If this is so, it can be argued against Nietzsche that he has given to the body too narrow an interpretation. His account cordons off a feature of corporeality intrinsic to it: the body's vulnerability. To be as embodied existence, as flesh, is to be vulnerable. This is not a property of diseased bodies but of bodies generally. While Nietzsche acknowledges and even celebrates death, he segregates the phenomena of vulnerability—sensitivity to temperature, fatigue, exhaustion, sleep, and the like—from death itself. These phenomena are treated metaphysically in the manner of nonbeing. Interpreting them this way makes them appear in the vitalist framework as manifestations of an etiolated or decaying life. Their role in the body's everyday corporeal existence is overlooked as if to manifest them at all is to express an excessively low threshold of sensibility.

Nietzsche interprets the living body as the body awake, as existence that never lets its guard down in order to avoid acknowledging the body's vulnerability. What does it mean for the body to exist as a body that is awake, and how does this condition contrast with sleep? Being awake is the foundation of ordinary existence, the standpoint from which the otherness of the world is grasped. Descartes' doubt begins when he can find no criterion to distinguish between dreaming, a phenomenon of sleep, and waking life. The discovery of the cogito can be interpreted as his finding a point of fixity that enables him to distinguish them and thus dispel his doubt. Wakefulness is the ground for the body's motility and sensory confrontations with the other, a condition that is suspended in sleep.

For Nietzschean vitalism, human existence is a perpetual self-overcoming, an activity that neither sleeps nor slumbers. Thus manifestations of vital somatic life, of its ascending tendency, preclude fatigue and exhaustion. But life thus interpreted is based on one of its pathological conditions, unceasing wakefulness or insomnia. Levinas writes:

[In insomnia] the ego is swept away by the fatality of being. There is no longer any outside or inside. Vigilance is quite devoid of objects. That does not come down to saying that it is an experience of nothingness, but that it is [an experience of anonymity]. The consciousness of a thinking subject, with its capacity for . . . sleep and unconsciousness, is precisely the breakup of anonymous being . . . to withdraw from being . . . to, like Penelope, have a night to oneself to undo the work [of] the day.[26]

The body presupposed by Nietzsche's thought lives in a ceaseless oscillation between a sensory inundation of forms that characterizes waking life and an anonymous wakefulness that cannot suspend itself even when it abandons the object structure of the visual field. This conception of the body refuses to acknowledge the body's slackness exhibited by phenomena such as fatigue and sleep. It is paradoxical that Nietzsche works to undermine the power of memory because, on his view, it makes possible a delay in the expression of affect. In remembering, consciousness holds on to its content and refuses to become slack. Yet Nietzsche confers normative value on the very phenomenon he criticizes with respect to memory, the phenomenon of unceasing activity when such activity is attributed to the body. A hypertrophied wakefulness is transvalued when it is ascribed to bodily life.

This objection to Nietzsche's *ressentiment* theory on the grounds of its faulty view of the body does not, however, dispose of another fundamental Nietzschean claim about the *origin* of *ressentiment*. Is there something in the character of existence itself that Nietzsche sees as bringing "the spirit of revenge" into being? If so, can the spirit of revenge be overcome? And, if Nietzsche thinks it can, how does his view affect the view of saintliness I have proposed together with the notion of time integral to it?

The origin of *ressentiment* for Nietzsche derives from the transiency of existing things. It is the rancor against time's passing, Nietzsche argues, that first devalues existence.[27] How can life be affirmed if all things pass away? Nietzsche treats the question of transiency genealogically in his historical analysis of the emergence of the spirit of revenge as a metaphysical doctrine; ontologically as a principle that generates revenge; and at an empirical level as a psychological motive.

Consider first the discovery that contingency is responsible for the birth of philosophy, especially, Nietzsche argues, as exhibited in the fragment of Anaximander. On Nietzsche's reading, Anaximander's Unlimited is posited as the matrix out of which things derive and to which they return in accordance with necessity. The primordial wound of coming-to-be is seen by Anaximander as a departure from the calm of eternity. An ethical reading is then added to the original metaphysical claim: passing away is *justified* as the price paid for existence.[28]

The ontological and psychological aspect of Nietzsche's account does not stress contingency so much as the directionality of time, time's irreversibility. Willing liberates, Zarathustra avers, but the will cannot undo what has already been done, is doomed to frustration, becomes "sullen" and "wrathful" because the irreversibility of time entails the will's inability to will backward. "This, yes, this alone," Nietzsche declares, "is *revenge* itself: the will's antipathy towards time and time's 'It was.'"[29] What is more, under the inexorable pressure of time, the will sees itself as responsible for its helplessness before time's directionality and superimposes a burden of guilt upon a prior condition of existence.

Nietzsche's resolution of the contingency dilemma is to posit the eternal recurrence of the Same. The elaboration of this theme is often seen as determinative for the way in which all of Nietzsche's writings are to be read and has generated a vast literature. Even the brief sketch that follows reflects an inordinately large commitment to basic suppositions about Nietzsche's work. The context of the problem of saintly altruism and its mode of temporalization do not exempt the interpreter from responsibility for the assumptions bound up with wider questions bearing on Nietzsche's writings. But the risks which are necessarily assumed in interpreting eternal recurrence are increased when the focus upon altruism precludes an extended justification of claims about Nietzsche.

In the analysis of revenge in the context of *Zarathustra* the spirit of rancor is overcome by bringing the creative will into play. Willing overcomes the rancor against time by bringing the will into concord with the order of time by willing that which was. "But I will it thus! Thus shall I will it," Zarathustra teaches.[30] This willing affirms one's own being, both backward and forward, for all eternity. It concentrates the whole of time, what Damascius thought of as the whole river from source to mouth, into the Moment. By bringing the will into conformation with the totality of time, the character of being is imposed on becoming. In a well-known passage in *The Gay Science*, Nietzsche writes:

[What] if . . . a demon were to sneak after you in your loneliest loneliness and say to you: "This is life, as you now live it, you will have to live once more and innumerable times more; and there will be nothing new in it, but every pain and every joy and every thought and sigh . . . must return to you—all in the same succession and sequence . . . even this moment and I myself. The eternal hourglass of existence is turned over and over—and you with it, a dust grain of dust!" . . . If this thought were to gain possession of you, it would change you as you are, or perhaps crush you. . . . Or how well-disposed would you have to become to yourself and to life to crave nothing more fervently than this ultimate eternal confirmation?[31]

Even if Nietzsche in his description of rancor has brought out to the fullest time's irreversibility, the question remains as to whether this irreversibility is to be construed as what I term dark diachronicity, lapse without recovery. Nietzsche, perhaps more than any other modern thinker, develops a phenomenology of time as physiological, cosmological, and cultural aging as well as of historical irreversibility. But superimposed on this construal of time is a notion of the power of human agency to trick time as it were while still retaining the truth of time's irreversibility and the innocence of becoming. By willing the same, the will wills for the future the ontological totality of what has been. The one who wills can know a "joyous affirmation," the Dionysian character of life "as that which is the same in all change, the same as the equally powerful, the equally blissful."[32]

Dark Diachronicity

Nietzsche's analysis of becoming and eternal recurrence is a precursor of what geologist Steven Jay Gould calls time's arrow, the irreversible sequence of unrepeatable events, and time's cycle, the fundamental states that are immanent in time as always present and never changing and in which the episodic and contingent character of time is overcome.[33] It could be objected that Gould's analysis is bound up with what he calls the discovery of deep time by geologists, time that is comparable to the vastness of Newtonian space. Nietzsche, on the other hand, belongs to a tradition that includes Bergson, Heidegger, Sartre, Jaspers, and others who see time not as the measure of motion, the punctiform and homogeneous clock time of a Newtonian universe, or even as the cyclical time inherent in the deep time of geological discovery, but as lived or experienced passage, the sense of time as long or short, heavy or light, joyous or sad. Like other proponents of lived time, Nietzsche views time to be driven by affect, but—and this is the important point—not only clock time but lived time too can be *both* directional *and* cyclical. Escaping from clock time into lived time may avoid the punctiform homogeneity and objectification of time, but it fails to overcome the deeper diremption of time, its character as directional and cyclical.

To see this, consider the way in which time's irreversibility and the recurrence of cycles affect Vladimir Jankelevitch's analysis of lived time in his account of the "pilgrimage of origins."[34] Human beings, Jankelevitch argues, have a double yearning expressed in archetypal stories of pilgrimage in which there is on the one hand the yearning for the homeland and on the other the pleasure of the journey itself. In the tale of Ulysses the pull of the homeland reflects a wish to return to the past, a longing for time's recurrence, whereas the joy of adventure fulfills a desire for ubiquity, for being everywhere at once. Because omnipresence is impossible, the voyager can visit only successively the places spread out contiguously in space. In sum, Ulysses yearns both for a substitute ubiquity to be found in the journey and for the return to his native Ithaca. The story of Ulysses' voyage is an expression of *lived* rather than *clock* time, yet it fleshes out the metaphor of arrow and cycle in one of its deepest and most primordial forms no less plainly than does geological time in Gould's account.

To say therefore that the dark diachronicity of saintly existence belongs to the modality of lived time does not yet release it from the diremptions of time expressed by arrow and cycle. Furthermore, the idea of lived time does not yet distinguish saintly time from that of ordinary work and language, for they too belong to the context of lived time. *The lived character of time is not what is peculiar to saintly time.* Recent philosophers (including even Nietzsche and Heidegger) who have developed qualitative analyses of time have not abandoned the concepts embodied in the metaphor of time's arrow and time's cycle. Heidegger has, to be sure, described the difference between Being and beings, but a crucial residue of this problematic, the temporalization of this difference, which cannot be described in terms of arrow or cycle, has awaited postmodern analysis. In sum, time's irreversibility, time's arrow, remains the dominant metaphor for qualitative explorations of time and, in complicity with the human anticipation of death, as what is dark in lived time. Time's cycle is an effort to mitigate the tragic character of this irreversibility.

But the dark diachronicity of saintly life circumvents time's arrow and time's cycle even if, superficially, it appears to fall on the side of time's arrow. Saintly existence, as I showed earlier, differs within itself, is fissured by a lapse and loss that are "structurally" rather than contingently irrecoverable by memory. Saints are also expert in "reversing" time's arrow in phenomena such as apology and repentance, a point to which I shall return in detail.

Recall that dark diachronicity is experienced as the unbridgeable chasm in sensation between the feeling and the felt. Only through the intervention of a quasi-cognitive intentionality or the conferring of signification through language is feeling harnessed, so to speak, and brought into correspondence with the felt, like the return of the pendulum's swing. But there is a residue that resists such incorporation that "ticks" diachronically, as it were, and cannot be brought into the present either in the Platonic sense of full recollection or, on Nietzsche's account, as willed recurrence. In the sphere of sensation, this residue is experienced as otherwise than present, as tactility, pressure, and pain.

Even if diachronicity is integral to sensing, is this experience of loss reflected in everyday existence? In the course of his phenomenological account of physical trauma, Erwin Straus develops a notion of newness in connection with complex experiences that roughly corresponds to what is physiologically integral to sensation as irrecoverable or lapsed.[35] First-timeness, Straus claims, determines the character of an experience, defines it in a particular manner. If it is vivid, decisive, or shocking in either a negative or a positive manner, an experience is unlikely to be repeated, and many positive experiences are disappointing when efforts are made to relive them. If an experience goes deep, it transfigures one's world orientation and effects a metamorphosis of personality. Religious conversion, Straus suggests, is an example of such a shock to an individual's world system. Its diachronicity lies in its irrecoverability. It is always already that particular newness that cannot be brought back with the fervor of something originary.

Intensity of experience is to be associated with its uniqueness, its passage, whether it is something flashing by—the final glimpse of the beloved Lara's face in Pasternak's *Dr. Zhivago*—or something of longer duration—the languid summer days with the beautiful girls at Balbec in Proust's *Remembrance of Things Past*. The *Sehnsucht* expressed in the lyrics of popular music reflect the grief of love gone stale, the yearning for repristinization, and, often, an acknowledgment of the hopelessness of this desire. Newness is adumbrated by being organized into a series of further reflections fanning out from an initial event or shock that has itself been constituted as such after the fact. Longing for a past *is* the fissuring of the present by what is lapsed and irrecoverable, a firstness riddled by an anterior difference.

Is there a way of annulling the past or engaging the future that takes time's dark diachronicity into account, that respects both the newness of experience and the irrecoverability of time? Repentance and apology, pardon, and forgiveness are phenomena that erase the past while maintaining time's irreversibility. Ordinary experience attests that the Other's vulnerability is generally received indifferently both at the microlevel of interpersonal relations and at the macrolevel of social, political, and economic affairs, that the rule of *homo homini lupus* prevails. Thus, ignoring the vulnerability of the Other is the rule so that the Other is often wounded bodily and psychologically at the microlevel, economically and politically at the macrolevel. The inflicting of injury is written into life histories.[36] In repentance the process is reversed not because the will wills backward in Nietzsche's sense but because the offense created by acts against the Other is undone so that the offense no longer exists. Unlike repentance, apology and forgiveness are social acts in which the undoing of past offense requires reciprocity: the Other must be complicit in granting pardon. In each of these phenomena, the offending events fall into the indifferent stream of becoming, with their offending character subtracted because the injury with which they were associated is expunged.

Traditional hagiographic narrative is rich in descriptions of saintly assistance in obtaining the forgiveness of those offended or in performing other irenic functions. A Chinese version of the *Upasaka Sila Sutra* about the Buddha's compassion reads:

> Because he saw them consumed by the fires of pain and
> sorrow yet knowing not where to seek the still waters of
> samadhi,
> For this he was moved to pity.
> Because he saw them living in a time of wars, killing and
> wounding one another: and knew for the riotous hatred in
> their hearts they were doomed to pay an endless retribution,
> For this he was moved to pity.
> Because he saw the men of the world ploughing their fields,
> sowing the seed, trafficking, huckstering, buying and selling:
> and at the end winning nothing but bitterness,
> For this he was moved to pity.[37]

Buddhist compassion and irenicism are directed to helping others in undoing *samsara*, the cycles of birth and death that endure for aeons. In fact, in most forms of Buddhism it is the realization that things are impermanent, that what exists is subject to birth and decay, that constitutes a perceptual and ontological change from suffering to insight. The unmaking or undoing of the past is crucial for the formation of new moral practices. The weight of the past is differently interpreted by the world's religious and intellectual traditions, for example, as karma in Hindu and Buddhist thought, as sin and guilt in Judaism, Christianity, and Islam, as viciousness of character in classical philosophy, and as a violation of conscience in modern thought. In each of these traditions the past must be repatterned and in some way neutralized before a change in moral practices is possible.

Nietzsche construed the Buddhist cycles of endlessly recurring existence without aim or purpose as a form of willing nothingness. He contrasted what he believed to be its nihilism with his own view that recurrence is to be affirmed. The relationship between Buddhism and Nietzsche's thought on this issue has been explored and resists easy summary. In the present context it suffices only to notice that the all-encompassing compassion of the Buddha makes possible behaviors that will ease the novice's mental suffering or "ill" (*dukha*) and lead to "ease" (*sukha*) through the cycles of time. Because there is no self to forgive or to be forgiven, the ills and misery of existence are expunged without personal reference.

The Neuter

The idea of neutrality first takes shape in the context of Heidegger's inquiry into the character of the being of human being. The object of any interrogation of human existence is not, he argues, a determinate being, man, but a being "prior to every factual concretion," a Dasein.[38] Such a being is sexless not because it is a nullity, an indifferently empty being, but because it is something prior to sexual differentiation. "Neutrality is not the voidness of an abstraction," Heidegger declares, "but precisely the potency of the origin, which bears in itself the intrinsic possibility of every concrete factual humanity" (*MFL*, p. 137). Neutral Dasein is not concrete human being but what makes such an existent possible. Still, the neutrality of the Dasein is not to be confused with a master concept but is to be taken as a concept that is both "thoughtful" and "historical." Cordoned off in its neutrality, the Dasein is isolated not in a factical but in a metaphysical way.

It would seem on this interpretation that the neutrality of the Dasein could be explained in Aristotelian terms as something potential that must be brought into actuality. The Dasein appears to be the essence of human being prior to its existence. But Heidegger's subsequent remarks make clear that this is not at all what is intended. The dispersion and disunity which constitute factical Dasein are not something incidental to it, "a mere formal plurality of determinations." Instead, "Dasein's essence already contains a primordial *bestrewal* [*Streuung*]" which is both temporally and spatially "a *dissemination* [*Zerstreuung*]" (*MFL*, 137–38).

It is against this backdrop that the fissuring of the saintly subject exhibited in the hagiographic tale must be examined. Consider again James's *Wings of the Dove* recast as hagiography in chapter 2. From the standpoint of literary technique, James's novel still belongs to the tradition in which the transparency of a consciousness is identified with the narrative voice, one that need not speak directly but whose point of view orchestrates the tale. Such voices, James's ambassadors, as Blanchot designates them, are deputized to speak for the author. Densher's standpoint is perhaps that of the panoptic consciousness that organizes the work into a totality. But if the novel is construed *hagiographically* so that Millie's altruism is made thematic, there is no such totality because her consciousness can no longer be unified by the narrative voice. Instead it is fissured, *bestreut*. On Heidegger's reading it is impending death that disseminates the origin, the Dasein. But in a hagiographic reading, dissemination occurs as the dispersal of egoity in the interest of the Other. This is not an innocuous difference but has the most profound consequences for hagiographic narrative.

It is crucial to recall that the hagiographic literature of many religious traditions follows conventional narrative schema in which the before and after of everyday time is governed by the anticipation of death even when death is followed by resurrection or, as in Hindu or Buddhist traditions, by rebirth.[39] But everyday time cannot be the focus as soon as the saint's encounter with the Other disperses present time and transgresses chronological sequence. This mode of temporalization could hardly be culled from traditional hagiographies by their contemporary readers or hearers but is revealed only now through the analysis of present time in postmodern criticism.

These recent interpretations do not focus on death but are the result of the entry into the literary works themselves of broken time, giving to the fictions of writers such as Kafka, Artaud, Bataille, Borges, Calvino, and Beckett their "irreducible strangeness."[40] "Characters," if there are any, are no longer instantiations of essences but float freely within narrative space. Nor is there a "correct" point at which the reader can be stationed with regard to the tale's events because narrative distance, the space between the work and its readers or writer, has been drawn into the interior of the work itself. There is no fixed "gaze" that can determine the horizon from which distance is measured, not outside it because contemplative or aesthetic distance that removed the reader from the work has been brought into the narrative's "interior" and not inside it because the outside is now in the inside or heart of narrative itself. There is only a destabilized exteriority that undoes every privileged vantage point. The elimination of a fixed point of view means that the ego or "I" previously stated or implied in narrative is unmoored but does not come to an end.

It is this new space or hole within literature itself, this estrangement from the center, that Blanchot speaks of as the neuter:

Narration governed by the neuter is kept in the custody of the "he," the third person that is neither a third person, nor the simple cloak of impersonality. The "he" of narration is not content to take the place usually occupied by the subject. . . . The narrative he dismisses all subjects, just as it removes every transitive action or every objective possibility. . . . [T]he speech of the tale always lets us feel it is not being told by anyone: it speaks in the neuter. . . . [I]n the neuter space of the tale, the bearers of speech, the subject of the action—who used to take the place of the characters—fall into a relationship of nonidentification with themselves: something happens to them, something they cannot recapture except by relinquishing the power to say "I."[41]

With the disappearance of the narrative "I," the tale itself has become forgetful. This does not imply that the tale is about a struggle to remember some forgotten incident even if this may contingently be the theme of some particular story. The present of hagiography is without memory because in the absence of the "I" there is only narrating speech but not a process of loss and recovery, of bringing up something contained within the repository of an "I."[42] The narrative he or illeity, the erring "subject,"[43] is the mark of postmodern narration. It stands on its head the last point of fixity in narration, the death of the Dasein. Now, strictly speaking, there can be no who. When dispersal is radical, there is no solidary Other and no I to constitute it. Instead, the who is neuter, that is, "neither one thing nor another," a void or hollow within the work itself. Speaking from no place, saying nothing, every trace of the neuter in the tale already betrays it.

Because the voice of illeity has no locale within the tale save as an outside that is inside, it is "radically exterior" to it. The neuter's "ghostly" voice which is nowhere undoes the character that speaks it, as, for example, Saint Teresa is undone when the hagiographic "I" becomes an empty nonplace "inhabited" by the Other. But how does hagiographic speech occur at all if it is always already displaced utterance? The spectral voice has, as it were, a kind of glamour that "attracts language [and] . . . allows the neuter to speak."[44] It signifies in a way altogether different from that of ordinary language, "opens another power in language." Everyday speech is a telling of what is or is not. The power of the neuter on the other hand bypasses ontological language "drawing language into a possibility of saying that would say without saying being . . . establishing the center of gravity of speech elsewhere."[45] Its obliqueness and evasion of solid ontic reference lead to a confusion of the neuter with madness.

In the last novel of the great tetralogy of Yukio Mishima, *The Sea of Fertility*, there is a Buddhist articulation of the neuter, of the self emptied of itself, without memory or present time. The saintly figure of Satoko illustrates this speaking through the voice of the Other. By contrast, all those who still belong to the everyday world characterized by the misery of endless cycles of birth and rebirth, death and redeath, inhabit a different narrative space. When the lawyer Honda, the narrative voice of all four novels, learns he is to die, he writes to Satoko, whom he remembers as the beautiful young woman who many years earlier was passionately in love with Honda's childhood friend Kiyoaki. Honda tells her of an old promise he made before Kiyoaki died that he (Honda) would see Satoko in accordance with Kiyoaki's last wish. With the failure of the love affair, Satoko had entered Gesshuji, an order of Buddhist women, where she is now its old abbess and where Honda travels to find her. To Honda's utter confusion Satoko denies ever having known Kiyoaki:

> "I fear I have never heard the name Kiyoaki Matsugae. Don't you suppose, Mr. Honda, there never was such a person? You seem convinced that there was. But don't you suppose there never was such a person from the beginning anywhere? I couldn't help thinking so, as I listened to you."
>
> . . . "But if there was no Kiyoaki from the beginning—"
>
> . . . He spoke loudly as if to retrieve the self that receded like traces of breath vanishing from a lacquer tray.
>
> "If there was no Kioyoaki, then . . . perhaps, there has been no I."
>
> For the first time there was strength in her eyes.
>
> "That too is as it is in each heart."[46]

"There never was such a person anywhere" echoes nearly word for word the great classical Buddhist formulations of the no-self doctrine as expounded in the *Samyutta-Nikaya* and the *Milindapanha*. There is no self underlying the sequence of mental events, only an impression of substantiality created by aggregates of feeling, perception, and consciousness that, taken together, create an illusory entity, an ego.[47] Language shores up this illusion with the act of naming, but the name is only an "appellation" or "convenient designation" when, in fact, "there is no ego here to be found."[48] The spectral voice of the abbess Satoko in Mishima's narrative is not the voice of the young Satoko, not because lapses of time destroy continuity but because there is no substratum that holds them together. Both the before and after of the order of time, time's arrow, and the endless round of rebirths, time's cycle, have been neutralized. Only the neuter that "shows" itself in the healing and compassionate voice of the abbess bears the traces of what Blanchot speaks of as radically other, the outside that is inside.

Not only does the neuter alter the order of time and place but, as one of the term's meanings indicates, it points to a loosening or decentering of sexual identity, as Heidegger's analysis already indicated. The word *neuter* refers to "a castrated animal or one having no sexual organs."[49] Feminist literature has described the condition of women as dislocated and errant, made other by historical circumstance, and given an identity that is exterior to or outside the logos. By recontextualizing the traditional question "What is woman's place?" Helene Cixous articulates a mode of temporalization that is neither linear nor cyclical but differential. She opens the space of a countermyth to the Ulysses story, the story analyzed by Jankelevich, in terms of linear and cyclical time. The story of Ariadne is a tale not of adventure and homecoming but of self-giving. "Ariadne, without calculating, without hesitating, but believing, taking everything as far as it goes—the anti-Ulysses—. . . advanc[es] into emptiness, into the unknown. [As woman, Ariadne makes Theseus secure while] she takes her leap without a line."[50] This is not to suggest that all women have been altruists (although many have) or that a historically determined passivity is desirable or can be equated with altruism. What Cixous' text helps to establish is the claim that both the de-hypostatizing of identity and the expression of passivity permit the neuter to speak.

It could be argued that Buddhist saints reflect modes of temporalization that are inherent in the metaphysical commitments of Buddhism so that it is not saintly altruism that is "articulated" as the neuter so much as the reflection in hagiography of prior philosophical notions of transitoriness and nonself. Similarly it might be maintained that it is not the condition of women that "speaks" the neuter but postmodern literature that creates the character of this utterance. If so, the preceding remarks about Buddhist and feminist texts may be seen as circular in that the result of their claims is built in from the start. But it can be argued, to the contrary, that Buddhism provides an ontological backdrop that supports altruism but that the structure of altruism is not parasitic upon Buddhist metaphysics. By the same token, feminist criticism recontextualizes older narratives and brings out the heretofore invisible condition of women inscribed in received traditions.

The sexual dislocation and decentering of the neuter are to be found not only in hagiographic and literary texts whose philosophical presuppositions are already deconstructive such as those of the Buddhist tradition, but as startling dissonances or counterdiscourses within conventional logocentric frameworks. Consider the tale of Saint Marina/us:

When Eugenius's wife dies, he leaves his young daughter with relatives and enters a monastery. He cannot forget her, so after some years he disguises her as a boy, "Marinus," and brings her to live in the monastery. When Marina/us is seventeen, Eugenius dies. Once, when running an errand for the monastery, Marina/us is accused of impregnating the daughter of an innkeeper where s/he was forced to spend the night. When the abbot confronts him/her with the charge of having fathered a boy s/he refuses to deny it, is expelled from the monastery, and is forced to live as a beggar. When his/her alleged boy is weaned, the child's mother deposits him with Marina/us. S/he again does not reveal the truth. After five years of caring for the boy s/he is readmitted to the monastery as a reward for having endured pain and humiliation with such patience. But Marina/us is made to do penance for her/his earlier sin. When Marina/us dies, her/his sex is discovered. The abbot is overcome with remorse and Marina/us is buried with honors.[51]

This extraordinary narrative of sexual transformation with its further intimations of incestuous longing decenters both time and identity and precludes straightforward reading. Is Marina man or woman? What is the nature of the longing of Marina's father? Is it the woman or the daughter that he yearns for? Or, in disguising Marina as Marinus, is it after all a young boy that he desires? When the unnamed woman is impregnated, is Marina/us the adoptive father or mother of the child? And what is the sexual status of the new couple, Marina/us and the unnamed woman? Into what time frame does the suppressed identity fall, the dark diachronicity of lapsed time or the self-identity of work and action? Whom does the abbot readmit to the monastery, who does penance, who is forgiven, and who dies?

The hagiographic body of Marina/us is a neuter. No sexual identity can be inscribed on its surface because the saintly body accommodates all sexual identities (in that sense it is polymorphous) and none.[52] The disinterested love of the Other requires the totality of the body of the one who loves as an ever shifting point of reference.

The Unconscious as a Language

Because sexual identity plays so crucial a role in this text, psychoanalytic interpretation that makes unconscious motives thematic may open the way to understanding the role of desire in saintly psychology. But standard psychoanalytic metaphors—such as those of displacement drawn from hydraulics or of force fields borrowed from physics as well as references to images and archetypes—as instruments of explanation are not homologous with the theological constructs of hagiographic discourse. If theological language is to be interpreted psychoanalytically, the content of the unconscious must be commensurable with the language of theology.

It is just here that Jacques Lacan's argument that the unconscious is "structured . . . like a language, that a material operates in it according to certain laws, which are the same laws as those discovered in the study of actual languages"[53] is fruitful. By treating the unconscious as a language, Marina/us can be viewed alternately as analysand and as text, a narrative made up of multiple voices, each—Eugenius, the dead mother, the abbot, the "seduced" woman, the child—an alienated voice of the unconscious. These "personages" can be construed as lines of force, as the "truth" of the patient Marina/us's desire covered by a carapace of alienated discourse that must be penetrated so that desire can find expression. For Lacan, "empty" or alienated speech must become "full" speech, a language in which the mirages of the subject dissolve through a recollection of the past.

Alienation begins with the by now familiar mirror stage, the age between six months and a year and a half when the child identifies with its specular image. At this stage the child sees himself in the "visual gestalt of his own body," an idealized version of his own unity. This, says Lacan, situates the active self, the ego "before its social determination, in an ideal direction" (*Ec*, p. 18). Because the specular image is an iconic or imaginary self, it is already an alienated fragment, an ego that will continue to obstruct the subject's desire. In the story of Marina/us the mirror image in which his/her desire will become manifest begins as an icon already broken: the body of Marina/us is both male and female and will forever alternate between that of the dead or absent mother and of the father who has abandoned her for the monastery so that he too is an absence.

A second and purely linguistic dimension of Lacanian analysis bound up with his interpretation of metaphor will orchestrate the next phase of the life of Marina/us. Metaphor, generally defined as the substitution of something concrete for an abstract notion, appears when "sense emerges from nonsense." Borrowing from the structural linguistics of Saussure, Lacan interprets metaphor in terms of the sign, a two-part construct made up of a signifier, a sound image—both the physical reverberation and the psychological impression—and a signified, the concept it refers to. Language is a chain of signs, each depending for its signification upon the adjoining signs, the significative context or setting into which it is inserted. The relationship between signifier and sign is arbitrary. For structural linguistics, metaphor is the creation of a new meaning when one signifier, related through similarity to another, substitutes for it. Adding a psychoanalytic dimension to the structuralist interpretation of metaphor, Lacan asserts that a signifier falls from the chain of signifiers, becomes latent, and is substituted for by another signifier but that a space or opening is left onto which a new signifying chain will be grafted.[54]

In the story of Marina/us what has been "forgotten," what has fallen from the chain of signifiers, is gender: Marina/us is biologically the girl child, Marina. This loss will occasion the emergence of Marinus with tragic consequences as manifested in the future misprisions of gender and the lifelong latency of the female, Marina. Disguised by Eugenius as a boy, Marina enters the social world of the monastery as male. During this period, either before or after entry into the monastery, the Oedipal phase of the psychosexual development of Marinus (for by now Marina has fallen from the chain of signifiers) would have taken place, the phase in which the child wishes to be everything to the mother, to substitute for what she is lacking, the phallus which for Lacan is not an organic referent but "the privileged signifier of that mark in which the role of the logos is joined with the advent of desire" (*Ec*, p. 287). But can the child Marina identify with the symbol of what she herself doubly lacks? As Marina she is missing what she hopes to provide, the absent phallus; as Marinus she is forever confronted by the dead or absent mother, the mother as lacking. The child Marina/us can only fail to identify with the symbol of maternal desire.

How is Marina/us to transform the object of desire into the truth of language? As Marinus, the oedipal conflict should be resolved in the encounter with the Law-of-the-Father, the law that proscribes identification with the phallus. But this is impossible for Marinus to achieve because he/she is also Marina. For Lacan, the Law-of-the-Father also prohibits the mother from returning the child to the womb, but a dead or absent mother cannot become the subject of such a prohibition. According to Lacan, the child is to surrender the phallus that he is in order to have a phallus so that he may enter the symbolic order of culture. The Father's law, attested through speech, must be recognized by the mother or the child will remain bound forever to the mother. Marina/us is doubly exiled, bound to the absent mother and cast out of the discursive symbolics of culture.

Recognition of the Father's law gives the child access to the Name of the Father, the *nom de père*. The homonymity of *nom* and *non* is meant to suggest name and the no-saying bound up with the Law-of-the-Father. For Marina/us, the Oedipal stage must end in a total collapse of meaning since as Marina she must fail to become an object of desire to the mother, a failure that, in turn, will exempt her from the Law-of-the-Father and bar her from entry into the world of culture. She can only continue to live as a bivalent body, as male and female, man and woman. The desire of Marina/us will be forever encoded in her body, given up to the inscribing of the language of desire upon the flesh of unspecified gender.

The desire of Marina is trapped between that of Eugenius for the boy Marinus and the desire of Marina/us for the dead or absent mother. For Lacan, desire is a "phenomenon" of the margin, born in the gap (*béance*) between need or biological lack and demand, what is urgently asked for or claimed. Desire cannot be self-determined in that the one that desires is at the mercy of the one who is to fulfill it, the Other. The dead mother can never fulfill the demand for love of this child because his/her demand is always *zweideutig*, ambiguous, alternating between Marina and Marinus, the broken icon of the mirror stage.

The Other for Lacan is also understood in a second, more complex sense. Because the unconscious is not known to consciousness, it too is Other and speaks the language of the Other. The analysand as the subject of desire can only desire insofar as he is Other because desiring belongs to the unconscious. The analyst must speak for the Other that desires but has been suffocated and does not dare to speak for itself. "Che vuoi?" ("What do you want?") is the question that must come to the fore (*Ec*, p. 316). The truth of the analysand's unconscious is the truth of the Other that has been barred, the barred Other [Ø]. This Other, the place of truth and of "the treasure of the signifier," is nonetheless grounded in lack, a nonplace, as it were, whose signifier is a signifier of lack that Lacan calls the signifier of the barred other [S(Ø)]. Yet this Other, unable to come into plenary presence and still remain Other, cannot fail to respond to the value of the treasure. It does so by inserting itself into the chain of signifiers, compelled to this course, Lacan argues, because "there is no Other than the Other" (*Ec*, p. 316). This is a point of cardinal importance for coming to grips with the character of Marina/us's desire.

Recall that each personage in the text is, in older non-Lacanian psychoanalytic terms, a projection, so that Eugenius, like the text's other voices, speaks for the desire of Marina/us. The Eugenius strand cannot forget Marina, loves her so deeply that he brings her to the monastery, where she will continue to live even after he dies, but the price paid for this love is her transformation into Marinus. With the death of Eugenius the desire of Marina/us is once more destabilized. She/he "runs an errand" which becomes the source of a deeper errancy when she/he is accused of impregnating the daughter of an innkeeper.

The crisis of identity is brought to a head: the abbot, a substitute in the chain of signifiers for Eugenius, forces the question of sexual identity by confronting him/her with the sexual infraction. But an advance has been made in self-understanding, for now she/he is dangerously close to the doubleness of desire. A space is opened for a new chain of signifiers that will speak for the barred Other.

However, the insight into her double desire is dangerous and the resistances begin to speak. Unable to betray either the father, Eugenius, who disguised her as a boy, or her biological gender, Marina/us remains silent. Expelled from the monastery, she/he begins to pay the price for desires so wildly extravagant. The boy she is said to have fathered is left with her by the mother after he is weaned. But could it be that the child's mother did not know the name of the father? This strange aporia in the narrative points to the "mother" as that strand of Marina/us's desire that has been barred from female speech during all the years spent in the monastery as Marinus.

In her grief over the death of Eugenius, Marina/us seeks frantically to replace the lost object of her desire with the boy, just as earlier Eugenius and perhaps the relative who briefly cared for her take the place in the chain of signifiers of the absent mother. But the substitute object (*l'objet petit a*, where "a" stands for *autre*) can never fill the primordial emptiness it comes to supplant.[55] What does Marina/us seek that is so quickly replaced by one finite object after another? Eugenius, the mother of the boy, the boy himself? The "obscure object of desire" (to borrow the phrase of filmmaker Buñuel) can never come to light because of language's relation to desire, a lack that can never attain discursive clarity. Yet, Lacan insists, the "I" can retreat to that nonplace where discourse is not by fading or withdrawing from the symbolics of language. This indeterminate place, or condition, is *jouissance*, a word linked both to the enjoyment of rights and to sexuality and that, in the present context, means boundless bliss. Bataille (as I hope to show in chapter 7) will speak alternately of continuity, plethora, excess, orgy, and sacrifice, metonymic substitutions within his frame of reference for this condition. The "I" comes to stand in the place where neither life nor death can be said to exist and from which the voice of the Other is heard. The "I" is a defect in this pure nonplace just as, Lacan insists, "the universe is a defect in pure non-being" (*Ec*, p. 317).

Now the Lacanian analysis must be carried beyond what it was originally intended to bear, the resolution of the tensions of an unconscious desire in the subject of a psychoanalysis, and enter the discourse of saintly altruism. Marina/us can never stand in that nonplace of desire "in this life," never be done with suffering, never come to terms with the brokenness of the icon in the mirror. Marina/us is barred from *jouissance*, from full bliss, because she is Marinus, subject to the Father's law, but as Marinus is barred from the substitute satisfaction of cultural symbolics because she is Marina.

To see the relevance of this analysis for the problem of saintly altruism, recall earlier Lacan's oracular utterance: "There is no Other than the Other." Marina/us is now thrown back upon corporeality as a field of inscription which becomes the body for the Other and, as such, a field of Marina/us's disinterested desire: the good of Eugenius, the nurturing of the boy, the good of the monastic community to which she/he returns. Marina/us works to fulfill the need of the Other through a saintly body that is both male and female. For the saint, there is no Other than the Other in the double sense of other persons whose need she/he heeds and the Other of a purely saintly unconscious desire. Because of the doubly gendered body of Marina/us, her/his desire at first oscillates wildly between genders but, as the narrative unfolds, becomes what it always already was, desire for the Other, disinterested desire.[56] The tensions of the analysand are never resolved because saintly life is not intended to be brought to closure, nor the body of inscription to be surrendered for the body of pleasure. The story of Marina/us is *narratively* resolved when, after death, his/her "true" sex is discovered, but it can never be *hagiographically* resolved in that the symbolics of a disinterested desire demand a doubly gendered nongender, as it were, and the infinite openness of inscription.

NEOPLATONIC CONCEPTIONS of time are generally interpreted as static and of little contemporary interest because they are grounded in an oppositional relation between an unchanging eternity and its mirror image, time. But remarkable anticipations within Neoplatonism of postmodern conceptions of time are developed by Plotinus and later Neoplatonists. Like Heidegger and Derrida, Plotinus alleges that time unfolds in errancy and dissemination, "squandering itself outside itself." Still another dimension is added, that of primary time, that enables the Neoplatonist, Damascius, to imagine radical becoming, thus presaging the conception I term dark diachronicity. To think the form of time as presence, he argues, destroys the radical character of becoming, thus anticipating the incompatibility of presence and radical diachronicity. Damascius sees too that the flow of time without the anchorage of the Now cannot even be thought and so cannot be time for us.

The temporalization of saintly labor is lived as the dark or differential time through which nothing can come to plenary presence, a mode of time attested by the corporeal structure of sensibility. Sensation has often been understood in terms of its cognitive function as an intention and a content that fulfills it. But sensibility also expresses the body's vulnerability as openness to exteriority or the Other, an exposure to alterity that does not yield cognitive content but instead breaks up the unity of the self.

Nietzsche offers several powerful objections that could count against a conception of altruism that is bound up with the dark diachronicity I have described and with the body's vulnerability. First Nietzsche's well-known *ressentiment* theory holds that pity reflects an animus of the weak against the strong, and second Nietzsche claims that this view is itself rooted in the human rancor against the passing of time. Max Scheler's attack on *ressentiment* is considered but found wanting because Scheler, by differentiating only the motives but not the fruits of altruism, leaves Nietzsche's view intact. Nietzsche also undermines the argument that the historical victory of the weak is the result of an actually superior will by showing the will of the weak to be subtractive and nihilistic.

Nietzsche's arguments can only be countered at a deeper level, that of his presuppositions about corporeality. Nietzsche's vitalism depends on a description not of the healthy body with its alternations of fatigue and exhaustion but of a pathological body, one that is always awake, tireless, and active or, in his terms, an ever active center of force or will to power. Thus Nietzsche's norms of strength and health are in fact parasitic upon an aberrant or diseased corporeality.

Nietzsche's view of time presupposes the pattern described by Stephen Gould as time's arrow and time's cycle. Time's arrow is the time scheme of the man of *ressentiment* who predicates its irreversibility, in contrast to the view of eternal recurrence or cyclical time put forward especially in the *Zarathustra* and *The Will to Power*. The dark diachronicity of saintly life and labor expresses the irrecoverability of time that does not generate resentment in that it always already belongs to the Other.

Once the diachronicity of saintly life is developed, its incursions into the relation between time and the hagiographic subject can be traced. Maurice Blanchot shows how the strategies of postmodern literature result in a neutering of the "I," a decentering that results in an impersonal "he." Language no longer makes claims about what there is but moves within a detemporalized textual space. The now unmoored subject speaks with the voice of another, the spectral voice that emerges from the dislocations of the text. This neutering is present in hagiography from the start not because hagiography is about a neutral subject, a Dasein, but because it expresses both the dark diachronicity of lapsed time and the sexually ambiguous saintly body. Not only are examples of the neuter to be found in Buddhist hagiography and feminist literature, but traditional hagiographic narrative is shown to offer striking instances of temporal and sexual neutering.

The story of a doubly gendered saint, Marina/Marinus, is analyzed in Lacanian terms as the subject of a desire that is ultimately neutral, a body upon which the needs and desires of the Other can be inscribed.

5

The little god o' the world sticks to the same old way,
And is as whimsical as on Creation's day.
Life somewhat better might content him,
But for the gleam of heavenly light that thou hast lent him:
He calls it Reason—thence his power's increased,
To be far beastlier than any beast.

Goethe, *Faust*, Prologue in Heaven

"What is dat keeps uh man from gettin' burnt on uh red hot stove—caution or nature?"

"[I]f it was nature, nobody wouldn't have tuh look out for babies touchin' stoves, would they? 'Cause dey just naturally wouldn't touch it. But dey sho will. So it's caution."

"How is de son gointuh be before his paw? Nature is de first of everything. Ever since self was self, nature been keepin' folks off of red-hot stoves. Dat caution you talkin' 'bout ain't nothin' but uh humbug. He's a inseck dat nothin' he got belongs to him. He got eyes lak somethin' else; wings lak somethin' else—everything! Even his hum is de sound of somebody else."

Zora Neale Hurston, *Their Eyes Were Watching God*

Otto Dix, The Seven Deadly Sins. Staatliche Kunsthalle, Karlsruhe. Marburg/Art
Resource, New York.

The Demand for Theory

AMONG THE questions raised by accounts of saintly life, particularly vexing are those bound up with how that life is to be justified. Can one act morally without recourse to prior reasoned reflection? Even in the absence of elaborate arguments, are there not at least loose commitments to moral protocols, such as the principle that one's actions ought to be determined by whether they are intrinsically right or wrong, the deontological view, or the notion that one should reflect about the consequences of one's acts before acting, the consequentialist position? Are not such tacit norms built into the process of arriving at moral decisions in everyday life even when they are not made thematic? In short, is there not some moral theory, at least a rule of thumb however inchoate, that is appealed to when an act is contemplated or judged in moral terms?

Connected with the first group of questions is a second, deeper question: *ought* one to act by appealing to general moral notions and frameworks to guide one's moral actions rather than to narratives? Has imitating the lives of others not led to grotesque and horrifying excesses, from the butchery of private crimes to the socially sanctioned destruction of whole peoples?

If saintly lives are useful, is it not because they are examples of right conduct derived from theoretical notions that are independent normative constructs? To be sure, once moral values are embodied in stories, narrative can serve an ancillary inspirational function, but are not the lives these stories recount paradigmatic because of the rationally justified norms they reveal?

Looking at the matter in another way, consider the view expounded in earlier chapters that hagiography is "grounded" in corporeal sensibility even if the body is described in terms of lapse, delay, and fissure, a claim about saintly lives even stronger than the positing of a mere tendency or disposition to goodness. If there is such a structure, there can be no reason for anyone to act other than altruistically, just as, for

127

example, there is no reason for anyone not to experience the world temporally and spatially. But experience shows the contrary. Far from behaving altruistically, individuals and societies observe another rule, that of reciprocal destruction. What is more, if there were a built-in structure and (per contra) compassion were the norm, no responsibility for benevolent actions would accrue, because such actions would be determined by the prior character of sensibility.

The question of saintly compassion raises still further issues. Does social injustice actually demand compassion or is another response required, one that would affect the realm of politics and economy? If so, should the saint become implicated in violence? And if not, how can saintliness become effective in the arena of social existence? And how is one to decide whether saintly intervention in the tangled world of political affairs is just if not by appealing to some nonnarrative moral norm? Do these problems not require the subordination of moral life to moral theory?

An ethic in quest of a postmodern response to these questions must meet them not by entering their frame of reference but by exposing their presuppositions, what postmodern thinking takes theory to be and how theory functions in moral matters. In so doing it must appeal to the strategies at its disposal: genealogical analysis and a hermeneutics of suspicion that exhibits the fissuring of theoretical discourse by delay and difference. At the same time it must account for the related problem of why saints are not best interpreted as moral exemplars, as specimens of definable moral properties such as goodness, justice, and the like, a matter that postmodern thinking can only decide by reaching into the historical root and metaphysical presuppositions of exemplarity.

The Metaphysics of Theory: Heidegger

Whether moral theory is necessary for leading a moral life cannot be determined without deciding first what is at issue when the notion of theory is invoked. A good starting point for deciding this question is common usage and the term's etymology. Theory has been defined as "systematically organized knowledge applicable in a wide variety of circumstances; especially a system of assumptions, accepted principles and rules of procedure devised to analyze, predict, or otherwise explain the nature or behavior of a specified set of phenomena."[1] The word also reflects a series of etymological shifts especially pertinent to a philosophical grasp of the term: the late Latin *theoria* is derived from the Greek verb *theorein*, "to contemplate," which, in turn, comes from *theo-*

ros, "spectator"; *theasthai*, "to observe," stems from *thea*, also the root of *theater*, and means "a viewing."[2] Its other root, *ora*, means "to be attentive to."[3]

It is not hard to see that the model of scientific understanding has been determinative in fixing the word's meaning in ordinary usage: the function of theory is to systematize phenomena that are not yet organized, to apply the results of this procedure to other phenomena, and to predict the future behavior of phenomena on the basis of what has thus been securely acquired. A related set of concepts grounds this account: first the idea that theory is a kind of knowledge, a body of propositions taken (at least provisionally) to be true; second the view that what is taken as true is subject to some mode of justification, a criterion in terms of which it is to be so interpreted; and finally the notion that, as something to be applied, theory is more general, broader, and more abstract than the facts or the phenomena to which it will ascribe signification in that the *interpretans* is wider than the *interpretandum*. The entire collocation of meanings that attributes to theory the creation of criteria for judging and the imposition of these criteria presupposes that theory is bound up with freedom as the freedom of interpretation.

From its etymology, theory can be seen to be linked to visibility, that which can be contemplated or seen, as in the case of viewing a theatrical performance. One who holds a theory is an observer of phenomena and a spectator before whose gaze the play of the phenomena, of what appears, is laid out. Such a gaze, disengaged from what it contemplates and separated from the object of contemplation by the distance that seeing imposes on the seen, is panoptic. Its field of visibility is interpreted as a whole and a heuristic meaning imposed upon the seen. The knower, the panoptic viewer of the phenomena, is like the spectator who watches the dramatic performance that issues from the productive intelligence of the writer and is brought to life by the mimetic efforts of the actors. In sum, a theory is seen to be "within" the true, capable of having truth or falsity ascribed to it, and as attributing signification to the phenomena, thus reflecting both formal and ontological characteristics.

In Heidegger's *Metaphysical Foundations of Logic* the properties of theory as summed up in its dictionary definition are made thematic: the ontological ground of the meaning of truth, the relation of this ground to visibility, and the notion of freedom that is bound up with the type of rationality integral to the development and application of truth criteria are brought to the fore. By uncovering the presuppositions to

which such a view of theory is committed, Heidegger's analysis provides reasons for abandoning moral theory as the basis for leading a
moral life, reasons that are bound up with Heidegger's own renunciation of ethics as axiology, or theory of values. But far from abandoning
ethics, I hope to show that Heidegger's analysis of theory has cleared
the way for a mode of signification other than ontological, for bringing
forth a discourse still in the process of formation, one that bypasses the
stilted and formulaic character of older hagiography but is parasitic
upon it in that it discloses pathways for moral action.

It will not be enough to say that hagiography is useful or worthwhile
because it fills in the gaps where theory has failed. So profound an
upheaval in moral discourse cannot leave the terms of the inquiry, the
notions of value and utility, untouched. They too are parasitic on
the theoretical constructs that Heidegger makes thematic. The task of
the present and the succeeding section then is threefold: first to analyze the idea of theory as an intellectual structure or concept, second to
demonstrate how this notion of theory fails to take into account the
being that theorizes in its freedom as human being, and third to go
beyond Heideggerian analysis by appealing to the work of Bataille and
Levinas to show how the being who theorizes is always already under
obligation. It is this final step that inaugurates any postmodern understanding of moral existence.

Heidegger proceeds by revealing on the one hand the chain of connections that subsists between what is claimed to be true and the way
in which these claims are justified in a given philosophy and on the
other the reality the claims and their justification presuppose. As Michael Heim argues in his Introduction to Heidegger's reflections on the
ontological presuppositions of logic, Heidegger brings to light the
deeper commitments of both traditional and modern logic by showing
"what reality structures are referred to by *implication*. . . . begin[ning]
with a rational system and proceed[ing] to the structure of reality implied by that system" (*MFL*, p. v). Theory must become self-reflexive
so that its hidden presuppositions are made explicit through the interrogation of its ontological ground. Modern philosophy, from Descartes
and Leibniz to the present, interprets the meaning of theory in a discourse already laid out by modern science, especially by mathematical
physics. "Science in general," Heidegger asserts, "may be defined as the
totality established through an interconnection of true propositions"
(*BT*, p. 32).

The view of knowledge integral to modern philosophy is grounded
in the notion that judgment is the real locus of truth, Heidegger con

tends. Tracing the meaning of the judgment to Aristotle's account of logos according to which propositions determine something as something, Heidegger maintains that judgments function as the affirmation or denial that something belongs to something. For Aristotle, the primitive constituents of reasoning are concepts that are subsequently linked to individual propositions that, in turn, are connected with one another by thinking. The linking up of propositions or judgments is inference (*MFL*, pp. 23f.). Because truth and falsity are attributes of propositions, and their inferential relations are logical relations, the inquiry into theory must take logic, understood as the judgment, as its starting point (*MFL*, pp. 100ff.). But recall that for Heidegger logic and its underlying ontological ground are inseparable:

[T]he task for logic . . . is to clarify the essence of truth. If, however, clarifying the essence of truth can only be carried out as a metaphysics, as an ontology, then logic must be conceived as *the metaphysics of truth*. (*MFL*, p. 102)

Once truth is defined in terms of logic, truth in every sphere of being is seen in terms of relations within and among propositions. When something is asserted to be true, the meaning of truth is reduced to relations of inclusion and exclusion and the reduction to identity such that the determinations asserted by the judgment are compatible with one another and interpreted as belonging together (*MFL*, pp. 102f.).

Heidegger contrasts his own position, that logic has metaphysical foundations, with the view that "logic is free-floating, something ultimate" (*MFL*, p. 103), and should be identified with thinking itself. Grounded in this misleading assumption is the related view that "logic has primacy over all the sciences" (*MFL*, p. 103). Posing as common sense, this perspective takes for granted that, without rules of thought, thinking could not take place at all. What is more, it is alleged that, in the absence of the science of logic, all argument is precluded and arguments such as Heidegger's about the ontological grounding of logic would themselves be impossible.

Although he acknowledges the inescapability of rule-bound reasoning, Heidegger denies that this admission entails the primordiality of logic. First, if the science of logic must preexist metaphysics, it must also preexist itself. Using rules, Heidegger argues, does not entail a systematic knowledge of them. If, per contra, such knowledge were entailed, justifying the rules of logic would be impossible without the prior existence of a fully formulated science of logic. Second, logic as the systematic laying out of the conditions for truth is itself the product of a tradition. If it is foundational, it must be able to justify and account for this tradition, a task that can only be undertaken by a metaphysics of truth. To maintain the primacy of the science of logic, Heidegger contends, is sophistical because such an assumption feigns an ultimacy for which it cannot provide the warrant. Appealing to what cannot receive its justification from the science of logic, the claim of primacy nevertheless creates the semblance that formal argumentation is the most rigorous and that all justification is therefore only satisfactory in the mode of formal argument (*MFL*, p. 106).

This is a point of considerable importance for my discussion. It was anticipated earlier in my account of Rawls's and Gewirth's moral theories and will appear again in my examination of Quine's and Davidson's views of language. By considering theory as a body of true propositions, a notion of truth is presupposed that depends on an assertion of identity within a structure of coherence established by the nature of the judgment. Not only is metaphysics reduced to logic, but with the development of symbolic logics, logic itself is equated with mathematics, which, in turn, becomes the master discipline for interpreting being.

The nature of the judgment, Heidegger contends, requires more penetrating inquiry. Not only is the judgment grounded in the operations of joining concepts through inclusion and exclusion, but this operation is itself subject to the grammatical structure of subject and predicate. When the subject and predicate of a proposition are construed as belonging together, their relation is "correct" and the proposition is said to be true. Relations of entailment are ascribed to propositions on the basis of their truth or falsity, and these propositions taken together are said to constitute arguments whose validity can be determined. But what accounts for the ascription of validity or the belonging together of a subject and predicate? Correctness and validity derive from the *correspondence* of thought or judgment (what is framed in the proposition) with the object of the judgment (*MFL*, p. 124). Truth is thought of as *adequatio ad rem*, "adequation to something, as measurement by something" (*MFL*, p. 124). Because this conception of truth is thought to apply to all truth, it embraces allegations about anything whatsoever, including the human inquirer who questions the meaning of truth and existence.

The intricacies of Heidegger's deconstruction of the modern conception of theory as based on the science of logic must be pursued several steps further because my proposed departure from his analysis takes these steps as its starting point. In his essays on technology, Heidegger remains faithful to his earlier account of modern philosophy's view of truth as calculation and being as that which is calculable. It cannot be overstressed that what Heidegger carries over from the earlier work is not only an interpretation of modern philosophy's equating of thinking with the science of logic but something more primordial, a certain construal of being, that makes it possible for the worldview of mathematical logic to dominate thinking. In the essays on technology, the intellectual hegemony of logic is seen to belong to a context of practices that dominates modern thought, the practices of modern technology (*QCT*, p. 116). For Heidegger, *praxis* means not only the planning and organization of production, but the *rationale* for the productive process so that the reflexive dimension of practice is included in its concept. I shall hereafter use the term *technique* to refer to the complex comprising both action and its rationale.[4]

Mathematical physical science is now disclosed as a mode of thinking ancillary to the more primordial grasp of being by way of technique. The rules of thought carried forward historically by a philosophical tradition and systematized as the science of logic are now joined to this construal of being by technique. Even if modern physical science antedates modern technology, from the standpoint of ontological interpretation, Heidegger contends, the cognitive character of modern science is parasitic upon the grasp of being integral to technique.

Consider first the essence of modern science, the manner in which it stipulates in advance an area of being to be investigated. To see how the foredisclosure of the meaning of being is understood by science, Heidegger returns to the Greek view of the *te mathemata*. He observes that the properties of beings laid out before their actual investigation includes among being's traits the capacity to be numbered (*QCT*, p. 118). Subsumed under the class of what is known prior to inquiry, number in Greek thought does not yet stand out as something independent of a nexus of traits ascribed to nature. In addition, the Greeks define physics as the knowledge of matter in motion. When number and matter in motion are taken together, a meaning of nature is configured that will come to determine the modern character of mathematical physics "as the self-contained system of motion of units of mass related spatiotemporally" (*QCT*, p. 119).

If nature is to become the subject of knowledge, it must now be governed by standards of exactitude, and the study of nature advanced by means of measurement, number, and calculation. This epistemology does not take calculation as its starting point; to the contrary, the ontological structure of nature is so patterned by technique that calculation as the access route to nature is foreordained. Observed change is made calculable by noting what perdures through change and formulating the constancies thus stipulated as laws of nature.

Science particularizes itself into fields of specialization by designating spheres of objects as domains of research. This outlining of spheres of activity opens up the need for each one to maintain itself and thus for scientific knowledge to become institutionalized.[5] The sciences are compelled to create fresh tasks for themselves, to branch out, while at the same time embracing calculative knowledge as the model for knowledge as such. Because the sciences are destined to grow and the activity of research to proliferate, they acquire dominance over other modes of inquiry.

Consider again, in the context of the new light shed by technique on the meaning of theory, the account of the derivation of the term from the Greek *theorein*. The two parts of the word were seen as belonging together: *theorein* comprises *thea*, the outward appearance of something, and *horao*, looking attentively at something (*QCT*, p. 163). When accented differently, Heidegger suggests, *Thea*, the name for goddess, and *ora*, respect or honor that is bestowed, opens the way for a new if related interpretation of *theoria*: "the reverent paying heed" to what was concealed but is now brought into unconcealment, "the unconcealment of what presences" (*QCT*, p. 163). Integral to the Greek conception is a prizing of *theorein* as the highest way of life in contrast to existential relations of utility, action, and production (*QCT*, p. 164).

The Greek view of theory is transformed, Heidegger argues, when seeing is rendered in Latin as *contemplatio*, seeing that breaks apart what is seen. Similarly the German *betrachten*, like the Latin *tractare*, connotes manipulation, working over, and striving (*QCT*, pp. 166f.). In that transformation lies the beginning of modern ontology dominated by technique: the construing of being as a system of causal nexus and as that which is set upon and willfully transformed.

This way of regarding the real as calculable, or as what can be surveyed as a causal sequence, is the decisive development in the recasting of the meaning of being by modern thought that only now has come into its own in technological culture. This way of seeing is more primordial than the manifestations of technology in war and ecological decline. It is the violent imposition upon nature of human willing:

The revealing that rules throughout modern technology has the character of a setting-upon in the sense of a challenging forth. That challenging happens in that the energy concealed in nature is unlocked, what is unlocked is transformed, what is transformed is stored up, what is stored up is in turn distributed, and what is distributed is switched about ever anew. (*QCT*, p. 16)

The process thus described is both endless and recursive in that it feeds upon itself: everything has become "standing-reserve or what is ordered so as to be at the ready for further ordering" (*QCT*, p. 17). But if beings are revealed as standing-reserve, must not human being also disclose itself in the same way? Heidegger argues that human being can never be transformed fully into standing-reserve because, although human beings do not choose the way in which being comes to presence in a given epoch, it is still they who propel the advance of technology (*QCT*, p. 17).

The dominance of the metaphysical foundations of the science of logic in Heidegger's early account of theoreticity achieves its full development in his analysis of technique. The pursuit of control leads to seeing individuals as homogeneous units that lend themselves to abstraction and formulaic manipulation based on the principle of parsimony. "Mathematics," Heidegger maintains, "is the reckoning that everywhere by means of equations, has set up the goal of its expectation, the harmonizing of all relations of order, and that therefore 'reckons' in advance with one fundamental equation for all merely possible ordering" (*QCT*, p. 170). It is no accident, Heidegger alleges, that Werner Heisenberg hoped to discover a single fundamental equation from which the behavior of matter could be derived (*QCT*, p. 172).

The view of theory that Heidegger describes governs moral philosophy not because moral philosophers have laid down its suppositions in advance—they are generally blind to these in any case—but because moral philosophy is in the grip of a metaphysics of truth that dominates the forms of rationality of the present age. By making the ontological ground of theory transparent to itself, Heidegger hopes to create a reflexivity in his own thinking that will exempt it from this controlling ontology.

Contemporary ethicists can argue that, while some moral theories exhibit the logical design of theoreticity described by Heidegger, a more subtle view of the moral life begins with praxis. Has not Western moral philosophy from its inception acknowledged the active dimension of morality? But for Heidegger, positing the primacy of activity does not free inquiry from entanglement in ontological matters because, as his account of technique shows, the model of praxis determinative for our epoch is that of the manipulation and control of nature.

It is useless to strive to evade the transformation wreaked upon practice by the present-day understanding of being and nature by taking the Kantian tack that human beings are never to be treated as means but only as ends. These are the terms of the process of analysis itself: one cannot think otherwise than through the categorial scheme of means and ends. Similarly utilitarian arguments that hope to demonstrate the maximization of happiness or the equitable distribution of goods borrow the practical notions of utility and happiness from the larger ontological context of calculable and manipulable being. On Heidegger's account, the limiting case is Plato's identification of being with the Good: "[T]he idea of the Good completes everything; it is that which embraces all beings as beings. . . . The idea of the Good is the basic determination of all order, of all that belongs together" (*MFL*, p. 116). That is why a new language heedful of these concerns must come to the fore with the help of both poets and thinkers attentive to this problematic.

Before turning to Heidegger's response to the malady he has diagnosed, it may be useful to summarize the achievements of his analysis up to the present point. First, the claims of the science of logic to be paradigmatic for theory as such are shown to fail because the alleged independence or free-floating character of logic reflects a neglect of its ontological ground. This ground remains invisible within the sphere of the science of logic itself so long as logic maintains its identity with thinking *tout court*. If it is argued that the rules of thought can be grounded by creating meta-languages with more reflexive properties, a Heideggerian response must note that further complexity only multiplies the levels of analysis and moves the rules of thought ever further from ontological self-understanding. Second, Heidegger's account of technique shows that inquiry cannot begin with practice in that the ontological root of practice in the present age is expressed as the manipulation and control of nature. Practice rooted in technique can only treat human beings as homogeneous objects of calculation.

Heidegger's description of science as the paradigm for a theory of the real is developed in the context of a pair of interlocking problems: first, the issue of the science of logic and the questions it poses for the understanding of theory *tout court* and second, the emergence of technology as the ruling thought form of the present epoch together with technology's harnessing of theory to its own practices for the domination of nature. The understanding of being that comes to the fore in modern science is imported into moral philosophy whenever the copula, some part of the verb *to be*, unites the parts of a proposition that asserts a value or describes the consequences of a contemplated moral act. Even the careful stipulation of these presuppositions cannot evade a falling into the dominant interpretation of being.

By showing that theory has lost sight of its ontological root and in so doing has transformed thinking into calculative reason, Heidegger has provided an answer to the first of the commonsense questions posed at the beginning of this chapter: Why can moral theories not provide a conceptual foundation for moral life?

Freedom and Being as Possibility

Heidegger's response to the ontological difficulties he has exposed corresponds to the twofold character of the problem. On the one hand, he shows that truth as coherence and adequation has lost sight of its more primordial ground to be found in the manner of being of the human existent, the Dasein. On the other, Heidegger points to the openness of the revealing or coming to pass of truth in contrast to the understanding of it that is integral to technology. Although these rejoinders seem unrelated, they are bound up with one another because both are grounded in Heidegger's interpretation of freedom, an account that remains consistent with his rejection of traditional moral philosophy. Although a postmodern ethic could not proceed without Heidegger's diagnosis of the maladies of theory, I shall argue that, to the extent that his thinking is deconstructive, it bars the possibility for developing an ethic in any received sense, but to the extent that it is insufficiently deconstructive, his thought remains paralyzed before everyday moral dilemmas as well as the enormities peculiar to the present age.

If this deconstructive element is to be brought out, Heidegger's negative response to the modern assumption that the science of logic is both ground and paradigm for all thinking must be placed in the context of the problem of the Dasein as a thinking being. The operational conditions for thought are not, Heidegger contends, the source of thinking but are grounded in the essence of the Dasein. Not surprisingly, Heidegger's interpretations of the Dasein do not confer univocal signification upon it but are dependent on the specific conceptual backdrop against which its structure is delineated. According to the familiar version of *Being and Time*, Dasein is an entity for whom Being is an issue. Heidegger elaborates:

[T]his means further that there is some way in which Dasein understands itself in its Being, and that to some degree it does so explicitly. It is peculiar to this entity that with and through its Being, this Being is disclosed to it. *Understanding of Being is itself a characteristic of Dasein's Being.* (*BT*, p. 32) (Text A)

Nearly the whole of *Being and Time* is devoted to an explication of the relation of the being that is Dasein to the Being of beings. What is essential is that, in Text A, Dasein's thinking is identified with the disclosure of being.

An earlier description of the Dasein, elaborated in the setting of Heidegger's criticism of Leibniz's theory of judgment, differs strikingly from that of *Being and Time*. Heidegger's starting point in this context is the nature of inquiry itself:

In its metaphysical essence, Dasein is the inquirer into the why. The human being is not primarily the nay-sayer (as Scheler said . . .), but just as little is the human being a yea-sayer. The human is rather the why questioner. But only because man is in this way, can he and must he, in each case, say, not only yes or no, but essentially yes and no. (*MFL*, pp. 216–17) (Text B)

On this account, the spirit of inquiry is defined nonteleologically in terms of a why that is freed from the logical canons that result in judgments of truth or falsity.

In Text A the ontological thrust of Heidegger's thinking comes to the fore and has been stressed in most critical interpretations, whereas Text B evinces an epistemological thrust bound up with the need to think transgressively against the canons of logical discourse. The nature of the difference is concealed in Heidegger's explication of the problem of freedom in each context, a difference that is of paramount importance for grasping the treatment of otherness in Heidegger's thought and for opening the way toward a postmodern hagiographic approach.

According to Heidegger, freedom is not bound up with ethics, as has been traditionally asserted, but is integral to the philosophical enterprise as such. There can be no mistaking this point. Heidegger stresses it repeatedly in numerous contexts and, in one of his most forceful statements, contends:

There is in fact a philosophical world-view, but it is not a result of philosophy and not affixed to it as a practical recipe for life. It resides rather in the philosophizing itself. Nor is it, therefore, ever to be read off from what the philosopher may say expressly about ethical problems, but it becomes manifest in what the philosophical work is as a whole. . . .

Philosophizing . . . is grasped in its genuine content only when in such knowledge the whole of existence is seized by the root after which philosophy searches—in and by freedom. (*MFL*, p. 18)

Freedom is not to be confused with a lack of conceptual rigor in contrast to the thinking of the special sciences or of the science of logic. But—and this is the main point—philosophical knowledge is possible only in and as freedom. Contrary to the received view that practical or moral philosophy is concerned with freedom and that metaphysics is the inquiry into the meaning of what is real, now freedom is asserted to be the root of philosophical thinking itself.

Consider the meaning of freedom from the perspective of *Being and Time* where Dasein is seen as the being for whom its being is an issue (Text A). In that context, anxiety is the mood of the Dasein that discloses it to itself as a being suspended in a world, a "wherein" in which the everyday existence of the Dasein is always already thrown. The anxiety before its thrownness exhibits its freedom to the Dasein, its existence as a Being-possible, as a choosing or taking hold of itself through the acceptance or concealment of its thrownness. Delivered over to itself as this self-disclosive, self-projective freedom, Dasein exists as its potentiality for Being (*BT*, p. 232).

Dasein can maintain itself "understandingly" and "concernfully" as "resolute" or "free for its world" and, in so doing, it can forward its ownmost potentialities and those of others. But, Heidegger warns, only when Dasein is most itself can it free others "to co-disclose this potentiality in the solicitude which leaps forth and liberates" (*BT*, p. 344). Heidegger distinguishes actions that spring from resoluteness from those that, depending on a prior ought, arise from guilt. In guilt it is assumed that if only Dasein conformed to an ought, it would actualize itself as a full presence without anguish or care, an interpretation that obscures the thrownness of Dasein and the nullity integral to its existence.

Still less does Heidegger equate solicitude with altruism, an issue about which there is no difference between his earlier and later explications. In *Being and Time* Heidegger argues:

[Solicitude] can take away care from the Other and put itself in his position . . . : it can leap in for him. This kind of solicitude takes over for the Other that with which he is to concern himself. . . . In such solicitude the Other can become one who is dominated and dependent. (*BT*, p. 158)

There is scarcely any distinction between this and Heidegger's comment in *The Metaphysical Foundations of Logic*:

Only because Dasein is primarily determined by egoicity can it factically exist as a thou for and with another Dasein. . . . The egoicity belonging to the tran-

scendence of Dasein is the metaphysical condition of the possibility for a Thou
. . . and for an I-thou relationship. (*MFL*, p. 187)

These assertions are not, for Heidegger, ethical claims but "existential-
ontological statements of essence" (*MFL*, p. 190).

The concept of freedom that is developed in connection with Heidegger's definition of the Dasein as inquirer in Text B has yet to be
considered before we turn to the postmodern hagiographic alternative.
The Dasein of Text B is the site of a crucial lack, of the absence of an
absence: the absence of alterity as an integral restraint to the voracious-
ness of the Dasein. Recall that Text B regards inquiry as issuing in a yes
and no. This formulation is worth pondering first, because it locates
the site of Heidegger's interpretation of inquiry well within the categorial framework of Hegelian dialectic in which the tension of op-
posites is sublated rather than within the polarized alternatives of a
Kierkegaardian either/or. Surprisingly this "yes and no" points to a
comportment of the Dasein treated at length in *Being and Time*, ambiguity (*Zweideutigkeit*), a kind of surmising along with others based on
idle talk or public discourse and, as such, a debased or inauthentic version of circumspection. How then can yes and no cohere with the spirit
of genuine inquiry as Heidegger demands in his early description of
Dasein?

The answer must be teased from Heidegger's account of freedom in
The Metaphysical Foundations of Logic in which Dasein understands the
other from the self outward. The Dasein's fundamental existential comportment is to choose itself, a mode of being Heidegger explicitly dis-
sociates from Kierkegaard's authentic self-choosing in faith as well as
from a narrow solipsistic-egoistic interpretation of the Dasein as a self-
enclosed monad (*MFL*, p. 190). But what then can the cryptic saying
"For-its-own-sake belongs to the essence of Dasein" (*MFL*, p. 191)
mean if it is not to be theologically or egoistically explicated? An egoistic account is especially perplexing because choice in modern philosophy is generally viewed as an expression of "self-spontaneity" in
contrast to mechanistic determinism. For-the-sake-of refers, Heidegger
concludes, to willing, not in its concrete manifestations in acts of will
but in its "intrinsic possibility of willing: freedom" (*MFL*, p. 191). Is
there anything in Heidegger's analysis that binds or tamps down this
freedom? If there is, it cannot be guilt grounded in an ought already
shown to be parasitic upon modern philosophy's "flawed" ontological
ground. The constraints on freedom, Heidegger avers, belong to the

Dasein itself: "Freedom makes Dasein in the ground of its essence responsible [*verbindlich*] to itself" (*MFL*, p. 192).

What can this mean, not only for the concrete comportments of the Dasein but for its essence? If Dasein is as a Being-possible and the strictures of an autonomously or theonomously derived law are ruled out, then the only constraints upon Dasein are factical, the limitations, such as scarcity or social and legal restrictions, imposed upon it by the order of existence. The only counterforce to the élan (*Uberschwung*) of the Dasein is the world itself (*MFL*, p. 193). If this is so, then apart from the world, Dasein is restricted only by its own desires and velleities. *The yes and no that Heidegger attributes to Dasein's inquiring belongs not to the structure of its thinking but to its desire.* What else can be meant by Heidegger's assertion: "Dasein [as a freedom] is in itself *excessive*, i.e. defined by a primary insatiability for beings—both metaphysically as such and also existentially, in factic individuation" (*MFL*, p. 192)? As evidence of the Dasein's "primary insatiability," he cites dissatisfaction and settling down as ontic nonprimordial behaviors of Dasein. The factical lack of freedom expressed in the paralysis of despair, the affective disclosure of the impossibility of the possible, in an inverse sense attests the limitless character of the Dasein's freedom.

If Heidegger's ontological analysis of theory and his account of technique provide grounds for rejecting moral theory, further inferences stemming from this analysis, specifically his rejection of altruism based on the notion of Dasein's freedom, cannot be dismissed. But if concealed in Heidegger's description of freedom there is yet another structure, other than Dasein's thoughtful interrogation of being, a structure of desire, then Heidegger's characterization of the Dasein will have shown itself to be fissured by an alterity it cannot extrude, an otherness or exteriority that is now inside the thinking of the Dasein. I shall call this "excessiveness of Dasein" (*MFL*, p. 192) Dasein's voluptuary structure or "wild" desire and its parallel ethical structure, desire for the Other. Both are exhibited in saintly life.

The Voluptuary Structure of Desire

Comparatively little attention has been paid to the absence both of desire or the erotic and of rage or violence in Heidegger's analysis of the Dasein. Although the Greek tradition from the pre-Socratics to Plato treats eros not only as a part of soul, a psychic disposition, but as a cosmic principle, for Heidegger eros is not a primordial structure of human existence. Similarly, *thymos*, or irascibility, a distinctive part of soul for Plato, has no place in Heidegger's description of the Dasein. Astounding too is the fact that Heidegger comments extendedly on the works of Hölderlin, Nietzsche, Rilke, and Trakl but attends almost not at all to the erotic dimension of their works. No less strange is Heidegger's analysis of economy in terms of the "ready-to-hand," of Dasein's relation to an instrumental nexus, without implicating desire in this structure of utility. Yet the trace of desire makes known its absence, fissures the Dasein in Heidegger's early account of the Dasein where it is described as "primary insatiability."

I referred earlier to desire's voluptuary structure. The term *voluptuary* derives from the Latin *voluptas*, "pleasure," and is related to the Germanic and Old English root *wel*, "to wish or will," the root of the Old English *willa*, "desire or will power." The Latin *velle* ("present stem vol") is the basis for the words *velleity*, *voluntary*, *benevolent*, and *malevolent*. It is not surprising that the root form *wel* has still another meaning expressed in the derivative stem *vol* and expands into a different chain of words. *Wel* can also mean "to tear, pull, or wound." The Old Norse *valr* means "the slain in battle" and is linked to Valhalla and Valkyria, the "chooser of the slain," one of twelve war goddesses.[6] Rage, ire, and irascibility (the traits incorporated in Plato's *thymos*) and desire (the Platonic *eros*) are borne in German and Old English by a single root *wel*. What signification does will as sheer force, thrust, or motion take on for a Dasein that is, on Heidegger's acknowledgment, "primally insatiable" and "responsible to itself," a Dasein untouched by the Other, if not that of voluptuary or wild desire and violence? The striking aporia in Heidegger's text, the absence of violence and desire as the primordial signification of will as "being-possible," cannot be explained by the thrownness of the Dasein without showing the transgressive character of that which always already infiltrates willing.

The unity of desire and violence, Plato's *eros* and *thymos*, ignored in Heidegger's account of the Dasein, is fundamental to Bataille's introduction of heterogeneity and difference into the subject and constitutes an entering wedge for a postmodern revisioning of Heidegger's thinking. Although the context for Bataille's social philosophy is the sociology and philosophy of culture deriving from Durkheim, Mauss, Lévy-Bruhl, and Roger Caillois, his description of subjectivity can be freed from its backdrop of outdated anthropological assertions when it is examined side by side with his coruscating aphorisms and subversive works of fiction. More germane to the present argument is Bataille's account of the relation of desire to the violent underside of the sacred, an analysis that I shall argue has been reconfigured in Levinas's description of two types of sacrality, ethics or the transcendence of the Other and the chaotic unboundedness of undifferentiated being that Levinas calls the *il y a*.[7] The analyses of Bataille and Levinas, taken together, provide a response to the second commonsense question cited at the beginning of this chapter: Why should one assume that stories of saints' lives can lead to altruism when hagiographic narrative so often recounts acts of terrifying violence and painful excess?

Bataille's account of desire is based upon the notion of expenditure whose protean expressions reveal themselves in every sphere of existence: in the radical profligacy of nature, in the violence of human societies, in the destruction of sumptuary objects, in cannibalism, in the erotic forays of the libertine, and in the ascetic practices of the mystic. The significance of consumption lies not in cumulative acquisition for its own sake but in the loss and negation generated by gratuitous and violent destruction: "[L]uxury, mourning, war, cults, the construction of sumptuary monuments, games, spectacle, arts, perverse sexual activity (i.e. deflected from genital finality)" constitute the real and symbolic artifacts of excess.[8] Citing the potlatch ceremony of the Northwest Coast Indians, Bataille asserts that relations of production and utility are secondary to those of sumptuary loss[9] and that integral to the destruction of wealth is the establishment of social hierarchy that degrades the producers of wealth and elevates the class that controls expenditure.

Human existence as the dialectical relation of work and desire must be seen against the backdrop of an expenditure that yearns for expression yet is reined in by the necessities of production, the very process that makes accumulation possible. Every human being is, for Bataille, a microeconomy always already torn apart by the polarities of a desire that is infinitized at every level of symbol and actuality on the one hand and by work and the rational constraint it imposes upon the sumptuary domain of desire on the other.

Human life, Bataille argues, is distinguished from animal existence by work. In order to make the effort to produce commensurate with output, calculative behavior is required: work and rationality go hand in hand as constitutive of human production. Yet the human subject is not a purely dianoetic and laboring being, a self-present individuality, but one riddled by erotic and violent impulses whose excess must be given expression. "I MYSELF AM WAR," Bataille cries in "The Practice of Joy Before Death."[10] These oppositions give rise to a second scission, the restrictions imposed by work and institutionalized by society, the taboos, the prohibitions or laws that only imperfectly control the infinite excess of the inner strivings of human beings. Instituted to restrain the desire and violence intrinsic to human life, taboos are only effective because they call upon the forces of the excluded sphere, relying on negative emotions for their power. But no exclusionary measures are enough for the total suppression of these strivings. Instead, they are permitted expression in socially sanctioned transgressions, the sacred or semisacred spheres of war, carnival, sacrifice, public feasts, and ceremonials. The sacred is to be thought of as an oxymoron: controlled free expression, whereas, by contrast, the profane is the domain of taboo and restriction.

Christianity, Bataille argues, overturns this arrangement by ascribing negative value to the profane realm of work and positive value to the sacred now cut off from its transgressive root of desire and violence. Because these forces are far too profound to suppress completely, they are transformed by Christianity into the experience of the divine. To see how this comes about, we must examine a final set of polarities, that of continuity and discontinuity. Human beings live as separate individuals, each identical to itself and discontinuous with every other individual. But death returns the separate existent to a continuity with the totality of what there is. Similarly eroticism, the distinctively human expression of biological sexuality, is equally fatal to discontinuity. The two, death and sexuality, are linked through the concept of expenditure and excess. In sexuality a "plethora" or superabundance of living material comes to the fore. In and through the distension of this plethora of material, "discontinuous individuals spring from the calm of repose to a state of violent agitation" from which they will emerge as separated beings once more.[11] In sexual encounter, individuals lose themselves briefly in an undifferentiated experiential continuum:

[T]he other individual does not yet appear positively, it is negatively linked to the disturbed violence of the plethora. Each being contributes to the self-negation of the other, yet the negation is not by any means a recognition of the other as a partner. . . . The violence of the one goes out to meet the violence of the other.[12]

With this analysis of continuity and discontinuity, it is possible to see how Christianity deviates from the general pattern of religion in the treatment of the forces struggling to come to the fore in sacrally sanctioned transgression. Christianity, Bataille argues, does not lose its religious character but stresses one of the aspects of religion, love, expressed as continuity "reached through the experience of the divine, . . . the essence of continuity."[13] Bataille describes a twofold process:

Basically the wish was to open the door to a twofold love. According to Christian belief, lost continuity found again in God demanded from the faithful boundless and uncalculated love, transcending the regulated violence of ritual frenzy. Man, transfigured by divine continuity was exalted in God to the love of his fellow. Christianity has never relinquished the hope of reducing this world of selfish discontinuity to the realm of continuity afire with love. The initial movement of transgression was thus steered by Christianity towards the vision of violence transcended and transformed into its opposite.[14]

Bataille argues further that the other source of continuity, death, is experienced as a threat to the discontinuous self of the workaday world. Christianity tries to accommodate both aspects of existence, continuity and discontinuity, by attributing endless postmortem continuity to the discontinuous individual. The Christian stress on love together with its promise of life after death has transformed the turbulent impulses of religion into their harmless and nonviolent aspect.

The benevolence of Christianity is contrasted with the religions of sacrifice in which both violence and desire find expression. The death of the discontinuous individual, the sacrificial animal, is seen to assure the continuity of the participants' lives in the sacrificial rites. What is more, Bataille asserts, "the act of love and the sacrifice" both reveal the flesh and replace the ordered life of the individual with a "blind convulsion of [the] organs."[15]

It can be argued persuasively that the theological and historical orchestration of the experience of the sacred is far more complex than Bataille's description allows. The worth of his analysis lies less in its examination of culture, although even here its influence has been considerable, than in bringing to the fore the duplicity and doubleness of the existing individual, the *Zweifaltigkeit* that Heidegger acknowledges in *The Metaphysical Foundations of Logic* but whose importance he represses in *Being and Time* by consigning it to the status of an ontic phenomenon, an inauthentic manifestation of the Dasein. (I retain the term *Dasein* for *human being* although, of course, it is not used by Bataille.) For Bataille to be a Dasein is to be it in the manner of not being it: that is to say, to work and to think are always already a resistance to what the Dasein "is," a fissured subjectivity. Teetering between humiliation and growth, orgy and abstinence, depravity and exaltation, Bataille's subject, unlike Heidegger's Dasein, can never get hold of itself. "Fixing existence in any given ipse," Bataille argues, is impossible.[16] Everywhere ipseity or selfness is constituted through negation as difference and determination. "Being in fact is found NOWHERE and it was an easy game for a sickly malice to discover it to be divine," Bataille writes.[17] Constantly displacing itself, being becomes a labyrinth in which the nonsubject shot through with loss and negation loses its way. In a characteristically scatological formulation triggered by a visit to the great apes in the London Zoo, Bataille writes in "The Jesuve," one of his best-known essays:

For it is not self-evident that the noble parts of a human being (his dignity, the nobility that characterizes his face) instead of allowing only a sublime and measured flow of profound and tumultuous impulses, brusquely cease to set up the least barrier against a sudden, bursting eruption, as provocative and dissolute as the one that inflates the anal protuberance of the ape.[18]

The distinction between debasement and the sublime is also stood on its head when Bataille in *Inner Experience* asserts: "The I is the expression of the universal," in contrast to the wildness of what he calls the *ipse*, the nondiscursive subject that cries out to the Other and annihilates the I in both self and Other.[19]

It is the phenomenology of desire as exorbitance that makes the excesses of saintly lives comprehensible. To rephrase a Freudian apothegm: where desire is there must excess be. So too the duality of excess is integral to saintliness because desire can only be exhibited through the two modes of continuity, death and eroticism. Saintly being cannot close itself off from the *negatitités*, the turbulent forces that strive for expression, because saintliness is always already situated within love and the risk of death. *Altruism is intrinsically excessive, the sumptuary expenditure of the life of the discontinuous individual.* Bataille does not mount a defense for religion despite its excesses or attack it because of them. Instead, he creates a meta-narrative that can be applied to saintly altruism and forges a language whose sinuosities comport with the character of hagiography. But Bataille insists that his meta-narrative does not exclude the reader from the oppositions of taboo and transgression, work and desire, continuity and discontinuity, from the extravagant subjectivity of *homo religiosus*, in that the reader is always already within the transgressive space of these polarities.

The commonsense question then about how saintly lives can generate altruism when they express violence or sexual license receives a partial answer in Bataille. By elaborating the meaning of the subject as excess, a language for the disclosure of an infrastructure of unending desire both in the macroeconomy of social existence and in the microeconomy of the desiring subject is developed. The pain and wounding of desire, its restlessness, its insatiability and obsessiveness belong also to the discourse of altruism.

The Indentured Subject

If Bataille accounts for saintly excess, he does not explain how altruism itself is generated, the question bound up with the value of saintly lives for ethics. It is here that the philosophy of Emmanuel Levinas helps to "fill in" what remains unthought in Bataille's thinking. If Bataille's economic metaphor of expenditure is extended, the point of intersection between Bataille's subject of excess and Levinas's account of altruism should come to the fore.

Recall that, just as Heidegger's Dasein is ahead of itself through anxiety and care, Bataille's subject not only nullifies what it has acquired but expresses its sumptuary losses even before it has incurred them. The concept of anticipatory expenditure must be applied to saintly life. *The saint is an extreme sumptuary, a subject that spends more than she/he has to the point of expending her/his own substance.* Every subject is always already in debt, but the saintly subject has consumed the capital of her/his own psychological and corporeal existence. Excluded from Bataille's analysis are the questions: "To what or to whom is the subject of expenditure indebted?" and "How does this indebtedness come about?" Perhaps the excess of violence and desire can be expressed in ways other than war and sacrifice, other than eroticism, without destroying itself as excess. It is to the question of nonviolent, nonnullifying alterity that Levinas directs attention.

Recall that Bataille's description of excess arises in his account of continuity, the abandonment of the separate self that comes about in the plethora or superabundance characteristic of sexual merger, although, he argues, even in the most all-consuming erotic experience the alterity of the Other is never fully lost. For Bataille, the social manifestations of such experience are expressed as orgy or sacrifice whereas Levinas interprets this excess in ontological terms, as the loss of separateness in anonymous, impersonal, and indeterminate being, the *il y a*, for which night is a primary metaphor and horror the mode of affective access to it.[20] This idea is adumbrated concretely in Blanchot's novel *Thomas the Obscure* in which Thomas (suggesting Saint Thomas and doubting Thomas, among other possible identities), already dead and therefore beyond the fear of actual death, experiences this horror: "On all sides night closed him in. He saw, he heard, the core of an infinity where he was bound by the very absence of limits."[21]

But excess can be opened up in an altogether different way. The other person is experienced not only as a visible form but as impinging on the self, as proximate to oneself.[22] In an obscure passage that requires explication but one that is important for making sainthood thematic, Levinas writes: "Immediacy is the excessive proximity of the neighbor, skipping the stage of consciousness, not by default but by excess. . . . It does not culminate in confusion [but in] an absence in which the neighbor abides."[23] Levinas's claim is that the Other is experienced as—to use an archaic formulation—a drawing nigh, a nearing that is not a merging with the self "in confusion" but an "excess" and an "absence."

As absence, the Other creates a restlessness in the self, "an insatiable desire, a contact, a love and responsibility," that can become neither the fulfillment of a sexual intention nor the content of a cognition.[24] But the Other is also an excess, the "more" of what, for Levinas, eludes intellectual grasp. Inscribed in the face of the Other is the trace of a transcendence that has escaped or, alternatively (from my point of view but not that of Levinas), the track or spoor of the totality of humankind or of all sentient beings, past, present, and future, none of which can be made fully present. In contrast to the false sublimity of the face that conceals the violence and desire of a self-aggrandizing egoity described by Bataille, a point to which I shall return in chapter 7, the face concentrates in itself the totality of human suffering.

But if both the *il y a* and transcendence are without positive determination, how is the *il y a* to be distinguished from transcendence? Blanchot asserts that, by imitating transcendence, the *il y a* "expose[s] the essential ambiguity of transcendence and the impossibility that this ambiguity be measured according to truth or legitimacy."[25] Is the usefulness of saints' lives to others not diminished when no clear line can be drawn between sheer or brute excess and saintliness? To be sure, there is no certainty about whether an allegedly saintly life is derived from obsession with the Other or from brute excess, but it has also been shown that there is no general agreement about which moral theories are to be preferred, which ends of human life to be endorsed, or which actions worth performing.

But is the uncertainty of saintly life not different from that bound up with moral theories in that theoretical uncertainty is attested against the ground of a prior certainty whereas the uncertainty of saintly existence is unsurpassable? Consider first the case of theoretical uncertainty. Suppose, for example, that an assertion about saintly altruism as a motive were integrated into a moral theory about saints. It might then be said that "X's saintly life derives from altruistic motives." But it could be argued that saints' motives, like motives generally, are inscrutable and therefore the statement could not be falsified: One could never be sure that altruism was the psychological force driving saints' lives. This type of uncertainty depends upon lack of access to what could falsify the proposition, knowledge of the saint's thoughts. But the uncertainty of saintly existence refers to the negation and absence within saintly subjectivity itself, an ungroundedness that does not rest on prior certainty, on something other than itself that is fixed, complete, and self-transparent. Like a detective novel in which the solution to the crime is never revealed because it is never clear that there has been a crime, saintly identity necessarily remains mysterious: it can never be established that there was a saint or proved that the primacy of the Other is the source of action.

Some further elaborations are demanded by the claim that uncertainty is an unsurpassable condition of saintly life. The first has already been aired in the discussion of Heidegger's account of theory. The demand for certainty is bound up with a conception of truth derived from the science of logic and the rationality of technique, metaphysical posits whose ontological ground can never be brought to light by logic and technique. The second reverts to the character of saintly Dasein itself. It is a strength rather than a weakness of hagiographic description that the will to certainty as self-will is supplanted by a transcendent or human Other because self-will obstructs saintly action.

This leads to the third related consideration, that of the egoity of the narrative's addressees. The hagiographic text lays hold of the reader so that the hermeneutics of reading—the addressee is after all a "reader" or recipient of the saint's story—is transformed into a struggle of writing. That is to say, the addressee must reinscribe, not merely re-present, the narrative as her/his own story. In the process of reinscription a new life is shaped. The "I" of her/his own story, like the "I" of the saint, is increasingly fissured by the Other, who is seen as "ordered to my responsibility, torn up from culture, law, horizon, context."[26] To be sure, saints sometimes surrender to temptation so that their lives may be rent by backsliding and self-doubt. But the reader may be better able to make the saint's motions after her/him when perfection is seen to be flawed. In following moral rules, the individual experiences each rule as a measuring rod and a possible occasion for failure. But the piecemeal approach bound up with rules that highlight moral failure is avoided when the differential nonstructure of a life claims its addressee.

Another question raised at the beginning of this chapter, "Why is altruism not a universal condition?" takes on added force in the light of the preceding analysis. Could it not be argued that the relations of ego and Other constitute a transcendental structure of the moral life so that responsibility for the Other simply becomes an attribute of the subject? In that case all lives should be lived altruistically even if experience regularly attests the contrary. Levinas's account of the face as an epiphany proscribing violence is open to this objection: if the face of the Other is posited as a universal condition of social existence, the rarity of altruism requires explanation.

It should be argued instead that a rudimentary sensitivity to others exists, but not everyone yields to the pressure of this primordial encounter. Uncontrolled desire and violence may be expressed by laying claim to the Other, by seeking to secure oneself against thrownness and ultimate nonbeing in all of its forms, social, psychological, and symbolic. Saints, to the contrary, like gifted composers or musicians are exceptional individuals, virtuosi of the moral life. Almost everyone can reproduce a simple melodic line upon hearing it, but not all are able perform a Bach cello suite, improvise a jazz harmony, or sing lieder. This analogy can be misleading if it is taken to imply that saintliness is something "natural," an inborn talent, rather than the result of copious exertion and self-sacrifice.[27] Although the capacity to expend egoity, to consume oneself, is a gift, it does not preexist what it becomes but is retrospectively so constituted in the practice itself. Because of its infrastructure of negations, saintliness, like talent, can never be fully realized.

Still another factor, the factuality of hagiography, precludes the notion of full saintly realization. The temporal horizon of factual interpretation intersects the saintly narrative so that the narrative can never be brought to closure. For the most part, the closer the historical events, the more pressing the existential claims upon the life of the interpreter. Yet, paradoxically, it is also more difficult to respond to the saintly address (the hagiographic vocative) because the outcome of immediate events is unforeseeable. To insert oneself into a hagiographic chain is fraught with the risk of misprision, of mistaking a demonic or simply indifferent narrative for a saintly one. On the other hand, to avoid a story's imperative opens another risk, that of a moral inertness that belongs to the nonhuman or to things. There can be no certainty of inscription because the meta-narrative that draws the tale into the future has not yet been written.

Political Saints

It is easy enough to "canonize" those who devote their lives to healing physical or psychological suffering, yet much present-day distress often emerges in a historical and political context from which this suffering is inseparable. The citizens of Chambon, for example, to be described later as risking their lives for others, were confronted with political quandaries peculiar to the twentieth century. Their stories belong to a new context and political climate in which man-made mass death brought about by human agency forms the backdrop of everyday existence.[28] Is it possible to speak of responses to these problems in terms of saintliness when the political sphere is already contaminated by relations of power?

These dilemmas are highlighted in the life of the South African opponent of apartheid Nelson Mandela. Consider Mandela's life in hagiographic transcription:

Nelson Rolihlahla Mandela is born into the royal family of the Tembu in Umtata in 1918. As a child, he absorbs stories told by tribal elders about the times before white settlement when the country was without distinctions of wealth or class. In 1941, Mandela comes to Johannesburg, where he encounters the urban poverty of the shantytowns, meets activists Walter Sisulu and Oliver Tambo, and is introduced to the African National Congress. In 1948, the Afrikaner nationalists assume power and implement the policy of apartheid by enacting laws that make possible the forcible relocation of persons and the breaking up of families. Mandela and Cachalia, the son of a supporter of Gandhi, inaugurate the Defiance Campaign of 1952, a program of nonresistance. Although acknowledged not to have been Communists, they are banned under the Suppression of Communism Act. In June 1955, the Freedom Charter stressing the equality of blacks and whites is drawn up and becomes the policy of many anti-apartheid groups. In December 1956, Mandela and 156 others are arrested for treason. Although tried in the heated atmosphere of the shooting of the Sharpeville protesters, they are nevertheless acquitted in 1961. During this period Mandela marries his second wife, Winnie Madikezela. Prior to South Africa's being declared a republic in May 1961, Mandela asks for a National Convention to draw up a nonracial democratic constitution and calls for a strike when this overture is rejected. With the failure of these efforts members of the *Umkhonto me Sizwe* (Spear of the Nation) replace nonviolence with sabotage. Mandela goes underground and is apprehended in August 1962. He is charged with inciting a strike and leaving the country illegally. Tried and convicted in Rivonia along with six others, Mandela tells the court "The government should be in the dock" and not he and that he is willing to die for the end of racialism in South Africa. Found guilty, he is imprisoned on Robben Island with the other Rivonia men, where he endures hard labor, and psychological and physical persecution. When possible he reads and studies and continues to assist other prisoners. In 1982, Mandela is transferred to Pollsmoor Maximum Security Prison on the mainland near Capetown. In 1985, President

P. W. Botha offers Mandela release if he will refrain from planning acts of violence. Mandela replies, "I cannot and will not give any undertaking at a time when . . . the people are not free." On 2 February 1990 President F. W. de Klerk announces Mandela's impending release. Two days later, Mandela is freed.[29]

This account is condensed largely from material in Winnie Mandela's autobiography, and, like many medieval hagiographic works, it is idealizing, reflects multiple authorship, and includes numerous hagiographic claimants: Sisulu, Twomba, Helen Joseph, and other antiapartheid activists. Winnie's life also takes on a semihagiographic character partly on its own account and partly through its linkage with Nelson's history. Recent charges against her have called her status into question, a point to which I shall return.

For hagiography, childhood is an impressionable age in which there is often a premonitory vision of a later mission articulated in terms of an earlier, more pristine tradition. The place of childhood visions of Jesus or the Virgin, frequent features of Christian hagiography, is taken up functionally by Mandela's encounter with the tribal elders. Adolescence is a preparatory phase of a life mission in the form of an encounter with the wider problems that will constitute later life tasks, and adulthood is a time when earlier and current challenges are met. The mature life reflects the tensions of temptation and resistance to temptation, of the conflict between the law and the subject's mission, often interpreted as a contrast between the law's hypocrisy and the saint's struggle to bring out the law's inner intent. Thus Derrida in an essay on Mandela writes: "The exemplary witnesses are often those who distinguish between the law and laws, between respect for the law that speaks immediately to conscience and submission to positive law (historical, national, institutional)."[30]

For Mandela, release from prison proffered on the condition that his mission be abandoned is a temptation, whereas the sublation of egoity in a larger black identity constitutes the structure of the overcoming of this temptation. In Christian hagiography saints may undergo lengthy periods of isolation in desert or monastery, whereas in Indian tales they may become forest wanderers, a sequestering that is often marked by painful self-scrutiny and self-mortification. Prison or slave labor camps serve this function in contemporary hagiography although of course such suffering is rarely self-imposed.

It can be objected that this or any structured interpretation of saintly life stations the interpreter outside the narrative thereby creating an interpretive meta-language that neutralizes its moral force. Thus those with critical consciousness appear to be uninvolved in the text's moral imperative of compassion and benevolence. Having understood the *form* of hagiography, the reader seems to be freed from the responsibility of attending further to its claims. But this argument reflects a double misreading, first of the grammar of hagiography and second of the addressee's situation.

Recall first that the grammatical property of voice in hagiography does not privilege the indicative of narration but the imperative. The reader is called forth by a story of saintly life even if she/he refuses the address of the imperative so that the very act of rejection already constitutes an acknowledgment and interpretation of the hagiographic summoning. Second, the text's addressee is not an observer, an onlooker, or a reader of others' stories but always already herself/himself a story, a Dasein (in the amended sense I have given the term) confronted by multiple narrative strands. To take the point of view of an onlooker is to posit the Dasein as either indifferently detached from the affairs of others or fearful of the consequences of engagement. This point is exhibited in Greek tragedy, for example in Sophocles' depiction of a submissive Ismene as contrasted with a defiant Antigone.[31]

It can be further objected that my account of altruism stipulates that all of mankind is the unit of significance for altruistic behavior. Political hagiography, to the contrary, defines altruism in terms of national or ethnic identity such that one group may benefit from an action whereas another may be harmed by it. But, it can be replied, the sphere of human action is by its very nature limited and inevitably involves proximate rather than remote persons or groups. What is more, even if the *stated* unit of hagiographic discourse is limited, the *implicit* unit may be the totality of humankind, both "black and white" in Mandela's terms. But have not narratives that stipulated the totality of humankind themselves, in practice, turned into the blood baths of history? When the logic of negation is interpreted as force and applied to a social entity designated as other, have not innumerable human beings been exterminated? Has not Stalinism, for example, with its promise of universal salvation, ended in the actual destruction of vast numbers of people just as surely as particularist ideologies?

Here too hagiography has an advantage over theoretical moral discourse with its remote abstraction and (frequently) its contrived examples. Not only does hagiography stipulate the unit of signification as "all humankind" or "all sentient beings" to which altruism is to apply but it reveals itself at the level of concrete factuality. Recall that it is not argued here that there is no *hors texte*, no factuality, but rather that what is outside the text is not open to unmediated grasp. Narrative factuality is the manner of hagiographic unfolding, and it is as story that the life of Stalin or of Pol Pot has been exposed as enmeshed in violence, mass death, and destruction. Because stories cannot be brought to closure, it is important to see that choosing to insert oneself into a hagiographic narrative carries considerable risks. At the same time, to be as a moral "Dasein" is to think and act in terms of narrative inscription and to remain open to the perils of historical incompleteness. Thus recent charges that Winnie Mandela's bodyguards were responsible for the death of an innocent boy and, during Nelson's imprisonment, that she acquired considerable wealth and lived lavishly show the difficulty bound up with political hagiography.[32]

The argument about altruism as excess invites a question that takes as its starting point not the degeneration of saintly life into violence but the possibility that violence itself is one of the imperatives of saintly existence. Can it not be argued that force is required when one's opponents use violence and, if so, whether this comports with the thesis that saintly altruism mandates the elimination of human suffering without inquiry into the moral character of the sufferer? Before addressing this question it is worth recalling the structure of vulnerability, the sensorium that not only registers sensations opening out into cognition but also expresses the body's vulnerability, wounding, and outrage discussed in chapter 4.

Levinas describes this structure in terms of the ego's prehistory. Before it knows or acts, egoity is always already hostage to the Other. Levinas declares: "It is through the condition of being hostage that there can be . . . pity, compassion, pardon and proximity. The unconditionality of being hostage is not the limit case of solidarity, but the condition for all solidarity" (*OBBE*, p. 117). What is more, suffering not only means the wounding and outrage undergone but includes within the outrage itself "an expiation for the other's fault" (*OBBE*, p. 118).

Actual narratives often bear witness to the traces of alterity that intersect with narrative factuality at the point where the restraints on violence are mandated intratextually. Excess (in Bataille's terms) expressed as expenditure in the interest of the Other will show itself in the narrative as a willingness to sacrifice oneself or to issue commands of self-sacrifice to the texts' addressees rather than in imperatives invoking the use of force. Gandhi, Martin Luther King, and Nelson Mandela (at least early in the anti-apartheid campaign), all of whom have, in various contexts, been hagiographically interpreted, are examples. Violence too will be seen as a strategy invoked in extremis in the absence of alternatives. The rejection of force may fissure the narrative structure itself by the insertion of a rule or principle: thus, Mandela says, members of the *Umkhonto* are told that "on no account are [resisters to apartheid] to injure or kill people."[33]

In his essay on Mandela, Derrida's question is: "Who is Nelson Mandela?" We cannot know whom to admire because, he suggests, Mandela is already captive to a historically determined identity but at the same time is always already free. Derrida writes:

We will never cease to admire him, himself and his admiration. But we don't yet know whom to admire in him, the one who, in the past, will have been the captive of his admiration or the one who, in a future anterior, will always have been free (the freest man in the world . . .) for having had the patience of his admiration. . . . The one refusing as early as yesterday a conditioned freedom.[34]

This obscure formulation brings to light the tension between a self that sees itself as having fulfilled its mission and therefore as satisfied or admiring of itself and a self that is other than itself and that has constituted itself as free. Both aspects are integral to the one who "is" and "is not" Mandela. In political hagiography, the self must inspect its conduct retrospectively, approve or disapprove of itself, and thus always admire or despise itself. What is deemed admirable, however, is the choice of political freedom, but the moment this freedom becomes the object of admiration it ceases to be free. The freedom that has become admirable undergoes yet another reversal: it cannot be the object of admiration because it is freedom for the Other who resists discursive articulation. "Your freedom and mine cannot be separated," Mandela tells black Africans when he refuses Botha's offer of release.[35]

The Logic of Exemplification

In considering the life of Mandela hagiographically, I argued that sensibility (in this case expressed as wounding and outrage) is the corporeal structure which enables saintly individuals to respond to suffering and others who witness the saint's work to be inspired by it. Still, it can be asked, because the lives of political saints are bound up with the exercise of political power, does not political charisma constitute a unique temptation, one that is best held in check by a prior conception of virtue? To be sure, this danger is inherent in the case of the saints, gurus, sages, and *tsadikim* of the world's religious communities both historically and at present, but it can still be argued that saintly excess is restrained by the saint's devotion to love and charity. Still, the problem of unchecked *political* saintly excess is especially vexing in the absence of prior normative constructs.

One account of the saint's power to engender imitation that appears to avoid this difficulty is that of the saint who is an exemplar of virtue. This view, as explicated by John S. Hawley, entails two senses in which the notion of exemplarity is to be understood. Hawley explains:

According to the word's first meaning, the saintly example instantiates and thus clarifies general principles of morality and qualities of character that can be articulated as meaningful and understood as possible for all participants in a society or community of faith. . . . In the second sense, by contrast, the saintly exemplar does not accord so easily with the moral standards that articulate a culture's highest sense of itself. Often saints do not heighten ordinary morality. They implicitly question it by seeming to embody a strange higher standard . . . [that] cannot be articulated in normal discourse.[36]

On the face of it, there is some resemblance between my argument that saints exceed ordinary morality by making extraordinary demands upon themselves and others and Hawley's view that they "embody a strange higher standard." But it is just this notion of exemplarity that I wish to challenge with a postmodern view of hagiography. Saintly individuals who fall under Hawley's first type, those who instantiate general principles, are examples or embodiments of qualities that are subordinated to a controlling and totalizing discourse, one that already takes for granted the relation of universal to particular. Saints of the second type, those who embody "a strange higher morality," are representative of a whole that is hard to define or, as Wittgenstein puts it, of something that could not be pictured or said. What Hawley means is that the saint's life is an embodiment of something unique and exalted that cannot be directly expressed in language.

In order to show what cannot be said, Wittgenstein had recourse to the idea of samples. This notion, employed by Nelson Goodman[37] to explain how values function, is a particularly well-developed account of the view of exemplarity that Hawley appears to advocate. Hawley's view can be restated in Goodman's terms: When we say that the saint is an exemplary figure (in Hawley's second sense), we mean that the saint's acts are samples of ethical behavior and the saint's life as a whole a sample of compassion, generosity, and love. Thus Mandela's life would be a sample of the virtues of courage and self-sacrifice and could be evaluated in terms of how effectively it "measured up" to prior notions of heroism and altruistic behavior. Because this account is a particularly powerful recent expression of the received view of moral conduct as exemplary, a postmodern challenge to it must examine its presuppositions and further implications.

Consider first Goodman's account of exemplarity in *Ways of World-making*. There, to be sure, Goodman focuses on aesthetic values, but the notion of samples can be transferred to an ethical context. The utility of samples, he argues, lies in the power they have to help us learn some properties of the whole of which they are samples.[38] In the case of Mandela, his behavior would, in Goodman's terms, be scrutinized to learn what goodness, compassion, and love are like.

One pitfall in considering things as samples is already anticipated by Goodman himself: if a sample is taken to learn about the whole of which it is a part, how can we tell if the sample is helpful? Must we not already know the character of the whole? Goodman counters this objection by showing that samples are useful if they are fair samples, those which have been produced in conformity with finely tuned inductive techniques.[39] Thus, although all the air in Los Angeles can never be tested for pollution, a good idea of what it is like can be formed by taking a fair sample. In adumbrating this idea, Catherine Z. Elgin writes:

Our problem is [one] of projection—of deciding under what circumstances the properties exemplified by a sample can be projected onto a larger whole. . . . And just as agreement with inductive practise is required to determine which predicates are projectable, agreement with sampling practise is required to determine which samples are fair. Both practises evolve over time as we learn more about the domain under investigation.[40]

But applying this notion of exemplification to an ethical context presents special difficulties. If the life of the saint is considered as a sample, what is that life to be considered a fair sample of? Perhaps of compassion or love, but surely also of justice and fairness. If so, there is something circular about the method of fair sampling that cannot be gotten round by the pragmatic argument Goodman employs: in practice, the use of inductive technique enables us to know the whole when we know a part. It can be argued against Goodman that the saint's life is, among other things, a fair sample of fairness. But to take a fair sample involves a prior notion of fairness so that an account of the saint's life based on the notion of fair sampling is circular. But, it could be countered, the term *fair* as applied to samples does not mean fairness in the sense of equity or justice, the notions appealed to when referring to saints. Instead, fairness means proportionality, context relevance, and the like.[41]

But it is just here that the genealogical analysis to which postmodernism can appeal points up the weakness of the sample paradigm in its amended form as proportionality and context relevance. The idea of fairness is set against the backdrop of inductive technique, a technique that is itself parasitic upon more primordial conditions of equity found in interpersonal relations such as sharing and returning what is not one's own. *A fair sample is one in which the part conveys the quality in question so that it does not mislead anyone about the whole.* This necessary recourse to concepts of equity arising in interpersonal relations shows that inductive technique is already bound to a prior order of social transactions. Fairness and equity emerge from an antecedent social order aptly described earlier by Bataille as encompassing both work and powerful currents of violence and desire, or by Levinas as the world affected by the advent of the Other.

Might it not be argued that Goodman's account has greater latitude than I have allowed, that, in fact, it can accommodate both an inductive and a qualitative view of fairness? In this connection Catherine Z. Elgin points to the multiple factors that determine rightness of exemplification. One requirement of rightness is that what a symbol exemplifies and the system to which the exemplified properties belong be appropriate to one another. When an intrasystematic conflict arises, the solution may involve adjusting the system to accommodate the antagonistic properties. If this is impossible, plural systems may be invoked without epistemologically privileging any. Epistemological tolerance of multiple systems, she claims, enriches understanding and, in any case, often resists inclusion in a single all-embracing system. Thus Elgin contends:

[T]he works of Jane Austen and those of Karl Marx contain telling descriptions of social conditions and of the ways economic and social factors constrain our options and limit our lives. . . . But the systems in which their accounts are cast employ different symbolic devices and . . . categories. Austen's descriptions are fictional, ironic, specific, and expressive. Marx's are factual, literal, general and descriptive. We cannot simply conjoin their accounts to arrive at a better understanding of social conditions, for we have no way to give a univocal interpretation to their conjunction.[42]

Can this spirit of tolerance be extended to notions of fair sampling by considering both equity as derived from a social context and aptness of procedure as arrived at through empirical investigation as equiprimordial? This notion of tolerance, parasitic upon the idea of what is context-appropriate, presupposes a notion of the proper, of what can be brought to plenary presence before a consciousness that judges. It takes for granted that, at bottom, there is a reality, namely, fairness, and that different modes of representation enrich one's grasp of it. Just as the behavior of light can be profitably interpreted in terms of waves or quanta, so too social conditions can be fruitfully described in a variety of ways.

Consider, Elgin urges, the writings of Marx and Austen. There is in both a core meaning, the social problems themselves, and a multiplicity of discourses that can bring these problems to light.[43] On Elgin's account, discourses are instrumental, the means for representing an underlying reality. The works of Austen and Marx become, on her reading, heuristic systems striving for intrasystemic coherence and representational fidelity. Thus the tolerance for differential conceptual practices leaves unquestioned the protocols and canons of systematicity itself: relations between part and whole, coherence of parts, elimination of cognitive dissonance by acts of extrusion or enlargements of the system.

It is worth noting that a phenomenological treatment of exemplarity is beset by similar difficulties. Max Scheler argues for pure types that he calls value-persons, of which the saint is the highest type.[44] Good and bad factual models are instances of value-persons. Thus Mandela would be an instance of the political saint as a value type. The historical model, the actually existing individual, originates in the exemplar:

It is certain that factual models originate for man *in* . . . other factual men as objects of some kind of experience. Yet these men, as they are experienced, *are* not the exemplars themselves. Although we frequently say, "This X is my model," what we mean by "model" is not at all this factual man in his flesh and blood . We mean that this X is an *exemplification* of our model proper. . . . The model itself is seen in men who function as exemplars. . . . But the model is not extracted or abstracted from the empirically contingent natures of such men, nor is it found as a real or abstract part of the exemplars.[45]

Like Goodman, Scheler thinks of the paradigmatic individual as exemplifying an ideal type although he does not have recourse to statistical or other scientifically derived norms in his description of types. In that respect, unlike Goodman, Scheler resists invoking the idea of fairness as fair sampling, an idea that can be traced to prior conceptions of equity and justice that, in turn, depend on interpersonal transactions from which values are subsequently derived. What is more, although he concedes that the order of experience precedes the order of reflection, Scheler fails to see the implications of this acknowledgment. If abstraction does not precede embodiment, then *something*—the proscriptive character of the human face, according to my argument—is prior to the *concept* of fairness or justice, and the saint's healing actions are prior to the concept of compassion. Were the converse true there would be no alleviation of physical or psychological suffering without antecedent conceptual values by means of which they could be justified, nor would there be saints without prior exemplary types. The saint opens the possibility for value types by providing the warranty for the values which are then brought to light.[46]

By no means am I suggesting that values and the rules and laws that express them are to disappear and that multiple intersecting narratives are totally to supplant them. Instead, it follows from what I hope has already been shown that contractual relations are possible only on the prior ground of the renunciation of violence. The making of compacts does not precede but can only supervene upon the total or partial elimination of force, for how can compacts emerge if the war of every man against every man is in progress? There must always already be at least two nonwarring parties who can come to agreement before there can be laws proscribing violence. Even those compacts that appear to be made under warlike conditions are, in actuality, forged when violence is suspended however briefly. Thus compacts do not end the state of nature; to the contrary, the state of nature must terminate before there can be compacts.[47] This means that a society's moral principles, beliefs, and legal system are incorporable within a previously existing archaic narrative of war and peace that is not yet hagiography but presupposes a cessation of pandemic violence and a recognition of alterity as the precondition of peace. Such a reorientation highlights the extreme fragility of compacts. Furthermore, it opens the way for considering hagiography as the reinscription of the ancient narrative of war and peace upon the finite body and psychological life of one who brings it to singular expression.

I ARGUE that hagiography is to be preferred to moral theory in shaping moral discourse and action not because there are difficulties associated with specific theories but rather because of the manner in which theory is grounded in modern philosophy. Heidegger shows that the notion of theory derives from a particular ontology, that of modern science. What is taken as true is determined by the science of logic, by what can be asserted in a proposition or, in Kant's terms, a judgment.

But the description of truth conditions laid down by the science of logic cannot be self-grounding. What is more, logic is the product of a tradition that cannot justify or account for itself. A second difficulty that attaches to the notion of theory, a difficulty described in Heidegger's later work, is that theory grows out of a specific two-pronged interpretation of the being of nature. Nature is regarded on the one hand as made up of calculable homogeneous units that can be manipulated at will and on the other as comprehensible in terms of causal laws. Human beings are construed as part of nature and, as such, open to the same mode of interpretation as other entities. This view of being and truth, transferred pari passu to moral philosophy, calls into question the preunderstanding of human existence which grounds its interpretations of value.

Showing the difficulties connected with theory does not yet explain why saintly altruism is to be preferred. Two accounts of the Dasein or human being in Heidegger provide an opening into this question. The first takes the Dasein as thrown or ungrounded being but does not preclude the Dasein's retrieval of itself in the free acceptance or rejection of its thrownness. In an earlier formulation, Heidegger suggests that the Dasein is not only free but also insatiable so that the way is prepared for interpreting human subjectivity as fissured by desire.

George Bataille's account of desire depicts the erotically traduced character of human existence, of life as governed by the tension between work and rationality on the one hand and desire and violence on the other. In many religions other than Christianity transgressive rites through which desire can express itself are found. For Bataille, desire and violence are interpreted in economic terms as excess, exorbitance, and inflated expenditure. Desire also articulates itself in the yearning for continuity with the whole of existence, a continuity that is attained with the death of the individual.

Although Bataille describes the structure of desire, he fails to account for its altruistic form. The philosophy of Levinas shows that excess can express itself in the disinterested desire for the Other who is in the trace of transcendence. But if everyone in encountering others experiences the disinterested desire for the Other, why is everyone not altruistic? I argue that saints are uniquely sensitive to others, that this endowment or talent is not to be construed as an a priori given but as a capacity that is constituted retrospectively, as it were, through saintly practice.

It can be further objected that one may never know whether saintly altruism is self-interested or the expression of a disinterested desire. In reply, it can be argued that certainty would nullify the character of existence as risk and constitute a misreading of life histories as self-certifyingly hagiographic. Whether there are political saints is a question that *en principe* cannot be decided. The narrative's addressee must risk making the motions after the story's protagonist or refuse to do so, itself a significant choice. Nelson Mandela's life can be read in the light of this analysis.

It can be argued that lives like that of Mandela are better interpreted as exemplars of positive human characteristics such as compassion and courage. Nelson Goodman and Catherine Elgin assert that exemplarity can be explained in terms of fair samples, that is, of parts that show the context-relevant properties of some specified whole. I argue that the notion of fairness in sampling is parasitic upon a prior notion of equity that, in turn, depends on the ungrounded relation to the Other. Values and rules are not excluded by my analysis but are seen as embedded in prior contexts of narrative and alterity.

6

"Think of your breed; for brutish ignorance
Your mettle was not made; you were made men,
To follow after knowledge and excellence."

Dante's *Inferno*, Canto VI

Under the shape of his sail, Ulysses,
Symbol of the seeker, crossing by night
The giant sea, read his own mind.
He said, "As I know, I am and have
The right to be."

"The Sail of Ulysses," Wallace Stevens

The canto of Ulysses. Who knows how or why it came into
my mind. . . . As if I . . . were hearing it for the first time: like
the blast of a trumpet, like the voice of God. For a moment I
forget who I am and where I am.

Survival in Auschwitz, Primo Levi

Hagaddah of German Rite. Italo-Ashkenazi 1478. The coming of Elijah on Passover
eve when the door is being opened for him upon the recitation of "Pour out thy wrath."
The illustration is symbolic not only of national but of personal redemption of each
member of the seder. Library of Congress, Washington.

Language without Alterity: The Suppression of Reference and Mood

IF SAINTLY work is distinct from everyday work, are saintly and quotidian language also different from one another? An inquiry into the structure of hagiographic narrative in chapter 2 yielded an account of the form in which saintly life is transmitted and influences others. But this analysis did not take up the questions of truth and meaning or their relation to a world apart from language. Contemporary accounts of language and reference may seem remote from the matter of saintly life. Yet what and how the saint comes to know what she/he knows, whether there are unique features that belong to the "truth conditions" of the language saints speak, and whether there is a discourse of alterity that differs from what can be said about material and conceptual objects—all are related to interpretations of language and truth generally, the subject of the present chapter.

No brief account could address even a single one of these questions in detail. I hope only to sketch the ontological commitments grounding some contemporary philosophies of language and to bring out the temporal infrastructure presupposed by their interpretations of truth and being. Thus, in considering the relation of formal languages to ontology, claims about existence and coherence that are of interest to those working *within* the framework of language philosophy will not come to the fore. Instead, an effort will be made to bring out the ligatures that bind the way truth is established to an implicit metaphysical ground, a question generally ignored by this philosophy.

Logic, no less than psychology or history, is rooted in pretheoretical, tacit modes of positing a world. The difference between the way the world is reflected in formal systems and in other modes of world projection is that formal systems are more remote from a lived matrix. But once a given logic and its justifying conditions are related to their pretheoretical roots, its ontological commitments can be brought out and these, in turn, interrogated with respect to their implications for the problem of saintly language.

In order to avoid later misconceptions about hagiographic speech, it is important to see the difference between recent and classical accounts of how language is bound up with the world. For Aristotle, logic reflects the orderly and hierarchical structure of being. Knowledge conforms to the organization of objects, beginning with objects of sense, moving to first principles and ultimately to the highest-order principle of intelligibility, the Unmoved Mover. Thus, for Aristotle, the warranty for propositional truth is not based on rules that determine coherence; instead, rules that determine coherence reflect a prior order of being. For the most part, the understanding of being in current logics is derived by considering the entities referred to intrasystematically rather than as reflecting features of what is antecedently real. In the present context what is at stake is not the ontic status of objects as internally ascribed but the intrinsic connections between the system's interpretation of truth and its tacit metaphysical supports. Despite deep and important differences, an analysis of this infrastructure links some basic claims about the nature of truth and language in the phenomenological philosophy of Husserl and in the analytic philosophies of Quine and Davidson to a common temporal framework, that of presence. The treatment of presence in these philosophies will be interpreted as excluding the distinctive temporalization of alterity integral to saintly life.

At the same time, these accounts will be shown to exclude or to evade the question of reference—of the world's extralinguistic being and the being of other persons—through a conceptual neutralization of sensation. Contemporary philosophies of language that domesticate the world's otherness are not wrong in any straightforward sense but instead reflect an ambiguity belonging to language: its capacity to evoke the world as other while suppressing that otherness. The order of concepts regiments sensation at the same time that it confers signification. How and why this is so is analyzed with considerable subtlety by Husserl, Quine, and Davidson, who, despite basic differences in their starting points, reflect the neutralization of reference in their descriptions of the linguistic web.

Saintly life, by contrast, presents a noncognitive relationship to sensation, one that will be interpreted not by introducing an older and discredited doctrine of sense data but by bringing to light one of sensation's primary functions: vulnerability, perviousness, or openness to the world's impingement on the self both as pain and as enjoyment. A crucial function of the connection of saintly life to sensation—the impact of the world upon corporeality—and the contrast this presents to the exclusion of sensation or to its neutralization in contemporary philosophies of language is a main theme of the present chapter. In addition to the problem of reference, Donald Davidson also considers the question of mood, analyzing the imperative as a distinctive verbal form. Despite this acknowledgment, imperatives are interpreted in terms of their factual core. Thus propositions in the indicative mood are thought to anchor imperatives, a contention that brings to light Davidson's sublation of the force of imperatives.

Once the meaning of imperatives is disentangled from the indicative, a phenomenological account of the imperative will be shown to reveal its doubleness. Commands not only are bound up with saintly life but, as dictating action, may also eventuate in violence. I hope to resolve this ambiguity by exploring the command's relation to self and other.

What is endorsed here is not a return to a realistic Aristotelian ontology on the one hand or a straightforward rejection of the regimentation of reference on the other. Instead, what is required is a reorienting of philosophical scrutiny so that the "custodian" of language, the Other who addresses me, comes to the fore. The intralinguistic traces of otherness demand an attentiveness to the communicative contexts of language, to links to alterity that enter hagiographic speech and leave their marks in ordinary language.

Phenomenology and Language

In his analysis of Husserl's writings, especially of the first of the *Logical Investigations* and of *Ideas I*,[1] Derrida asserts that a view of being and time common to the Western philosophical tradition grounds Husserl's thinking. Far from being a presuppositionless philosophy as Husserl claims, phenomenology takes for granted that being means being present, and this in two distinct ways: First, being is ascribed to a thing when it presents itself to consciousness as the object of a sensible intuition. Second, a subject or self is (exists) only insofar as it is present to itself. The being of the subject is its immediate self-presence in conscious acts. The task of phenomenological analysis is to gain apodictic (certain) evidence, a knowledge of objects through immediate and intuitive apprehension of them. Husserl distinguishes the intuiting consciousness present to itself from an empirical stratum, what stands outside of and is opposed to the self-presence of mental life.[2]

This stratification is reflected in Husserl's account of language. An empirical level or *indication* is a movement of consciousness toward a content not yet present and therefore still outside consciousness, and *expression* is a purely linguistic function tied to the logical powers of language.[3] This distinction roughly approximates Frege's use of reference and sense, respectively. Because Husserl determines the model of language on the basis of theory, he subordinates the indicative level to expression. Primordial indication is dumb, a mere pointing out (*Zeigen*), but the alterity of what is thus shown comes to fruition in the unity of indication proper (*Anzeigen*) with what is expressed (*Hinzeigen*). If expression is to fulfill its function of making objects present, it must itself be a transparent medium which mirrors or re-presents the preexpressive level. Its task is to protect and restore the stratum of sense by transforming it into an ideal conceptual and universal form. The object, now divested of its empirical content, can be expressed without having to pass through the world and, as such, is indefinitely repeatable. Having transcended empirical determination, its ideal being requires a medium that can preserve it. This medium is the voice speaking to itself. The model for expression which, for Husserl, *is* meaningful discourse is the interior monologue, the inner conversation that preserves signified meaning by relying on the silent voice of solitary mental life.

Derrida thinks of the action of voice for Husserl as an "auto-affection" promoting a conception of being as identical with itself, present to itself forming the substance of a subject. Derrida writes:

The operation of hearing oneself speak is an auto-affection of a unique kind. On the one hand it operates within the medium of universality; what appears as signified therein must be idealities that are *idealiter* indefinitely repeatable or transmissible, the same. On the other hand the subject can hear or speak to himself and be affected by the signifier he produces, without passing through an external detour, the world, the sphere of what is not "his own."[4]

While speech *appears* to unfold in time, the ideal objects that emerge in speech are "omnitemporal." Even the source point of indication, the primordial impression which speech ultimately expresses, is already atemporal. It is, Husserl says, "spontaneously generated." Without past or future, when this now is no longer, it is constituted through auto-affection as a past *now*. Two conclusions can be drawn from Husserl's analysis of indication and expression: first, signification depends on intrasubjective speech, the voice that communes with itself, and, second, the temporal framework of silent speech is the present.

Husserl's analyses of language sublate two modes of difference, each through the deployment of a distinctive strategy: the difference of one event from another in the stream of staggered temporal events[5] and the difference between the world's exteriority and consciousness.[6] Temporal dispersion is controlled by synchronizing events into constellations of meaning such that each pattern is governed by a single significative intention. Consider as a case in point a theory about the cooperating behavior of several viruses. Single observations of virus behavior in which viruses act simultaneously as they attack living cells become significant only when a sufficient number of instances is considered and these instances understood as exhibiting a general pattern. Similarly an organizing theme that functions as the end or purpose of a story, such as the didactic purpose of a fable, suppresses the temporal dispersion of its events. Fables, as I argued in chapter 1, display theoretical rather than narrative intent.

The second mode of sublating alterity in Husserl subordinates the world's immediate presence to the intentionality of a consciousness that bestows meaning on or intends its objects.[7] What is present to consciousness does not unfold before the passive gaze of consciousness like the unwinding of a film but receives its identity through an intention *as* some specific this or that. The fact that objects are meant (*Gemeint*) or intended does not entail their construction by the subject but rather the coming to fruition of a content by way of intending acts of consciousness. Nor does intentionality deprive experience of vividness. Thus the redness in Matisse's painting of a woman in red is not dimmed when this redness fills out a specific perceptual intention but is instead affirmed as brilliantly and strikingly crimson. Every bestowal of perceptual or cognitive meaning, every affirmation of truth and falsity, presupposes relations of intentionality.

Each of the ways in which alterity is undermined, the suppression of temporal dispersion and the sublation of the world's otherness, exhibits what I should like to call bad faith, a kind of hypocrisy built into language itself. In the case of temporal and spatial dispersion, the apparent transparency of consciousness, its claim to deliver truth and presence, covers over the way in which objects actually manifest themselves. Objects come to be for the intending consciousness spatially through a successive showing forth of facets of the object, or temporally in the succession of events. Yet, across the dispersion of their appearing, a single meaning is conferred "always promising to be *other* and other, yet always identifiable."[8]

The bad faith of the self's subordination of the world's otherness also overlooks the way in which the world impacts upon the self. Not only is a meaning bestowed on discrete conceptual and material objects, but also the world weighs on the subject, impacts on sensibility as lived quality or as sensation that may express itself as painful wounding or trauma. For example, the world's alterity might be experienced positively in actual physical contact with the elements by plunging into them, into air and wind in skydiving or the water's depths in scuba diving. Negatively the trauma of a car crash is an unmediated and crushing impingement of the world upon corporeality. Even if an overlay of cognitive significations accrues to these bodily transactions, their apprehension is not mediated primarily by thinking or representing but is directly experienced as the pleasure of immersion in the world or as painful contact with it.

Language must suppress alterity if it is to express general significations. Ideality, identifiable threads of meaning that crosscut individual events, is required if there are to be meanings at all. Language touches on singularity only through the word's power to confer signification through a process that first sublates individuals. The bad faith of ideality that can be discovered in Husserl's view of language is not simply the extrusion of the level of indication, of unrepeatable and discrete events from the linguistic web. Such exclusion is necessary if meaning is to be conferred. Instead, it is the rendering invisible of the infrastructure of otherness through whose means, as it were, language speaks. The traces of alterity that find their way into language as well as experiences that occur otherwise than as cognitively or linguistically mediated are ignored or stretched to fit models of linguistic ideality.

The Absent Other: Quine and Davidson

Like Husserl in the Fifth and Sixth of the *Logical Investigations* and in *Ideas I*, Quine believes in normative epistemological discourse, governed by canons of objectivity and rationality. For Quine, these canons are continuous with those of science. But scientific language, he argues, depends upon intralinguistic contexts far removed from the impingements of experience. At the same time, Quine also appeals to fixed stimulus meanings which both precipitate and cash out at least those utterances which are reports of observations:

Observation sentences peel nicely; their meanings, stimulus meanings, emerge absolute and free of all residual verbal taint. Some sentences such as "Neutrinos lack mass," are different from observation sentences in that no hint of the stimulatory conditions of assent or dissent can be dreamed of that does not include verbal stimulation from within the language.[9]

The referential stratum of Quine's account (like Husserl's indication) is excluded from the intralinguistic web when the sentence's subject, for example, the term *neutrinos* in the preceding citation, reflects a level of theoreticity and abstractness that precludes its being cashed out by an appeal to stimulation.

In order to see how much weight stimulus situations can bear in establishing meaning, it would be futile to look to intralinguistically determined sentences. Instead, Quine constructs a *Gedanken* experiment in which he stations himself inside an existing language at the periphery of a hitherto unknown language to determine how, in the absence of intralinguistic clues, the unknown language is to be translated. Perhaps stimulus situations can provide a core of common meanings. But if so, how would one go about determining this? Because there are many admissible linguistic correlations with stimulus situations, the stability of stimulus meanings is questionable. This drives Quine to appeal to a common human nature to establish the parameters of admissible correlation: "What provides the lexicographer with an entering wedge is the fact that there are many basic features of men's way of conceptualizing their environment, of breaking the world down into things common to all cultures."[10] Stimulus meanings are limited to occasion sentences, those which command assent or dissent when accompanied by prompting stimulation.

In sum, just as Husserl domesticates reference through the ideality of expression, Quine limits the role of stimulus meaning to occasion sentences. When confronted with an unknown language, stimulus situations may be correlated with some linguistic bit but this is a measure taken in extremis with no assurance of accurate correlation. (In the absence of a common intralinguistic web, there is, in any case, nothing but stimulation to appeal to.) Without a reference language which permits cross-checking, the accuracy of translation cannot be determined. Stimulus situations are to be called upon as needed and regimented by the supplement of a known language if meanings are to be fixed. At no point is alterity permitted to pierce the fabric of intralinguistic signification.

The unreliability of reference is also maintained in Quine's account of synonymy. It had long been noticed that a common referent may elicit different meanings. Consider Frege's by now standard example: two names, each having a different meaning, are applicable to the same referent. "Morning Star" and "Evening Star" may be ascribed to the identical celestial body but are not synonymous. In the absence of complete knowledge about the object, reference fails to establish sameness of meaning. Quine suggests that collateral information may cash out the meaning of sentences when stimulus meaning alone does not suffice. For example, assent to the sentence "Bachelor," he asserts, may be prompted by a glimpse of an appropriate face but still requires collateral information to round out the meaning. What is more, the same stimulus (the physical face) may fail to elicit "Bachelor" if there are two or more speakers, an objection that Quine sees as fatal for regarding stimulus situations as determining conditions for intersubjective synonymy.[11]

In sum, stimulus meaning, the referential stratum of linguistic signification, cannot by itself establish synonymy intersubjectively. Could it not be argued that at least the collateral information required to "round out" meanings introduces the otherness of persons because such information is a social product? Is this not all the more so in that Quine claims a speaker's understanding of a word or sentence depends not on some specifiable sector of language but on the funded lingual capacities of a speech community, on language as a whole? Similarly, in the case of ontic commitments, the *totality* of our warranted beliefs about what there is, is for Quine "the unit of empirical significance."[12]

This contention provides the support for Quine's by now familiar critique of classical empiricism's account of sensation. One of the dogmas of empiricism, Quine claims, is reductionism, "the belief that each meaningful statement is equivalent to some logical construct upon terms which refer to immediate experience."[13] But, he continues, it is all of our funded beliefs taken together that allow the meaning of individual statements to come to the fore. If alterity cannot be attributed to reference in the reductionist sense of correlating stimulus situations with linguistic bits, Quine thinks that at least language and belief are communally grounded. And, if signification is intersubjectively established, does this not avoid the solipsism that Derrida attributes to Husserl's account of meaning?

Far from affirming the alterity of other persons, Quine's view of socially grounded signification interprets the Other as another self. To be sure, collateral information is relied on to ground meaning because consensus can be secured about what there is and such accord is, in turn, the result of a common human essence. But for Quine, the Other is commensurable with the self because of structural identities that characterize human beings. This homogeneity is accounted for by a theory of evolution: the emergence of a common human nature developed through geological time as the result of environmental stresses. The hypothesis of a human nature together with the notion of progressive human development is never problematized nor its naturalistic implications explored. Instead, a complex theory of language is grafted onto a philosophical anthropology that leaves the relations of self and world unexamined. The ineradicability of the problem of reference is the intratheoretical sign of what is not made thematic in Quine's discussion of language, an account that stands or falls with the way in which human existence is understood.

The suppression of alterity occurs at yet another level of Quine's description of synonymy. He argues that collateral information may supplement stimulus situations for the same speaker, but the same stimulus may fail to elicit an identifying word, for example "Bachelor," from two different speakers. How then is intersubjective synonymy to be established? This difficulty can be overcome, Quine claims, if we think of "Bachelor" and "Unmarried Man" as intrasubjectively synonymous first. These terms may then be synonymous for each and every member of the community although the stimulus triggers that elicit them will vary from person to person. But, and this is the point I have been leading up to: there is no bypassing the single speaker constraint since here alone the sameness of stimulus meaning criterion functions unchecked. The price for intrasubjective synonymy is, just as it was for Husserl, a solipsistic version of reference. If synonymy is to be established, the differential character of reference open to intersubjective accord must be tamed and alterity excluded from the web of language. Thus Quine writes:

What we find is that, though the concept of stimulus meaning is so very remote from "true meaning" when applied to the observational occasion sentences, "Bachelor" and "Unmarried Man," still synonymy is defined as sameness of stimulus meaning just as faithfully for those sentences as for the choicest observation sentences—as long as we stick to one speaker. For each speaker "Bachelor" and "Unmarried Man" are . . . alike in stimulus meaning without having the same meaning in any acceptably defined sense of meaning (for stimulus meaning in the case of "Bachelor" is nothing of the kind). Very well, let us welcome the synonymy and let the meaning go.[14]

Not only is synonymy intrasubjectively grounded, but the holistic view of language, the backdrop for our warranted beliefs, is, in the end, equally dependent on the single person constraint. Michael Dummett, in his criticism of Quine, contends that holism is itself parasitic upon intrasubjective conditions:

Total holism as appears to be advocated in "Two Dogmas" is necessarily solipsistic. . . . [because] it must give an account of adoption of beliefs by any one individual which may not be shared by others. We have thus to think of a total theory as representing the totality of beliefs held at any one time: others may speak the same language as he; but each man's theory is his own.[15]

By contrast with the sublation of reference in Quine's view of language, in saintly life sensation (Quine's "stimuli") has an altogether different function, that of exposure to world and Other. Language confers notional order upon sensation in order to complete and stabilize its meaning. But for hagiographically mediated existence, the Other is a primordial "stimulus situation," an impingement of exteriority upon self. Saintly corporeality as exposure to the world apprehends the Other as a pressure, even a wound or trauma, replete with moral meaning. This openness to the world uproots the self's interests and supplants them with the needs of the Other.

To be sure, the saint speaks in everyday fashion about everyday matters but her/his language is subordinated to a more primordial layer of significations. For saintly life, this other constellation of meanings is not expressed in sentences whose signification is warranted by a backdrop of socially secured collateral information. Instead, what is definitive is the context-specific need of the Other that intrudes into the pattern of quotidian concerns with the Other's demands that set the saint's life on its way and open the discursive space of hagiography.

Reference in the context of saintly existence is a function of the interface of world and Other, a nearness that is corporeally felt rather than conceptually cognized. This sensing of the Other through the body as a whole deposits traces in ordinary language. Many languages contain expressions such as "Her fate weighed heavily on me" or (more strongly) "I felt his pain" and negative expressions such as "His presence was an imposition." These locutions are not a mere *façon de parler* but must be construed as metonymic substitutions for what is primordial in the encounter with another. Even if the regimentation of reference is required by the language of factuality, the extension of the ontological commitments of factual language to language generally subordinates the Other of hagiographic discourse to unexamined beliefs bound up with reference.

Classical empiricism, by contrast, presupposes an uninhibited reliance on reference as the foundation of signification. Because the saint relies upon the absolute otherness of other persons in establishing meaning, the saint carries the philosophical suppositions of empiricism to an extreme. To be sure, saintly life is not an effort to adapt the epistemological agenda of empiricism to the conditions of moral existence. Instead, it relocates the source of alterity from the exteriority of the object of experience to the Other. Derrida's remarks about empiricism help to clarify the point:

The true name of the inclination of thought to the Other, of this resigned acceptance of . . . incoherence inspired by a truth more profound than the logic of philosophical discourse, the true name of this renunciation of the concept, of the a prioris and transcendental horizons of language is *empiricism*. For [empiricism] has committed . . . the fault of presenting itself as a philosophy. And the profundity of the empiricist intention must be recognized beneath the naivete of certain of its historical expressions. It is the dream of a purely heterological thought at its source. A *pure* thought of *pure* difference.[16]

The reinstating of reference in the sphere of moral action opens the possibility for the renewal of empiricism along lines that avoid the difficulties bound up with reference in theories of language. In saintly life the Other is the ultimate referent that can never be brought into plenary presence.

Reference and Mood: Davidson

Further implications of Quine's account of stimulus meaning and the establishment of synonymy are drawn out by Donald Davidson. Reluctant to abandon a theory of reference to account for meaning, Davidson nevertheless believes that stimulus meaning is notoriously unreliable as an anchorage for establishing sameness of meaning. Quine had already stressed the indeterminacy of translation and reference but had not gone far enough. Davidson explains:

I think Quine understates his case. If it is true that the allowable evidence for interpreting a language is summed up when we know what the acceptable translation manuals from His to Ours are, then the evidence is irrelevant to questions of reference and ontology. For a translation manual is only a method of going from sentences of one language to sentences of another, and we can infer from it nothing about the relations between words and objects.[17]

Reference is defined as "a relation between proper names and what they name, complex singular terms and what they denote and predicates and the entities of which they are true,"[18] and appears to be an indispensable aspect of language. On the face of it, it is counterintuitive to hold that sentences can be meaningful, true or false, without further grounding their semantic content in extralinguistic elements. Davidson explains that, although a theory of meaning must include an account of truth, a piecemeal theory of truth that appeals to the selected semantic features of names and predicates fails because it omits two strategic factors. First, it cannot account for other aspects of the theory's basic vocabulary such as specifying the truth conditions for conjunction or disjunction. Second, equally intractable but deeper, it cannot resolve the problem of relating a nondiscursive function, reference, to language. Thus Davidson elaborates:

To "live with" the concept of reference means . . . to take it as a concept to be given an independent . . . interpretation in terms of non-linguistic concepts. . . . [T]he essential question is whether it is *the*, or at least one, place where there is direct contact between linguistic theory and events, actions or objects described in non-linguistic terms.[19]

These difficulties, especially those bound up with the problem of reference, lead Davidson to appeal to the concept of satisfaction, an intralinguistic relation "between predicates and n-tuples of entities of which the predicates are true."[20] But an absolute theory of truth, one that is not relative to some particular conceptual scheme or model, can only show that the truth conditions of a sentence are *satisfied* if and only if the condition stipulated by the predicate can be applied to the entity about which it is predicated. Thus, for example, "an entity satisfies the predicate 'x flies' if and only if that entity flies."[21] It is futile to ask for any further cashing out of the relation.

Davidson's departure from Frege's account of reference is, as Michael Dummett argues, radical. For Frege, Dummett insists, "we really do succeed in talking about the real world, a world which exists independently of us, and it is in virtue of how things are in that world that the things we say are true or false."[22] What is more, Dummett contends, Frege relies on the name/bearer relation rather than semantic role as the model for reference. "The referent of an expression is its extralinguistic correlate in the real world."[23]

If an absolute theory of truth cannot shed further light on names and predicates, Davidson thinks, it can show how the truth of a sentence in some natural language depends on the sentence's structure. There need be no concern about the theory's failure to account fully for the preanalytic concept of truth. Once no nonlinguistic account of reference is possible, the best a theory of truth can do is to "state the extension of the concept of truth for one or another language with a fixed vocabulary." But the felt need for extralinguistic anchorage leads Davidson to offer the hope that a distinction between the account of truth conditions "*within* the theory" and "explanation *of* the theory" will supplement or take up the theory's internal ontological slack by supplying a meaning for reference.[24] Outside the truth theory, reference is to be construed as a "*posit*," a supplement to the theory of truth. A theory of meaning "should take the form of absolute truth. If it takes this form we can recover a structure of sentences . . . with ontological implications of the usual sort. Reference, however, drops out. It plays no essential role in explaining the relations between language and reality."[25]

The difficulties described earlier in connection with Quine's description of meaning can be ascribed a fortiori to the more stringent regimentation of reference in Davidson's discussion of meaning. But the cordoning off of reference makes an explanation of its function all the more pressing. Davidson is obliged to append a codicil or supplement to his general theory, the interpretation of reference as supplementary, a "posit" to round out his view of truth. But the role of the supplement in a theory of truth is not peripheral to its ontological commitments. Derrida has analyzed the function of supplementarity to cover the aporias that come to light when some form of ideality is found wanting. He argues that the supplement is something added on to a theory's self-proclaimed fullness that reveals its built-in fault lines and absences.

Applying Derrida's account to Davidson, what is declared to be an innocuous addition—reference as a posit—is an essential element of the theory without which its explanatory force would be dissipated. Because the refractory element destabilizes the theory, it is extruded from it but remains a linchpin of the theory as an organized whole. Derrida writes in connection with Rousseau's concept of grammar in *The Essay on the Origin of Language*:

There must (should) have been plenitude and not lack, presence without difference. From then on the dangerous supplement . . . adds itself from the outside as evil and lack to happy and innocent plenitude. It would come from an outside which would simply be the outside. This conforms to the logic of identity. . . . but not to the logic of supplementarity, which would have it that the logic be inside, that the other and the lack add themselves as a plus to replace a minus, that what adds itself to something takes the place of a default in the thing.[26]

Difference is not the only property linked to language that resists inclusion in an absolute theory of truth. Frege had held that, apart from sense and reference, sentences may also exhibit *force*. J. L. Austin noticed that sentences not only say but also do something. Sentences are speech acts that depend upon the conditions of utterance.[27] Davidson holds that force is expressed in the grammatical mood of a sentence, indicative, imperative, interrogative, and so on. The interpretive question raised by mood is how the meaning of sentences is changed as a result of shifting from the indicative to other moods. "To the whole array of attitude-attributing locutions," expressions conveying orders, hopes, commands, expectations, and the like, Davidson claims to offer a new approach.[28]

Attitude-ascribing sentences are to be interpreted paratactically, decomposed into an indicative core together with an expression that syntactically represents the nonindicative part that Davidson designates as the mood-setter.[29] Like the function keys on computer templates that by themselves do nothing, mood-setters as described by Davidson give force to something else, the sentences's indicative core. The mood-setter is itself interpreted as a sentence and is thus rendered "semantically tractable," conforming to a standard theory of truth. The truth conditions of the mood-setter are said to hold when the indicative core has the specified illocutionary (performative) force.

Integral to Davidson's theory of mood is the preservation of the indicative core in the relations between indicative sentences and corresponding sentences in other moods. This core remains stable as moods vary. Force, expressed by moods other than the indicative and especially by the imperative, is subordinated to indication, the verbal form that denotes acts or states as an *objective fact*. The concept of factuality, the making present of some object (in Davidson's version detached from the idea of consciousness integral to Husserl's discussion), transposed to a linguistic frame of reference, dominates the understanding of being and time. The paratactic decomposing of imperatives is especially significant in the context of saintly life in that the imperative is the grammatical mood that dominates hagiographic narrative.

Violence and the Imperative

In the phenomenological and analytical philosophies of language just considered, reference was seen to be neutralized as a condition of both truth and meaning. The alterity of the world barred the possibility of propositional conformation to the way the world is without the mediation of ideal constructs. Kant had already concluded that the world is accessible only through the spatial, temporal, and categorial conditions of cognition with which phenomena appear to be in accord. But for Kant, there is no assurance that what is open to the understanding is what there is.[30] Husserl expanded and deepened Kant's account by refining the description of the access routes to phenomena, directional pathways, or intentions that originate in consciousness. Husserl's perspective reflects an intensification of the turn to the subject characteristic of modern philosophy.

For Quine and Davidson the notion of an intentional consciousness is superfluous, a residue of the Cartesian ghost in the machine. Instead, they respond to a worry about the world's unknowability by focusing on language's internal coherence, the way in which the conditions of representation are intralinguistically distributed. For Quine and Davidson (as for the early positivists) speculation[31] about an unknowable core of things is a philosophical disease whose symptoms mark the language of metaphysics. The task of linguistic philosophy is therapy: to limit the pathology of metaphysics so far as possible by regimenting philosophical language—stipulating the truth conditions of propositions and how they are to be satisfied. For reasons already shown, the conditions of truth and meaning thus established sacrifice the otherness of world and other persons.

Science, to be sure, establishes referential relations with the world not in piecemeal fashion but as a whole. Yet the propositions of science are, as Dummett shows, dependent on intrasubjective conditions in that theories incorporate beliefs about the world that do not float in linguistic space but must be adopted by individual subjects. It would not be far from the mark to characterize linguistic philosophies whose conditions of truth and meaning are in important respects intrasubjectively established as egologies.[32]

These accounts of language bring to light the *unavoidability* of language's subordination of the world's otherness. For Husserl, if meaning is to be communicated, the level of sense must be transposed into an ideal conceptual form. Similarly, stimulus situations are seen to be nearly worthless in determining meanings for Quine and Davidson in that such situations become intelligible when supplemented by intralinguistic information. But their accounts fail to describe traces of otherness that inscribe themselves into language because radical alterity resists direct communication. What is other cannot become the subject of a descriptive proposition because descriptions form part of a discourse whose formal conditions are established and controlled by the subject. Alterity must communicate itself otherwise than predicatively.

Other persons present themselves not only as subjects of assertions but, more primordially, as moral "stimulus situations": the sheer existence of the Other challenges the self with moral force and inflicts upon it disquieting moral demands. Traces of the Other are incised (as it were) in language in the form of grammatical mood, specifically the imperative, which functions within language as attesting the corporeal "presence" of the Other. The way in which the Other is revealed was discussed in detail in chapters 2 and 4. At present it is enough to notice that, in subordinating the imperative to the indicative, most language philosophies privilege the factual rather than the moral stratum of language.

But is it not the case that the imperative mood more often than not expresses a command that sublates the interest of the Other? Is not the imperative voice a grammatical property of legal language, an expression of power even when justified, and, as the grammatical mood of unjust laws, a manifestation of the abuse of power? And what of imperatives that enjoin or inflict violence apart from the context of positive law?

The purpose of imperatives is to act on a will, generally to cause another to initiate or refrain from some action which may or may not belong to a moral context. Propositional clusters like "Close the door. It's cold outside" or "Don't water the garden. It rained only yesterday" are examples of imperatives mandating morally neutral actions. Less usual is the command that alters belief or reinforces what is already believed. "Listen to the opposition candidate. You may change your mind" and "Don't believe the accused. He is probably lying" are such propositions. For the most part imperatives mandating belief are bound up with the initiation of action. To command another generally implies the basic freedom of the Other to refuse what is ordered.[33] But there is the appearance of paradox in the issuing of imperatives, even of nonmoral imperatives. The moment the Other conforms to the command, the two-sidedness of freedom, the freedom to refuse commands, is undermined. A freedom that maintains itself as freedom cannot conform to the will of the one commanding without losing itself as freedom.

Many philosophers from Plato to Kant have treated the problem of the relation of imperatives to freedom on the model of Plato's analysis of knowledge as recollection: knowledge is the recovery of what is already known but has been forgotten. The analysis is imported into the sphere of morality when the clash between imperatives and freedom is resolved by interpreting the command as an accord achieved in advance between the one who commands and the will that is commanded. In Plato, for example, the ruler always already (antecedently) has the interest of his subjects in mind when he rules. Such prior accord is possible because the ruler and the ruled are bound by a common rationality so that only an irrational order will be resisted. The courageous person will risk death rather than obey a command that is contrary to reason.

Socrates' refusal to disobey the laws of the state on the assumption that they are rationally grounded is a premier case in point.[34] It is better to die than to undermine the principles of rationality.

Yet, as Levinas argues, "Things are not so simple."[35] There appears to be an instance of perfect freedom, of a will that does not need to submit to rationally grounded imperatives because it alone can issue them. This is the freedom of the tyrant whose will is unimpeded and who does not have to surrender to another will. Is the tyrant then not the only free being? The classical picture of tyranny as unreason that can nevertheless be subordinated to rational control is undermined, first because the imperatives of tyranny are backed by the political, social, and economic power of the polis and second because tyrannical power is sustained by the fear of the ruler on the part of the ruled. Pain or its prospect is the ultimate guarantor of this power.

Contemporary existence has witnessed an extension of force wielded by the state on an unprecedented scale. It is a commonplace that vast increases in the technological capacity to inflict suffering and death on ever-increasing numbers of persons have accrued to the interest of the tyrant. Levinas writes: "Tyranny has unlimited resources at its disposal, those of love and wealth, torture and hunger, silence and rhetoric."[36] The emergence of totalizing structures that sublate all semblance of the other's freedom has become a part of the taken-for-granted backdrop of everyday life. The idea that the discursive "space" for adjudicating intrasocietal conflict as well as conflict among world societies has decreased is a commonly accepted observation.

With the tendency toward an absolutization of the sources of power, the role of language, especially of imperatives, has taken on new dimensions. Grammatical mood can express the will to power and, where such power is absolute, speak with an authority that is able to arrogate rationality to itself. Here, as in the case of classical rationality, an appeal is made to common discursive principles but, in contrast to the classical case, the rules of discourse are allocated and regimented by fear. Levinas argues that "[fear] can exterminate in the tyrannized soul even the very capacity to be struck, that is, even the ability to obey on command."[37] Simone Weil refers to this condition as affliction, prolonged physical suffering, "an uprooting of life, a more or less attenuated equivalent of death, made irresistibly present to the soul by the attack or immediate apprehension of physical pain. . . . [But] there is not real affliction unless the event that has seized and uprooted a life attacks it . . . in all its parts, social, psychological and physical."[38] In the case of political torture, the pain of the tortured is not even permitted expression because the purpose of the infliction of pain is to bring the will of the tortured into conformity with that of the regime. The one who undergoes torture is made to endorse the regime's imperatives and speak with its voice.[39]

Imperatives are not subordinated to indicatives as in the case of Davidson's linguistic philosophy; to the contrary, a strange reversal occurs. The factuality of the indicative is harnessed to the imperative so that totalizing imperatives are made to express indicative force. Thus unrealizable goals may be dictated by totalitarian power. As an example, consider the order that forty thousand slave laborers at the Buna factory during World War II produce synthetic rubber for the German war effort. Complex technical and economic conditions made it impossible for the factory to produce even a single pound. Such ignoring of practical circumstances that limit the carrying out of imperatives leads Michel Foucault to assert: "Truth is linked in a circular relation with systems of power which produce and sustain it, and to effects of power which it induces and which extend it."[40]

In the context of total power, imperatives mandate facts. Contemporary saintly action inserts itself into a field of imperatives authorized by competing wills to power, each of which strives for totalization. Generally, saintly altruism does not oppose these fields of force with counterforce of the same type, although counterforce cannot be ruled out. When there is an extreme imbalance of power, such action is fruitless in any case. Instead, saints are likely to examine how totalizing wills to power obtain endorsement by using the grammar of pain and social humiliation and to develop counterstrategies. The form these counterstrategies may take requires further inquiry.

Consider first how power expresses itself: wills to power aim at immediate discharge. By contrast, saintly counterstrategy must sustain itself over time. This perdurance is effected in traditional hagiography as patience and, in the case of Buddhist narrative, as endurance through many lives. A Buddhist Mahayana text explains:

For I have taken upon myself, by my own will, the whole of the pain of all things living. Thus I dare to try every abode of pain, in . . . every part of the universe, for I must not defraud the world of the root of good. *I resolve to dwell in each state of misfortune through countless ages* . . . for the salvation of all beings . . . for it is better that I alone suffer than that all beings sink to the worlds of misfortune [emphasis mine].[41]

Although Gandhi does not appropriate the Buddhist position in any straightforward fashion, its spirit of endurance is expressed in the claim that his notion of resistance against racial policies in South Africa during the early part of the century and later against British rule in India designated as "soul force" (*Satyagraha*) is characterized by patient suffering.[42]

Instead of making the corporeal vulnerability of the Other a manipulandum so that it is made to speak the language of power, saints issue imperatives only *after* being affected by the material condition of the Other. At first the Other is experienced as mandating a proscriptive principle, that of noninjury or avoiding positive harm to the Other. But as hagiographies so often show, the difficulties and suffering of others increasingly impact on saintly lives so that the imperative issuing from the other's presence becomes a positive injunction to mitigate her/his situation.

Consider the case of the rescue of thousands of Jews during World War II by French Protestants in the Nazi-occupied town of Le Chambon. The growth of altruistic consciousness is expressed in Christian terms in a sermon that describes the move from simple noninjury to radical altruism:

Many of the obligations laid down in the Bible involve avoiding doing harm. The Ten Commandments, for example, lay down such negative obligations. You shall not kill . . . and so on. Ordinarily people have strong obligation only to avoid doing harm themselves; they are not usually obliged to go out of their way to *prevent others* from hating, hurting or deceiving. It is usually enough if they simply sit quietly within the limits laid down by the "you shall not's" and do nothing to violate those limits. People are not often *required* to help. We are not often obliged to obey the Ten Commandments and do *more*.

But the spirit of the [biblical] passages about the cities of refuge [places] a heavy obligation upon those who live as regular inhabitants of those cities . . . as if they were all commanded to be the Good Samaritan of Luke 10:30–37.[43]

Once the grammar of imperatives is acquired, saintly lives cannot extricate themselves from the hagiographic imperative. Thus William Hart MacNichols, who spends all of his time in volunteer work with AIDS patients, explains the religious experience he had in which his vocation to alleviate suffering was revealed to him: "'I didn't want to get into it. It's messy. There's all kinds of hysteria and fanaticism. . . . [but] . . . I thought I can't get away from this.'"[44]

Saints are "native speakers" of the language of alterity, poets of the imperative. Unlike most others, they experience the power of the imperative, grasping not only its force in political contexts but also its everyday debasement by those who most frequently resort to it. When they deploy the grammar of mood didactically, it is by way of an integral relation between speech and action undertaken on behalf of the Other. Moral exhortation without attendant other-directed action may become empty sermonizing, a misuse of saintly grammar; when backed by physical force, it may become violence against the Other.

The Philosophy of Reflection

The incongruities and paradoxes generated when reference does not circulate freely within a theory of truth are the results of the requirement of the theory itself, sameness of meaning and repeatability. This holds as much for Husserl's account of expression as for Quine's and Davidson's theories of truth. What is to count as an object, whether intralinguistically stipulated by a theory of truth (Quine and Davidson) or the product of intentional acts of consciousness (Husserl), is a representation from which the unmanageable alterity of reference has been excluded. The philosophy of reflection provides the historical and conceptual backdrop for the emergence of representation as the ground of truth although, of course, it does not provide either an "explanation" or anything like an exhaustive account of this view.

Rodolphe Gasché thinks of reflection as "designating the action of a mirror reproducing an object." It is also the "mirror's mirroring itself, by which process the mirror is made to see itself."[45] Gasché distinguishes two ways in which the mirror works. The first type of reflection refers to the method consciousness uses in acquiring self-knowledge in Kantian philosophy and in Husserlian phenomenology. Reflection is manifested in the recursive action of the mind upon its own acts as they function to constitute the objects of thought. The second type of reflection, logical reflection, is a turning away from thought's own relation to objects, including the self considered as an empirical entity, in order to consider the relation between objects and the concepts of these objects.[46] Although Gasché does not consider the relevance of this description to analytic philosophers of language, this aspect of reflection is integral to the work of Quine and Davidson. For both, the relation of word and object is an intralinguistic matter in which world, subject, and Other are reworked to fit the truth conditions of a symbolic language.

Elements of both types of reflection appear in Hegel's remarkably prophetic account of reflection in *Faith and Reason*, an early essay on Kant, Fichte, and Jacobi.[47] To be sure, Hegel could not be expected to foresee the complex evolution of reflection, but his description nonetheless highlights many of the salient features of later philosophies of reflection. Hegel characterizes reflection as subjectivism and formal thinking. Subjectivism is manifested when knowledge is limited to the phenomena, the appearances of things, by the structure of the subject. This mode of reflection is grounded in Kant's view of the a priori forms of sense knowledge, forms contributed by the subject. Reflection also exhibits a formal aspect because thinking does not consist of intuited sense content alone but also of relational elements. If attention is withdrawn from the object's sensuous content, what remains is the scheme of their thinkability, the categories, elements of thought which bind together the empirical content of our concepts. Kant bases the categories on the subject-predicate form of language expressed in judgments or propositions. For Hegel the subjective mode of reflection goes deeper because the categories are features of the synthesizing intelligence and, as such, are attributable to the subjective character of Kant's ordering. Lacking a theory of the object, Kant's categorial scheme cannot account for the being of the thing.

Contemporary attention has shifted from the finite epistemological subject to the problem of language. The former has to a considerable extent become the province of the psychology of cognition whereas the schemata of intelligibility have been absorbed by philosophies of language. In Davidson's philosophy, reflection is exhibited not in the mirror play between consciousness and its objects but in the relation between second- and first-order languages. In an intralinguistic mirroring in which the object language is reflected in the formal constructs of the meta-language, the extralinguistic grounding of the object language is excluded. Along with the exclusion of the object and mirrored within this reflexive intralinguistic play is a transformed conception of the subject. Thought is now linked to language in that "each requires the other in order to be understood, but the linkage is not so complete that either suffices . . . to explicate the other. . . . What is . . . needed . . . is to show how thought depends on speech."[48]

For Davidson, just as reference becomes parasitic on truth, thought is bound up with language. Once thought is identified with propositional form, its semantic potentialities are regulated by the absolute theory of truth described earlier. Recall too that attitudinal elements are redescribed paratactically so that expressions of mood are subordinated to an indicative core. On this interpretation of the relation of thought to language, it can be argued (quite apart from the theory's intent) that to know the subject is to know what sentences the subject holds to be true.

The philosophy of reflection, whether in its transcendental or in its logical form, assures the total transparency of the subject, either as the sum of its intentional acts and their content or as the sum of true utterances together with a paratactic redescription of attitudinal locutions. Such a subject can, at least theoretically, be grasped by the objective observer. In describing this situation with reference to Husserl, Levinas writes:

The I that thinks the sum of the angles of a triangle is . . . also determined by this object. . . . Whether it remembers or has forgotten, it is determined by the fact of having passed through the thought of the sum of the angles. This is what will be visible to the historian [objective observer] for whom the I representing to itself is already something represented. At the very moment of representation, the I is not *marked* by the past but *utilizes* it as a represented and objective element. . . . Representation is a pure present.[49]

Saintly life exhibits an altogether different temporal structure, the dark diachronicity that is the time scheme of saintly labor described in chapter 4. The atemporality of reflection departs from the time-tied encounter with the Other by taking the standpoint of thought elevated to omniscience, thought without heart, without the *karuna* or compassion of Buddhism, the *rachamim* or mercy of Judaism, or the *agape* of Christianity.

LANGUAGE IS considered from the standpoint of its suppression of the otherness of world and persons. Some aspects of the truth theories of Husserl, Quine, and Davidson are examined, and all three are seen to exclude or radically regiment what cannot be incorporated into language. This difficulty is referred to in all three as the problem of reference.

Derrida reads Husserl as subordinating indication, the referential stratum of language, to expression. Quine begins by ascribing a significant role to reference as exhibited in stimulus situations but finds them refractory to univocal interpretation. Because stimulus situations fail to anchor meaning, collateral information is required. This is best seen in the context of translating an unknown language, a case in which stimulation appears to offer a stable reference for words in both languages but in fact fails to anchor linguistic correlation. Otherness is also sublated when sameness of meaning within a language is considered. Because the same stimulation may evoke different responses from two or more speakers, Quine shows that synonymy can only be established intrasubjectively.

Davidson retains Quine's preference for an extensional logic, but the intractability of reference leads him to formulate a theory of truth in which reference is neutralized by its interpretation as an extratheoretical posit. What is more, Davidson's analysis of grammatical mood privileges the indicative, thus further subordinating the force of an utterance to its factuality. On these accounts of language, alterity is sublated in the interest of intralinguistic criteria of truth and coherence.

I have continually referred to the imperative as the grammatical mood of hagiography. It is now shown that the imperative bears a relationship to violence. It is the grammatical mood of a political language that reduces the other's freedom, restricting that freedom to accord with some totalizing will to power that is grounded in the body's susceptibility to pain. Totalizing political power succeeds by supporting its commands with the fear of physical pain and psychological humiliation whereas saints issue imperatives only after experiencing the commanding presence of the Other. Human vulnerability is what lends force to the grammar of imperatives.

All three philosophers, Husserl, Quine, and Davidson, are shown to fit a pattern whose outlines Hegel described in his account of the philosophy of reflection, a mode of thought that sees the subject reflected in the objects of cognition. In contemporary language philosophies, reflection is exhibited when the subject is seen as the sum of its true utterances, when intrasubjective constraints rather than the Other determine meaning, and when the temporal framework of existence is the present. Saintly life, by contrast, bypasses the logic of presence and exhibits a structure of becoming that is opened up through saintly compassion for the Other.

7

Who is my father in this world, in this house,
At the spirit's base?

My father's father, his father's father, his—
Shadows like winds

Go back to a parent before thought, before speech,
At the head of the past.

Wallace Stevens, "The Irish Cliffs of Moher"

[I]s not a readiness for flight a kind of weakness too, since it
consists in a wavering, an unsteadiness, a fluttering? Something of that nature characterizes my son. These are not, of
course, the characteristics to rejoice a father; they tend obvi-
ously to destroy a family. Sometimes he looks at me as if he
would say "I shall take you with me, Father." Then I think:
"You are the last person I would trust myself to."

Franz Kafka, "Eleven Sons"

Saint Nicolas, Tavant, Personification of Lust. Romanesque fresco. Marburg/Art Resource, New York.

Depravity, Sanctity, and Desire

THE DOMAIN of politics described in chapter 5 overlaps with another that I call the *discourse of depravity*, a discourse of limitless desire often identified with postmodernism. Because the theme of desire is also central to any revisioning of saintly life, a significant postmodern approach to this theme will be the focus of the present chapter. The idea of a desire that streams without restriction raises critical questions for the position argued here, that desire is an end and instrument of saintly moral action. How can the free flow of desire which may aim at anything whatsoever give rise to a moral life? And if unhampered desire cannot generate moral lives yet drives the lives of saints, does this not preclude the interpretation of hagiographic narrative as a moral discourse? Must hagiography not reverse itself to become a discourse of depravity?

My purpose in this chapter is to answer these questions by analyzing Deleuze and Guattari's view of desire as something material, productive, and unlimited and by considering some crucial difficulties their position entails. The main thrust of my criticism is that, although desire is necessary to radical altruism, *unlimited* desire that has become productive is an expression of power and is incompatible with altruism because the Other, always already presupposed, constitutes a limiting condition of desire. The Other can never coincide with the desire that intends her/him.

The approach of Deleuze and Guattari must be contrasted with some versions of postmodernism considered earlier and that present a different order of challenge to both the *logos* of metaphysics and the *ethos* of moral philosophy. Levinas and Blanchot stress the constraint imposed upon power by the Other. The pattern of free-flowing desire described by Deleuze and Guattari is exhibited in the work of Jean Genet, whose fiction is a teratology of twisted saintly lives that explode in episodes of uncontrolled eroticism. These lives are marked, however, not only by transgression and numinous intensity but also by generosity as it is understood by Levinas. Genet's saints of depravity serve to highlight the ambiguities of contemporary sainthood—the intertwining of compassion and erotic desire, betrayal and love. I turn to Genet's saints not as models of contemporary sanctity whose lives Genet's readers are exhorted to follow but rather as bringing to the fore the excesses of sanctity and the deceptiveness of saintly purity that contemporary psychology and literary analysis can help display.

In chapter 2, I argued that saintly experience as described in a variety of hagiographic traditions, especially in Western Christian tradition from the medieval period to the seventeenth century, brings together contemplative and active, mystical and moral strains. Saintly life when defined as radical altruism requires the separability of these strands even if they are often interwoven in hagiographic narrative. Although I analyzed these strains from a postmodern perspective, their historical grounding reflected the often multilayered metaphysical suppositions of the times in which the various strands—often of Neoplatonic provenance—originated and were brought together.

It might be imagined that no contemporary metaphysic could be further removed from the plenum of Neoplatonism with its hypostatized and hierarchical layers than the eclecticism of much postmodern thought. This is indeed the case for Levinas, Blanchot, and Derrida. But in the analyses that follow, I hope to make plain that there is a comparable philosophical position in the works of Deleuze and Guattari, one that constitutes the ecstatic ground of a postmodern "mystical" metaphysics that has been recontextualized in psychological, sociological, and economic terms. This metaphysical backdrop is to be discerned not in the altruistic works of contemporary saintly lives but in the fictions concerning the saints of depravity who will be considered at the end of this chapter.

The Material Forces of Production: Deleuze and Guattari

Radically reinterpreting received notions of desire, Deleuze and Guattari treat it not as an attribute of the subject but as a force that circulates within an economy and is socially apportioned in accordance with specifiable laws of distribution. Desire is removed from the sphere of affect, transformed into an economic resource like hydroelectric or nuclear power, and its modus operandi decided by those who possess sufficient force to control its circulation. There is no mistaking the thesis: not only is desire social before it is individual, but desire is capital and revolution is its redistribution. What is heretical in Deleuze and Guattari is the insistence that an erotic ideality be treated as a commodity and subjected to the laws of political economy. As such, a hermeneutic of desire is not at bottom psychological or philosophical but an economic and political discourse.

One obstacle to the de-individualizing and collectivization of desire is the interpretation it has been given by the Oedipus myth so that desire is pressed into serving the individualization process itself. In the intrafamilial drama of desire and its frustration as described in Freudian psychoanalysis, the triangulated patterning of desire, "daddy-mommy-me," not only stamps the growing child with all of his future repressions but provides the ideological legitimation for the individualism of capitalist societies. The attack on the Oedipus myth is an important part of Deleuze and Guattari's argument, and I shall consider it in detail in a subsequent section. At present it is enough to notice that, for them, "Oedipus is always colonization pursued by other means, it is the interior colony, . . . it is our intimate colonial education."[1]

It is not hard to see that Bataille's conception of the sumptuary economy and of ritualized transgression, as described in chapter 5, opens the way for delineating desire as a vast macroeconomic force that the authority of the state seeks to bring under control by tolerating its restricted expression within the safe confines of the family. Less visible is the reliance of Deleuze and Guattari on Heidegger's interpretation of human being in the present epoch as standing-reserve, a calculable and manipulable commodity. This view of human existence that, for Heidegger, derives from the essence of technology for Deleuze and Guattari is attributable to the working of economic forces. On Heidegger's account, the meaning of being in the present age is expressed in willing that can be surmounted only by an attentiveness to the way in which being is given. Deleuze and Guattari argue that it is better to will the overturning of the system of distributing desire, to revolutionize the circulation of "spiritual" commodities, than to listen passively to the voice of being. The first step in such a revolution, they believe, is to examine schizophrenic thinking so as to draw from the structure of breakdown its implications for revolutionary breakthrough.

Although Deleuze and Guattari are critical of the implementation of Marxism in numerous present-day Marxist societies, their thinking is an effort to extend Marxist analyses to psychic life, socializing the productions of that life. Marxist too are the stylistics of a text that reads as a manifesto encompassing both arguments and plans of action. As Foucault notes in his Preface to *Anti-Oedipus*, the work is "an *ars erotica*, *ars theoretica* and *ars politica*," less concerned with the etiology of social phenomena than with how to proceed (*AO*, p. xii). It is a foray against Marxist theoretical purists who forget desire and psychoanalysts who distort it, and the majority who misdirect desire toward the very structures that repress it (*AO*, pp. xii–xiii).

Because Deleuze and Guattari's approach to desire in *Anti-Oedipus* is dominated by the Marxist view of production, it may be useful to organize the work's disparate strains in terms of the Marxist categories that underlie their analysis. I shall treat what they designate as the body without organs and desiring-machines (terms soon to be explicated) as *forces of production*; the Oedipus myth as the ideology of an outworn *mode of production*; schizoanalysis as a cognitive and practical scheme for revolutionizing the *relations of production*; and the schizorevolutionary manufacture of desire as the nonrepressive *mode of production* that will characterize the new society. Thus Marx writes in a well-known passage in the Preface to *The Critique of Political Economy*:

In the social production of their life, men enter into definite relations that are indispensable and independent of their will, relations of production which correspond to a definite stage of their material productive forces. The sum total of these relations of production constitutes the economic structure of society, the real foundation on which arises a legal and political superstructure and to which correspond definite modes of social consciousness. . . . The bourgeois relations of production are the last antagonistic form of the social process of production.[2]

Traditional Marxism has addressed social production but has left the psychic life of individuals untouched, thus leaving a space for the seepage of an ideality that will ultimately penetrate and poison social and political action. Just as Democritus, turning against the ideality of Greek concepts of being, posits atoms and void as ontic simples, so too Deleuze and Guattari rearticulate psychic life in material terms[3] (*TP*, pp. 161–64). Such rematerialization is not achieved by resorting to some tangible "stuff"—for example, by adopting the materialist argument that the mind is the sum of its brain states—because philosophical ultimates not only must be material but must be able to enter into social relations. They therefore take the novel path of interpreting psychic life as a production process in which desiring-machines are both the agents and the final products of the process. "A truly materialist psychiatry," they argue, "introduce[s] desire into the mechanism and . . . production into desire" (*AO*, p. 22). If being has become mechanism, as Heidegger's analysis that thinking is calculation seems to imply, then the machinic character of the epoch is inescapable and the repudiation of mechanism in the name of the human is a futile and retrograde gesture.[4]

The genuineness of the machinic character of desiring production is attested on two quite different grounds, first because desiring-machines work in the same way as machines generally, and second because they, no less than technical machines, are "real." Consider first the function of machines as "a system of interruptions or breaks" (*AO*, p. 36) that cut into an otherwise uninterrupted material flow. The mouth that cuts off or disrupts the flow of milk, air, or sound is an example of a desiring-machine. Equally important is the continuity of the flow that is itself the product of another type of desiring-machine. There are only machines breaking and producing flows constituting a unity of process and product (*AO*, pp. 36–37).

It is clear that goods in the usual sense do not result from the operations of this system. Instead, the machinic "schematism" refers to the way in which bodies intermingle in a society organized by two systems or regimes that regulate corporeal relationships, the functions of alimentation and sex (*TP*, p. 72). Like Heidegger, who argues that tools are organized into a nexus, Deleuze and Guattari contend that machines can be considered only in their mutualities and interdependencies, "inseparable from symbioses or amalgamations defining a nature-society machinic assemblage" (*TP*, p. 90).

Recall next the problem of the genuineness of desiring-machines. By interpreting the real as material, the factuality of desiring-machines is defended, and by considering it at the same time as social, desiring-machines can be viewed as part of the productive process and as creating reality itself.

Desire produces reality, or stated another way, desiring-production is one and the same thing as social-production. It is not possible to attribute a special form of existence to desire, a mental or psychic reality that is . . . different from the material reality of social production. Desiring-machines are not fantasy-machines or dream-machines, which supposedly can be distinguished from technical and social machines. Rather fantasies are secondary expressions deriving from the identical nature of the two sorts of machines. . . . [F]antasy is never individual: it is group fantasy. (*AO*, p. 30)

At stake is the radically novel concept that matter is socially produced and that, depending on the *mode* of production, it can be invested with "fascist" or "schizorevolutionary" meaning, one a consequence of idealization, the other the result of "group fantasies" and thus a genuinely collective product. For Deleuze and Guattari *homo natura* or unrepressed humanity is not the starting point in the revolution of desire but the end of a revolutionary process that overturns the repressive strategies of the old mode of production. Thus, contrary to the received state of nature theories, *homo historica* precedes rather than supervenes upon *homo natura*.

Desiring-machines do not float about freely but, instead, attach themselves to what Deleuze and Guattari call the body without organs. This concept acquires three distinct but related meanings: the nonplace of counterproduction, breakdown and death; the surface upon which production is recorded; that which is related to so-called partial objects (a concept elaborated in the work of Melanie Klein and others) as the ground of these objects. Consider the breakdown of the productive process such that the break-flows come to a halt and "everything freezes in place" (*AO*, p. 7). The body's organs that heretofore articulated production seem to drop away, leaving an undifferentiated mass. This is the body without organs, "the unproductive, the sterile, the unengendered, the unconsumable" (*AO*, p. 8), and, as such, the indeterminate, distinctionless body of death. The entire biological organization, the structure of the organs, causes suffering to the body without organs. Antonin Artaud is cited as saying "'The body is the body . . . and has no need of organs . . . / organisms are the enemy of the body'" (*AO*, p. 9). It is not that the organs as such stand opposed to the body without organs; it is rather that their organization must be restructured so that, taken together, they do not constitute an organism, the forms and functions imposed upon the body so as to stratify and exact labor from it. To organize the body differently than in accordance with some prevailing set of social rules is to be cast out or defined as depraved (*TP*, pp. 158f.). When the body without organs is interpreted privatively, it is thought of as a formless counterflow that repels the productive process of the desiring-machines. Construed positively, it takes on the character of the mode of production that will be projected upon it: the body of the earth in primitive societies, that of the tyrant in despotic society, and that of capital in the present-day Western world.

Notice next the second meaning of the body without organs, that of a surface of inscription. Capital is such a surface, although in capitalism, it is argued, the productive process is alienated because the achievement of labor is inscribed upon the body without organs so as to make capital appear the cause of production. As a plane of inscription the body without organs is an enchanted or bewitched skin across which the productive process has been stretched so that it takes on the features of the macrocosmic social body's mode of production (*AO*, pp. 12–14).

It might well be imagined that the transcendent Other as described in classical theological frameworks has simply been recast as the body without organs. Saintly ascetic practice could then be imagined as a machine-like arrangement inscribed upon an all-powerful, undifferentiated transcendent source and saintly desire as an assemblage of desiring-machines, of break-flows magnetized by a divine body without organs. The break of the flow of desire in saintly life would then appear as the torment of ascetic practice and the continuity of the flow as the outpouring of saintly compassion and generosity. But Deleuze and Guattari reject the divinization of the body without organs. "The body without organs is not God" in that the term *God* designates an absolute source of truth, "God defined as the *omnitudio realitas*" (*AO*, p. 13). By contrast, it is the energy that sweeps through the body without organs in its guise as earth, despotism or capital, an energy that disjoins and redistributes desire, that is divine. Crisscrossed by bands of differential forces, the schizophrenic too is traversed by this divine energy and is "brought as close as possible to matter, to a burning living center of matter" (*AO*, p. 19).

It is worth noting in the context of the problematic of saintly life that the distinction drawn by Deleuze and Guattari—a distinction between God as an ultimate principle of being and truth as well as the energy of the productive forces—can be reframed in traditional theological language. The God of love has been distinguished from the God of wrath, the God of Abraham from the God of the philosophers, the God beyond God from the creator and governor of the universe, the *arhat* or the *pratyeka* buddha who seeks individual release from suffering from the bodhisattva who works for the release of all. These disjunctions were intended to mark off differences between normative theological constructs and the burning center of things. To be sure, each pairing requires careful historical elaboration and arises in a unique socio-cultural context.

What crosses over into the postmodern discourse of desire is that *agape, rachamim* ("mercy"), *karuna* ("heart") expressed as one of the aspects of the traditional polarities points to a wellspring of transfigurative power that breaks down egoistic boundaries. The energy coursing through the body without organs suggests a functional homology with the divine as a source of transforming love. This is reflected in the contrast drawn between "God as the master of exclusions and restrictions that derive from the disjunctive syllogism" and a "subject that passes through all predicates," a subject described in Nijinsky's cited comment: "'I am God. I was not God. I am a clown of God; I am Apis. I am an Egyptian. I am a red Indian. I am a Negro. I am a Chinaman. I am a Japanese. I am a foreigner, a stranger'" (*AO*, p. 77).

The third meaning of the body without organs relates it to partial objects as that which is nondifferent from them. According to the psychoanalytic theory of Melanie Klein, partial objects are formed by projecting libido and aggression outward and attaching them to objects while at the same time taking objects into the self. The first of these objects is the mother's breast introjected either as "good" or "bad" in accordance with the infant's experience of pleasure or pain. In this way, a nexus of internalized entities is built up that enriches and amplifies psychic life.[5] Nevertheless, for Melanie Klein partial objects function as fragments of a lost whole or of a totality yet to be constructed, whereas for Deleuze and Guattari "partial objects are molecular functions of the unconscious" (*AO*, p. 324) that remain prepersonal and dispersed singularities. What is more—and this is the decisive point—there is no difference between the partial objects and the body without organs: "Partial objects are the direct powers of the body without organs and the body without organs, the raw material of the partial objects" (*AO*, p. 326). The two are bound together as matter and the degrees of intensity with which that matter fills space, as the "immobile motor" is bound to its "working parts" or as the "giant molecule" is bound to the "micromolecules" that constitute it (*AO*, p. 327).

In yet another account, the body without organs is defined as something that is manufactured through one's desiring practices. It is not a fundament that can be reached but a limit that one is in the process of attaining, a material version, as it were, of Kant's regulative ideal (*AO*, pp. 149–50). In an essay entitled "How Do You Make Yourself a Body without Organs?" Deleuze and Guattari declare:

So what is this BwO—But you're already on it, scurrying like a vermin, groping like a blind person, or running like a lunatic: desert traveler and nomad of the steppes. On it we sleep, live our waking lives, fight—fight and are fought—seek our place, experience untold happiness and fabulous defeats; on it we penetrate and are penetrated; on it we love. (*TP*, p. 150)

The body without organs is "a Place, a Plane, a Collectivity" on which specific intensities constituting body types are orchestrated, for example, the icy body of the addict (*TP*, p. 161). The potential totality of all the bodies without organs is designated as "the plane of consistency," (*TP*, p. 72), a nonstructure described in geological terms as a plateau upon which the repressive strata of socially legislated signification are arranged.

Although the word *plane* is used as a geological term, it also designates a level or arena of ecstatic experience and, as such, resonates with Neoplatonic connotations. The plane of consistency can refer to the body without organs when that body has not been appropriated by capital or hypostatized as paranoia and the like. Neither void nor chaos, the plane of consistency beneath its stratigraphic patterns generates continuous intensities (*TP*, p. 72). Changes in intensity result in deterritorialization, a polysemic term that means a milieu in which the desiring flows are in flight; a process of disappropriating desiring flows; a condition or place that reaches its absolute state as the plane of consistency.

When considering the design of the plane of consistency, it is useful to invoke again Neoplatonic cosmology with its multiple spheres of emanations. It is by no means farfetched to think of Deleuze and Guattari as Sufi adepts who are also Neomarxists or as materialist or empirical ecstatics who revision the emanations of light in Neoplatonism as the body's multiple capacities for experience, a body that has become transpersonal, material, and cosmic.[6] It is the ecstatic aspect of Deleuze and Guattari, their demand for the transformation of the multiple planes of existence, that is relevant to saintly life and action.

In what may be a softening of the political radicalism of *Anti-Oedipus*—its cry of "Destroy, destroy"—Deleuze and Guattari announce in their later writings that enough organismic structure must be kept to initiate action. Total destratification may, after all, result in a catastrophic collapse of the assemblage of machines: "You don't reach the BwO and its plane of consistency, by wildly destratifying. . . . Lodge yourself on a stratum, experiment with the opportunities it offers . . . find potential movements of deterritorialization, possible lines of flight, experience them" (*TP*, p. 161). It is only through this tentative step-by-step clambering over the strata that it becomes possible to pass beyond them and on to the plane of consistency.

One further consideration of paramount importance for a critique of desiring production to be undertaken in a later section of this chapter is the treatment of lack in the context of the productive forces. How, it could be asked, can desire be thought of as the production and allocation of the flows and breaks of desiring-machines, if desire, at least in its everyday meaning, is bound up with lack? Does not Deleuze and Guattari's entire analysis founder once desire is interpreted in the received sense as an intention aimed at that which is absent? How is it possible to consider desire simultaneously as sheer nullity and as process and product of production? Only by suppressing the negative character of desire, its nonbeing as lack, and by reinterpreting desire quasi-materially can this objection be overcome. Deleuze and Guattari's definition of desire must be pondered not only because it so fundamentally reworks the received view but also because other postmodern positions I have described take an opposing tack in describing being and presence in terms of gap, fissure, void, negation—in short, in terms of lack.

Deleuze and Guattari assert that traditional readings of desire rest on a misunderstanding of its material nature:

If desire produces, its product is real. . . . Desire is the set of *passive syntheses* that engineer partial objects, flows and bodies, and that function as units of production. The real is the end product, the result of the passive syntheses of desire as autoproduction of the unconscious. Desire does not lack anything; it does not lack its object. It is, rather, the *subject* that is missing in desire, or desire that lacks a fixed subject; there is no fixed subject unless there is repression. (*AO*, pp. 26f.)

They go on to claim that there is no difference between desire and its object: "They are one and the same thing" (*AO*, p. 27).

But surely, it can be urged, there must be basic needs rooted in nature. Deleuze and Guattari contend, however, that desiring production is more primordial than need so that need supervenes upon rather than grounds desire. Needs are "counterproducts within the real that desire produces [and] lack . . . [is] a countereffect of desire . . . distributed . . . within a whole that is natural and social" (*AO*, p. 27). That desire may turn into the *fear* of lack is not denied. But, they argue:

[Desire and lack] are not "phrase[s] uttered by the dispossessed. . . . [S]uch people know that they are close to grass, that desire needs very few things . . . the very things that are continually taken from them, . . . not things the subject feels the lack of somewhere deep down inside himself, but the objective being of man, for whom to desire is . . . to produce within the realm of the real." (*AO*, p. 27)

This analysis reveals desire as instantly productive with no gap or fissure between desiring and its product. It may seem that when Deleuze and Guattari speak of the minimum that desire "needs," they have conceded that there is, after all, an irremediable lack within nature that cannot be transcended. But such an inference is misleading because, for them, lack is a phenomenon made to appear through the manipulation of production by a ruling elite (*AO*, p. 28). Sartre had warned that scarcity must be the starting point of economy because if, per contra, scarcity is denied, its effects are blamed on human agents, an ascription of responsibility that, in totalitarian societies, is generally followed by the most draconian measures.[7] Deleuze and Guattari nonetheless endorse Maurice Clavel's view that to acknowledge scarcity's irreducibility is to abandon Marxism because, if scarcity is unsurpassable, then social action is in many cases futile. For them there can be nothing but desiring production and social production, the determinate form that desiring production takes, "only desire and the social and nothing else" (*AO*, p. 29).

It is not difficult to see in this account a radicalization of Marx's view of need as developed in "Saint Max," the attack on Max Stirner, in *The German Ideology*.[8] To Stirner's account of the way that desires become fixed, Marx, in a crossed-out portion of the original manuscript, replies that communism alone can bring about an alteration in the fixedness of desires by changing their material basis.[9] Marx distinguishes between fixed desires whose form will become normalized but will nevertheless persist, come what may, and those desires that originate in the social system itself. Pragmatic criteria will determine which desires will merely be altered and which eliminated. He goes on to say that desires by their very nature are fixed, as are the needs on which they are based. The sex instinct "will cease to be fixed only as the result of castration or impotence," and no one will be freed from the necessity of having to eat at fixed intervals. "The communists," Marx declares, "have no intention of abolishing the fixedness of their desires and needs but to so reorganize production as to make their normal satisfaction possible."[10]

Deleuze and Guattari agree about the ineradicability of sex and alimentation, but see them not as lack but as modes of production. Furthermore, because the main thrust of their work is to liberate desiring production, the idea of what norms could supplant the Oedipal mode, if any, is far from clear.

Oedipus and the Codes of Production

The harsh law of capitalism, Deleuze and Guattari declare, can function only because it has infiltrated psychic life so that the unconscious is captured by macroeconomic forces. Their argument that this process is invisible to the subjugated conforms to Marx's view that a historical period cannot be made transparent to itself. Marx writes:

With the change of the economic foundation, the entire immense superstructure is rapidly transformed. . . . In considering such transformations, a distinction should be made between the material transformation of the economic conditions of production . . . and the ideological forms in which men become conscious of this conflict. . . . Just as our opinion of an individual is not based on what he thinks of himself, so can we not judge of such a period of transformation by its own consciousness.[11]

The paradigm that colonizes the psychic life of the child, the psychoanalytic reinterpretation of the Oedipus myth, provides the rationale for grasping the individual's place in society by locating him within the intimacy of the family. The child desires the mother but is prevented from fulfilling his wishes under threat of castration by the father. By surrendering the longed-for object and recognizing paternal authority, the subject emerges as an individual self, an ego that has been preformed for later social existence.[12] The family drama of "daddy-mommy-me" is destined to be replayed throughout the child's life, with the symbol of Oedipus functioning proscriptively as a limit beyond which desires cannot be extended. The very familiarity of the Freudian account attests the degree of its acceptance.

The failure of psychoanalysis lies in its blindness to the Oedipal drama as a secondary formation, a symbol or icon of more primordial productive functions. The Oedipus myth is ideology masking the repressive distribution of desire. "'So, it's your father, so it's your mother, so it's you': the familial conjunction results from the capitalist conjunctions, insofar as they are applied to private persons" (*AO*, p. 265).

If Oedipus is an instrument of the capitalist mode of production, Deleuze and Guattari do not draw back from the Marxist question, "What is to be done?" Classical Marxism, they believe, has been tarnished by the repressive character of many actual Marxist states and Freudianism by the system that has annexed it. The new thinking must come from heretofore rejected or undervalued sources outside present formations of power: the thought processes of schizophrenics and the strategies for encoding the incest taboo in certain nonliterate societies.

Consider first the process of schizoanalysis that Deleuze and Guattari hope to transform into a therapeutic discourse that will uncover the sickness of the age and, by painful means if necessary, liberate the production of desire from normative constraints. The neurotic lives in accordance with the Oedipal code but the schizophrenic, by standing outside it, is able to penetrate its true character, to repudiate its cognitive polarities and its repressive rules, in short, to "schizoanalyze" it. For the schizophrenic, "There is no such thing as man or nature now, only a process that produces the one within the other and couples the machines together. Producing machines, desiring machines everywhere. . . . the self and non-self, outside and inside no longer have any meaning whatsoever" (*AO*, p. 2).[13]

To see the difference between Oedipal and schizoid production, Deleuze and Guattari distinguish between two forms of social investment, the one repressive, the other liberating. The segregative social field, identified as paranoid and fascist, centralizes power and views authority as a pyramidal hierarchy that "counterinvests" those at the bottom and neutralizes "every free 'figure' of desire" (*AO*, p. 277). By contrast, the schizorevolutionary is seen to follow the escape mechanisms, the lines of flight, of desire by creating hatchways through which desire can flow.

Schizoanalysis is intended not only to reorient the social field affectively and cognitively but to revolutionize the relations of production by a forcible recoupling of desiring-machines. Thus Deleuze and Guattari declare "Destroy, destroy. The task of schizoanalysis goes by way of destruction—a whole scouring of the unconscious, a complete curettage. Destroy Oedipus, the illusion of the ego, the puppet of the superego, guilt, the law, castration" (*AO*, p. 311). This curettage can be achieved only be resorting to extreme measures:

[S]chizoanalysis must devote itself with all its strength to the necessary destructions. Destroying beliefs and representations, theatrical scenes. And when engaged in this task no activity will be too malevolent. . . . [B]rutally intervening each time the subject strikes up the song of myth or intones tragic lines, carrying him *back to the factory*. (*AO*, p. 314)

"Back to the factory" is not a mandate to return to the manufacturing plant but a strategy for forcing the imagination or desiring production to think otherwise than Oedipally. Far from being less coercive than the straightforward command to go back to the workplace, this strategy aims at penetrating the structure of desire by collectivizing it. René Girard in his extended commentary on *Anti-Oedipus* remarks:

When they leap over a dangerous pass, the two authors seem to raise their voices. One could say they are speaking in a stage whisper in order to precede some formidable red guard who must be encamped nearby, blindly devoted to the cause of the molecular unconscious. [Translation mine][14]

There is, to be sure, a vast difference between the schizophrenic and the schizorevolutionary, between illness and revolution, between breakdown or the ultimate arrest of desire and breakthrough or its full expression. The desideratum is not the birth of a schizophrenic society but rather that schizophrenic experience provide an entering wedge into an encrusted ideological structure, one that seals in the flows of desire. Schizoanalysis is the first of a series of therapeutic designs for desire's reinscription and recirculation.

Consider next another controversial therapeutic measure, the reinscription of the incest code. If schizoanalysis uncovers the repressiveness of the Oedipal mode of socialization, could it not be argued that, bereft of its code, the social field is open to unrestricted desiring production? Can schizoanalysis so radically scramble a society's codes that the incest taboo no longer holds? To be sure, schizoanalysis replaces the ideality of Oedipus with the materiality of desiring-machines and partial objects, but in so doing, it permits desiring production to run amok. What had become material by becoming machinic must now undergo social transformation and a nonrepressive way must be found for placing limits upon desire.

The first step in this process is the deprivatization of the individual body. In Western societies body parts are the possessions of individuals, but this perspective is to be replaced by a collective investment of meaning in the body's organs. In many primitive societies body parts become collective property, are seen as products of the earth and are so marked:

The essence of the recording inscribing socius, insofar as it lays claim to the productive forces and distributes the agents of production, resides in these operations: tattooing, excising, incising, carving, scarifying, mutilating, encircling and initiating. (*OE*, p. 144)[15]

The body as a surface of writing demands the cruelty of a corporeal wounding without which there would be no codes, no culture, and no memory, a Nietzschean point not lost on Deleuze and Guattari.[16] "The first signs are the territorial signs that plant their flags in bodies" (*AO*, p. 145).

This argument is elaborated in terms of a distinction between two codes that determine kinship, the biological or filiative code, and the social code or the code of alliance. Deleuze and Guattari argue that ties of alliance are more primordial than chains of biological filiation because codes of alliance, the product of collective decision and fantasy, *determine* the laws of consanguinity, the manner of reckoning biological descent. Thus there are social agreements that allocate the way bloodlines are to be reckoned. A kinship system is not a biological structure but a social practice. Deleuze and Guattari hope not to replace filiation with alliance but to call attention to the contractual, as it were, character of kinship. A kinship system "comprises both qualitative alliances and extended filiations" (*AO*, p. 155). The purely biological is neutral and must be given positive or negative social signification. From the moment that putatively biological distinctions appear, there must always already have been alliances to apportion and construe them (*AO*, p. 167). Thus, for example, "mother" and "sister" do not exist as biological categories but arise only after they are prohibited as spouses.

The consequences of this repristinization are of fundamental importance to a grasp of the Oedipal function in society: it does not describe already existing relationships but constitutes them. Oedipus does not exist as a built-in biological constraint but as a social determinant that restricts the production of desire. In that sense Oedipus as the icon of limit is universal because its "displacement . . . disfigures what all societies dread absolutely, as their most profound negative: namely the decoded flows of desire" (*AO*, p. 177).

The psychoanalytic version of limit expressed by the Oedipus myth is seen by the authors as especially pernicious because not only does it set the limit for prohibited action but it legislates what the individual *should* wish for. But this position conceals a deep difficulty for a materialist psychology. On the one hand, Deleuze and Guattari concede that limits are set by all societies so that the Oedipus myth cannot be faulted simply because it is repressive. It can only be repudiated because of the character of the repression, specifically the suppression of fantasy and uninhibited imagination. An Eskimo, they say, can dream about Oedipus without guilt (*AO*, p. 177). But if all that is meant by lifting the Oedipus proscription is the freedom to fantasize in the sense of *imagining* or *dreaming*, such liberty is, from a materialist standpoint, worthless. On the other hand, if fantasy production is *real* production as they insist, then they have not disposed of the question of whether they mean *actually* to lift the incest taboo, to lift it in practice. Either they must concede that fantasy is nonmaterial or they will be forced to acknowledge that they have removed the incest prohibition in a factical sense. This criticism highlights what I shall call the fallacy of misplaced materiality: the mistake of treating fantasy production as physical production.

Nomad Thought

If their interpretation of economy is drawn from Marxist analysis, Deleuze and Guattari derive their cognitive strategies from a deconstructive reading of Nietzsche, for it is he, they argue, and not Freud who has a grasp of "how it stands with our age in regard to health and sickness."[17] One aspect of Nietzsche's importance would seem to lie in his proclamation of the death of God. But according to Deleuze and Guattari, it is not the release of human beings from the tyrannical rule of a divine despot but the astonishing revelation that there never was any such rule in the unconscious in the first place that establishes Nietzsche's significance. On Freud's view, the death of God requires God's replacement by the living father so that, in the name of the living father, the repressions of a divinely sanctioned law may be continued. But Nietzsche goes further not because of the jejune pronouncement that God is dead but because he brings to light "that what takes so long in coming *to consciousness* is the news that the death of God makes no difference *to the unconscious*" (*AO*, p. 106). Generally hailed as the prophet of the death of God, Nietzsche shows instead that the whole matter can be dispensed with because, by never having entered the unconscious, God does not belong to the primordial order of desiring production. In attributing to Nietzsche the removal of God from the unconscious together with the theological cortege that attaches to this concept, Deleuze and Guattari can proclaim: "It is not a matter of saying that Oedipus is a false belief, but that belief is necessarily something false that diverts and suffocates effective production" (*AO*, p. 107).

Not only has Nietzsche freed the unconscious from the burden of transcendence but, it is argued, he has invented nomad thought, a mode of thinking that is without logical or metaphysical precedent. In a series of writings that are more ripostes than essays, especially *On the Line*[18] and a brief sketch of Nietzsche's style, "Nomad Thought,"[19] Deleuze and Guattari claim that nomad thought brings about a counterphilosophical thinking and speaking. Attention to some of its properties— its impulse to decodify, its rejection of interiority, and its preoccupation with pulsions of power rather than intellectual constructs—suggests for them the birth of a new a/philosophical impulse.

In "Nomad Thought," Freud and Marx are described as representing hierarchical linear thinking because of their efforts to recodify the codes of modernity already undermined by previous criticism. Freud tries to breathe new life into the nuclear family and Marx to recentralize sovereignty at least until socialist production is consolidated. Nietzsche's thinking alone undoes encrypted philosophical concepts by transmitting uncodifiable states of experience not to a new notional language but to a new body, Nietzsche's own or that of the earth.[20] Such thought suggests a line of flight, a thinking away from received philosophical distinctions, especially those pertinent to envisaging a moral or cognitive subject. Differing from both representation and formal argument that take the subject or consciousness as a starting point, crisscrossed by a movement that comes from outside, Nietzsche's thought and writing are grounded in "an immediate relation with the exterior."[21] A Nietzschean aphorism does not originate in the mind of a subject but is "an amalgam of forces" that neither cohere nor agglutinate into recognizable conceptual patterns but, instead, are "always held apart from one another . . . carrying us away ever further outside."[22] In the endless play of forces, the force that is final at any given moment is the most outside force even if outside cannot be further stipulated because there is no interior point of reference. The human subject too is a play of forces and proper names are merely designations for pulsional intensities inscribed upon a body that may be individual, collective, or terrestrial.

Nomadism is not only a way of thinking for Nietzsche but also, Deleuze claims, a political style. In *Genealogy of Morals*, for example, Deleuze asserts that Nietzsche shows that imperial and bureaucratic machines spring from primitive proto-Asian rural communities but that, at the periphery of this centralized power, a new phenomenon occurs: "Whole groups depart and . . . become nomads."[23] Philosophic discourse is the superstructure first produced by an imperial state, whereas pitted against traditional philosophy is the new socio-political counterdiscourse of nomadic thought. For Deleuze, nomadism names a *style* of counterconceptual thinking rather than the actual migration of peoples: "The nomad is not necessarily one who moves" because "some voyages take place in situ."[24]

In *On the Line* nomadic thought is articulated in terms of a double set of images: segmented line/line in flight and radicle/rhizome (a term that will be explicated) in accordance with whether the image articulates capitalist or schizorevolutionary relations of production. The line can either "segment," "stratify," and "territorialize" or express "flight, movements of deterritorialization and of destratification."[25] The rhizome is preferred to the root because the root is an image of the tree structure and the tree is an icon of hierarchical power relations. Nature, Deleuze and Guattari argue, works differently. "The radicle system, or fasciculated root," may become rhizomatic when an incision in the main root stimulates new growth at the periphery.[26] But bulbs and tubers that can connect at any point are already rhizomes.[27] The language of schizoanalysis is rhizomatic in the sense that semiotic chains are eclectic, mimetic, and gestural as well as cognitive whereas spoken languages take on rhizomatic form as "dialects, patois, argots and special languages."[28] Multiplicity, the growth of connections and ruptures,

flows and breaks, characterize rhizomatic discourse. Ever wary of a reconstituted unity, Deleuze and Guattari caution:

The multiple *must be made*, not by continually adding a higher dimension, but,
on the contrary . . . by force of restraint, at the level of dimensions already
available, by making n-1. Only thus does the one become part of the multiple:
by being always subtracted from it.[29]

This effort to escape unity will be shown ultimately to fail because of
the attack waged against the notion of lack.

Three Myths of the Anti-Oedipus

Postmodernists such as Derrida, Blanchot, Levinas, and de Certeau
strongly stress the problem of language whereas, by contrast, Deleuze
and Guattari do not shrink from positing metaphysical ultimates,
quasi-material micromolecular infrastructures, that operate in accordance with a principle of breaks and flows. The motions of desiring-
machines and their parts are subject to appropriation by social forces
and indeed exist as already preempted. There are not and never were
neutral desiring-machines but only socially channeled break-flows. The
machines' actions, when they are not captured by repressive social
forces, produce powerful material currents, praxes of ecstasy. Insofar as
many radically altruistic saints have been ecstatics, the lifting of repressive codes would seem to reinstate the inexpressible ecstasy of the spiritual adept that Lacan and Kristeva have called *jouissance* and that
Deleuze and Guattari leave unnamed. But can the free break-flows they
describe account for *saintly* ecstasy?[30]

Desiring-machines, partial objects, and the body without organs are
"*metaphysical*" constructs at the same time that they are *social products*.
This doubleness of desiring production opens the possibility for a
"metaphysical" critique of Deleuze and Guattari's analysis of desire. I
shall consider the difficulties of maintaining a life of unrepressed desire
not in the name of another law or another politics but as bound up
with a cortege of constructs that thwart the flourishing of saintly altruism. I shall designate these constructs the myth of the plenum, the myth
of the tabula rasa, and the myth of the absent absence.

Before turning to these myths, it is important to credit the positive
contributions of Deleuze and Guattari to the interpretation of saintly
life. First, although hagiography is not made thematic in their work,
the way is paved for developing a discourse of ecstasy that incorporates

the material aspect of desire. In chapter 3, I distinguished between mystical and altruistic dimensions of saintly life and argued that not all saints are mystics. In that context, I also suggested that mystical experience is not composed of brute "feels" but is organized and articulated in terms of cultic, institutional, and linguistic frameworks that give form to this experience. Deleuze and Guattari now offer a way of distinguishing between the ecstasy of the experience and the codes of its inscription. Reports of mystical states belong to the strata of articulation, to the chain of signifiers whose differential structure constitutes meaning. With the molecularization, the dissemination, and the breaking up of ordinary meaning and with the deterritorialization of repressive modes of desire, even the ecstatic stream as something given beyond framing discourse can be glimpsed, if only obliquely, and described, just as the qualitied world is reducible to particulate atomicity in Democritus and Lucretius or to number in Pythagoras.

Although not explicit in their work, saintly lives can be read in terms of production and distribution: the saint alters the *relations of production* by producing the alleviation of suffering among the physically and psychologically destitute; the *means of production* by including in a society's resources the saint's own body; and *surplus value* by producing an excess of desire that spills over into the lives of others. The reinscription of hagiography as social discourse would construe saintly generosity as an assemblage of desiring-machines that exert their force against the material determinations of history that cause suffering. Saints' lives could also be construed in terms of micromolecular structure organized in accordance with the laws of nature so long as such laws were understood to determine dispersed singularities rather than general forms.[31] Saintly action, for example, could be thought of as a material counterforce that, like air resistance that slows the descent of an object drawn by gravity, obstructs and undermines affliction (*TP*, p. 380).[32] Although saintly existence is not made thematic in their work, Deleuze and Guattari facilitate the revisioning of saintly experience as a metaphysics and as an economy of desire.

To be sure, these positive contributions bring to light the material and productive aspects of desire, but the price paid for a material metaphorization of desire may be the imposition of suffering greater than that which has been lifted. *It is not the minimization of pain and suffering that determines for Deleuze and Guattari how desiring production is to be controlled but rather a predelineated view of how power is to be allocated.* By legislating how desire is to express itself, the manner in which pain and suffering are to be experienced is also enjoined. "Back to the factory" constitutes a cultural revolution of the psyche that bids one to suffer, dream, imagine, fantasize, take joy in, despair, only in authorized ways.

In addition to the issue of allocating suffering, there are also metaphysical obstacles to interpreting saintly altruism in terms of desiring production. Consider first what I have designated as the myth of the plenum. Recall that Deleuze and Guattari mount an attack upon lack as a psychological construct and scarcity as an infrastructure of economy. Their argument is founded on the premise that production and lack are incompatible. Because there is nothing but the fullness of desiring production, they cannot, strictly speaking, explain disease and natural catastrophe, only the suffering caused by the inequities of distribution. The remedy proposed for socially caused suffering would consist in the forcible seizure and reorientation of the means of production, but even if the results of natural calamity can be ameliorated by human action, disease, earthquakes, and the like can rarely be avoided through such action.

A second difficulty parasitic upon the elimination of lack, not in its material form as scarcity, but in its conceptual structure, is one that goes to the heart of disseminative critical thought. How is inequity to be envisaged without giving conceptual expression to privation? How can there be differences of desiring intensity without experienced lack? By reinterpreting desiring production as without delay or lack, they have, inadvertently and counter to their intentions as postmodern disseminative thinkers, reinstated the plenum of Neoplatonic metaphysics now reinterpreted as a material fullness. This point is made but is left oddly undeveloped in an ironic remark by René Girard: "There are [for Deleuze and Guattari] souls so vile as to claim desire can lack something. They dare inject religion into the unconscious."[33]

The "reversed Platonism" of Deleuze sets out to recast Platonic being as a materialism, a move that requires a radical reworking of the notions of true being, the being of appearances, and nonbeing. But because for Deleuze nonbeing is excluded, a new ontic level is created that supplants nonbeing, that of the simulacrum which is made to do both metaphysical and epistemic work. In his reading of Plato, Deleuze declares that Plato's interest is not taxonomical, the discovery of divisions and difference—for example, the difference between tiger and lynx—but rather a quest for authenticity: "Who is the *true* X?" This question is asked *before* the world of the forms is posited so that the forms are set in motion as a solution to this anterior question. Deleuze shows that the traditional interpretation of Plato, the separation of the world into the transcendent world of essences and the everyday world of the cave, actually reflects a misunderstanding of the process by which this dichotomy is activated. Instead, Deleuze distinguishes between what receives its being from the forms and the pure becoming that escapes the action of the forms. Deleuze writes:

Plato has invited us to distinguish two dimensions: 1. that of finite and measurable things, of fixed qualities, whether they be permanent or temporary, but always presuming stops as resting places, as establishing presence, as assigning subjects . . . ; 2. and then a pure becoming beyond all measure, truly maddening that never stops, in two senses at once, always eluding the present, making the future and the past coincide, the more and the less, the too much and not enough in the simultaneity of a refractory matter (. . . "the younger becomes older than the older, the older younger than the younger." (*Parmenides*, 145–55]) [Translation mine][34]

This dualism transcends that of idea and its sensible copies. It is instead the distinction between what receives the action of the forms and what eludes the forms, between the copy and what Deleuze calls the simulacrum. "Pure becoming, the unbounded, is the matter of the simulacrum insofar as it escapes the action of the Idea, insofar as it contests at the same time both the model and the copy."[35]

As Foucault shows in his analysis of Deleuze, Plato's ontology begins with the "sorting operation which precedes the discovery of essences,"[36] a process of probing what appears that will extrude the nomad, the false "appearance," the simulacrum, from the crowd of appearances. This process of extrusion is made possible only by establishing the world of essences which will separate the simulacrum, the "false" appearances, from the multitude of appearances. *Before* the establishment of essence, predelineated, as it were, are the contenders for true being. All are eliminated as being that is not genuine save one, the nomad or simulacrum, the nameless one, because it eludes classification. The form or essence exists preeminently so that the false copy, the nomad, the unclassifiable simulacrum, may be reduced to nonexistence. The simulacra are outside of or beyond the appearances in that the appearances are what they are, are given their sham being, in the wake of the true.

Thus a reversal of Platonism can never take place by rehabilitating the appearances as modern empiricisms have tried to do. Instead, Deleuze borrows a strategy consigned to the edge of the history of Western philosophy, the materialism of the Epicurean theory of perception. There are, Epicurus argued, emissions that bounce from the surface of bodies, *phantasms*, that are received by the sensory receptors. Perception is rematerialized by Deleuze as a relation between the surfaces of bodies that both fully corporealizes perception and causes the interior of things to pass to the outside through the emissions. Two goals of the reversal of Platonism are achieved at once: materiality and the breaking up of the received distinction between inside and outside. Phantasms and simulacra undermine not only the world of essences but the appearances that are their shadows. The result, says Foucault, leads "joyously to . . . a metaphysics freed from its original profundity . . . revolving around atheism and transgression."[37]

What account can be given of the temporalization of the phantasmatic? Deleuze links his explanation to the notion of event defined as an *effect* of the collisions of bodies and, as such, without causal efficacy. Instead, as Foucault commenting on Deleuze shows, events form another kind of metaphysical succession best exemplified by death:

Death supplies the best example being both the event of events and meaning in its purest state . . . It is that of which we speak as always past or about to happen and yet it occurs at the point of extreme singularity. A meaning event is as neutral as death: "not the end but the unending; not a particular death but any death."[38]

To recast the matter in grammatical terms, the event infinitizes itself by displacing the present and circulating endlessly within language. "It puts the interiority of language in contact with the exteriority of language with being . . . and univocity is transmitted from the exteriority of being to the interiority of language."[39]

Neither the brilliance and flair of Deleuze's "reverse Platonism" nor that of Foucault's interpretation should blind the interpreter to a result of this analysis: a material fullness that, in reconceptualizing nonbeing in corporeal terms, can only think nonbeing as extruded being. Like most ecstatics, the terror of nothingness, the *horror vacui*, is a dark night of the soul that must be avoided at all costs. It is realizable only through a cordoning off of nonbeing (Neoplatonism) or the positive ontologization of lack as reframed in postmodern terms (Deleuze).

In chapter 5, I spoke of the resources hidden in Neoplatonism for the analysis of temporality as dispersion and dissemination. There, I also alluded to what is no longer viable in this thought, its insistence upon the plenary presence of the One and the explanation of difference and multiplicity as privation. Deleuze and Guattari, who begin from the opposing perspective of many modern and virtually all postmodern epistemologies, posit multiple differential forces of varying intensity. But by denying both lack, ideal nonbeing, and scarcity (material nonbeing), they have in fact replicated the ontological structure of the One as envisioned in Plotinus with its attendant difficulties in accounting for multiplicity. The positing of simulacrum, phantasm, or event multiplies entities but does so without delineating a differential structure that would permit their discrimination.

Consider the place of the One in Plotinus's system. It is the primary and ultimate principle of reality, the "unoriginating," "the spaceless," for which "we abolish the notion of any environment: . . . circumscribe him within no limit . . . no quality; since [there is] no shape, [there can be] no relationship" (*En* VI.8.11). So great is the unitive impulse in Plotinus that he enjoins: "Think of the One as Mind or as God, you think too meanly" (*En* VI.9.6). Its self-sufficiency is the essence of its unity. "Even self-mastery is absent here, [because] self-mastery begins with Being while the supreme is to be set in a higher order" (*En* VI.8.12). It is not difficult to read *in nuce* in this account a version of the body without organs, "the immobile motor" that is "unproductive" and "sterile" to which the partial objects attach themselves.

Recall that not only is the body without organs immobile, but it is a plane of inscription, an enchanted surface that arrogates the productive process to itself. To what then can differentiation be attributed? The structural problematics of Neoplatonism and of Deleuze and Guattari necessitate the positing of a second principle to render plausible the engendering dynamism that results in multiplicity. Unlike Plato, who posits ideal forms to explain the origin of things in the world of sense, Plotinus argues that activity in the One is the function of will insisting that a thing's "will and itself must be the same thing" (*En* VI.8.13). In the case of the One, if the will were other than the One it would become a manifold. If this posited identity of will and the One does not strictly avoid duality, "we must be patient with language . . .; everywhere we must read 'so to speak'" (*En* VI.8.13). Particularly striking is the connotation of yearning that Plotinus attaches to will, a territory retraversed by nineteenth-century Romanticism and twentieth-century postmodern ecstatics. The Plotinian longing that sweeps through the One—"lovable, very love, the Supreme is also self-love" (*En* VI.8.15)— becomes the *Sehnsucht* of Faust and his successors.[40]

Almost imperceptibly, Plotinus has assigned to the One functions he generally attributes to the Intellectual Principle or *nous*, the whole that comprises all beings, the objects that are known and the mind that knows them.[41] In order to avoid further conflation Plotinus is forced to assert that being belongs to the manifold of *nous* and, as such, unity cannot belong to being. "In sum, unity cannot be the totality of beings for so its oneness is annulled" (*En* VI.9.3). This leads to the conclusion that the One is beyond being, greater in perfection. But if the notion that the One transcends being is taken to the end, a startling postmodern position emerges: *the One and the nihil are the same*. Plotinus draws back from this possibility and attributes the threat to unity as stemming from need or lack: "Something there must be supremely adequate . . . most utterly without need" (*En* VI.9.6). The absence of need in the One precludes the generation of multiplicity in it and makes necessary the positing of the hypostases in order to account for the multiple ideal and material entities comprised in the cosmic whole.

Desiring production considered from the standpoint of the body without organs is functionally analogous to the One, and the partial objects to the manifold of the Plotinian *nous*. But because Deleuze and Guattari's account of desiring production in the *Anti-Oedipus* is radically materialistic, the body without organs and the partial objects must be taken together as constituting a material plenum without spatial aperture or temporal delay, without Derridean *différance*. Repression may simulate lack, but in actuality there is only the machinic plenum. This is what I referred to earlier as the fallacy of misplaced materiality.

The whole language of stratigraphy of Deleuze and Guattari's later work, the inadvertent substitution of geological strata for the Neoplatonic hypostases, replicates the strategies of Neoplatonism in order to save the level of multiplicity that, as empirical and postmodern epistemologists, they must preserve. The notion of gaining footholds on the body without organs leaves the way open for praxis but precludes the ecstasy of the plenum; ecstatic experience, on the other hand, undoes repression but offers no starting point for action. Since the reconciliation of fullness and motility is impossible, both are allowed to stand side by side: The plenum—"the plane of consistency," the "seamless" totality of the bodies without organs—is without aperture but because it is beset by a ceaseless restlessness, it is always already negating itself. Because desiring production is truly full, it is without lack, but because it is a fullness of pure motion, of pure-break flows, it is a plenum that cannot be other than pure void: it is, so to speak, an *empyrean* void opened as the abyss-al nihilism of the present epoch described by Nietzsche and Heidegger.

This has the most serious consequences for the interpretation of sainthood: saintly action can only be desiring production inscribed upon a void of break-flows that, like ocean waves, meet, merge, disintegrate, and are swallowed up by other break-flows. There are no transactions, only collisions of forces.

If these metaphysical "postulates" result in self-divestiture—a breakup of repressive constellations of desire—in the absence of anything other than desire, this dispossession of self leaves open the gaping ground of pure nihilism. It is the same fear that Lyotard attributes to Marx in his extraordinary essay "Le désir nommé Marx" in *L'économie libidinale*,[42] a text constructed in the free-wheeling style of a Marx brothers film. Lyotard argues that Marx is a fiction writer whose work is not to be interpreted theoretically but as a form of madness. First, one must "stroke the beard" that adorns the martial head,[43] but in order to discover the libidinal Marx, one must envisage him as a split personality: "The Old One" is also a young girl, "a strange bisexual composite." The girl is "upset by the polymorphous body of capital, and yearns for a great love."[44] Marx the public prosecutor is to indict capital and imagine a new love for her, the proletariat.

Because capitalism is bound up with prostitution for Marx, Lyotard identifies the little Miss Marx of Marx's alternate persona with Edwarda, the prostitute of Bataille's novel.[45] The exchangeability of everything in capitalist society into money gives desire an exchange value so that it too is freed from older controlling forms. Thus capital releases aleatory and uncontrollable pulsions of desire:

> Madame Edwarda is not just a prostitute [in an economic order of prostitution] who authorizes a semiotics and a sociology of prostitution; she is also a madwoman. In what does her madness consist? In the excess of enjoyment (*jouissance*) in her professional position. The rule of frigidity is not respected.[46]

The depiction of desire with nothing to stop it save further pulses of desire turns Edwarda's professional activities into a chaotic free-for-all of pleasure.

I have designated those who practice unconstrained desire but in whom the altruistic impulse remains intact *saints of depravity*. Desiring production is not without love, but in the absence of the Other this eros turns itself inside out like a glove and exposes itself as pure negation. These ecstatics, the imagoes of saints and buddhas to which an age of nihilism gives birth, are depicted in the fiction of such writers as Genet, Klossowski, Mishima, Burroughs, and Duras. No postmodern account of radical altruism can afford to ignore the relation of depravity to sainthood as it shows itself in postmodern fiction. I shall turn to Genet's fiction after considering two other related myths in Deleuze and Guattari, that of the tabula rasa and that of the absent absence.

A consequence of the demythologization of the Oedipus myth is an emptying of the conceptual space it occupied and the supplanting of

Oedipus by the molecular structure of free desire. Only the neurotic remains trapped by the Oedipal mode of socialization. Plotinus describes failed visionaries in terms that might well be applied to the neurotic: they are those "who have not attained to see . . . come to know the Splendour There; . . . felt and clutched to itself that love-passion of vision known to the lover come to rest where he loves; . . . the vision is frustrate" (*En* VI.9.4). By contrast, the schizophrenic of Deleuze and Guattari attains liberation by "destroying beliefs, representations, theatrical scenes" (*AO*, p. 314), short-circuiting historical memory and replacing *homo historica* with *homo natura*. But vertical or deep memory is excluded and, with it, the stories of antecedent events so that schizo-analysis precipitates a forgetting that results in a cognitively clean slate.

It's not our function to account for the dead, the victims of history, the martyrs of the Gulag in order to conclude: "Though the revolution is impossible, we thinkers must think the impossible, since this impossibility only exists in our minds!" It appears to us that the Gulag would never have existed if the victims had spoken out the way those who mourn them do today. The victims would have had to think and live very differently, in order to provide subject matter for those who cry in their name, who think in their name and give lessons in their name. It's the life force that pushed them and not their sourness."[47]

In speaking for the victims and against the voices of conventional wisdom, Deleuze and Guattari become the very voices they excoriate, spokesmen for the dead. What is most significant, however, is not the apparent contradictoriness of their position but a break in the connection between historical narrative, in this case the stories of the victims, and later historical action. It is worth noting a response cited in a slave narrative to the view that victims themselves should have avoided their fates: "'I have heard a heap of people say they wouldn't take the treatment what the slaves took, but they woulda took it or death. If they had been there, they woulda took the very same treatment.'"[48]

For Deleuze and Guattari radical change is self-justifying, a function of the socio-metaphysical structure of desiring machines, of the "law" of their production and distribution. The pain and suffering recounted in historical narratives is irrelevant. "Thinking the impossible" is a recommendation for action without recourse to the action's antecedents as if human practice were born afresh each day.[49] This is the myth of the tabula rasa. It derives not from dissemination and difference but from the hidden structure of presence, the *immediacy* of desiring production which produces itself without temporal delay, gap, or fissure.

The third of the three myths is that of the absent absence. In chapter

5, I argued that the saint experiences the impingement of the Other, a pressure exerted by virtue of another's sheer alterity. The Other, absent in any strict sense both from language and from sensation, is discerned in the traces of alterity that show themselves grammatically as the imperative voice and corporeally in the capacity for feeling pain. The Other's absence is necessary because, should the Other come to presence in a sensation or concept, her/his alterity would be reduced to the same. But for Deleuze and Guattari such a "conceptualizing" of the Other is simply precluded because it requires the thinking of absence. For them, there is either a positive plenum, a cosmological body without organs, or an infrastructure of total negation upon which it would be meaningless for another negation, namely lack, to supervene. The rejection of lack entails the disappearance of the Other and constitutes the myth of the absent absence.

I argued earlier that the human face gives itself as the material "form" in which the trace of an absence that can never be made present is inscribed. But Deleuze and Guattari develop an opposing view of the face claiming that it signals repressive perceptual and semantic structures. Far from revealing alterity, the face is, for them, another form that repression assumes reinforcing the absence of alterity or the myth of the absent absence. A version of this myth is also in force in the fiction of Genet.

Genet and the Saints of Depravity

In a premonitory comment that anticipates Genet's role as a schizo-revolutionary writer, Sartre remarks in the Preface to *Our Lady of the Flowers*, "[Genet] rejects reality and, in order to be even more certain that he will not be recaptured, logic itself. He is going to find his way back to the great laws of the participationist and autistic thinking of children and schizophrenics."[50] Yet Sartre continued to demand of Genet what a prophet of the nihil could not grant, as Derrida, in the oblique and broken text of *Glas*, reveals:

An alliance not easily explicable with Sartre. And yet: "Sartre himself noted a curious difficulty at the basis of Genet's work. Genet, the writer, has neither the power to *communicate* with his readers nor the intention of doing so. The elaboration [evidently not deliberate] of his work has a sense of the negation of those who read it. Sartre saw, though he drew no conclusions, that in these conditions the work was not entirely a work, but an *ersatz*, half way from the major *communication* at which literature aims."[51]

Sartre's insistence that Genet become the sovereign author of his text and that literature communicate an author's message is rejected in *Glas*. Instead, Genet's aim, the *negation* of his readers, is sustained and endorsed, as it were, as the strategy of Derrida's own transgressive writing designed to thwart the notion of chronology and authorial intention. Derrida declares:

> Above all do not go on thinking that I am here telling you . . . the story of a *genêt* whose dye [*genette*, form of *genêt*, means "dyer's greenweed"] . . . interests me before anything else. And it is true that I will have done nothing if I have not succeeded in affecting you with *genêt*, in coloring, smearing, gluing [*encoller*] you, making you sensitive, transforming you, beyond all that is combined here, out of the proper affect of this text.[52]

If this text is taken as Derrida's "own" commentary, then the imperative voice has infiltrated it: Be affected, smeared, glued, transformed with *genêt*.

There is in Genet and his protagonists an unconcealed doubleness, the antinomian hero and the saints and martyrs of medieval hagiography, a point repeatedly stressed by Sartre in *Saint Genet*. The protagonists in Genet's fiction are "perverts" (*pervertis*) with the full range of significations carried by the word: those who turn from standards of rectitude, who interpret incorrectly, and who practice sexual perversion. To pervert (*pervertir*) still carries many connotations of older forms of the root *wer* from which it derives such as *wert*: Germanic, "value or worth"; Old English, "fate or destiny"; Latin, to turn or bend." Generally the derivatives of *wer* mean "to turn or twist," an Old English version of which, *writhan*, from *wreit*, means "to twist or torture."[53] The standards that govern saintly life are reversed by Genet so that asceticism becomes total and unrestrained sexual indulgence in practice and in fantasy, pain in the service of God becomes torment in the interest of pleasure, and its brute need becomes concentrated sexual desire. Genet's characters are often types of saintly existence reinscribed, to use the language of Deleuze and Guattari, upon the body without organs.

In *Our Lady of the Flowers*, the most clearly hagiographic of Genet's works, the embellishments of saintliness that have become kitsch—its gilt, its flowers, its stylized drops of blood, its severed heads—all are transformed once more into modes of ascent that reanimate Parmenides' dictum: "The way up and the way down are the same." Traditional religion is never fully abandoned. "Darling still goes to mass [with Divine] because of its luxuriousness" (*OLF*, p. 85). The homosexuals and the criminals, pimps, thieves, and murderers are types for the saints of traditional hagiography. Our Lady is a solitary whose martyred existence replicates the asceticism of the desert fathers but expresses itself in the eroticized structure of her existence. As a prisoner, Sartre remarks in the Preface to *Our Lady*, she is bored in her cell and "boredom makes for amorousness." "No wonder," he continues, "Our Lady horrifies people: it is the epic of masturbation" (*OLF*, p. 2).

Genet's fiction is certainly transgressive, but is it also postmodern? Is its "logic" disseminative and differential in Derrida's sense or nomadic, rhizomatic, and alate as Deleuze and Guattari demand? Sartre's account of two tendencies in recent poetry provides a useful foothold in attempting to assess Genet's relation to postmodernity. One tendency "discovers plurality everywhere, exaggerates it" but presents this plurality as something serial which is then "congealed" in an abstract moment (*OLF*, p. 24). The other, Genet's perspective, does not "present externality as an expansive power but as a nothingness [upon which] the perceptible appearance of secret unities" is conferred. If this description holds, it would seem that Genet's art is politically and socially rebellious but that he remains metaphysically logocentric.

Yet Sartre also insists that the erotic scenes of Genet's fiction are "frequentative," that is, although innumerable recurring events are gathered into a single narration, the resulting story is not a condensation of these. Instead, "the identity is posited at the very beginning; it is the concept that is temporalized, the sacred essence that is projected into and developed in duration. . . . The tale changes into a ritual" (*OLF*, p. 36). It is clear that the unity and static character of concepts is broken up and disseminated. In Derridean terms, their notional "polysemy is infinite."[54] At the same time Genet's tale changes into a ritual, in conformity with Deleuze's description of rhizomatic thinking as praxis.

If postmodern hagiography is necessarily transgressive, in contrast to nineteenth-century hagiographic fiction such as Henry James's *Wings of the Dove* or George Eliot's *Middlemarch* that appear straightforwardly to endorse altruism, does this entail accepting the infliction of pain and violence and outbursts of sheer velleity as a postmodern ethic? Genet's work is particularly significant in this regard because the sovereign subject is broken up, disseminated, and cast aside through the humiliations and sufferings of the protagonists. And for many of them, anything goes, as it were, so long as erotic pleasure is enhanced. Is Genet's work to be read in the imperative as soliciting entry into its narrative chain? It is not enough to say that the text is intentionally self-parodying and as such does not solicit the reader. One could reply that the text merely replicates the parodic and "camp" features of contemporary life and that, far from constituting an obstacle, these features draw the reader into its world. Closer investigation is required.

Before turning to *Our Lady of the Flowers*, consider first the work's stratigraphy. Just as in standard hagiography there is often the admiring narrator whose life intersects with that of the saint, so too Genet enfolds the story of the homosexual queen, Divine, and her circle into the novel's autobiographical strand that repeats and reinforces imaginary episodes, a technique discussed in chapter 1 in connection with the twelfth-century story of Saint Mary the Egyptian. Sometimes saints' lives intersect within a single narrative so that the aura of sanctity attaching to the principal life is reinforced. The numinous episodes in the life of Our Lady cast shadows over Divine's degradation and martyrdom, as well as over the lives of those who have merely incidental contact with her. Thus, like Jesus and the Roman soldiers, after Our Lady is sentenced, "The guards spoke to him and served him as if, knowing he was laden with the weight of the sins of the world, they had wanted to bring down upon themselves the benediction of the Redeemer" (*OLF*, p. 291). Then too the tales of Divine's childhood with its premonitory visions of later events establish etiological relations between childhood happenings and her later martyrdom and miracles in the manner of standard Christian hagiography.

The events recounted in *Our Lady* are adorned with traditional sensory embellishments: "decaying flowers," the "odor of candles and incense," "bouquets of violets," and the "black haloes" of the mourners' umbrellas (*OLF*, p. 580). The most scatological and violent doings are treated allegorically and paired with their sacred equivalents. Thus the sentence depicting Divine's depravity, "[Divine] robs and betrays her friends," is followed through a process of transvaluative slippage by its allegorical equivalent: "I am Bernadette Soubiroux in the Convent of Charity long after her vision. Like me, she lived an ordinary life with the memory of having spoken familiarly with the virgin" (*OLF*, p. 295).[55]

Genet's allegories, unlike allegories governed by point-for-point similitude that are brought to closure when the salient similarities are established, are determined by difference. The allegorical pairing is based upon dissimilarity, upon a making contiguous of transgressive act and Christian counterpart so that one side of the allegory can never actually sink into the other. Thus, for example, in New Testament allegory Paul can speak of Hagar as representing the Old Testament and

Sarah the New, whereas Genet's use of Bernadette can never be thought of as somehow factually prefiguring the life of Divine. The allegorical elements can only endlessly reflect one other in a mirror play of transgressive and salvific acts. Because "depraved" desire in Genet's work carries the weight of its "sacred" double, the narrative cannot dispense with love in the sense of *caritas* but often invests this love with a new and material meaning, the relief of sexual need. Thus in the prison at Mettray the older men served by young catamites remark: "They're right, they relieve suffering humanity," to which Genet adds that he "associat[es] the expression with that of the Church: 'the humanity of Good Suffering.'"[56]

The discourse of depravity can be brought to light through the strategy of hagiographic recasting so that the duality of Genet's narrative, its sin and sanctity, can be made to appear. Transgressive events are to be read as if the "original" of which they are now the nonnuminous double is placed under erasure (*sous rature*), a strategy of reading I borrow from Heidegger and Derrida. Genet's text is to be read in the light of its own self-effacement in that its transgressive events are written as self-annulling so that, together with the events recounted, the saintly "original" appears. But this is not at all because the "original" is, as it were, a historical algorithm, a canonical Christian schematic of which the narrative's "facts" and "characters" are the simple obverse. Divine's story is a palimpsest, not merely of its histories writ small—the composite of events and characters of the Paris underworld—but also of Western Christian history, of the idealizing rules of its historiography, their Romantic-transgressive reinscription in recent literary culture, and the dissolution and dissemination of these forms into molecular pulsions of desire. Consider a possible recasting of *Our Lady*—one among innumerable possible reworkings—with its strategies of erasure and self-annulment. I shall highlight these by placing the hagiographic "original" in brackets and the bracketed constructs under erasure.

The narrator/Genet is alone in his prison [~~monastic cell~~], where he invents the story of Divine and her circle of criminal friends [~~the circle of saints~~] based on news photos of murderers [~~icons~~]. Posted on the wall, these photographs become the subject of Genet's erotic fantasies [~~contemplation~~]. Divine has just died of consumption [~~martyrdom~~], and the pimps, queens, murderers, and thieves [~~saints and church luminaries~~] have come to pay their respects [~~apotheosis~~]. Now, after her death, Divine's legend [~~hagiography~~] can come into being. Twenty years earlier she arrived in Paris from the provincial town where she was born [~~sacred childhood~~] and where she met and fell in love with the homosexual pimp and stoolie Darling Daintyfoot [Judas]. Divine is introduced to the life of the streets, to hustling, cocaine, and imprisonment [saintly trials]. After six years of life together [trials, corporeal works of mercy], Darling Daintyfoot leaves Divine [betrayal] for a treacherous rival queen, Mimosa [demon], but returns to Divine [repentance and forgiveness] and remains for five more years [further trials and works of mercy]. At this time Darling meets Our Lady of the Flowers [meeting of the saints], who is a boy of sixteen and who has just murdered an old man for his money [redemptive act, sacrifice]. When Our Lady accidentally drops the money at the railroad station, Darling picks it up [miracle]. The two become friends, and Darling moves into an elegant hotel with Our Lady [monastic seclusion]. When the twenty thousand stolen francs give out [saintly poverty], they return to the attic and to Divine, who comes to love Our Lady [renewal of saintly bonds]. Later Divine meets and falls in love with Gabriel or Archangel [one of the beatified], who is killed in the war and is replaced in her affections by Seck Gorgui [one of the beatified], a giant black whom she serves [corporeal works of mercy]. In thinking of her childhood Divine remembers her friend Alberto, who places her hand on the body of a snake so that she will loathe whatever she comes to love [vision]. When Our Lady returns to Divine's attic for the last time, Divine is jealous at her gradual exclusion from the erotic triangulation of Seckui, Our Lady, and herself [trial]. Meanwhile, Our Lady during routine police questioning about a cocaine seizure inexplicably confesses to the murder of the old man [expiation]. A much publicized trial is conducted [trial], and Our Lady is given the death penalty. Forty days later she is guillotined [martyrdom and apotheosis]. Divine is in despair [trial]. When the two-year-old child of a neighbor comes to visit, Divine contrives to have the child fall from the balcony of her flat [redemptive sacrifice]. Convicted for involuntary manslaughter, she serves three months [trial], contracts tuberculosis [trial], has a final vision of the snake-handler Alberto [beatific vision], and dies [death and apotheosis]. The narrator, Genet, recalls that his case is to be heard the next day [trial]. If he is not released, he will continue to "refashion lovely new lives for Darling, Divine, Our Lady and Gabriel" [adoration of the saints].

Genet illuminates the yearnings of saintly life within the postmodern framework of a fully material immanentism and radical transiency. His work brings to the fore one of the perquisites of a magical plenum in which individuality is lost and wholeness without fissure seems to be attainable: ecstasy. On the one hand, there is an exterior plane, the body-cosmic, a surface of pleasure unimpeded by alterity. Consider Divine's remarkable description of her body turned into cosmic exteriority: "I wanted to swallow myself by opening my mouth very wide and turning it over my head so that it would take in my whole body, and then the Universe, until all that would remain of me would be a ball of eaten thing" (*OLF*, p. 75). On the other hand, there is the endless nihilatory stream of productive becoming. The cosmic surface so seemingly full is pure emptiness. The most extreme possibilities of the body's capacities for pleasure and pain—sadomasochistic love, murder, the putrefaction of death by disease, drug-induced euphoria—must be played out against the glacial ridges, icy peaks, and crevasses of the void, not the One, but the -1, negation beyond being. In a remarkable paraphrase of Saint Catherine of Siena, Genet comments that his criminals "are as at home in infamy as a fish is in water."[57]

This strand of postmodernism, expressed by Deleuze and Guattari, Genet, and others, must be distinguished from the positions of the later Heidegger, Derrida, Levinas, and Blanchot, for whom difference, delay, fissure, break, gap, trace, spoor predominate. Thus there are alternative strands of postmodernism. First there is the tendency in which delay and difference as disruptive of cognitive, axiological, and metaphysical wholeness are stressed.[58] The other thread, which includes Deleuze, Guattari, and Genet, posits desire as kind of plenum with nothing to stop its headlong rush other than lines of flight that turn the plenum into its obverse. Genet's genius is to have written a gospel of unimpeded desire, desire brought to a halt only when it collides with another desire that will devour it or that it will itself devour.

Faces

I have argued that desire for the Other imposes a responsibility for the Other that is especially strong in the lives of saints. How can this interpretation of alterity be sustained in a postmodern context when an alternative postmodernism allows for the ecstatic character of saintly life, the mystique of a pleroma that becomes a nihil? I maintained (with Levinas) that the face is the an-iconic material expression of the Other that provides the warranty for language and that saints' lives, far more than others, respond to the impingement of alterity. But in the broken plenum of Deleuze and Guattari there can be no faces in the sense I attribute to the term. For them as well as for Genet, there is always already void upon which no further negation can supervene. Desiring production can only redistribute its products or reconceive them. Like Democritus and Lucretius, Deleuze and Guattari interpret death not as negating but as reallocating preexisting particulate ultimates. Their arguments must be carefully weighed because, if they are right, saintly ecstasy as described by Genet would constitute the imperative of postmodern hagiography.

Deleuze and Guattari's analysis is a response both to earlier phe-

nomenological accounts of faciality and to a perceived if unacknowl-
edged resistance of the human countenance to deconstruction. In his
remarks on official portraits, Sartre comments that the portrait "recognizes neither weakness nor strength but is concerned only with
merit."[59] They belong, says Sartre, "at the top of a pole like a totem . . .
[to be] bowed down to."[60] Living faces, in contrast to objects that exist
in the form of physical mass, project themselves in time and space, a
capacity Sartre calls *transcendence*.[61] What is more, he argues, the face
is an entryway for the world and is "filled with greedy holes which snap
at everything that passes within reach."[62] Eyes, ears, nostrils are not
mere receptors but, in reaching out toward the world, display the property of "voracity."

For Deleuze and Guattari, faces present a particularly vexing problem in that the face is without question something material and yet it
gives itself as something ideal. It is, as such, a taxonomical anomaly, an
ersatz material icon whose ideality must be deconstructed and its pre-
tenses uncovered. The face must be shown up for what it is: a material
surface that, on the one hand, reveals interiority described as a "black
hole" and, on the other, a surface of inscription, a "white wall," to be
read by others (*TP*, p. 167). For Deleuze and Guattari, "the face constructs the wall that the signifier needs in order to bounce off of; . . .
the frame or screen. The face digs the hole that subjectification needs in
order to break through; . . . the black hole of subjectivity as consciousness or passion" (*TP*, p. 168).

By allowing only typological significations to emerge, faces never
give themselves as individuals. The white wall/black hole system is a
"machine of faciality (*visageité*)" that produces existing faces by ma-
nipulating the relationship of hole to wall (*TP*, p. 168). Deleuze and
Guattari's analysis carries over the Sartrean view of the face's voracity
and stylization that were, in Sartre, confined to portraiture, to living
faces. For them faces overwhelm the body, organize its significations,
and dominate its codes. Far from representing what is human in human
beings, the face is inhuman from the start. "If human beings have destiny, it is . . . to escape the face, to dismantle the face and its facializa-
tions" (*TP*, p. 171) by loosening the characteristic organization of its
features. The human countenance must be disarticulated so that it becomes "asignifying" and "asubjective," deterritorialized and reencoded
so as to become one with the body without organs.

Because faces express social roles as well as inner states, it is contended that faces have political significance. Even if all people have
faces, it does not follow that the face has a universal meaning. To the

contrary, Deleuze and Guattari contend, "The face . . . is White Man himself. . . . The face is Christ. . . . The face is the typical European" (*TP*, pp. 176f.), both absorbing other faces and excluding from power those that do not conform to dominant racial, class, or sex types. Racism, it is asserted, is measured by the degree from which other faces deviate from white faces. Yet, as Deleuze and Guattari concede, in painting from the medieval period to the Renaissance, Christ himself appears in diverse figures: the Christ of Mannerist painting, Christ as the child of the Black Virgin, and the like. But the polysemic force of the tribal or primitive visage as well as that of Christian medieval and early Renaissance painting disappears when new power constellations impose significations on faces so that they become fetishized commodities. "The face," they argue, "is a politics" (*TP*, p. 181).

Although it is difficult to resist the conclusion that this interpretation of faciality is posited as much for its shock value as for its usefulness in uprooting stubborn structures of ideality, I shall consider the argument in detail. Deleuze and Guattari concede that the escape from faciality cannot be achieved by repristinization, the deployment of strategies invoked in nonliterate societies for socializing the subject, as they had maintained in their early work. Instead, in the essay on faciality, they appeal to nomadic thinking as it appears, for example, in the Anglo-American novel—the works of Melville, D. H. Lawrence, Henry Miller, and others—in which new horizons are discovered (*TP*, p. 186). Schizoanalysis encourages the transcending of horizons through recognition of the lines of force determined by black holes and white walls: "Know them, know your faces; it is the only way you will be able to dismantle them and draw your lines of flight" (*TP*, p. 189).

Some crucial difficulties that beset this account of the face can now be considered. Earlier I suggested that there is no place for alterity in Deleuze and Guattari's metaphysics of desiring production but only a surface of inscription, the body without organs, and the desiring-machines that break or produce desiring flows. Faces take on the character of the mode of production and the being of parts that are heuristically organized by the productive process. But on this view, there can be no nonrepressive reconstellating of faces, no transformation of the visage into an extension of the body as required by Deleuze and Guattari. Because the existence of lack is precluded, there is no fissure in desiring production, no place for an entering wedge to initiate change. Faces only produce and break down like the machines of Chaplin's film *Modern Times* or those of Fernand Léger's paintings. In a field of pure positivity or of pure negativity, there is nothing to stop the production of desire as a positive force except another desire. The metaphysics of desiring production by itself can no more provide a foothold for favoring the wretched of the earth than can the theory of ancient atomism. Desiring production functions with the indifference of a neutral force. Yet Deleuze and Guattari do not hesitate to appeal to repression as a reason for redistributing the products of desire.

In grasping the materiality of the face, they have convincingly brought to the fore the possibility of the face's becoming an icon of power.[63] But the despotic face masks what is common to faces: the manifestation of mortality that, irrespective of race, gender, and class, is expressed in every face, a mortality that the attitudinal specificity of each face either allows to become transparent or conceals. Even when faces express types—the artist, the soldier, the schoolgirl—there is always already a primordial signification attributable to them, the mortality of the existent. Faces express everything but finitude for Deleuze and Guattari because death is itself missing in the metaphysics of a desiring production that endlessly redistributes break-flows, endlessly deterritorializes and reterritorializes upon the plenum/void of the body without organs.

Because they always already manifest mortality, faces are an-iconic expressions of negation and cannot be further deconstructed. To be sure, facial expressions can be altered or the face brought into closer affinity with the body. *But the face is impervious to deconstruction because it is always already deconstructed insofar as it always already bespeaks finitude.* To attempt to further deconstruct the face as Deleuze and Guattari undertake to do is to act upon it with violence, to commit murder, so to speak. The guillotine is so often regarded with horror not only because it kills but because in concentrating its attack on the head, it violates the source of the proscription against murder, the face, whose power of negation is, for Deleuze and Guattari, precluded by the metaphysics of desiring production. Genet, in interpreting execution by guillotine as conferring a singular honor, indirectly acknowledges this power: "My aspiration to a saintliness of muted brilliance . . . made me choose decapitation which has the virtue . . . of reproving the death that it gives . . . of illuminating its beneficiary with glory. Such glory is not human."[64]

The doubleness of Genet's discourse (unlike that of Deleuze and Guattari), its simultaneous appeal to depravity and sanctity, opens a reading of the face that at least does not preclude interpreting faces as resisting integration into concepts and as carrying proscriptive weight.

This is borne out by an episode in which the child, Jean, has been asked to draw a face:

Faces are defended by respect. They resemble each other in that they are images. Drawing the main lines aroused no emotion in me, but when it came to achieving resemblance, I was paralyzed by a difficulty that was not only material, physical, but one that was of a metaphysical order. The face remained there in front of me. And the resemblance escaped. Finally my skull suddenly burst. I had just seen that its chin was individual, its brow was individual. . . . I was advancing in knowledge.[65]

All faces are negative ethical icons "defended by respect" whose specificity—the attitudinal expression that points up the particular route each life has taken in living its finitude—eludes representation.

Hagiographic fiction may contain the most astute observations about the affective expressions of faces as well as the social roles faces display. But these meanings supervene upon a more primordial layer of signification expressed in the always already deconstructed face. The otherness of the face rather than the chain of signifiers superimposed on it is the object of disinterested saintly desire. Faces lay claim to saints who substitute for or become the hostage of the Other.

SAINTLY DESIRE has in preceding chapters been interpreted as desire on behalf of the Other. A radically new perspective put forward by Deleuze and Guattari indirectly challenges the possibility not only of desiring in another's interest but also of discerning the traces of alterity that would attest the Other's claim upon the self.

In their Marxist hermeneutic of desire, Deleuze and Guattari treat desire as a mode of production and claim that present-day relations of production must be altered. If social and economic change is to occur, such change must be intrapsychic because the psychic and the social are inseparable. They see the obstacle to such transformation in the imposition of individuality by means of the socializing power of the Oedipus myth. Production itself is not the usual manufacturing and distributing of commodities and information but a process that is at once metaphysical and social, metaphysical in that an ultimate reality composed of desiring-machines is posited, and social in that material reality is a form of desire.

Desiring-machines are the "system's" ultimates. They are attached to a body without organs that is at once a surface of inscription upon which the mode of production is inscribed and a counterflow that repels the desiring-machines. The body without organs can be compared to the God beyond God of many mystical traditions and, when cosmicized as "Place" or "Plane" or "Collectivity," resembles the Plotinian One, a plane of experience where ecstasy is freed. The resemblance to Neoplatonism is stronger still when lack is extruded from the cosmic body, in the case of Deleuze and Guattari, because it is a vestige of ideality. The relation of the body without organs to desiring-machines can be seen as an unintentional recasting of the connection of Plotinus's One to the *nous*, the level of being and the manifold.

In order to release the dammed up forces of desire, Deleuze and Guattari recommend radical cognitive, affective, and practical measures, elimination of the Oedipus myth, the treatment of the body's parts as having collective rather than private significations in the manner of primitive societies, and substituting Nietzschean thought for Freudian myth.

Despite its ingenuity, important difficulties obstruct the usefulness of this version of postmodernism for an account of saintly life, most of them parasitic upon the treatment of lack. It is convenient to designate these weaknesses as the myth of the plenum, the myth of the tabula rasa, and the myth of the absent absence. First, Deleuze and Guattari treat desiring production not as lack but as something positive and full, as immediate unfissured creation. But because desiring production is also unceasing motion, the plenum is turned in upon itself, as it were: the cosmic whole becomes the cosmic void. This is the myth of the plenum. Second, schizoanalysis—the elimination of the Oedipus myth—mandates the erasure of historical memory, thus creating a tabula rasa. This practice is both coercive and counterproductive in that the past is required if only as a starting point for change. Finally, and especially important for its bearing on saintly life, is the myth of the absent absence. Without positing that which is missing, materially as scarcity and ideally as that which remains to be done, it is impossible to generate change. What is more, in the absence of lack, in a world of plenary presence, there can be no Other because the other's mode of givenness is always by way of what is absent, hidden, or withheld.

Jean Genet's fiction is an effort to construct saintly lives on the basis of unrepressed desire thwarted only by another's desire. His fiction is transgressive and, in borrowing the trappings of older hagiographic traditions, also proto-Christian. The result is a broken narrative, a backdrop of desiring production on the one hand and altruism on the other. Genet's characters are saints of depravity: those who desire on behalf of the other's transgressive desire.

Postmodernism appears to have split along a crucial fault line: on one side the stress on alterity, temporal and spatial diffraction in the work of Derrida, Levinas, Blanchot, and others, on the other Deleuze and Guattari's reversed plenum with its substitution of lines of flight for lack and difference. This split shows itself in the treatment of faciality, an issue discussed by early phenomenologists and taken up by postmodern thinkers. Deleuze and Guattari argue that the face is a stylized icon, a type, that reflects the mode of production and, as such, requires deconstruction. I argue, to the contrary, that the face is always already deconstructed in that it expresses the other's vulnerability and mortality. Other meanings may supervene, but the face exhibits the possibility of its own negation. Saints experience the claim of this negation more radically than others and respond to it with generosity and compassion.

8

Behold I am about seventy years old. And I have never been worthy [of finding a reason as to] why the Exodus from Egypt should be mentioned at night-time until Ben Zoma expounded it to me: for it says: thou shallt remember the days when thou camest forth out of the land of Egypt all the days of thy life. [Had the text said] "the days of thy life" it would have meant only the days; but "all the days of thy life" included the nights as well. The sages, however, say "the days of your life" refers to this world; "all the days of thy life" is to add the days of the Messiah.

Mishnah Berakoth 12 b

Moses stayed up on the mountain so long because it takes a long time to learn God's secret words that have the power in them to see and to do. Moses learned ten words from God. So he took the ten words of power and he made ten commandments out of them. On the back side of the words there were seals and these seals had the power of all destructions, besides more power to create and to do.

Zora Neale Hurston, *Moses, Man of the Mountain*

MOSES: My love is for my idea. I live just for it.
AARON: You also would have loved this people
Had you only seen how they lived
When they dared to see and feel and hope.
My folk is not faithful unless it feels.

Libretto for *Moses and Aaron*, Arnold Schoenberg

Relief of Moses and the Burning Bush. Reims Cathedral. Marburg/Art Resource.

Saintliness and Some Aporias
of Postmodernism

MY AIM in the present study has been to bring together two strands of inquiry, first the strand of saintly existence as a focus for moral life, and second the strand of postmodernism as an attack on the totalizing power of reason. The starting point of the first line of inquiry is a question asked by everyday common sense: "Why have ethical theories so persistently failed to solve moral dilemmas, not only as these dilemmas assault us in life but also as they occur in theoretical reflection?" Earlier this mode of questioning led to an investigation of the limits of theory and to a turn toward life narratives, particularly hagiography, defined in terms of saintly self-sacrifice on behalf of the wretched of the earth. Saints' lives were considered as nonfounding, nonoriginative points of departure for the moral lives of their addressees.

It is here that the second line of inquiry, the radical strategies of postmodern "critique" for outwitting the cunning of reason—strategies that are stratagems—came into play. Because theory is under attack, postmodernism as a "philosophical" and "literary" discursive style cannot straightforwardly appeal to the techniques of reason, themselves the instruments of theory, but must forge new and necessarily arcane means for undermining the pieties of reason.

I have throughout the present study stressed four such strategies. First, the concept of social epistemology, reason's *Sitz im Leben*, was discussed to demonstrate how reason's good faith and neutrality are embedded in historical and social contexts. Second, language was shown to contain capacities for condensation and double entendre through the use of tropes salvaged from a rhetorical tradition that both rationalist and empiricist philosophies alike had trashed. Not only are these powers of language exposed by postmodernism but they are postmodernism's own argot and they account, at least in part, for the peculiarities of its language, for the fact that, if reason's pratfalls are to be made known, one must speak an idiolect one is still in the process of

creating. Third, postmodernism was seen as both appealing to and rejecting Freud's discovery of the unconscious. It endorses Freud's account insofar as Freud interprets the unconscious as a reservoir both of
desire, a polysemic term that includes the notion of appetite (especially
sexual appetite), and of differential forces that act as resistances against
intrapsychic repression. But postmodernism rejects the Freudian notion
that desire can be brought under the jurisdiction of an ego that is *fons
et origo* of thought and action because there can be no vantage point
other than desire itself for acquiring purchase against desire. Fourth,
postmodernism was depicted as henophobic, as repudiating the One as
the foundation of thought and being. The attack on unity is bound up
with postmodernism's antifoundationalism, its antipathy toward the
notion that there is a privileged source of truth and meaning, whether
a transcendent divine Other or human consciousness.

These last two characteristics of postmodernism raise formidable
problems for the enterprise of a postmodern hagiographic ethics. The
third characteristic, the pandemic character of desire, appears to allow
for nothing but the free flow of desires, for, in the absence of legitimat-
ing structure, what could stop desire except its collision with another
desire? This difficulty is bound up with the fourth "canon" of postmodernism, henophobia, a fear of the One. When consciousness is no
longer an identifiable locus of being and action but dissolves into the
free play of desire, a radically disseminative or pluralistic description of
meaning, truth and practice must be given. The unity of the subject is
then reduced to impersonal pulsions of desire or force. Could it not
then be argued that postmodernism, far from facilitating an account of
saintly life, is especially damaging to it? The comparable position in the
context of the Indian metaphysical tradition is expressed in the words
of Krishna in the *Bhagavad Gita*, "There is no slayer and there is no
slain." There are only the forces of existence in endless permutation.
Could it not be maintained that from a postmodern perspective if there
are only pulsions of desire, there are in *sensu strictu* no saints, no needy
sufferers, and no acts of compassion? There can be saints only if there
is singularity, if each and every time there is compassion there are
more than disseminated drops of desire, if each and every time there is
suffering there is more than unanchored affliction. If this objection
holds, does not the argument for a postmodern hagiographic imperative
founder?

Saints were introduced to begin with because moral reason was seen
to be subject to the same damaging criticisms as theoretical reason and

therefore unable to establish a univocal view of moral action. Yet now the dissolution of standard theories of truth and reason appears to preclude the appeal to saintly lives because, with the attack on reason, the principle of the individual subject is itself destroyed.[1] I hope to show that hagiography can be saved by preserving saintly singularity. By distinguishing *singularity* which expresses difference from what many postmodernists are actually attacking, the concept of *particularity*, an account can be given of saintly life that is recognizably both postmodern and altruistic.

The matter is complicated by a problem brought out in the preceding chapter where I described a strand of postmodernism that posits a metaphysics of the nihil. This version of postmodernism reinstates a unity that it purports to dissolve. There is, however, another interpretation of postmodernism that is in keeping with its expressly differential and disseminative intent, that avoids reintroducing unity and presence and appeals to difference. I shall return to this latter version of postmodernism in the present chapter.

The conflation of nihilistic and differential postmodernism has pernicious consequences for ethical existence not only in the work of Deleuze and Guattari but even in the less clearly nihilistic work of Sloterdijk and Kristeva. By adhering to the postmodern "canons" of limitless desire and the indistinguishability of moral from literary discourse, Kristeva can neither endorse nor excoriate the racist work of Céline, to which she appeals on other grounds. I shall consider the moral ambiguity into which such literary discourse, however well-intentioned, falls when the commitment to difference falters.

In this chapter I hope to pick up the two strands of thought that have guided this inquiry so far. First, there is the issue of saints' lives as a response to the ethical worries of ordinary people and as supplanting theories about altruism. Second, there is the approach to saintly life by way of a postmodernist interpretation of hagiography. Postmodernism in art, architecture, and painting has served as a critique of a modernist aesthetic impulse that is experienced as having become effete and detached from life. Even if postmodernism's language is on occasion arcane, it can and does address the moral worries of its time.

I want to return to what can be thought of as the commonsense view of altruism that sometimes arises as a "natural" solution to vexing moral dilemmas. This standpoint is sharpened and brought into focus by analytic ethicist Nicholas Rescher but remains rooted in the dogmas of common sense. I shall consider Rescher's view in some detail as reflecting in pointed and sharply argued fashion the concerns of common-sense altruism, concerns that remain opaque and unreflexive without close scrutiny of its presuppositions.

Before a "last" look at postmodernism's treatment of radical altruism, I consider again but from a new perspective the difficulties of nihilistic/ecstatic postmodernism that precludes moral discourse. In chapter 7, I distinguished empirical ecstatics Deleuze and Guattari from differential postmodernism. Here I hope to show, principally through a critique of Julia Kristeva's work, especially her analysis of abjection, how ambiguity in the service of postmodern ecstaticism can undermine the political discourse it wants to support. I conclude that there is another strand of postmodern discourse that allows for a singularity that does not replicate the unity that, in certain postmodern thinkers, rears its head from within difference to suppress the radical character of differencing.

Differential postmodernism does not bring the matter of singularity to closure despite the henological or unifying tendency within language itself. At the level of moral existence, the postmodernism of difference always already undermines and abrades the effort to suppress the alterity of the Other. Although it sides with the *impulse* that leads to theoretical articulations of moral altruism, at the same time it undermines the pretensions of theoreticity and moral reason.

The Altruism of Common Sense: Rescher

I take a commonsense view to mean first, one that posits everyday experience as its starting point; second, one that presupposes that the position being defended already has acquired or will acquire through the force of the argument itself some degree of social consensus; and finally, one that takes the meaning of being and truth for granted without seeing the need for further explication. Thus it is not only the rough and ready disputes of ordinary life but also the far more refined discussions of altruism undertaken by analytic philosophers that reflect the commonsense view.

As representative of the commonsense view in support of unselfishness, more radical and more compelling than the views of Nagel and Gewirth discussed earlier, consider Nicholas Rescher's clarification of some widely held beliefs about altruism. Rather than focusing exclusively on the limitations of his position as I did when examining other analytic treatments of altruism, I shall treat his position as proffering clues concealed in the language of argument that can lead to a postmodern understanding of the Other. Thus Rescher's argument will be used in much the same way as Heidegger deploys the *existentiell*, the ontic or everyday behaviors of the Dasein in order to bring out its ontological structure. In the course of defending unselfishness against egoism, Rescher comes surprisingly close to disclosing the breaks and fissures in common sense. However, his defense of person-differentiated altruism, a theme to be considered later, obstructs an even closer rapprochement with the radical altruism I attribute to saintly life.

Rescher's work belongs to a familiar genre, that of the theory of moral sentiments. His aim is "to explore . . . the significant place that must be accorded . . . to the operation of unselfishly sympathetic affections among people," specifically to the sentiment of sympathy.[2] We can, he maintains, enter into the positive and negative feelings of others. These "vicarious affects" take the form of deriving satisfaction from the happiness of others (*U*, p. 5) and dissatisfaction from their unhappiness, are generally learned rather than innate, and—of particular importance—operate "in the order of reasons rather than causes" (*U*, p. 6). Thus, says Rescher:

What is at issue is not just a matter of being pleased or displeased *when* someone enjoys or suffers—for example by a peculiar blood transfusion or by being somehow cross-connected with that person by wires. The crucial factor is being happy *at* another's happiness by way of *motivation*, being pleased for him, valuing someone's good fortune *just because it is his*. (*U*, p. 6)

The issue for Rescher is that the other's unhappiness or happiness does not *cause* mine, which would be the case were the other to be thought of as an extension of myself. Rather, I care about the other's good fortune precisely because it is the other's and it is this which is the motive of my actions. "The factor of motivation," says Rescher, "is crucial" (*U*, p. 6). It is "because the other's welfare is at issue" that I am concerned for him" (*U*, p. 6). Altruistic motivation can be thwarted in extreme circumstances where saving oneself becomes a primary concern. But this is not the rule, Rescher stresses, and so is of little interest in framing a general theory.

In the next phase of the argument, Rescher correlates the vicarious affects with the degree of relationship to those toward whom these affects are directed. The "closeness or distance of social and psychic linkage that subsists between [persons]" (*U*, p. 7), including persons in future generations, will determine the sort of affect that is to be directed toward them. One will, for example, delight in one's child's joy but be only mildly pleased upon hearing of a stranger's happiness (*U*, p. 7). Rescher points to the destruction of impartiality as the price that is paid for such affective discrimination (*U*, p. 8). Nevertheless he endorses differential treatment based on person-discriminating acts against the utilitarian claim that "'each [person] is to count for one, no one for more than one' as a precept for everyday human interactions" (*U*, p. 14). To treat all alike indicates a kind of moral blindness unless, in one's social or professional capacity as doctor, judge, teacher, and so on, one is obliged to do so.[3] The fact that one takes satisfaction in one person's gains rather than another's legitimates the principle of differentiation, because as soon as I opt for X's gains, I choose to better her/his situation rather than Y's (*U*, p. 17).

Not all vicarious affects are desirable from an ethical standpoint. Thus *Schadenfreude*, any satisfaction I might derive from another's loss or unhappiness, does not redound to my credit. What is more, Rescher declares, it is less desirable to help others out of duty alone in the absence of emotional involvement than out of sympathy (*U*, pp. 15f.). Emotions do not simply fall upon one but actually can be cultivated.[4] Rescher concludes that "To be a person is correlative with recognizing the personhood of others and with standing in morally appropriate sorts of relationships with them" (*U*, p. 15).

Rescher's quarrel is with those who base morality upon prudence, who argue that acting morally pays. This regularly turns out to be false, he argues, and leads to the unpersuasive Socratic retort that, when the wicked thrive, it is because they fail to recognize the difference between their apparent and their actual self-interest. To the argument that one undertakes moral action in order to reap the benefits of living in a moral society, Rescher replies that such self-interested morality does not work because the really prudent person would simply weigh the disadvantages against the advantages and act morally only when convenient (*U*, pp. 98–99).

Rescher acknowledges a more compelling argument against the vicarious affects. It could be contended that the emotion of sympathy might be expended on unjust social relations, thus increasing rather than mitigating social injustice (*U*, pp. 100–101). Examples are whites who sympathize with apartheid in South Africa, Sudeten Germans who were sympathetic to Nazi expansionism in 1939, and Cambodians who are in sympathy with Pol Pot's forces on nationalist grounds.[5] Rescher concedes that the vicarious affects cannot be established as "ultimate, wholly sacrosanct, and totally indefeasible" (*U*, p. 101). He resorts to the notion of an impartial arbiter who would sort matters out and mediate between general social concerns such as justice and the "idiosyncratically diversified proliferation" (*U*, p. 101) of personal interests.

Although in the present state of affairs there is a gap between personal and social interest, things ought to be otherwise: "From the moral point of view we ought to strive individually to realize a morally well-ordered society. And in a morally well-ordered society the correlation of action for individual advantage and for the social good ought to obtain" (*U*, p. 103). But such a correlation between the individual and society is a social construct. At the level of the community "only society can foster the interests of the general good. The individual agent is impotent to do more than contribute his mite towards shifting society in this direction" (*U*, p. 105).

Rescher goes on to justify the positive vicarious affects along Hegelian lines arguing that they lead to social order, which, in turn, results in the development of individual potential and lives that are morally gratifying. What is more, individuals are entitled to be satisfied (*U*, pp. 105–6). This argument brings out the idealistic aspect of Rescher's theory, the quality of life as the telos of social order in which excellence and a sense of personal worth can be realized. Not only must life hold felt satisfactions but it must make possible the actualizations of social ideals. What, in sum, do the vicarious affects contribute to this goal?

Despite [their] relatively modest roles as a mode of motivation in human affairs, their *theoretical* implications are nevertheless strikingly significant. Like the *aqua regia* of little intrinsic value, which reveals the presence of true gold, the vicarious affects yield a yardstick by which to measure some of the strengths and deficiencies of various social theories. (*U*, p. 111)

Consider first the most important aspect of Rescher's account of altruism, from a postmodern point of view: its treatment of the Other. According to Rescher one can enter into another's feeling so that, from the outset, the Other is another myself whose interests can be reduced to my own: the starting point of my affect is my ego. But Rescher is careful to insist that the other's affects are not wired to my own or linked to mine as in a blood transfusion but remain the Other's. I am motivated by the other's affects simply by virtue of the fact that they are hers/his. What is at stake in my encounter with another is the other's welfare.

Written in the idiom of common sense, Rescher's view shares three crucial dimensions with Heidegger's account of other persons. First, Heidegger argues that an understanding of others is not derived from knowledge about them but is of a different kind that makes subsequent "knowledge and acquaintance" possible (*BT*, p. 161). Rescher achieves the same end by distinguishing between motives and causes: if the other's happiness were a *cause* of my own, the being of the other would be homogeneous with that of objects. When, instead, I am *motivated* by the other's happiness because it is his, the difference between being together with others and being in a world of causal relations is noted. Second, according to Heidegger I am from the start related to the Dasein that I am through concernful solicitude. Unfortunately, Heidegger continues, being-with-others "understandingly" is often interpreted psychologically so that the other is "a duplicate of the self" (*BT*, p. 161). Although Rescher uses a psychological locution, sympathy, the nub of Heidegger's distinction is taken into account when sympathy is defined in terms of concern for the other's welfare. Third, Heidegger pinpoints deficient ways of being-with-others: aloofness and self-concealment that are self-serving or egotistical. Rescher captures the sense of these properties of behavior when he speaks of prudential modes of relating to another. Often, he argues, conduct based on prudence is taken as a natural mode of action.

The "prisoner's dilemma"—a puzzle invented by game theorists in which various alternatives for gaining freedom based on a willingness to incriminate one another are offered to two prisoners held incommunicado—is a highly contrived example that highlights the point.[6] It is assumed that each prisoner will calculate how best to gain his release irrespective of the outcome for his fellow prisoner. But Rescher contends that "the dilemma present[s] a paradoxical circumstance in social interaction [only when one is] dragooned into assuming the stance of the theory of games itself" (*U*, p. 34), that of self-interested prudence. While Rescher argues that the position of self-interest is not natural, nevertheless his account of benevolence is an outcome of a debate between prudential and other-directed moralities within the theoretical framework of practical reason.

Although Heidegger's discussion moves beyond the commonsense view, recall the argument advanced in chapter 6 that Heidegger's position in regard to the *Mitsein*, the being-with-others of the Dasein, is far from postmodern. Despite his description of the Dasein as "thrown," it retains a unity characteristic of the subject that is intrinsic to modern and not postmodern philosophy. Heidegger's account of Dasein's death-anticipating character is, so to speak, only halfway there because the Dasein, anticipating its own death, gathers itself in resoluteness, thus ensuring its wholeness. The Dasein lacks the fissuring that comes into play only with the introduction of desire. Rescher's formulation of the commonsense position in the next phase of his argument, however darkly and intuitively, grasps the importance of what many postmodernists mean by desire: libidinal affect as it is socially encoded and distributed, allowing libidinal energy to gravitate in patterns of preference.

Recall Rescher's contention that benevolence is person-discriminating, a notion that governs the everyday thinking of many who think of themselves as altruistic. This concept is embodied in its radical form in the popular NIMBY (not in my backyard) imperative: keep social ills at a maximum degree of remoteness from self, family, and neighborhood. Rescher does not support person-discriminating altruism in this negative form in which a putative benefit accrues to one's friends.[7] Even when stated positively, Rescher concedes, person-discriminating altruism is bound to destroy impartiality. But he maintains that evenhandedness is impossible because, in most cases when one chooses to invest vicarious affect in one person, it is diverted from another. For example, if I decide to be happy on A's behalf, I have opted for A's gains rather than B's.

The result of a differential altruism is, however, the reinstatement of self-regarding prudence rejected earlier. The dichotomy between public and private, individual and social, family and state, that has governed moral and social discourse is interpreted by common sense in terms of interests to be balanced. Instinctive preference based on kinship is weighed off against the commonweal as determined by prior social accords. Thus the family (or other kinship structure) is assumed to provide the natural object for the expression of benevolence whereas, by contrast, institutional or social concerns are objects of disinterested principle. The hope of common sense is that a balance will be struck between a person-discriminating altruism and a morally well-ordered society.

The postmodern analysis of Deleuze and Guattari explicated in chapter 7 undermines the balance put forward by common sense by uncovering the contractual character of kinship allocation. Their position implies that the satisfaction in the joy of those who are related by kinship cannot be something natural because the allocation of kinship is always already socially coded and the hierarchy of preferences predelineated by an invisible social structure. While Rescher grasps the ineradicability of desire, he misses its programmatic character.

Then too Rescher's commonsense view of desire, including its person-differentiating character, takes as its starting point the satiability of desire. Common sense begins with the view that the other's dissatisfactions arise on the ground of a prior fullness or satisfied desire. One's own vicarious affects are directed principally toward enjoying the other's satisfactions. But I argued earlier that, to the contrary, the Other manifests herself/himself primordially as need or destitution. How, it could be demanded, does the primordiality of destitution alter the person-differential character of altruism? Will I not generally choose to alleviate the suffering of those closest to me rather than that of those who are more remote no matter how proximity is socially allocated?

The likelihood is that most would indeed give preference to those closest, but saintly lives operate in accordance with different "laws." The topographical markers of alterity can be read by anyone—the crumpled body as a signifier of pain, the expressionless face as a signifier of depression—but for saints the Other's destitution is a vortex, a centripetal force, as it were, into which saintly desire on the Other's behalf is drawn. The more fissured the life of the Other, the greater the other's lack, the weightier its claim upon the saintly self. Saints are person-differentiating, but it is lack and not proximity that is encrypted in the body or "group body" of the Other that decides who receives preference. Thus the AIDS patient, the injured of the Armenian earthquake, the sub-Saharan victims of famine are "in the trace of alterity" and "speak" in the imperative. Although the Other cannot be incorporated in a concept, from an *instrumental* point of view victims take on the character of signifiers whose signified is lack and destitution. The hagiographic imperative gives rise to practical questions, "What is to be done?" so that victims acquire secondary significations within an instrumental nexus.

In sum, the argument that the Other is the source of my vicarious satisfaction is parasitic upon a conception of the Other's prior destitution. Rescher's defense of commonsense altruism falls short of acknowledging this even when he avers that "To be a person is correlative with recognizing the personhood of others and standing in morally appropriate sorts of relationships with them" (*U*, p. 15). Common sense has come halfway in recognizing that what "persons" are is bound up with moral existence but has not yet grasped that "to be a person" begins with a conception of alterity that overcomes common sense's blindness to the nonconceptualizability of the Other and the Other's being as lack.

Rescher's most compelling argument for unselfishness is his assessment of its efficacy. Although he is for the most part a de-ontologist (holding that some acts are morally obligatory irrespective of their outcomes), paradoxically his most significant contribution is bound up with the *consequences* of altruism. Recall that he argues forcefully for altruism as the "aqua regia" which reveals the "presence of true gold" because it is the measure of the strengths and deficiencies of social theories. It is not surprising to find, couched in the language of theory, theory's subversion: *social theories do not measure altruism but altruism measures social theories*. It is, to use postmodern language, the saint's response to the Other—not, as Lyotard puts it, the grand meta-narratives of theory—that addresses me and mandates benevolence in everyday life.

Saintly exertions have this effect because the extremism of saintly life compels attention. This passive coercion, altruism's radical side, also finds a place in common sense. In an analytic account of saintly radicalism, J. O. Urmson contends that saints' actions are those that "exceed the limits of their duty, whether by control of contrary inclinations and interest or without effort."[8] Although Urmson distinguishes between saints and heroes, his description of heroism as the suppression of fear either through willful control or simply without any effort is often attributed by common sense to saints.[9] Urmson incorporates the dimension of excessiveness in describing saintly action absent from Rescher's account of moderate altruism. Yet, because Urmson's standpoint demands extraordinary self-sacrifice but remains within the framework of common sense, it is difficult to support without appealing to the traditional rationale for saintliness, that of a transcendent ground.[10] Rescher's more tepid benevolence is, on the face of it, more workable, yet his position fails to take account of the extremes of contemporary historical circumstance and the responses that such extremes may elicit on the part of some individuals. Thus Rescher's position is persuasive to those who think of their society as just and for whom the dream of wholeness still persists. Rescher subscribes to the principle of limited altruism applicable to manageable problems in the hope that benevolence will expand, whereas Urmson begins with expansive altruism believing that generosity will trickle down. In that regard Urmson's failed common sense is closer to the hagiographic imperative I have described.

Postmodern Ecstatics and Saintliness: Kristeva

Postmodernism's appeal to context, to social epistemology, contextualizes commonsense arguments endorsing altruistic action. It highlights the extreme situations of the twentieth century that bring into high relief the contrast between the radical altruism of those who place themselves totally at the disposal of the Other, become hostage to the Other, and those who respond with tepid benevolence or, worse yet, contribute to harming others.

At this point, after the long route of analyzing saintly life in postmodern terms has been traveled, three charges leveled against postmodernism can be weighed. The first is postmodernism's attack on the lawful, the second its assault on the past, and the third its unmaking of the subject or self. Critics of postmodernism argue that in unburdening itself of nomological structure it has thrown away morality, that in shedding the past it has created a historical vacuum upon which totalitarianism can supervene, and that in attacking the self or subject it has opened the possibility of an abuse of the Other because there is in *sensu strictu* no Other and no self to be held responsible. Is postmodernism not an expression of moral decadence rather than a solution to the problem of decline?

Consider postmodernism's antinomianism, an attack on the lawful. For some postmodernists thought is the captive of a politics that shapes it so that thought qua thought is discredited when its embedding politics is rejected. This case is stated in an extreme form by Deleuze and Guattari: "Thought as such is already in conformity with a model that it borrows from the State apparatus, and which defines for it goals and paths, conduits, channels, organs, an entire *organon*" (*TP*, p. 374). Behind this critique is the historical example of the radical injustice of National Socialism and what Deleuze and Guattari believe to be elements of Fascism that infiltrate many contemporary states. "From thought to *l'univers concentrationnaire*" appears to be the political motto of those who see in the old metaphysics an urgent need for a new politics.

Less radical is the notion that thought qua thought is "legitimated" but separated from morality, and the latter cordoned off as undesirable. Thus Sloterdijk writes:

Under a sign of the critique of cynical Reason, enlightenment can gain a new lease on life and remain true to its most intimate project: the transformation of being through consciousness. To continue enlightenment means to be prepared for the fact that everything that in consciousness is mere morality will lose out against the unavoidable amoralism of the real. (*CCR*, p. 82)

Both types of antinomianism, that of Deleuze and Guattari and that of Sloterdijk, are manifestations of the will to ecstasy, both texts the work of postmodernism in its empirical ecstatic form. The will to joy, the "transformation of being through consciousness," is, for Sloterdijk and Deleuze and Guattari, the "telos" of metaphysics. Joy is to be enhanced by contributions from the arsenal of modernism so that the machinic is harnessed to the flesh. Such ecstasy is expressed, for example, in the new worldwide culture of music—rock, new wave, and their successors—in which the body as a whole is both sensorium and medium for aesthetic expression. I argued in chapter 7 that Deleuze and Guattari's antinomianism derives from an account of desiring production that conceals a metaphysical monism beneath the differential and pluralistic character of their version of the real. I shall not go over this ground again except to notice that the single-minded quest for ecstasy by way of a hidden monism is bound up with the coercive seam in the otherwise an-archic postmodernism of Deleuze and Guattari.

The character of Sloterdijk's antinomianism is the result not only of a broken metaphysics but also of a broken politics in that two quite different and opposing political wills are the starting point of his work. On the one hand, there is the postmodern expression of the will to joy derived from Nietzsche; on the other, there is as the work's immediate backdrop, the historical experience of a National Socialism that Sloterdijk unequivocally rejects. His use of Nietzsche stemming from the first consideration is modified by the second. "It was perhaps Nietzsche's theoretical recklessness that allowed him to believe that philosophy can exhaust itself in provocative diagnoses without . . . thinking seriously about therapy" (*CCR*, p. 206).

Yet is there not a danger in the fact that postmodernism draws upon the immediate past? And once "morality" has been repudiated and eclecticism enjoined as a principle of selection, does not a strange contiguity and juxtaposition of elements become likely? Sloterdijk's repudiation of National Socialism is strongly voiced in his work. It is hard to imagine a more forceful expression of revulsion than his endorsement of Adorno's remark: "'All culture after Auschwitz, including the penetrating critique of it, is garbage'" (*CCR*, p. 287). Yet there is a quasi-unconscious deployment of a Fascist detritus that fissures this critical discourse.[11] For example, in the context of a discussion of Hitler's SS as Death Head (*Todtenkopf*) units, he writes:

Fascism is the vitalism of the dead . . . embodied in [Western culture] in vampire figures that, for lack of their own life force, emerge as the living dead among the not yet extinguished to suck their energy into themselves. Once the latter are sucked dry they too become vampires. Once they become devitalized they crave the vitality of others. (*CCR*, p. 286)

Is the contagion of vampirism spread to its victims so that all become vampires? Does Sloterdijk know that vampirism was attributed to Jews and does he intentionally reverse this discourse by attributing it to the SS? If so, how can one explain the contagion that allows the attribution of the "disease" to its victims? Who are the victims? People in general, the German populace that accepted Nazism, the victims of the SS? The ambiguities of Sloterdijk's discourse persist within the ambit of his broader quest for ecstasy.

Ecstatic postmodernism's ambiguities arise in part from its failure to go deep enough and in part from its wresting from the ruins a metaphysics that will allow for the return of an all-encompassing unity not, of course, without first paying homage to topographical difference (Deleuze) or the "kynical" absurd (Sloterdijk). It is noteworthy that there is no mention, critical or otherwise, in Sloterdijk's work of the discourse of alterity beginning with the dialogical philosophies of Buber, Rosenstock-Huessy, and Marcel or of the recent analysis of this tradition by Michael Theunissen.[12] Suffice it to say that ambiguity pervades the discourse of postmodern ecstatics insofar as alterity remains an absent absence.

Julia Kristeva's work is especially disquieting in this regard. Repelled by National Socialist discourse, she is nevertheless led by the ecstatic empirical thrust of her thought to bring this discourse into the closest contiguity with the language of ecstasy or *jouissance* in a way that ultimately renders their discrimination nearly impossible. The compelling reasons she believes exist for this doubleness come to the fore in the course of her analysis.

Rejecting the inside/outside and self/other dichotomy, Kristeva develops a phenomenology of the abject, a new psychological type that experiences itself as the discarded refuse, the trash, of the psyche. Neither an object—objects provides a locus for the establishment of homologous meanings—nor an other—others flee signification altogether—Kristeva's abject is a liminal being. "What is abject [neither object in the strict sense nor other], the jettisoned object, is radically excluded and draws me towards the place where meaning collapses" (*PH*, p. 2).[13] Thus, for example, the infant who rejects its food as separating it from its desire for the parents identifies with the loathed object, spits it out, and in ejecting the food ejects itself (*PH*, p. 3). It will, Kristeva contends, continue to see itself as something loathsome because the ego and the superego have driven it away. Hounded into exile, as it were, "from its place of banishment, the abject does not cease challenging its master. Without a sign it beseeches a discharge, a convulsion, a crying out" (*PH*, p. 2). It is not difficult to interpret saintly anorexia described by Weinstein and Bell and discussed in chapter 2 as a version of saintly abjection. The saint can be viewed as an abject loathsome to herself/himself but taken up into the compensatory love of God. This interpretation would reduce the role of alterity, the appeal of the other's destitution in saintly life, to an endless quest for overcoming abjection.

Kristeva argues that in abjection a certain uncanniness appears which comes to acquire independent existence but whose origin is forgotten. "[I]t harries me as something radically separate, loathsome. Not me, not that. But not nothing either. A weight of meaninglessness about which there is nothing insignificant and which crushes me. On the edge of non-existence and hallucination" (*PH*, p. 2). Compounded of Kierkegaard's dread as well as Freud's and Heidegger's *Unheimlichkeit*, Kristeva's uncanniness nevertheless differs from the uncanniness of all of them in that the abject's lack is allowed no subsistence. Thus, in her interpretation of Freud's famous case of little Hans, no sooner does the child recognize the phallic lack of his mother and perhaps himself than it is replaced with the horse, "a hieroglyph having the logic of metaphor and hallucination" (*PH*, p. 35). Little Hans creates, in the manner of the abject, what is absent. The principle of hieroglyphic substitution opens the possibility for "the subject of abjection" to develop a language of her/his own and, as such, to be "eminently productive of culture. Its symptom is the rejection and reconstruction of languages" (*PH*, p. 45).

Abjection challenges theories of the unconscious that are sustained by negation. The abject, unable to locate herself/himself, unsituated, self-exiled, becomes a "deject." Like Deleuze's nomad, Kristeva's abject asks not "'Who am I?'" but "'Where am I?'" and, like the schizorevolutionary, is "a deviser of territories" (*PH*, p. 8). To be sure, for Kristeva it is "a space that is never *one*, nor *homogeneous* nor *totalizable*" (*PH*, p. 8), a place of exclusion upon which the abject/deject will live her or his *jouissance*. Despite this affirmation of difference, Kristeva has strayed onto the pleasure plateaus of Deleuze and Guattari, onto the territory of a body without organs, a body, as I argued earlier, without alterity which, on the one hand, is declared to be nontotalizable but, on the other, is the hypostatic pleroma of *jouissance*.

This homogeneity is attested in her treatment of the Other, that Other who no longer has a grip on the stray: The abject/deject is an *Auswurf* (my term), a castaway, that enters "an abominable real . . . through jouissance" (*PH*, p. 9). The *jouissance* of abjection is without alterity, the ecstasy that comes from a repeated iteration of self-loathing. Like the other empirical ecstatics, Kristeva's is a broken discourse, one in which the plenum becomes not a nihil but the abject's sick and sickening plane of *jouissance*. The abject, repugnant to others and having no "clean and proper" self, replaces the desired Other with internal fluids such as urine or blood (*PH*, p. 53). An older phenomenology of qualities—Sartre's analysis of the sticky, for example—is now applied to the abject's plane of ecstasy.[14]

Kristeva relates this analysis of psychological abjection to the history of religions, which she interprets as a nexus of collective expressions of abjection, paganism or Greek religion, Judaism and Christianity, each with its own means of purifying the abject (*PH*, p. 17). Mark C. Taylor observes that her analysis "recalls Hegel's tripartite interpretation of religion."[15] Unlike Hegel, however, the dialectical relation of Western religious patterns in Kristeva does not culminate in their resolution:

> Advancing from the Greek, through the Jewish, to the Christian, the sacred is transformed from exteriority to interiority. While the Greek suffers the sacred from without and the Jew encounters it in and through willful transgression, the Christian experiences the sacred as an outside that is inside, forever faulting his identity.[16]

For Kristeva, arguing against Hegel, the tension between Greek and Jew is not reconciled in Christianity.

The Hegelianism that is rejected in the irreconcilability of religious oppositions reenters through the backdoor in Kristeva's understanding of the historical route taken by abjection. Thus, she maintains, the move from a naive and unmediated paganism, matrilinear in character, is succeeded by biblical Judaism's fear of a matrilineal power that could threaten the paternal Law and its distribution of the categories of pure and impure (*PH*, p. 91). What is extruded, the maternal, does not disappear but builds a victimizing and persecuting machine by ascribing sanctity to a people and segregating it from the nations of the world (*PH*, p. 112). The theme of exclusion is further elaborated in the Christian conception of sin and retribution in which the righteous are cordoned off from the sinners and the whole played out as a scenario of eternal bliss and eternal punishment. This, in turn, leads to the "final" stage of Kristeva's dialectic: "the catharsis par excellence called art" that purifies and is "destined to survive the historical forms of religion" (*PH*, p. 17). Sin, Kristeva claims, is transcended when, as Nietzsche revealed, it becomes integral to the beautiful (*PH*, p. 122).

Although Kristeva's discourse breaks with Hegel on the matter of the dialectical sublation of the religious moments, she replicates Hegel's ordering of Western religions. In his analysis of Hegel's early theological writings, Taylor shows that, for Hegel, Old Testament religion is not merely dialectically overcome but despised as representing the nadir of Spirit. Hegel declares: "'How were [the Jews] to recognize divinity in a man, poor things that they were, possessing only a consciousness of their misery, of the depth of their slavery, of their opposition to the divine?'"[17] Yet, for Kristeva, because abjection is subversive, there is a certain *pli* or fold in her analysis that distinguishes it from the early Hegel's description of Judaism as the religion of stones and fecal matter.[18] Despite this difference, Kristeva writes:

In opposition to Apollonian . . . Greek corporeality, flesh here signifies according to two modalities: on the one hand close to Hebraic flesh (*basar*), it points to the body as eager drive confronted with the law's harshness; on the other it points to a subdued body, a body that is pneumatic since it is spiritual, completely submersed into divine speech in order to become beauty and love. (*PH*, p. 124)

Biblical monotheism, argues Kristeva, is to be exorcised by a Christianity that is the penultimate stage before the *jouissance* of aesthetic quietism.

There is in this account a forgetting of postmodernism's perspectivalism. Kristeva fails to notice that the Exodus, for example, may have been interpreted by classical Christianity through the symbolics of prefigurement, but as the epigraphs of this chapter attest, it is an epic of freedom for Jews and, to a considerable extent, has become so for Afro-Americans against the ground of a quite different metaphysics.

The matter is even more complex because Kristeva goes on to declare that it is one of Christianity's insights that both "perversion and beauty" belong to the same libidinal economy. It would seem that, for Kristeva, the multiple modes of expressing abjection are determined not by moral concerns when these concerns are proscriptive but, as in the case of Genet, through the transformation into beauty: "[S]in is the requisite of the Beautiful. . . . the Law of the Other becomes reconciled with Satan" (*PH*, p. 122). It is the *aestheticization* of the Law that is, for Kristeva, therapeutic both at a psychological and at a metaphysical level rather than the surrender of nomological discourse to the discourse of the Other. The joker or wild card (Derrida), the simulacrum (Deleuze and Guattari) that might be invoked as tropes for the saint as quick change artist of social and personal transformation could be borrowed by Kristeva to describe the being that belongs to the Other. But the implication to be drawn from Kristeva's account of the Other is that the Other is a floating signifier to be transformed into beauty. Her discussion of the abject is a double discourse: an explanation of abjection in its many forms but also a subtle endorsement of it through a certain break in the discourse of abjection. This manifests itself in a particularly puzzling way in her extended analysis of Céline.

Céline's anti-Semitism, and Kristeva's treatment of it, is an exceedingly complex matter, and my remarks will bear only on its relevance for the problematics of saintly life. There is, on the one hand, Kristeva's exposure of Céline the "Fascist ideologue" who rages against Jewish monotheism and displaces this by Fascist mystic positivity. And yet Kristeva, through an almost invisible conceptual slippage, avers: "It is impossible not to hear the liberating truth of [Céline's] call to rhythm and joy, beyond the crippling constraints of a society ruled by monotheistic symbolism and its political and legal repercussions" (*PH*, p. 179). To be sure, "the liberating truth" is bound up with "the deadliest of fantasies" (*PH*, p. 174), as Céline's pamphlets show. Yet she asks:

Do not all attempts . . . at escaping from the Judeao-Christian compound . . . to return to what it has repressed, converge on the same anti-Semitic Célinean fantasy? [T]his is because . . . the writings of the chosen people have selected a place, in the most determined manner, on that untenable crest of manness seen as symbolic fact—which constitutes abjection. (*PH*, p. 180)

The entire discourse of the chapter "Ours to Jew or Die" is written with an abhorrence of Fascism that is at the same time a lure, a willing subjection to its seductive power not only to disclose it but to speak the transgressive and unspeakable discourse with pleasure through the mouth of another.

Yet it could be argued there is a concept of saintly existence that shows itself in Kristeva's work apart from her analysis of abjection. Lacan, she insists, connects saintliness to the psychoanalyst (*PH*, p. 27), the witness to abjection, to its decoding, and to its cathartic explosion in the patient. If this is the case, the further question must be asked, "Who is the analyst?" Not the psychoanalyst but the writer of genius is the "master" analyst, who reaches the point where writing transcends itself: "the sublime point at which the abject collapses in a burst of beauty that overwhelms us—and that 'cancels our existence' (Céline)" (*PH*, p. 210). It is the writer, Céline, who appropriates the discourse of abjection in its most violent form and who transforms it into beauty.[19]

It is not inapposite in the context of Kristeva's transcendence of abjection through its aestheticization to recall Kierkegaard's admonition to "reason from existence not towards existence, whether moving in the palpable realm of fact or in the realm of thought" (*PF*, p. 31). The consequences for existence of this aestheticization cannot be ignored for the Other since abject/deject is not only "a hieroglyph" marked by the sign of negation but a flesh and blood existent for whom this negation is nihilation.[20] To bestow a shadowy existence on the Other is to exert the power of negation.

Kristeva's docetism, her failure to treat the Other as a creature of flesh and blood, leads indirectly to a certain general inattentiveness to the distribution of discourse, to the question, "Says who?" the liberating question of postmodernism posed compellingly by Foucault and Sloterdijk among others. She explicates the abjection of paganism, Judaism, and Christianity and the abjection described in Céline's Fascist idiolect but forgets that men and women who wield or lack power, who kill or are killed, are both the objects of these discourses and their controllers. In the context of contemporary history, to be an abject of another, not least of all an abject in the writing of Céline, is to be implicated not in a speculative but in an actual chain of death.

The preference for a joy beyond pleasure, for an ecstaticism that is different from solicitude, shows itself elsewhere in Kristeva's work, in her preference for the madonnas of Giovanni Bellini over those of Leonardo Da Vinci on the grounds that, in the distanced look of Bellini's Virgin, "unlike the solicitude in Leonardo's paintings, [there is] ineffable jouissance" (*DL*, p. 347).[21] The face of the Virgin is averted, the gaze is "never center[ed] in the baby."[22] It seems that there is in Bellini's madonnas "a shattering, a loss of identity, a sweet jubilation where she is not."[23]

Ecstaticism does not require temporal difference and deferral but a reinstatement of that very present that postmodernism has rejected. Yet, in repudiating both classical and modern metaphysics to which they attribute a logic of presence, Deleuze, Kristeva, and other French postmodernists posit difference *en principe*. This conflict can come to the surface in the work of Peter Sloterdijk, for example, because, by refusing to totally reject the intellectual aims of the Enlightenment, he is less embarrassed by signs of the logic of presence in his work than are most postmodernists. Thus in the last sentence of the *Critique of Cynical Reason* he concludes: "[C]ourage can suddenly make itself felt as a euphoric clarity or a seriousness that is wonderfully tranquil within itself. It awakens the present within us. In the present, all at once, awareness climbs to the heights of being. . . . No history makes you old" (p. 547).

To gain the pleromatic fullness of ecstasy requires a present that forgets history for the reasons discussed earlier, because who in the century of man-made mass death could attain ecstasy without amnesia?

The Problem of Saintly Individuation

The discourse of postmodernity is a language of desire, its economy a libidinal economy, its ethic often bound up with a conatus toward satisfaction. In considering postmodern "metaphysics," differential forces, quanta of power or desire, are stipulated but there is considerable variation in the way these forces have been interpreted by postmodern thinkers. Desire may be described in terms of difference and yet may function as a hypostatic plane of libidinal satisfaction, not seamless yet without alterity. I have argued that the reverse Platonism of Deleuze attempts to maintain difference while sublating the Other. Where lack or negation appears to be mandated, phantasmatic being is made to take its place in order to maintain the differential character of discourse. But if postmodernism is to be differential, then alterity must be thought of in terms of lack, absence, and negation. On the other hand, it could be asked, is alterity nothing but negation and lack, a nonplace from which a certain speech, the speech of the Other, issues? And, depending on the answer, how does lack bear on the altruism of saints?

The question for saintly life is not only "Can there be difference without lack?" but also "How is the object of saintly life and action to be described in terms of lack?" Must there not be a positivity bound up with living for the Other? And if differential postmodernism, in contrast to pleromatic postmodernism, allows the nonconceptualizable Other to be the object of saintly work, must there not also be a "subject" of saintly life? If saint and Other are segregated by the radical character of alterity itself, how can the saint come into relation with the Other?

For there to be a saint who initiates action, who relieves suffering, who experiences compassion, there must in some sense be singular beings who are saints. Yet both ecstatic and differential postmodernisms are fairly well agreed that an account of the subject as an originary consciousness fails to grasp the "infrastructures" that fissure metaphysical conceptions of consciousness. The conditions for saintly life as something singular must be stipulated and the kind of ideality deconstructive analysis undermines must be detached from the term *singularity* by bringing to light the difficulties connected with individuation.

Much of the critical work has already been done in the examination

of reference and exemplarity of chapter 4. It remains only to suggest
how positive singularity can avoid the logocentric implications so pene-
tratingly exposed by postmodernist critics. To distinguish naively construed individuality from saintly singularity, it is convenient to apply
the term *particularity* to the received notion and the term *singularity* to
saintly existence.

The concept of particularity is bound up with the problem of reference. To see this, it may be useful to retraverse some old ground. In
chapter 4, I argued that, for recent analytic and phenomenological philosophies of language, the question of how propositions re-present the
world poses difficulties resolved only at the price both of neutralizing
the world's otherness and of introducing mediating notions that explain
and stipulate the connections between language and the world. Phenomenological philosophy posits a consciousness that provides access
to phenomena whereas analytic philosophies of language specify conditions of intralinguistic coherence. What is to count as a particular is
established within the constitutive frameworks of consciousness on the
one hand and propositional truth conditions on the other.

For phenomenology, particulars are constituted as such by a consciousness that is intentional. They acquire signification through their
relation to a generic universal, an essence, an *eidos*, a form of unity
constituted by a consciousness that bestows meaning on them by creating assemblages, a unity that conjoins both material and ideal objects.
Particulars are what is presided over by the eidos.[24] Because the eidos is
something purely conceptual, it extends over an infinity of possible particulars which "fall under it as its 'particular exemplifications.'"[25] For
Quine's linguistic philosophy, particulars conform to the pattern established in his famous dictum: "To be is to be the value of a variable."
One meaning that can be ascribed to particulars then is that they are
whatever can be substituted for a variable in a proposition. Like Husserl, Quine envisions particulars as multiplying ad infinitum, a problem
that arises when one thinks of counterfactuals or unrealized particulars,
those that did not and could not come into being. Both Quine and
Husserl have a horror of the infinite—of the runaway flow of particulars—and so have recourse to universals.[26] For both Husserl and Quine,
particulars derive their meaning from the constructs that regiment them
and are homogeneous with one another with respect to the properties
stipulated by the ordering construct. Particulars are monadic in a
double sense: first, as part of what is heuristically united by the construct, for example, the relation of the eidos of red to the assemblage of
red objects brought together by it (Husserl), and second, as freestand-

ing wholes themselves—at least when they are time-tied particulars—in the sense of being numerically distinct from one another (Quine).

On either view of particularity, saints could be interpreted as particulars, as living specimens of the virtues of compassion, generosity, and courage. The notions of exemplarity they presuppose have already been subjected to extended criticism in chapter 5. In the present context, it suffices only to notice that, were the relation between universal and particular, however liberally construed, to determine the character of saintly acts, saintly behavior could be thought of as a series of acts, if not homogeneous, at least commensurable with one another, regimented by the essence of saintliness and saints themselves could be thought of as members of an ideal social whole: a tribe, a militia, or a club.

How is saintly singularity to be described if we are not to fall back into some premodern or modern notion of particularity? How is the Other to be construed if we are not to resort to the notion of a larger whole characterized by suffering and privation? How then is the singularity of the Other to be preserved if it can be preserved? Can the Other simply be without further elaboration the One who I am not?

"Negativity Is Not Transcendence"

I have repeatedly stressed the extirpation of lack in ecstatic postmodernism.[27] The reason for this insistence is *not to show that the Other is what I am not*, for this only reinstates the Other as another myself, as the obverse of my fullness and positivity. Such a relationship is one in which I am interchangeable with the Other so that the arena of social transactions is flattened out into a single terrain of homogeneous parts. When this situation is pushed to the extreme, as it is in Blanchot's novel *Aminadab*, as Levinas shows, it becomes absurd:

Between the persons circulating in the strange house where the action takes place, where there is no work to pursue, where they only abide—that is, exist—this social relationship becomes total reciprocity. These beings are not interchangeable but reciprocal, or rather they are interchangeable because they are reciprocal. And then the relationship with the Other becomes impossible.[28]

If neither I nor the Other is *constituted* as lack, the Other *manifests* negativity as a destitution that is "parasitic" upon lack. For the saint, need is expressed in the Other's very existence as well as in concrete manifestations of suffering through war or natural catastrophe, through poverty, illness, or psychic injury. Every Other is different from a "self" that is seen as a hollowed-out interiority (Levinas), excessive expenditure (Bataille), desiring production (Deleuze), or a textual marginality, the result of spatial deflection and temporal delay (Derrida). The negativity of destitution is not a secondary "phenomenon" of lack but something primordial, the always already riven character of suffering, and displays itself as such to the saint. This mode of negation is to be distinguished from the negation that belongs within the totality of a system such as the negation of labor that overcomes the resistance of material being and is dependent upon anterior material existence. Nothing whatsoever precedes the destitution of the Other.

If the Other manifests herself/himself through destitution yet does not gain identity through being an alter ego or what I am not, is there some alternative way in which the Other is distinguishable and which will, at the same time, display the Other's singularity? This brings to the fore the question of the Other's positivity, her/his *supra-ontological* or *me-ontic* being in that the Other is always already the object of a desire that exceeds any expectation of fulfillment. The saintly desire for the Other is excessive and wild. In traditional Christian theological language, the saint desires not only the welfare of the Other, the cessation of another's suffering, but also the Other's beatitude; not only to sit at the right hand of God oneself but to desire the elevation of the Other.

Recall too that saintly struggle on behalf of the Other is a wrestling with time, the mode of temporalization I called earlier "the time that is left." If saintly action is to be effective, suffering must cease before the saint's life and the life of the Other come to an end, in Jewish and Christian hagiographic language, the time of earthly life when change is still possible before the fixity of eternal life begins. The problem of an ever-diminishing time span bears directly on saintly singularity in that this singularity is definable in part as the complex of occurrences that come to pass between the beginning and the end of the saint's activity. The time of a saintly life as expressed in hagiographic narrative is the time-before-it-is-too-late that is, as Kierkegaard claims, lived forward but remembered backward. Each telling of the saint's story, so long as the tradition in which the narrative is embedded remains vital, is an ever-renewed soliciting of the narrative's addressees. To those situated within this tradition, hagiography hammers home its own mode of temporalization, the-time-before-it-is-too-late.

Nowhere is this time scheme more forcefully interpreted than in Kierkegaard's tale of the subjection of choice to the compression of time. Imagine, he declares, that a child is offered the alternative of buying a book or a toy. The choice is open so long as the child is still deliberating, but once he selects the toy and the money is spent he cannot go back to the beginning before the choice was made and buy the book. Similarly the knight errant who throws his destiny in on the side of one army over another and then loses cannot turn around and offer his services to the winner. The victor can only say, "'My friend, you are now my prisoner; there was indeed a time when you could have chosen differently, but now everything is changed.'"[29] The saintly future is the-time-that-is-left in which to alleviate suffering before it is too late.

To return to the problem of singularity, the suffering of the Other is, *from the standpoint of the saint*, always greater than the intention that strives to relieve it. The singularity of the Other speaks from the non-place of the difference between the saint's desire and the Other's own suffering so that the Other's singularity is always an excess, more than can be encompassed by saintly intention. What is absolutely Other gives itself to the saint as this excess. The Other, then, as seen by the saint, is the one whose suffering exceeds any saintly effort at amelioration. This is neither a factual description, since saintly effort is often effective, nor an expression of psychological pessimism, which could only paralyze action, but rather a depiction of the infrastructure of saintly experience.

This is a crucial point missed in the theoretical accounts of altruism considered earlier. Rescher believes that moderate benevolence is an adequate response to the need of others whereas Urmson considers a more extreme saintly response desirable. For both, the need of the Other is inherently satiable. To put it otherwise, when need dries up, altruism is no longer required so that it must be generated afresh with each new situation. A postmodern reading attributes to the Other an unceasing impingement upon saintly existence.

Saintly singularity *as seen from the standpoint of the saint's "flock" and addressees* takes as its starting point the visible manifestations of saintly desire for the Other, the saint's acts of generosity and compassion. From this perspective, saintly singularity is desire released from the bonds of a unifying consciousness, a desire that is unconstrained and excessive yet guided by the suffering of the Other. Despite the pain of saintly existence, the addressees of saintly discourse (if not always the saint) see the Other not as a weight or burden but as light, to borrow the oxymoron of Kundera, with the unbearable lightness of being.[30] In actuality, no saint can always carry such generosity through to the end.

I have also maintained that postmodern saintliness is not premodern saintliness, because inscribed in postmodern saintly life is the weight of recent history. Hagiography, when written in the idiolect of the postmodern saint, bears the trace of the rational and egalitarian suppositions of the Enlightenment as well as the force of the Kantian moral law and the criticisms and appropriations of it in utilitarian and pragmatic ethics. If liberal theories of justice (Rawls), phenomenological ethics (Scheler), and contemporary Kantianism (Gewirth) referred to in this study fail to persuade, it will not do to return nostalgically and uncritically to an older ethos. Nostalgia is amnesia, a wiping out of both the sea-changes brought about by recent history and the sins of older communities such as slavery in ancient Greece and the persecution of Jews, Moslems, and heretics by medieval Christianity. This backward thrust is an example of what I called earlier the myth of the tabula rasa and leads to impossible dreams such as Alasdair MacIntyre's hope for the restoration of a monastic ethic or a return to an Aristotelian version of the good life as one governed by the classical virtues.

The postmodern saintly life as a new path in ethics is not a proposal to revert to an older hagiographic discourse, least of all to hide behind its metaphysical presuppositions. It is instead a plea for boldness and risk, for an effort to develop a new altruism in an age grown cynical and hardened to catastrophe: war, genocide, the threat of worldwide ecological collapse, sporadic and unpredictable eruptions of urban violence, the use of torture, the emergence of new diseases. In an epoch grown weary not only of its calamities but of its ecstasies, of its collective political fantasies that destroyed millions of lives, and of its chemically induced stupors and joys, the postmodern saint shows the traces of these disasters. Just as postmodern art forswears the aesthetic purity of modernism, just as postmodern philosophers are only now beginning to forge the instruments for bringing vastly different philosophical languages into discursive contiguity, postmodern saints derive their modes of action from their immediate modernist predecessors as well as from traditional hagiography. Borrowing the compassionate strands of the world's religious traditions, the absurdist gestures of recent modernist art and literature, and modern technologies, saints try to fashion lives of compassion and generosity. They may remain uncanonized, for postmodernism does not encourage institutional canonization, but this does not mean that they need to go unrecognized or unappreciated. The names of saints, revealed under the "rotten sun" (Bataille) of postmodern existence, are written *sous rature*, under erasure (Derrida), and show as faint traces of alterity (Levinas) beneath the catena of altruistic actions that constitute postmodern hagiography.

Notes

Abbreviations

I have abbreviated works referred to most frequently. For full information concerning the source of the citation, see the first endnote that mentions the work. Where English translations are available, I have cited them for ease of reference. I have translated passages from works for which there is no English version and in cases where I found it necessary to do so in the interest of style or clarity.

AO	Deleuze and Guattari, *Anti-Oedipus*
BT	Martin Heidegger, *Being and Time*
CCR	Peter Sloterdijk, *Critique of Cynical Reason*
CPP	Emmanuel Levinas, *Collected Philosophical Papers*
Ec	Jacques Lacan, *Ecrits*
En	Plotinus, *Enneads*
Gen	Friedrich Nietzsche, *Genealogy of Morals*
MFL	Martin Heidegger, *Metaphysical Foundations of Logic*
OBBE	Emmanuel Levinas, *Otherwise than Being and beyond Essence*
OLF	Jean Genet, *Our Lady of the Flowers*
PH	Julia Kristeva, *Powers of Horror*
QCT	Martin Heidegger, *The Question concerning Technology*
TI	Emmanuel Levinas, *Totality and Infinity*
TP	Gilles Deleuze and Felix Guattari, *A Thousand Plateaus*
U	Nicholas Rescher, *Unselfishness*

Prelude

1. Ihab Hassan, "The Question of Postmodernism," in Harry R. Garvin, ed., *Romanticism, Modernism, Postmodernism* (Lewisburg, PA: Bucknell University Press, 1980), p. 22.

2. Edith Wyschogrod, *Spirit in Ashes: Hegel, Heidegger, and Man-Made Mass Death* (New Haven: Yale University Press, 1985), pp. 15–16.

3. Joseph Caputo in *Radical Hermeneutics* (Bloomington, IN: Indiana University Press, 1988), pp. 236–67, discusses some dilemmas faced by a "post-

metaphysical" ethics. James L. Marsh in "The Post-Modern Interpretation of History: A Phenomenological Hermeneutical Critique," *Journal of the British Society for Phenomenology*, 19 (May, 1988): 112–27, discusses the implications of philosophical postmodernism arguing that it significantly highlights the abuses of modernism but "ontologizes alienation" (p. 123). Mark C. Taylor in *Erring: A Postmodern A/Theology* (Chicago: University of Chicago Press, 1984) attributes the death of the self, the sense of "loss and fault," as well as liminality, to postmodernism: "We are in a time between times and a place which is no place. Here our reflection must begin" (p. 6). Michael David Levin in *The Opening of Vision: Nihilism and the Postmodern Situation* (London: Routledge, Chapman & Hall, 1988), pp. 404–5, interprets the death of the self in post-modernism as the death of the modern self rather than of the self *tout court*. Charles Altieri in "Judgment and Justice under Postmodern Conditions; or How Lyotard Helps Us Read Rawls as a Postmodern Thinker," in Reed Way Dasenbrock, ed., *Redrawing the Lines: Analytic Philosophy, Deconstruction, and Literary Theory* (Minneapolis: University of Minnesota Press, 1989), pp. 61–91, suggests that Lyotard shows the incommensurability of different juridical narratives because of power inequities, thus providing a bottom line account of injustice, but suggests too that we must look to Rawls for positive recommendations with regard to distributive justice.

    4. Julia Kristeva, "Postmodernism?" in Garvin, *Romanticism, Modernism, and Postmodernism*, p. 141.

    5. Benjamin H. D. Buchloh, ed., *Broodthaers: Writings, Interviews, Photographs* (Cambridge, MA: MIT Press, 1987), originally published as *October 42*, Fall, 1987, p. 173.

    6. François Lyotard, *The Postmodern Condition: A Report on Knowledge*, trans. Geoff Bennington and Brian Massumi (Minneapolis: University of Minnesota Press, 1984), p. 81.

    7. Ibid.

    8. Ibid., pp. 31–32. For a history of the term *postmodern* see Ihab Hassan's overview in Garvin, *Romanticism, Modernism, Postmodernism*, pp. 117–18.

    9. Charles Jencks, *What Is Postmodernism?* (London: Academy Editions and New York: St. Martin's Press, 1986), p. 14. Deconstructivist architecture can be distinguished from postmodernist architecture as defined by Jencks in that it does not stress the reintroduction of traditional and vernacular forms. Instead, its practitioners such as Frank O. Gehry, Bernard Tschumi, Peter Eisenman, and Daniel Libeskind use "'warped' images in contrast to the 'pure' images of the old International style," as the well-known modernist architect Philip Johnson, suggests. Johnson goes on to contrast the "icon" of the perfect ball bearing of high modernism with the jagged formlessness of the planks of an old spring house in Nevada. "The sphere is pure; the jagged planks make up a deformed space. The contrast is between perfection and violated perfection." See Philip Johnson and Mark Wigley, *Deconstructivist Architecture*, published on the occasion of the Deconstructivist Architecture exhibition, Museum of Modern Art, 23 June to 30 August 1988 (Boston: Little, Brown & Co., 1988),

pp. 7–8. The difference between what is intended by the terms *postmodern* and *deconstructive* in architecture requires extended study. In the context of the present work, both eclecticism and fissuring ascribed to postmodern and deconstructive architecture, respectively, will be attributed to literary and philosophical postmodernism.

10. Richard Rorty in his remarks about philosophy as conversation in *Philosophy and the Mirror of Nature* (Princeton, NJ: Princeton University Press, 1979) endorses the separation of ethics and science, leaving intact ethics' structure of argument but removing the sting. Thus, on the one hand, he wants to think of philosophers as "conversational partners" and to "prevent conversation from degenerating into inquiry" (p. 372); in short, he wants to think of philosophers as providers of "useful kibitzing" (p. 393). On the other hand, the enabling source of this playfulness is "their historical background of arguments on similar topics" (p. 393).

11. Garvin, *Romanticism, Modernism, and Postmodernism*, p. 125. There is disagreement not only about definitions of postmodernism but about whether it is a manifestation of modernism. See in the same volume David Antin, "Is There a Postmodernism?" pp. 127–136, or Wallace Martine, "Postmodernism: Ultima Thule or Seim Anew?" pp. 142–155.

12. Ibid., p. 124.

Chapter 1

1. Nadejda Gorodetzky, *Saint Tikhon of Zadonsk: Inspirer of Dostoevsky* (Crestwood, NY: St. Vladimir's Seminary Press, 1976), p. 221.

2. Ibid., pp. 223–24. The relevance of saints' lives for moral philosophy has remained almost unnoticed by contemporary philosophers and theologians. Noteworthy exceptions are Lawrence Cunningham, *The Meaning of Saints* (New York: Harper & Row, 1980); Robert Neville, *Soldier, Sage, Saint* (Albany: State University of New York Press, 1978); Patrick Sherry, *Spirit, Saints, Immortality* (Albany: State University of New York Press, 1984). Neville stresses the complementarity of the ideal types he develops, Sherry the problem of immortality. Using William James's analysis of religious experience as his starting point, Cunningham emphasizes narrative, saintly transfiguration, and the appeal of saintly life to others. Analytic treatments by Robert M. Adams and Susan Wolf are considered in chapter 7, note 8.

3. Bernard Williams, *Ethics and the Limits of Philosophy* (Cambridge: Cambridge University Press, 1985), pp. 200–201.

4. Alasdair MacIntyre, *After Virtue: A Study in Moral Theory* (Notre Dame: Notre Dame University Press, 1981), p. 140. In *Philosophy and Historical Understanding* (London, 1964), pp. 202–207, a pioneering effort in Anglo-American philosophy to show the narrative character of history, philosophy, and moral life, W. B. Gallie argues to the same effect when he challenges the possibility of universalizing moral judgments because differences in people's fundamental concepts of rationality give rise to incompatible moral laws. Nev-

ertheless Gallie supports the willingness to argue rationally about any given moral issue as itself a distinguishing mark of the moral life.

5. *Oxford English Dictionary* (Oxford: Oxford University Press, 1971).

6. Jacques Derrida, "Living On: Border Lines," in Harold Bloom, ed., *Deconstruction and Criticism* (New York: Seabury Press, 1979), p. 87.

7. Maurice Blanchot, *The Gaze of Orpheus and Other Literary Essays*, trans. Lydia Davis (Barrytown, NY: Station Hill Press), p. 109. Although W. B. Gallie in *Philosophy and Historical Understanding* generally interprets narrative representationally, like Blanchot, he argues that the reader or listener is pulled forward almost against his will by the development of the characters' actions, thoughts, and feelings.

8. Pierre Delooz, "Towards a Sociological Study of Canonized Sainthood in the Catholic Church," in Stephen Wilson, ed., *Saints and Their Cults: Studies in Religious Sociology, Folklore, and History* (Cambridge: Cambridge University Press, 1983), p. 195.

9. Ibid.

10. John Stratton Hawley, ed., in *Saints and Virtues* (Berkeley: University of California Press, 1987), p. xiv, contends that Aesop, originally a didactic writer, enters Muslim hagiographical literature as an ancestor of Muhammad.

11. Paul Nelson, *Narrative and Morality; A Theological Inquiry* (University Park, PA: Pennsylvania State University Press, 1987), considers the role of narrative in Anglo-American moral philosophy and contrasts the utility of one's personal story for moral theory with rule-governed morality. Ronald Hepburn's interpretation that life stories are fables supporting a person's value decisions is compared with Iris Murdoch's view that fables are expressions of people's moral natures and conflict with rule-based conceptions of morality. In considering the uses of narrative in theology, Hans Frei distinguishes between narrative as the alleged "'built-in constitution of human being'" and "narrative specificity through which we describe an experiential-agential world and ourselves in it" (p. 77). Nelson concludes that both narrative and rule are necessary. I argue that, without attention to the structure, sociology, and genre distinctions of narrative as currently considered in literary criticism, philosophers like Hepburn fail to distinguish fables from other stories and consequently tend to blur the differences between stories and laws (see esp. pp. 20–47). A distinction between narrative and rule-governed discourse comparable to Nelson's is made by Gary L. Comstock in "Two Types of Narrative Theology," *Journal of the American Academy of Religion* 55 (Winter, 1987): 687–717. Comstock distinguishes between the pure narrative theology of Frei, Lindbeck, Hauerwas, and David Kelsey, a position maintaining that Christian faith is best grasped by the "grammatical rules and concepts" of its texts, and the impure narrative theology of Ricoeur, Tracy, Hartt, and McFague, the view that narrative is infiltrated by historical and philosophical concerns.

12. Mikhail Bakhtin, *The Dialogic Imagination*, trans. Caryl Emerson and Michael Holquist (Austin: University of Texas Press, 1981), p. 344.

13. Phyllis Johnson and Brigitte Cazelles, *Le Vain Siècle Guerpir: A Literary Approach to Sainthood through Old French Hagiography of the Twelfth Century* (Chapel Hill: North Carolina Studies in the Romance Languages and Literature, 1979), pp. 278–81. I have further condensed the narrative summary provided in this work. Both source material and historical interpretations in this study have proved invaluable in treating literary documents of the period.

14. Bakhtin, *Dialogic Imagination*, p. 114.

15. Ibid., p. 119.

16. Ibid., p. 110.

17. Wallace Martin, *Recent Theories of Narrative* (Ithaca, NY: Cornell University Press, 1986), p. 135, offers a useful inventory of narrators including first- and third-person narrators and embedded narration (stories told intratextually by a protagonist). Classical hagiography is rich in narrative voices that often mark levels of sanctity. (For example, Zozima is holier than the final narrator because he is closer to Mary, but the final narrator mediates between higher levels and the community.)

18. Lyotard, *Postmodern Condition*, p. 19.

19. Bakhtin, *Dialogic Imagination*, pp. 262–63.

20. Rudolph M. Bell, *Holy Anorexia* (Chicago: University of Chicago Press, 1985), p. 101.

21. Ibid., p. 125.

22. Bakhtin, *Dialogic Imagination*, p. 276.

23. "St. Theodosius," trans. Helen Iswolsky, in *A Treasury of Russian Spirituality* (Gloucester, MA: Peter Smith, 1969), p. 19. In *The Russian Religious Mind: Kievan Christianity* (Cambridge, MA: Harvard University Press, 1946) Fedotov claims that the kenotic school of Saint Theodosius rejected radical asceticism. With some exceptions, antinomian protest does not generally express itself in radical self-mortification in Russian piety (pp. 387–88).

24. Lyotard, *Postmodern Condition*, p. 81.

25. Ibid.

26. Jean-Jacques Rousseau, *Emile ou l'éducation* (Paris: Flammarion, 1966), p. 205.

27. Peter Brown, *The Cult of the Saints: Its Rise and Function in Latin Christianity* (Chicago: University of Chicago Press, 1982), p. 65.

28. Johnson and Cazelles, *Le Vain Siècle Guerpir*, p. 250.

29. Donald Weinstein and Rudolph M. Bell, *Saints and Society: The Two Worlds of Western Christendom 1000–1700* (Chicago: University of Chicago Press, 1982), p. 154.

30. Maurice Merleau-Ponty, *Phenomenology of Perception*, trans. Colin Smith (London: Routledge & Kegan Paul, 1962). See esp. pp. 203–42.

31. Ibid., p. 67.

32. Ibid., p. 69.

33. Ibid., p. 67. Thomas Nagel uses the phrase "the view from nowhere" as the title of a book that tries to explain the value of objectivity.

34. Ibid., p. 139.

35. William James, *Essays in Radical Empiricism* (Cambridge, MA: Harvard University Press, 1976), p. 86.

36. Vincent Descombes, *Modern French Philosophy*, trans. L. Scott-Fox and J. M. Harding (Cambridge: Cambridge University Press, 1980), p. 68.

37. Richard Kieckhefer, *Unquiet Souls: Fourteenth-Century Saints and Their Religious Milieu* (Chicago: University of Chicago Press, 1984), p. 92.

38. Teresa of Avila, *The Life of Teresa of Jesus: The Autobiography of St. Teresa of Avila*, trans. and ed. E. Allison Peers (Garden City, NY: Doubleday, Image, 1960), p. 197.

39. Ibid., pp. 194–95.

40. Michel de Certeau, *Heterologies: Discourse on the Other*, trans. Brian Massumi (Minneapolis: University of Minnesota Press, 1986), p. 160.

41. Jacques Derrida, "Plato's Pharmacy," in *Dissemination*, trans. Barbara Johnson (Chicago: University of Chicago Press, 1981), p. 109.

42. Jacques Derrida, *Positions*, trans. Allen Bass (Chicago: University of Chicago Press, 1972), p. 12. For an extended discussion of the terms used by Derrida in connection with texts and textuality see Rodolphe Gasché, *The Tain of the Mirror* (Cambridge, MA: Harvard University Press, 1986), pp. 278–93.

43. Derrida, *Positions*, pp. 64–67.

44. Jacques Derrida, "The Double Session," in *Dissemination*, p. 257. For a discussion of the relation between alterity and negation, absence, blanks, and marginality see Mark C. Taylor, *Altarity* (Chicago: University of Chicago Press, 1987), esp. pp. 241–43, 295–303.

45. Derrida, *Dissemination*, p. 258.

46. Ibid.

47. Derrida, *Deconstruction and Criticism*, p. 83.

48. The remarks on *différance* are a slightly modified version of several paragraphs taken from Edith Wyschogrod, "Time and Non-Being in Derrida and Quine," in *Journal of the British Society for Phenomenology* 14, no. 2: 114–16.

49. Jacques Derrida, *Speech and Phenomena and Other Essays on Husserl's Theory of Signs*, trans. David. B. Allison (Evanston, IL: Northwestern University Press, 1973), p. 138.

50. Ibid., p. 139.

51. Jacques Derrida, "Structure, Sign, and Play in the Language of Human Sciences," in Richard Macksey and Eugenio Donato, eds., *The Structuralist Controversy* (Baltimore: Johns Hopkins University Press, 1972), p. 260.

52. Derrida, *Speech and Phenomena*, p. 141.

53. Ibid.

54. Ibid., p. 86.

55. Paul Ricoeur, *The Rule of Metaphor: Multidisciplinary Studies of the Creation of Meaning in Language*, trans. Robert Czerny (Toronto: University of Toronto Press, 1975), p. 147. The citation is from Gerard Genette, *Figures 1* (Paris: Editions du Seuil, 1966), p. 108.

56. Derrida, *Deconstruction and Criticism*, p. 84.

57. Arthur Danto in *Narration and Knowledge* (New York: Columbia University Press, 1985), p. 318, argues that, in its description of the relation between language and event, the correspondence theory of truth is "intuitively correct." On this view, the truth conditions of a sentence are satisfied by some satisfier extrinsic to the sentence, usually some nonlinguistic item. In describing the events to which it refers, history follows this pattern. It "aims at the truth [and] may be spoken of as history-as-science" (p. 323). Danto affirms the openendedness of historical interpretation but attributes it to the situation of the historical observer in relation to the past. Temporal distance forces the historian to apply new descriptions to earlier events.

58. Johnson and Cazelles, *Le Vain Siècle Guerpir*, pp. 258–61.

59. Diana Dewar, *Saint of Auschwitz: The Story of Maksymilian Kolbe* (London: Darton, Longman & Todd, 1982). My account of Kolbe is a summary of his life by Dewar, who writes as an admiring non-Catholic biographer.

60. Claude Lévi-Strauss, *The Savage Mind* (Chicago: University of Chicago Press, 1966), pp. 16–22.

61. Mircea Eliade, *The Sacred and the Profane*, trans. Willard R. Trask (New York: Harcourt & Brace, 1959), pp. 21–113.

Chapter 2

1. See W. T. Stace, *Mysticism and Philosophy* (London: Macmillan, 1961); R. C. Zaehner, *Mysticism, Sacred and Profane* (Oxford: Clarendon Press, 1957), and *Concordant Discord* (Oxford: Clarendon Press, 1970); William James, *The Varieties of Religious Experience* (New York: Longman Green & Co., 1902).

2. Carl A. Keller, "Mystical Literature," in Steven T. Katz, ed., *Mysticism and Philosophical Analysis* (London: Oxford University Press, 1978), pp. 75–101.

3. Steven T. Katz, "Language, Epistemology, and Mysticism," in Katz, *Mysticism and Philosophical Analysis*, pp. 22–74.

4. Ibid., pp. 32–35, 45–50.

5. Wayne Proudfoot, *Religious Experience* (Berkeley and Los Angeles: University of California Press, 1985), p. 125.

6. Michael Goodich, "Politics of Canonization in the Thirteenth Century," in Stephen Wilson, ed., *Saints and Their Cults: Studies in Religious Sociology, Folklore, and History* (Cambridge: Cambridge University Press, 1983), pp. 169–87, argues that the political function of canonization trials in the thirteenth century was primarily to thwart the recurrent threat of heresy but that the *imitatio Christi* reflected in saintly life remains of paramount interest.

7. Teresa of Avila, *Life of Teresa of Jesus*, p. 170.

8. Michel de Certeau, *Heterologies*, p. 94. Cf. his *La fable mystique XVIe–XVIIe siècle* (Paris: Gallimard, 1982), pp. 257ff.

9. Ibid., p. 95.

10. Ibid.

11. Tzvetan Todorov, *The Poetics of Prose*, trans. Richard Howard (Ithaca: Cornell University Press, 1977), p. 114.

12. Michel de Certeau, *Heterologies*, p. 96.

13. Teresa of Avila, *Life of Teresa of Jesus*, p. 191.

14. Ibid., p. 174.

15. Ibid., p. 127.

16. Catherine of Siena, *The Dialogues*, trans. Susan Noffke (New York: Paulist Press, 1980), p. 27.

17. Ibid.

18. Ibid.

19. Ibid., p. 29.

20. Robert L. Cohn in "The Case of Judaism," in John Stratton Hawley, ed., *Saints and Virtues*, suggests that "the primacy of the community over the individual . . . works against the production of saints" in Judaism (p. 92). This is true if the merger with transcendence and the cultic veneration of saints are stressed. But as Cohn shows, both the *Zadik* (the morally virtuous person) and the *Hasid* (the boundlessly generous and religiously fervent individual) are exemplars of Jewish piety. If saintliness is identified with radical altruism, then it is a key element in Judaism.

21. Thomas Nagel, *The Possibility of Altruism* (Princeton, NJ: Princeton University Press, 1970), pp. 145–46. Nagel's analysis does not refer only to radical altruism but to "any behavior motivated by the belief that someone else will benefit or avoid harm by it" (p. 6n).

22. Ibid., pp. 143–45.

23. See Wyschogrod, *Spirit in Ashes*, pp. 57–62, for an account of the historical a priori.

24. Peter Sloterdijk, *Critique of Cynical Reason*, trans. Michael Eldred (Minneapolis: University of Minnesota Press, 1987), pp. 3–9.

25. Ibid., p. 4.

26. Ibid., p. 5.

27. Ibid.

28. Ibid.

29. Ibid., p. 4.

30. This interpretation is found in *The Notebooks of Henry James*, pp. 102–3. The *Notebooks* are not intended to justify any given reading but in this case offer support to a hagiographic recasting.

31. Ibid., p. 106.

32. Henry James, *The Wings of the Dove* (New York: New American Library, 1964), p. 202.

33. Ibid.

34. Leon Edel, *The Life of Henry James: The Master* (New York: J. B. Lippincott, 1969), p. 114, points out that conversation at Lamb House during the year when *The Wings of the Dove* was being written and where Henry James

often resided centered on William James's *Varieties of Religious Experience* with its stress on conceptions of mystical and saintly life.

35. Henry James, *Wings of the Dove*, p. 369.

36. Todorov, *Poetics of Prose*, p. 114.

37. Ibid.

38. Henry James, *Wings of the Dove*, p. 496. The nature of Millie's innocence can be brought out by an unlikely analogy. The psychologist Oliver Sacks in "The Twins," *New York Review of Books*, 28 February 1985, describes a pair of idiot savant twins with physical and neurological difficulties who nevertheless play a mathematical game beyond the competence of the most sophisticated mathematicians. When one utters a prime number the other responds, a game sometimes resulting in an exchange of twenty-figure primes. Sacks concludes that they do not form abstract notions of numbers but experience them in some sensuous and immediate way. "They have a most singular imagination—and not the least of its singularities is that it can imagine only numbers" (p. 36). Saints can be thought of as *idiot savants of the ethical* in the unmediated character of their moral responses. Of course Millie's saintliness does not exclude considerable psychological insight and social intelligence.

39. Todorov, *Poetics of Prose*, p. 145.

40. Ibid. Todorov uses this analysis to interpret James's tales rather than the major novels.

41. Ibid., p. 161.

42. Ludwig Wittgenstein, *Culture and Value*, trans. Peter Winch (Chicago: University of Chicago Press, 1980), pp. 69e–70e.

43. Henry James, *Wings of the Dove*, p. 496.

44. Ibid.

45. Michel de Certeau, *Heterologies*, p. 160.

46. Maurice Merleau-Ponty, *The Visible and the Invisible*, trans. Alphonso Lingis (Evanston, IL: Northwestern University Press, 1968), p. 10.

47. Merleau-Ponty, *Phenomenology of Perception*, p. 365.

48. The concrete universal as the embodiment of an archetypal or general structure plays a pivotal role in Hegel's system. See G. W. F. Hegel, *Logic*, pt. 1, of *The Encyclopedia of the Philosophical Sciences*, trans. William Wallace (1894; reprint, Oxford: Clarendon Press, 1975), pp. 22ff. For Husserl, material essences are significant only in connection with grasping the character of physical objects. See Edmund Husserl, *Ideas: General Introduction to Pure Phenomenology*, trans. W. R. Boyce Gibson (New York: Collier Books, 1962), pp. 56ff.

49. Maurice Merleau-Ponty, *The Prose of the World*, trans. John O'Neill (Evanston, IL: Northwestern University Press, 1973), p. 20n.

50. Merleau-Ponty, *The Visible and the Invisible*, p. 139.

51. Emmanuel Levinas, *Totality and Infinity*, trans. Alphonso Lingis (The Hague: Martinus Nijhoff, 1981), pp. 173ff.

52. Michel de Certeau, *Heterologies*, p. 199.

53. Aristotle, *De Interpretatione*, 21b–23a. All Aristotle citations are from *Basic Works of Aristotle*, ed. Richard McKeon (New York: Random House, 1941).

54. Ibid., 21b.

55. Ibid., 23a.

56. Ibid.

57. Soren Kierkegaard, *Philosophical Fragments, or a Fragment of Philosophy*, trans. David Swenson, revised Howard V. Hong (Princeton, NJ: Princeton University Press, 1962), pp. 90–93.

58. Ibid., p. 91.

59. Ibid.

60. Aristotle, *Nichomachean Ethics*, 1111b.

61. Ibid.

62. Aristotle, *Poetics*, 1454a.

63. Ibid., 1451b.

64. Henry James, *Wings of the Dove*, p. 396.

65. Mark C. Taylor, *Altarity*, p. 243.

66. Michel de Certeau, *Heterologies*, p. 202.

67. Ibid.

Chapter 3

1. Emmanuel Levinas, *Otherwise than Being or Beyond Essence*, trans. Alphonso Lingis (The Hague: Martinus Nijhoff, 1981), p. 4. Hereafter cited in the text as *OBBE*.

2. In many state of nature theories self-interest is expressed as the desire for possessions and, in the case of Hobbes, also as a desire for recognition by others. The problem of self-preservation comes to the fore when the satisfaction of needs is threatened by scarcity. For Hobbes the state of nature is a state of war, for which three sources are posited: "first, competition; second, diffidence; thirdly glory. The first maketh men invade for gain; the second for safety; and the third for reputation." The reason for human enmity lies in the fact that "two men desire the same thing, which nevertheless they cannot both enjoy." It is this which gives rise to "continual fear and the danger of violent death." See *Leviathan*, in *The English Philosophers from Bacon to Mill*, ed. Edwin A. Burtt (New York: Random House, 1939), pp. 160–61. Locke denies that the state of nature is a state of war but agrees that there is ownership in the state of nature stemming from the ownership of one's body. Whatever "[man] hath mixed his labor with becomes his property. . . . where there is enough and as good left in common for others." *Concerning Civil Government*, in *English Philosophers from Bacon to Mill*, p. 414. Rousseau in *The Social Contract*, trans. Willmore Kendall (Chicago: Henry Regnery, 1954), p. 26, argues that prior to the social contract "man loses his natural liberty, along with an unlimited right to anything that he is tempted by and can get."

3. Rawls, *A Theory of Justice* (Cambridge, MA.: Belknap Press of Harvard University Press, 1971), p. 302.

4. Ibid.

5. Ibid., p. 303.

6. Alasdair MacIntyre, *After Virtue: A Study in Moral Theory*, p. 232. MacIntyre makes the even stronger claim in *Whose Justice? What Rationality?* (Notre Dame, IN: University of Notre Dame Press, 1988) that an appeal to a rationality that is independent of some tradition is impossible. For the bearing of this view on Rawls's liberalism see pp. 344–48.

7. Emmanuel Levinas, "Meaning and Sense," in *Collected Philosophical Papers*, trans. Alphonso Lingis (The Hague: Martinus Nijhoff Publishers, 1987), p. 85. Hereafter cited as *CPP*.

8. Martin Heidegger, *Being and Time*, trans. John Macquarrie and Edward Robinson (New York: Harper & Row, 1962), I:10, pp. 144–45. Hereafter cited in the text as *BT*.

9. Jean-Paul Sartre, *Being and Nothingness*, trans. Hazel Barnes (New York: Philosophical Library, 1956), p. 228.

10. Alan Gewirth, *Reason and Morality* (Chicago: University of Chicago Press, 1978), esp. pp. 129–61.

11. Ibid., p. 135.

12. Ibid., p. 218.

13. Kai Nielsen, "Against Ethical Rationalism," in Edward Regis, ed., *Gewirth's Ethical Rationalism* (Chicago: University of Chicago Press, 1984), p. 165.

14. Ibid., p. 66.

15. Gewirth, *Reason and Morality*, p. 91

16. Ibid., p. 229.

17. Ibid., pp. 229–30.

18. Eric Mack, "Negative Causation and the Duty to Rescue," in *Gewirth's Ethical Rationalism: Critical Essays with a Reply by Alan Gewirth* (Chicago: University of Chicago Press, 1984), p. 164, writes that Gewirth's "ambitious use of the immorality condition [transgressing a moral norm entailed by PGC] makes causal truths dependent upon moral duties, and in turn upon the conditions for these duties." Mack stresses Gewirth's deontological bent but adds that Gewirth wants to eat lotus with the consequentialists. Thus Gewirth interprets agency as intentional in much the same way that Donald Davidson does in the context of action theory when Davidson asserts: "To say someone did something intentionally is to describe the action in a way that bears a special relation to the beliefs and attitudes of the agent; and perhaps further to describe the action as having been caused by those beliefs and attitudes" (*Essays on Actions and Events* [Oxford: Clarendon Press, 1982], p. 121). Both Gewirth and Davidson go to considerable lengths to breach the gap between the intentional aspect of agency and the causal nexus of events. For a discussion of Davidson's view of language in relation to radical altruism see chapter 6 of the present work.

19. Alan Gewirth, "Replies to my Critics," in *Gewirth's Ethical Rationalism*, p. 234.

20. Ibid.

21. Aristotle, *Metaphysics*, 1047a.

22. Martin Heidegger, *The End of Philosophy*, trans. Joan Stambaugh (New York: Harper & Row, 1973), pp. 10–19.

23. Descartes, *The Philosophical Works of Descartes*, trans. Elizabeth R. Haldane and G. R. T. Ross (New York: Dover Publications, 1951), I:151–52.

24. Ibid., II:219

25. Ibid.

26. Ibid.

27. Ibid., II:201.

28. Gilbert Ryle, *The Concept of Mind* (New York: Barnes & Noble, 1949), pp. 11–24.

29. Martin Heidegger, *Basic Problems of Phenomenology*, trans. Albert Hofstadter (Bloomington: Indiana University Press, 1982), pp. 122–40.

30. Martin Heidegger, *The Question concerning Technology and Other Essays*, trans. William Lovitt (New York: Harper & Row, 1977), p. 128. Hereafter cited in the text as *QCT*.

31. Emmanuel Levinas, *Existence and Existents*, trans. Alphonso Lingis (The Hague: Martinus Nijhoff, 1978), p. 68.

32. Ibid.

33. Ibid., pp. 73–77. Levinas stresses the role of the instant in coming to oneself as well as the instant's evanescence. Because my starting point is the analysis of work, I examine the relation of the instant to utility.

34. Jacques Derrida, "*Geschlecht* II: Heidegger's Hand," in John Sallis, ed., *Deconstruction and Philosophy: The Texts of Jacques Derrida* (Chicago: University of Chicago Press, 1987), pp. 161–96.

35. Ibid., p. 168.

36. Ibid., p. 170.

37. Ibid.

38. Ibid., p. 173.

39. Ibid., p. 168.

40. Ibid., p. 173. Cf. Heidegger's discussion of the question of the essence of man in *An Introduction to Metaphysics*, trans. Ralph Manheim (New Haven: Yale University Press, 1959), p. 140: "The determination of the essence of man is *never* an answer but essentially a question. The asking of this question and the decision in this question are historical. . . . The question of what man is must always be taken in its essential bond with the question of how it stands with being."

41. Sallis, *Texts of Jacques Derrida*, p. 180.

42. Martin Heidegger, *Existence and Being*, trans. Werner Brock (London: Vision Press, 1959), p. 268.

43. Levinas, *CPP*, pp. 18ff., treats violence as the application of force but not as presenting a structure comparable to that of work.

44. Techne and its transformation into technique are a fundamental issue in Heidegger's thinking. Thus objects of handicraft differ from manufactured objects not only in form but also in their ontological ground. Preliminary to a lengthy analysis of the Kantian view of the thing, Heidegger writes that things can be understood narrowly as "that which can be touched, reached or seen i.e. what is present-at-hand" and in a wider sense as "every affair or transaction . . . occurrences, events." Still another use, Heidegger claims, is introduced in the eighteenth century, that of "a thing-in-itself" not approachable in experience as well as things as they are for us. See his *What Is a Thing*, trans. W. B. Barton, Jr., and Vera Deutsch (Chicago: Henry Regnery, 1967), p. 5.

45. In his critique of Levinas, Derrida considers what is entailed in claiming that the Other as Other cannot be the object of violence: "The movement of transcendence towards the other . . . would have no meaning if it did not bear within it, as one of its essential meanings, that . . . I know myself to be other for the other. Without this, 'I' . . . , unable to be the other's other, would never be the victim of violence. The violence of which Levinas speaks would be a violence without victim." See "Violence and Metaphysics," in *Writing and Difference*, trans. Alan Bass (Chicago: University of Chicago Press, 1978), p. 126.

46. Blanchot's use of the term *désoeuvrement*, translated as "worklessness" and "unwork," carries some of the connotations I attribute to labor. Literally "idleness," *désoeuvrement* is turned by Blanchot into a kind of occupation. In connection with a discussion of the meaning of the book, he speaks of writing as worklessness, as something between reason and unreason that passes into and disappears in the book. See Pierre Joris's "Introduction" to his translation of Maurice Blanchot, *The Unknowable Community* (Barrytown, NY: Station Hill Press, 1988), pp. xxiii–xxv.

47. "A Mission to Heal," in *New York Newsday*, 22 December 1987, pt. 2, p. 3.

Chapter 4

1. Plotinus, *The Ethical Treatises* (*Enneads* I–VI), trans. Stephen MacKenna (Boston: Charles T. Branford Co., n.d.), III.7.11. Hereafter cited in the text as *En.*

2. Martin Heidegger, *Early Greek Thinking*, trans. David Krell and F. A. Capuzzi (New York: Harper & Row, 1975), 26, 337.

3. Ibid.

4. Derrida, *Dissemination*, pp. 330–66.

5. Ibid., p. 338.

6. Ibid., p. 304.

7. S. Sambursky and S. Pines, eds., *The Concept of Time in Late Neo-Platonism* (Jerusalem: Israel Academy of Sciences and Humanities, 1987), p. 83.

8. Ibid.

9. Ibid.

10. Ibid.

11. Ibid., p. 79.

12. *Vissudhi Magga* xvi, trans. W. C. Warren, in Sarvepalli Radhakrishnan and Charles A. Moore, *A Sourcebook in Indian Philosophy* (Princeton, NJ: Princeton University Press, 1957), p. 289.

13. Ibid., p. 34.

14. In his account of asceticism as a constant in culture, Geoffrey Galt Harpham, *The Ascetic Imperative in Culture and Criticism* (Chicago: University of Chicago Press, 1987), argues that Nietzsche attacks asceticism as an ideal but treats it as a practice (p. 218) and that Nietzsche hopes to "'make asceticism natural again'" (p. 219).

15. Aristotle, *Poetics*, 1453a.

16. Friedrich Nietzsche, *The Genealogy of Morals*, trans. Francis Golffing (Garden City, NY: 1956), 1, 7, p. 155. Hereafter cited in the text as *Gen.*

17. Michel Haar, "Nietzsche and Metaphysical Language," in David Allison, ed., *The New Nietzsche: Contemporary Styles of Interpretation* (New York: Dell Publishing Co., 1977), p. 20.

18. Max Scheler, *Ressentiment*, trans. William W. Holdheim (New York: Schocken Books, 1972).

19. Nietzsche's *ressentiment* argument can be understood as a contest of wills to power. For a brief account of the Will to Power as "World, Life, Being," see Michel Haar's "Nietzsche and Metaphysical Language," in Allison, *The New Nietzsche*, p. 8.

20. Gilles Deleuze, "Active and Reactive," in Allison, *The New Nietzsche*, pp. 80–106.

21. Ibid., p. 93

22. Scheler, *Ressentiment*, p. 90.

23. Nietzsche is crucial for the work of postmodernity. See Mark C. Taylor, *Altarity*, pp. 238–41.

24. Sloterdijk, *Critique of Cynical Reason*, pp. 44–45.

25. Walter Kaufmann, *Philosopher, Psychologist, Antichrist* (New York: Random House, 1968), p. 342.

26. Levinas, *Existence and Existents*, p. 65. For Levinas, wakefulness is a kind of pressure that readies the psychism for reception of the Other.

27. Richard Sugarman, *Rancor against Time: The Phenomenology of Ressentiment* (Hamburg: F. Meiner, 1980), p. 57, argues compellingly that Nietzsche's aim is to overcome the rancor against time stemming from the will's inability to will backwards. "This indeed, this alone is what revenge is."

28. Ibid.

29. Friedrich Nietzsche, *Thus Spake Zarathustra*, in Walter Kaufmann, ed., *The Portable Nietzsche* (New York: Viking Press, 1954), pp. 161–62.

30. Ibid., p. 163.

31. Friedrich Nietzsche, *Die Frohliche Wissenschaft*, in *Gesammelte Werke*, Musarion Edition, 1882, vol. 12, as translated by Walter Kaufmann in *Nietzsche*, p. 324.

32. Frederick Nietzsche, *The Will to Power*, trans. Walter Kaufmann and R. J. Hollingdale (New York: Random House, 1968), 1050, p. 539.

33. Stephen Jay Gould, *Time's Arrow, Time's Cycle: Myth and Metaphor in the Discovery of Geological Time* (Cambridge, MA: Harvard University Press, 1988), pp. 10–11.

34. Vladimir Jankelevitich, *La mort* (Paris: Flammarion, 1966), pp. 347–67.

35. Erwin Straus, *Man, Time, and World: Two Contributions to Anthropological Society* (Pittsburgh: Duquesne University Press, 1982), pp. 33ff.

36. Abigail Rosenthal, *A Good Look at Evil* (Philadelphia: Temple University Press, 1987), p. 17, compellingly explicates evil as a frustration of narrative intentionality: "In the living out of a story there are two ways to be in default on what the story promised. . . . the default on ideality, the failure to see the further story . . . [and] the deliberate thwarting of the story. The latter is what I take to be evil."

37. *Upasaka Sila Sutra, Takakusu* XXIV: 1036, trans. in A.D. 428, in Edward Conze, I. B. Horner, David Snellgrove, and Arthur Waley, eds., *Buddhist Texts through the Ages* (New York: Harper & Row, 1964), p. 285.

38. Martin Heidegger, *The Metaphysical Foundations of Logic*, trans. Michael Heim (Bloomington: Indiana University Press, 1984), p. 136. Hereafter cited in the text as *MFL*.

39. For shifts in the social, cultural, and institutional treatment of death in Western civilization see Phillipe Ariès, *The Hour of Our Death*, trans. Helen Weaver (New York: Knopf, 1981); for a consideration of the conceptions of life after death that govern Christian articulation of the problem see Krister Stendahl, ed., *Immortality and Resurrection*, the Ingersoll Lectures of 1955 (New York: Macmillan, 1965). An account of death in some Eastern religions can be found in Fredrick R. Holt, ed., *Death and Eastern Thought: Understanding Death in Eastern Religions and Philosophies* (Nashville, TN: Abingdon Press, 1974).

40. Maurice Blanchot, "The Narrative Voice," in *The Gaze of Orpheus* (Barrytown, NY: Station Hill Press, 1981), p. 138.

41. Ibid., p. 140.

42. Ibid.

43. Emmanuel Levinas uses the term *illeity* defined as "The detachment of the Infinite from the thought that seeks to thematize it and the language that tries to hold it in the said" (*OBBE*, p. 147).

44. Maurice Blanchot, "Literature and the Right to Death," in *Gaze of Orpheus*, p. 48.

45. "The Narrative Voice," in *Gaze of Orpheus*, p. 143.

46. Yukio Mishima, *The Decay of the Angel*, trans. Edward G. Seidensticker (New York: Washington Square Press, 1974), p. 246.

47. *Samyutta Nikaya*, iii: 66, in *Sourcebook in Indian Philosophy*, p. 280.

48. Ibid., p. 281.

49. See *neuter* in *The American Heritage Dictionary*, p. 883.

50. Helene Cixous and Catherine Clément, *The Newly Born Woman*, trans. Betsy Wing (Minneapolis: University of Minnesota Press, 1986), p. 75.

51. Herbert Thurston, S.J., and Donald Atwater, eds., *Butler's Lives of the Saints* (New York: P. J. Kennedy & Sons, 1956), pp. 313f.

52. Caroline Walker Bynum, *Holy Feast, Holy Fools: The Religious Significance of Food to Medieval Women* (Berkeley and Los Angeles: University of California Press, 1987), pp. 290–91, argues against the view that stories of transvestite saints indicate that women must assume "symbolic maleness" if they are to make spiritual progress. She contends that for men cross-dressing is freighted with religious symbolism whereas for women it is a practical measure. Her account is an advance over the view that cross-dressing is compensatory. My argument is that the psychological "space" in which altruism occurs is one of both male and female symbolism because the saint must, to remain Other for the Other, take on the corporeal significations of both genders.

53. Jacques Lacan, *Ecrits: A Selection*, trans. Alan Sheridan (New York: W. W. Norton, 1977), p. 234. Hereafter cited in the text as *Ec*.

54. Anika Lamaire, *Jacques Lacan*, trans. David Macey (London: Routledge & Kegan Paul, 1977), p. 197.

55. Ibid., p. 174.

56. Bynum, *Holy Feast, Holy Fools*, pp. 265ff.

Chapter 5

1. See *theory* in *The American Heritage Dictionary*, p. 1335.

2. Ibid.; see *wer*-4 in "Table of Indo-European Roots," p. 1549.

3. The root *ora* is stressed in Martin Heidegger, *The Metaphysical Foundations of Logic*, trans. Michael Heim (Bloomington: Indiana University Press, 1984), pp. 164–65. Hereafter cited in the text as *MLF*.

4. Jacques Ellul, *The Technological Society*, trans. John Wilkinson (New York: Random House, 1964), p. xxv, speaks of technique as having efficiency as its sole aim.

5. Michel Foucault in "Truth and Power," in *Power/Knowledge: Selected Interviews and Other Writings, 1972–1977*, trans. Colin Gordon (New York: Pantheon Books, 1980), pp. 109–33, interprets knowledge as power and, as such, as having an interest in maintaining itself.

6. See *wel*-2 in "Table of Indo-European Roots," in *The American Heritage Dictionary*, p. 1548.

7. Levinas, *Existence and Existents*, pp. 57–64. See also *TI*, pp. 140–42.

8. George Bataille, "The Notion of Expenditure," in *Visions of Excess: Selected Writings, 1927–1939*, trans. Allan Stoekl (Minneapolis: University of Minnesota Press, 1985), p. 118.

9. Ibid., p. 121.

10. George Bataille, "The Practise of Joy before Death," in *Visions of Excess*, p. 239.

11. The resemblance to Arthur Schopenhauer's account of the individual is striking: "Why is our consciousness brighter and more distinct the further it reaches outward, so that its greatest clearness lies in sense perception . . . [and] becomes more obscure as we go inwards, and leads . . . into a darkness in which all knowledge ceases? . . . [C]onsciousness is possible only where the true inner being runs out into the phenomenon. . . . As soon as consciousness forsakes us—in sleep, in death . . . in magnetic or magic activity; for all these lead through the center. . . . where eternity lies . . . [there is] profoundest peace." See his *The World as Will and Representation* (New York: Dover Publications, 1966), vol. 2, pp. 325–26.

12. George Bataille, *Erotism: Death and Sensuality*, trans. Mary Dalwood (San Francisco: City Lights Books, 1986), p. 106.

13. Ibid., p. 118.

14. Ibid.

15. Ibid., p. 92.

16. George Bataille, "The Labyrinth," in *Visions of Excess*, p. 173.

17. Ibid.

18. George Bataille, "The Jesuve," in *Visions of Excess*, p. 78.

19. George Bataille, *Inner Experience*, trans. Leslie Anne Boldt (New York: State University of New York Press, 1988), pp. 115–16.

20. Levinas, *Existence and Existents*, p. 58.

21. Maurice Blanchot, *Thomas the Obscure*, trans. Thomas Lamberton (New York: David Lewis, 1973), p. 37.

22. Emmanuel Levinas, "Language and Proximity," in *CPP*, p. 119.

23. Ibid., p. 120.

24. Ibid., p. 119.

25. Maurice Blanchot, *The Writing of the Disaster*, trans. Ann Smock (Lincoln: University of Nebraska Press, 1986), p. 65.

26. Levinas, "Language and Proximity," in *CPP*, p. 121.

27. Kant in the *Critique of Judgment*, trans. J. H. Bernard (New York: Hafner Press, 1951), p. 150, defines genius in connection with the fine arts as "the talent (or natural gift)" or "the innate mental disposition (*ingenium*) *through which* nature gives the rule to art." Kierkegaard in *Concluding Unscientific Postscript*, trans. David F. Swenson and Walter Lowrie (Princeton, NJ: Princeton University Press, 1941), p. 348, in his discussion of the religious personality, can be viewed as overturning the Kantian notion: "To hymn a hero of faith is quite as definitely an aesthetic task as it is to eulogize a war hero. If the religious is in truth the religious, if it has submitted itself to the discipline of the ethical and preserves it within itself, it cannot forget that religious pathos does not consist in singing and hymning and composing verses but in existing." A saintly "genius," like Kierkegaard's believer, "differs from the ethicist in being infinitely interested in the reality of another" (p. 288). Kierkegaard's ethicist in this context is understood as one who lives in conformity with the moral law.

28. See Jacques Derrida, "No Apocalypse, Not Now (full speed ahead,

seven missiles, seven missives)," *Diacritics* 14, no. 2 (Summer, 1984), p. 24, and Wyschogrod, *Spirit in Ashes*, pp. 15–16.

29. My recasting is based on Winnie Mandela, *Part of My Soul Went with Him*, ed. Anne Benjamin, adapted by Mary Benson (New York: W. W. Norton, 1984), p. 148. There are other biographies of Mandela that are less hagiographic. As Gail M. Gerhart remarks in a review of Fatima Meer's *Higher than Hope: The Authorized Biography of Nelson Mandela* (New York: Harper & Row, 1990) that appeared in the *New York Times Book Review*, 11 March 1990, p. 17: "Any biography of Mr. Mandela published today is a work in progress."

30. Jacques Derrida, "Who Is Nelson Mandela?" in Jacques Derrida and Mustapha Tlili, eds., *For Nelson Mandela* (New York: Henry Holt & Co., 1987), p. 36. The idea of political sanctity is considered by Leonardo Boff in "The Need for Political Saints: From the Spirituality of Liberation to the Practice of Liberation," trans. Linda Rivera and Leon King, in *Cross Currents* 30, 4 (Winter 1980–81): 369–76. He suggests that current conditions open the way for "struggle against the mechanisms of exploitation" and the destruction of community to "work for a society not yet visible and will perhaps never be enjoyed" (p. 376). From my perspective, that of a narrative view of hagiographic altruism, liberation theologies cannot resolve the tension between "solidarity with one's class" and "overcoming of hatred against those who are agents of the mechanisms of impoverishment" (p. 376). This tension is embedded in a larger context, that of interpreting political sanctity on the model of the logic of exemplarity: the saint is seen as an example of a class. I criticize this logic in the latter half of the present chapter. Furthermore, without stipulating that radical altruism as manifested through narrative is a precondition of political sanctity, the danger of misappropriating the interests of the oppressed on the grounds of class remains open.

31. In Sophocles' *Antigone*, trans. R. C. Jebb, in Whitney J. Oates and Eugene O'Neill, Jr., eds., *Seven Greek Plays* (New York: Random House, 1950), p. 190, Ismene responds to Antigone's reminder that divine laws have been violated by admitting, "[T]o defy the State—I have no strength for that." Hegel, in *The Phenomenology of Mind*, trans. A. V. Miller (Oxford: Oxford University Press, 1979), pp. 283–89, interprets the *Antigone* as a conflict between the divine law reflected in the law of the family and the law of the state but does not take account of Ismene's obedience by default to the law of the state.

32. In the *New York Times*, 17 February 1989, p. A 1, Christopher S. Wren reports that "Winnie Mandela was effectively cast out . . . by the anti-apartheid movement," because of the "killing of a 14-year-old youth [Stompie Moeketsi] whom Mrs. Mandela's bodyguards are accused of abducting."

33. Winnie Mandela, *Part of My Soul Went with Him*, p. 36.

34. Derrida and Tlili, *For Nelson Mandela*, p. 41.

35. Winnie Mandela, *Part of My Soul Went with Him*, p. 148.

36. John Stratton Hawley, Introduction, in John Stratton Hawley, ed., *Saints and Virtues* (Berkeley and Los Angeles: University of California Press, 1987), xvi.

37. Nelson Goodman, *Ways of Worldmaking* (Indianapolis: Hackett Publishing Co., 1978), pp. 63–70, 133–37.

38. Ibid., pp. 63–70.

39. Ibid., pp. 133–37.

40. Nelson Goodman and Catherine Z. Elgin, *Reconceptions in Philosophy and Other Arts and Sciences* (Indianapolis: Hackett Publishing Co., 1988), p. 22.

41. Ibid., pp. 19–23.

42. Ibid., p. 26.

43. Ibid., p. 25.

44. Max Scheler, *Formalism in Ethics or Non-Formal Ethics of Values: A New Attempt towards the Foundation of an Ethical Personalism*, trans. Manfred S Frings and Roger L. Funk (Evanston, IL: Northwestern University Press, 1973), pp. 584–85. Harold Alderman in "By Virtue of a Virtue," *Review of Metaphysics* 26, 1 (September 1982): 127–53, argues for a Scheler-like view of exemplary individuals but "correcting" for cultural factors. He suggests that "[t]here is a trans-cultural dimension of character, one most clearly manifest in the paradigmatic individual" (p. 129). Alderman also sees that this view must be embedded in a narrative, literary, and historical context. This is a significant advance over acontextual characterizations of exemplarity, but the conceptual terrain of Alderman's account is that of a virtue theory, which is itself a kind of goodness theory culminating in the idea of the paradigmatic individual. Thus Alderman's view leaves the infrastructure of moral theory untouched.

45. Ibid., p. 582.

46. Irene E. Harvey in "Doubling the Space of Existence: Exemplarity in Derrida—The Case of Rousseau," in John Sallis, ed., *Deconstruction and Philosophy: The Texts of Jacques Derrida* (Chicago: University of Chicago Press, 1985), pp. 60–70, points to Derrida's double treatment of examples as superfluous additions, mere examples, on the one hand and as essential additions on the other. Examples become signs, a transformation necessitated by the very structure of argument.

47. I first encountered this point in the lectures of the late Henry M. Rosenthal. It is stated in his posthumously published *The Consolations of Philosophy, Hobbes's Secret, Spinoza's Way*, ed. Abigail L. Rosenthal (Philadelphia: Temple University Press, 1989), p. 50: "All these positivities or credit features of the human condition [worth, dignity, honor, and so on]—which we began with some knowledge of, if we began with anything—call for description: because nothing can be described at all unless it is morally described."

Chapter 6

1. Published as *Logische Untersuchungen*, 2 vols. (Halle: Max Niemeyer, 1900; 2d ed., 1913); English translation by J. H. Findlay, *Logical Investigations*, 2 vols. (New York: Humanities Press, 1970). And *Ideen zu einer reinen Phänomenologie und phänomenologische Philosophie*, *Husserliana III* (The Hague: Mar-

tinus Nijhoff, 1913); English translation by W. R. Boyce Gibson, *Ideas: Introduction to Pure Phenomenology*, trans. W. R. Boyce Gibson (New York: Collier Books, 1962).

2. Derrida, *Speech and Phenomena*, p. 78.

3. Ibid., pp. 17–22.

4. Ibid., p. 78.

5. Edmund Husserl in appendix IV of *The Phenomenology of Internal Time Consciousness* (Bloomington: Indiana University Press, 1964), p. 144, writes in regard to time: "The identity of temporal objects, therefore, is a constitutive product of the unity of certain possible coincidences of identification of recollections. Temporal Objectivity is established in the temporal flux, and to be identifiable in recollections and hence to be the subject of identical predicates is an essential art of this Objectivity."

6. "To the cogito itself belongs a 'glancing towards' the object, which from another side springs forth from the 'ego' which can henceforth never be absent." See Husserl *Ideas I*, p. 109.

7. Ibid., pp. 83–84.

8. Levinas, *CPP*, p. 111.

9. "Meaning and Translation," originally in A. Brouwer, ed., *On Translation* (Cambridge, MA: Harvard University Press, 1959). This essay, an adaptation of *Word and Object* (Cambridge, MA: MIT Press, 1960), was written while the latter was a work in progress. It is in Jerry A. Fodor and Jerrold Katz, eds., *The Structure of Language* (Englewood Cliffs, NJ: Prentice Hall, 1964), p. 477.

10. Willard van Orman Quine, *From a Logical Point of View* (New York: Harper & Row, 1963), pp. 61–62.

11. Willard van Orman Quine, "Meaning and Translation," in Fodor and Katz, *Structure of Language*, p. 468.

12. Willard van Orman Quine, *From a Logical Point of View*, p. 42.

13. Ibid.

14. Willard van Orman Quine, in Fodor and Katz, *Structure of Language*, p. 468.

15. Michael Dummett, *Frege's Philosophy of Language* (2d ed., London: Gerald Duckworth & Company, 1981), p. 598.

16. Derrida, *Writing and Difference*, p. 151.

17. Donald Davidson, *Inquiries into Truth and Interpretation* (Oxford: Clarendon Press, 1984), pp. 220–21.

18. Ibid., p. 216. The intralinguistic interpretation of reference leads Samuel C. Wheeler III in "Metaphor according to Davidson and De Man," in Dasenbrock, *Redrawing the Lines*, to claim that both Davidson and De Man "hold that . . . linguistic meaning is not reducible to non-language like meaning bearers" (p. 116).

19. Ibid., p. 219.

20. Ibid., p. 217.

21. Ibid.

22. Dummett, *Frege's Philosophy of Language*, p. 198.

23. Ibid.

24. Davidson, *Inquiries into Truth and Interpretation*, p. 221.

25. Ibid., p. 225.

26. Jacques Derrida, *Of Grammatology*, trans. Gayatri Chakravorty Spivak (Baltimore: Johns Hopkins University Press, 1976), p. 215.

27. J. L. Austin, *How to Do Things with Words* (Cambridge, MA: Harvard University Press, 1975), p. 11.

28. Davidson, *Inquiries into Truth and Interpretation*, p. 118.

29. Ibid., p. 119. Derrida alludes to this problem in his analysis of case rather than mood in connection with Levinas's philosophy. See his *Writing and Difference*, p. 95.

30. "Doubtless indeed there are intelligible entities corresponding to the sensible entities; there may also be intelligible entities to which our sensible faculty of intuition has no relation whatsoever; but our concepts of understanding, being mere forms of thought for our sensible intuition, could not in the least apply to them," Kant writes. See *The Critique of Pure Reason*, trans. Norman Kemp Smith (London: Macmillan, 1958), B 309, p. 270.

31. Donald Davidson in *Inquiries into Truth and Interpretation* explicitly endorses Tarski's positivist account of truth (Convention T): "We recognize sentences like 'Snow is white,' is true if and only if snow is white, to be trivially true. Yet the totality of such English sentences uniquely determines the extension of the concept of truth for English. Tarski generalized this observation and made it a test of theories of truth" (p. 194). Davidson goes on to show its limitations as applied to natural languages but endorses it as "desideratum of a theory" if not as "a formal test" (p. 204). In a variety of contexts, he prefers Tarski's to Carnap's interpretations of truth and meaning.

32. The term *egology* is scattered throughout Levinas's work. For an extended analysis of the guilt and innocence of the ego see "The Ego and the Totality," in *CPP*, pp. 25–45.

33. Ibid., pp. 15–16.

34. See Wyschogrod, *Spirit in Ashes*, pp. 3–6, for an account of Socrates' death as establishing the dominant model for understanding death in Western thinking, the "authenticity paradigm."

35. Levinas, *CPP*, p. 15.

36. Ibid., p. 16.

37. Ibid.

38. Simone Weil, *Waiting for God*, trans. Emma Crauford (New York: Harper & Row, 1951), pp. 118–19.

39. Elaine Scarry, *The Body in Pain: The Making and Unmaking of the World* (Oxford: Oxford University Press, 1986), pt. 1.

40. Michel Foucault, *Power/Knowledge: Selected Interviews and Other Writings, 1972–1977*, trans. Colin Gordon, Leo Marshall, John Mepham, and Kate Soper (New York: Pantheon Books, 1980), p. 133.

41. From the *Siksamuccaya*, in Theodore de Bary, ed., *The Buddhist Tradition* (New York: Random, House, 1969), p. 85.

42. Mohandes K. Gandhi, *Satyagraha in South Africa* (Ahmedabad: Nasvajivan Publishing House, 1950), p. 115.

43. Philip Hallie, *Lest Innocent Blood Be Shed* (New York: Harper & Row, 1978), p. 110.

44. "A Mission to Heal," in *New York Newsday*, 22 December 1987, pt. 2, p. 3.

45. Gasché, *Tain of the Mirror*, pp. 16–17. The analysis of reflection is restricted to phenomenological philosophy and is not applied to analytic philosophy by Gasché.

46. Ibid., p. 19.

47. G. W. F. Hegel, *Faith and Knowledge*, trans. Walter Cerf (Albany: State University of New York Press, 1977), pp. 67ff.

48. Gasché, *Tain of the Mirror*, p. 156.

49. Levinas, *Totality and Infinity*, p. 125.

Chapter 7

1. This is the orientation in Gilles Deleuze and Felix Guattari, *Anti-Oedipus: Capitalism and Schizophrenia*, trans. Robert Hurley, Mark Seem, and Helen R. Lane (New York: Viking Press, 1977), p. 170. Hereafter cited in the text as *AO*.

2. Karl Marx and Frederick Engels, *Selected Works* (Moscow: Foreign Languages Publishing House, 1962), vol. 1, pp. 362–64.

3. Gilles Deleuze and Felix Guattari, *A Thousand Plateaus: Capitalism and Schizophrenia* (Minneapolis: University of Minnesota Press, 1987), pp. 161–64. Hereafter cited in the text as *TP*.

4. Martin Heidegger in his well-known "Letter on Humanism," trans. Edward Lohner, in Nino Langiulli, ed., *The Existentialist Tradition: Selected Writings* (Garden City, NY: Anchor Books, 1971), pp. 204–45, writes "To think of the truth of being means at the same time to think of the *humanitas* of the *homo humanus*. What is at stake is *humanitas*, in the service of the truth of Being but without humanism in the metaphysical sense" (p. 235).

5. Melanie Klein, *Envy and Gratitude and Other Works, 1946–1963* (New York: Delacorte Press, 1975), p. 58.

6. I am indebted to Dr. Lucia Lermond for the phrase "empirical ecstatic."

7. Jean-Paul Sartre in *Search for a Method*, trans. Hazel Barnes (New York: Knopf, 1963), argues that scarcity is a given but is "lived" in terms of the mode of production. The way in which scarcity is treated may create antagonisms in the relations of production. Thus, he writes: "Whatever men and events are, they certainly appear within the compass of *scarcity*; that is, in a society still incapable of emancipating itself from its needs—hence from nature" (p. 131).

8. Karl Marx and Frederick Engels, *The German Ideology* (Moscow: Progress Publishers, 1964), in the section "Saint Max," a critique of Max Stirner as ego phenomenologist, attack the position that one can master both needs and thoughts through voluntary control (esp. pp. 274–80).

9. Ibid., p. 277n.

10. Ibid.

11. Karl Marx, *Selected Works*, vol. 1, p. 363.

12. There is no account of either a comparable or a different process of socialization for women in *AO* although its antihierarchical analyses have been influential in French feminist thinking. See Brian Massumi's Foreword to *TP*, pp. xi–xii.

13. Deleuze and Guattari's claim that the schizophrenic process is useful for the understanding of present-day capitalist society is anticipated in the antipsychiatry movement of R. D. Laing in *The Politics of Experience* (New York: Ballantine Books, 1967) and in David Cooper in *Psychiatry and Anti-Psychiatry* (New York: Ballantine Books, 1971). Michel Foucault in *Madness and Civilization: A History of Insanity in the Age of Reason* (New York: New American Library, 1965), esp. pp. 241–78, interprets as punishment both the hospitalization of the mentally ill and the silence of the analyst who, in the course of psychoanalytic therapy, judges the patient. Thomas Stephen Szasz in *Psychiatric Slavery: The Dilemmas of Involuntary Psychiatry as Exemplified by the Case of Kenneth Donaldson* (New York: Free Press, 1977), pp. 133–39, sees institutionalization of the mentally ill as a violation of rights and argues for the parallel between involuntary servitude and psychiatric incarceration. In their estimation of conventional psychiatry as repressive and punitive, these writings belong to the same spectrum of opinion. For an explicit expression of indebtedness to Michel Foucault and R. D. Laing, see *AO*, pp. 132n.

14. René Girard, "Système du délire," in *Critique dans un souterrain* (Lausanne: Editions l'âge d'homme, 1976), p. 196.

15. For a materialist ecstatic reading of the body as a source of collective meaning see Alphonso Lingis, *Excesses: Eros and Culture* (Albany: State University of New York Press, 1983).

16. The meaning of the body as a surface of inscription and pain as the instrument of writing in the sense ascribed to inscription in Deleuze and Guattari can be traced to Nietzsche. For example, in the *Genealogy of Morals*, trans. Walter Kaufmann and R. J. Hollingdale (New York: Vintage Books, 1969), p. 61, Nietzsche writes "If something is to stay in the memory it must be burned in: only that which never ceases to *hurt* stays in the memory."

17. Friedrich Nietzsche, *Untimely Meditations*, trans. R. J. Hollingdale (Cambridge: Cambridge University Press, 1983), p. 174.

18. Deleuze and Guattari, "Rhizome," in *On the Line*, trans. John Johnston (New York: Semiotext(e), 1983), esp. pp. 10–13.

19. Gilles Deleuze, "Nomad Thought," in Allison, *The New Nietzsche*, pp. 142–49.

20. Ibid., p. 142.

21. Ibid., p. 144.

22. Ibid., pp. 144–46.

23. Ibid., p. 148.

24. Ibid., p. 149.

25. Deleuze and Guattari, *On the Line*, p. 2.

26. Ibid., p. 7.

27. Anticipation of the possibilities of rhizomatic thought as opposed to the putative security of logocentric thinking can be found in Dostoevsky and Kafka. The nameless narrator in Fyodor Dostoevsky, *Notes from the Underground*, trans. Mirra Ginsburg (New York: Bantam Books, 1974), p. 36, declares: "What makes you think human desires must be corrected? . . . [W]hy are you so absolutely convinced that not going against true normal advantages, guaranteed by reason and arithmetic, is really always to man's advantage and a law for all mankind?" Franz Kafka in "The Burrow," trans. Willa and Edwin Muir, in *The Complete Stories* (New York: Schocken Books, 1976), p. 352, writes that, when threatened by an unknown noise, the burrower declares: "Once more I let my passages lead me where they will. . . . A complete reversal of things in the burrow; what was once the place of danger has become a place of tranquillity, while the Castle Keep has been plunged into the melee of the world and all its perils" (p. 352).

28. Deleuze and Guattari, *On the Line*, pp. 12–13.

29. Ibid., p. 10.

30. Michel de Certeau in *La fable mystique XVIe–XVIIe siècle* (Paris: Gallimard, 1982), pp. 165–79, defines the problematic involved in encoding ecstatic experience in the sixteenth and seventeenth centuries. He writes: "Articulated through Scholastic metaphysics or detached from but still presupposing it these [later] theories lead every inquiry back to a first Speaker. Words and things spell out a language organized by a Word to be heard in the noise of the world, this body of metaphors . . . where a listening . . . knows how to recognize the ruses of a founding voice" (p. 168) (translation mine).

31. Deleuze and Guattari distinguish between types of law designated as *dispars* and *compars* in connection with the nomological structure of science: "The compars is the legal . . . model employed by royal science. . . . extracting constants, even if these constants are only the relations between variables . . . an invariable form for variables. But for the dispars as an element of nomad science the relevant distinction is material-forces rather than matter form . . . not extracting constants from variables but of placing the variables themselves in a state of continuous variation" (*TP*, p. 369).

32. Cf. Simone Weil's account of gravity in *Gravity and Grace*, trans. Emma Crauford (London: Routledge & Kegan Paul, 1952), pp. 1–4. Gravity is the law of self-preservation and self-aggrandizement from which we can escape only through grace. How does one overcome gravity? By "ris[ing] in the domain of moral gravity. Moral gravity makes us fall towards the heights" (p. 4).

33. Girard, *Critique dans un souterrain*, p. 196.

34. Gilles Deleuze, *Logique du sens* (Paris: Editions de minuit, 1969), pp. 9f.

35. Ibid. Cf. Gilles Deleuze, *Différence et répétition* (Paris: Presse Universitaire de France, 1968), pp. 166f.

36. Michel Foucault, *Language, Memory, Practise: Selected Essays and Inter-

views, trans. Donald F. Bouchard (Ithaca: Cornell University Press, 1977), p. 167.

37. Ibid., p. 171.

38. Ibid., p. 174.

39. Ibid., p. 175.

40. M. H. Abrams in *Natural Supernaturalism: Tradition and Revolution in Romantic Literature* (New York: W. W. Norton), pp. 143–95, traces a line of development from Plotinus and Proclus through the hermetic tradition, Renaissance Kabbalism, and German and English Romanticism, especially in Coleridge, Hegel, and Schelling.

41. Arthur Hilary Armstrong, *The Architecture of the Intelligible Universe in the Philosophy of Plotinus: An Analytical and Historical Study* (Cambridge: Cambridge University Press, 1940), p. 2.

42. François Lyotard, "Le désir nommé Marx," in *L'économie libidinale* (Paris: Editions de minuit, 1974). In extended interviews with Lyotard by Jean-Loup Thebaud, in *Just Gaming*, trans. Wlad Godzich (Minneapolis; University of Minnesota Press, 1985), Lyotard, speaking of *L'économie libidinale*, states that the book is not dialogical, that it is "more like the bottle tossed into the ocean" than a conversation that fulfills the dialogical requirement of "return[ing] the effects of the statements to their author" (p. 5).

43. Ibid., p. 117.

44. Ibid., pp. 119–20.

45. George Bataille, *Madame Edwarda* (Paris: Jean Jacques Pauvert, 1956).

46. Lyotard, *L'économie libidinale*, p. 171.

47. Deleuze and Guattari, *On the Line*, pp. 108–9.

48. James Mellon, ed., *Bullwhip Days: The Slaves Remember* (New York: Weidenfeld & Nicolson), p. 240.

49. For an account of how this position might be developed see Arthur Danto, *Narrative and Knowledge*, pp. 77–82. Danto cites Bertrand Russell as suggesting that it is not logically impossible for the world to have come into existence five minutes ago and for people to remember a past that is totally unreal. No logical necessity, Russell continues, connects temporal events so that putative knowledge of the past is logically independent of the past and analyzable in terms of present content. Danto proposes historical instrumentalism as one strategy for neutralizing problems of reference in connection with statements about the past. "For instrumentalism, it does not matter whether sentences refer or not. . . . We would only have converted certain sentences from fact-stating to organizational instruments and, in the latter capacity, truth or falsity are rendered logically inappropriate" (p. 81). These instruments would function like the theoretical terms of science. For an analysis of the neutralization of reference from a postmodern point of view see chapter 6.

50. Jean Genet, *Our Lady of the Flowers*, trans. Bernard Frechtman (New York: Bantam Books, 1964), p. 2. The Introduction by Jean-Paul Sartre is from his *Saint Genet, comédien et martyr* (Paris: Librairie Gallimard, 1952).

51. Jacques Derrida, *Glas*, trans. John P. Leavey, Jr., and Richard Rand (Lincoln: University of Nebraska Press, 1986), p. 217.

52. Ibid., pp. 104–5. On the name Genet, Derrida writes: "Genet names a plant with flowers—yellow flowers (*sarothamnus scoparius, genista*; broom, *genette, genet-à-balais*, poisonous and medicinal, as distinct from the dyer's broom, *genista tinctoria, genestrolle*, dyer's greenweed, woodwaxen, an herb for dying yellow); *genet* a kind of horse. Of Spain, a country of great importance in the text" (p. 35).

53. *American Heritage Dictionary*. See *pervert* (p. 980) and root *wer* in "Table of Indo-European Roots" (p. 1549).

54. Derrida, *Dissemination*, p. 253.

55. Michel de Certeau in *La fable mystique XVIe–XVIIe siècle*, p. 196f., shows that seventeenth-century European mystical writers cannot overcome linguistic heterogeneity and stabilize practice rather than language.

56. Jean Genet, *Miracle of the Rose* (New York: Grove Press, 1966), p. 171.

57. Jean Genet, *Funeral Rites*, trans. Bernard Frechtman (New York: Grove Press, 1969), p. 171.

58. Gasché, *Tain of the Mirror*, p. 176, concludes his subtle analysis of deconstructive methodology as tracing the inner limits of philosophy with the remark, "Deconstruction opens philosophy to its Others."

59. Jean-Paul Sartre, *Faces, Preceded by Official Portraits*, ed. Maurice Natanson (The Hague: Martinus Nijhoff, 1969), p. 158.

60. Ibid.

61. Ibid., pp. 162–63.

62. Ibid., p. 161.

63. Levinas's account of faciality lacks a description of the face as domination. By arguing for the primordiality of the face as vulnerability, I try to show that such an account need not be fatal to Levinas's view. That the face of the torturer, for example, is a still a face is not considered by Levinas.

64. Genet, *Miracle of the Rose*, p. 2.

65. Ibid.

Chapter 8

1. Reservations about postmodernist critiques of the self are found in David Michael Levin, *The Opening of Vision*, pp. 404–5, where both the death of the modern self and the continuation of personal growth are defended, and in John Caputo, *Radical Hermeneutics*, pp. 289–90, where the term *persona* is suggested instead of *self* as expressing the mystery of the person.

2. Nicholas Rescher, *Unselfishness: The Role of the Vicarious Affects in Moral Philosophy and Social Theory* (Pittsburgh: University of Pittsburgh Press, 1975), p. 3. Hereafter cited in the text as *U*. Rescher's work follows a strain in American philosophy beginning with William James's *Varieties of Religious Experience* in which saintliness is extolled as the culmination of the religious life. Pitraim Sorokin in *Altruistic Love: A Study of American Good Neighbors and Christian Saints* (New York: Beacon Press, 1950), pp. 197–213, views altruism in the form of good-neighborliness and saintliness as related to one another. "Masters

and creators of love energy," saints are seen as necessary to society. Rescher, F. O. Urmson, and Thomas Nagel are, in differing degrees, representative of the Jamesian view.

3. The argument for partiality based on lines of familial proximity is the foundation of Confucian ethics. Tu wei Ming in *Humanity and Self-Cultivation: Essays in Confucian Thought* (Berkeley: Asian Humanities Press, 1979), pp. 27–30, shows that the virtues of humanity or goodness (*jen*) and propriety (*li*) in Confucianism depend upon self-cultivation that, in turn, is bound up with family relationships that open into widening spheres of social relations. Confucians argue that Mo tzu's advocacy of universal love, love that is not person discriminating, ignores a psychological reality, the strength of family bonds. The problem of kinship altruism is explored in C. R. Braddock, *The Problem of Altruism: Freudian-Darwinian Solutions* (Oxford: Basil Blackwell, 1986), pp. 71–119. A key source for the argument against preferential benevolence in Western philosophy is the Socratic attack on the notion of doing good to one's friends and harm to one's enemies. See Plato, *Republic*, 332a.

4. For an account of the thesis that there is a rational aspect in emotion see Robert Solomon, *The Passions* (New York: Anchor Press, 1977).

5. Examples are mine, not Rescher's.

6. In a concise summary of the prisoner's dilemma Rescher writes: "Two prisoners, held incommunicado, are charged with being accomplices in the commission of a crime. For conviction, the testimony of each is needed to incriminate the other. If each confesses, the result is mutual incrimination, and both will divide the twenty years' imprisonment. If only one turns state's evidence, thereby incriminating the other (who maintains silence) the whole penalty will fall on [him]. But if both maintain silence and neither confesses, both will suffer a much-diminished penalty. . . . The prisoners [must choose whether to confess] or opt for the benefit of silence accompanied by an even greater risk" (*U*, p. 33).

7. The colloquialism NIMBY came into general use in connection with housing AIDS victims and homeless persons in middle-class neighborhoods some years after Rescher's study was written.

8. J. O. Urmson, "Saints and Heroes," in A. I. Melden, ed., *Essays in Moral Philosophy* (Seattle: University of Washington Press, 1958).

9. Ibid., p. 201.

10. Robert M. Adams in "Saints," in *The Virtue of Faith and Other Essays in Philosophical Theology* (New York: Oxford University Press, 1987), pp. 164–73, maintains that Susan Wolf's contention that saints are boring and joyless holds only for moral saints defined by her as those whose actions are morally as good as possible. Adams contends that this is not true of actual saints such as Saint Francis, Gandhi, or Albert Schweitzer because the lives of such persons are grounded in transcendence: "What interests a saint may have will depend on what interests God has, for sainthood is a participation in God's interests. . . . As the author of all things and all human capacities he may be regarded as interested in many forms of human excellence" (p. 170). For Wolf's position

see her "Moral Saints," *Journal of Philosophy* 8 (August, 1982): 419–39. A post-modern perspective rules out the boredom argument not on grounds of the saint's relation to transcendence but first, because boredom is a function of sameness, and difference and alterity are the "foci" of a postmodern ethic; second, because contemporary life conditions are likely to force saints to lead risk-ridden lives; and third, because saintliness often necessitates the acquisition of instrumental skills that are interesting and demanding in order for saints to live out their stories.

11. The indiscriminate juxtaposition and appropriation of historical elements has been seen as a danger even in postmodern architecture. Thus Charles Jencks in *What Is Postmodernism*, p. 20, writes that postmodern architect Leon Krier's plan for the reconstruction of Washington, D.C., has been unfairly compared with the urban planning of Albert Speer under National Socialism. This characterization misses the "irreducibly plural reality" of Krier's work.

12. Michael Theunissen, *The Other: Studies in the Social Ontology of Husserl, Heidegger, Sartre, and Buber*, trans. Christopher Macann (Cambridge, MA: MIT Press, 1984), situates the notion of alterity as a critical focus in the history of phenomenological and dialogical philosophy.

13. Mary Douglas in *Purity and Danger: An Analysis of Concepts of Pollution and Taboo* (Harmondsworth and Middlesex: Penguin, 1970) addresses the problem of liminality in terms of the fear aroused by borderline forms of life in nonliterate societies.

14. Jean-Paul Sartre, *Being and Nothingness: An Essay on Phenomenological Ontology*, trans. Hazel Barnes (New York: Philosophical Library, 1956), pp. 600–615, analyzes such qualities as the soft, the sticky, the slimy as revelations of being.

15. Mark C. Taylor, *Altarity*, p. 167.

16. Ibid., pp. 167f.

17. Cited in Mark C. Taylor, *Altarity*, p. 9.

18. Ibid.

19. On violence as productive of beauty see Yukio Mishima, *Sun and Steel*, trans. John Bester (Tokyo: Kodansha International, 1970). "To combine action and art is to combine the flower that wilts and the flower that lasts forever" (p. 50).

20. That the body becomes a hieroglyph can be seen in Kafka's "The Penal Colony," trans. Willa and Edwin Muir, in Kafka, *The Complete Stories*, ed. Nahum Glatzer (New York: Schocken Books, 1976). The Harrow inscribes into the flesh of the condemned man a script "that cannot be deciphered with the eyes" but is deciphered, as it were, with his wounds (p. 150).

21. Julia Kristeva, *Desire in Language: A Semiotic Approach to Literature and Art* (New York: Columbia University Press, 1980), p. 247.

22. Ibid.

23. Ibid.

24. Edmond Husserl, *Experience and Judgment: Investigations in a Genealogy of Logic*, trans. James S. Churchill and Karl Ameriks (London: Routledge & Kegan Paul, 1973), p. 350.

25. Ibid.

26. Willard van Orman Quine, "Meaning and Translation," in Fodor and Katz, *Structure of Language*, p. 462.

27. The title of this section is found in Levinas, *TI*, p. 40. Levinas denies the primordiality of negativity because, for him, negativity requires a being that is prior to it. Thus negativity has its place in the world of totality, for example, in connection with work that transforms the world that sustains it, but "metaphysics does not coincide with negativity" (*TI*, pp. 40–41).

28. Emmanuel Levinas, *Time and the Other*, trans. Richard A. Cohen (Pittsburgh: Duquesne University Press, 1987), p. 83.

29. Kierkegaard, *Philosophical Fragments*, p. 20 n.

30. Milan Kundera, *The Unbearable Lightness of Being* (New York: Harper & Row, 1987).

Index

(bolding indicates subject is found in an illustration)